Politics and Trade in the Indian Ocean World

Publisher's Note

Professor Ashin Das Gupta passed away on 4 June 1998. The editors, contributors and the Publishers of this volume deeply regret that he could not see it in print.

Ashin Das Gupta

Politics and Trade in the Indian Ocean World

Essays in Honour of Ashin Das Gupta

edited by

Rudrangshu Mukherjee
and
Lakshmi Subramanian

DELHI
OXFORD UNIVERSITY PRESS
CALCUTTA CHENNAI MUMBAI
1998

Oxford University Press, Great Clarendon Street, Oxford OX2 6DP

Oxford New York
Athens Auckland Bangkok Calcutta
Cape Town Chennai Dar es Salaam Delhi
Florence Hong Kong Istanbul Karachi
Kuala Lumpur Madrid Melbourne Mexico City
Mumbai Nairobi Paris Singapore
Taipei Tokyo Toronto

and associates in

Berlin Ibadan

ISBN 0 19 564420 4

Typeset by Sheel Arts, Delhi 110 092
Printed in India at Wadhwa International, New Delhi 110 020
and published by Manzar Khan, Oxford University Press
YMCA Library Building, Jai Singh Road, New Delhi 110 001

Contents

Note on Contributors

S. ARASARATNAM is retired Professor of History, University of New England, Australia. He is the author of *Merchants Companies and Commerce in the Coromandel Coast 1650–1740* and *Maritime India in the 17th Century*.

MUZAFFAR ALAM is Professor of Medieval Indian History, Jawaharlal Nehru University and is the author of *Crisis of Empire in Mughal North India*.

RUCHIRA BANERJEE completed her Ph.D. from the University of Bombay.

BHASWATI BHATTACHARYA is at the Centre for European Expansion, Leiden University.

P. J. MARSHALL is former Rhodes Professor of Imperial and Commonwealth History, University of London. He is the author of *The Impeachment of Warren Hastings; East Indian Fortunes: The British in Bengal in the 18th Century* and *Bengal: The British Bridgehead*.

KENNETH MCPHERSON is Executive Director of the Indian Ocean Centre for Peace Studies, Curtin University and Universiy of Western Australia. He is the author of *The Indian Ocean: A History of the People and the Sea* and *The Muslim Microcosm: Calcutta, 1918–1935*.

RUDRANGSHU MUKHERJEE was Reader in History, Calcutta University. He is at present the Editor: Editorial Pages, *The Telegraph* and is the author of *Awadh in Revolt 1857–58: A Study of Popular Resistance* and editor of *The Penguin Gandhi Reader*.

M.N. PEARSON is Adjunct Professor, Faculty of Arts, Southern Cross University, Australia. He is the author of *Merchants and Rulers in Gujarat: The Response to the Portuguese in the 16th Century* and *The Portuguese in India*.

OM PRAKASH is Professsor, Delhi School of Economics and the author of *The Dutch East India Company and the Economy of Bengal, 1630–1720* and *Precious Metals and Commerce*.

LAKSHMI SUBRAMANIAN is Reader in History, Calcutta University. She is the author of *Indigenous Capital and Imperial Expansion: Bombay Surat and the West Coast*.

SANJAY SUBRAHMANYAM is Director d'etudes, Ecole des hautes etudes en sciences sociales, Paris. He is the author of *The Political Economy of Commerce: Southern India 1500–1650; The Portuguese Empire in Asia 1500–1700: A Political and Economic History* and *The Career and Legend of Vasco da Gama*.

1

Introduction

Ashin Das Gupta's work has moved, as Rudrangshu Mukherjee notes in his essay in this volume, from merchants to the port to the ocean. All the essays which follow, save one, are on areas which Das Gupta nurtured as fields of historical research. As admirers of Das Gupta know, he also writes in Bengali on a wide range of subjects. This volume of essays does not touch upon those themes. (A full bibliography of his writings prepared by Uma Das Gupta is included.)

The essays cover two very broad themes. One is the relationship of the ports (or coastal areas) to their hinterland and of trade to politics in the eighteenth century, a period of transition and turmoil. This, of course, is a subject close to Das Gupta's heart. Bhaswati Bhattacharya and Lakshmi Subramanian look at the Coromandel coast and Surat respectively. Malabar, which was the area which Das Gupta studied in his first book, is the subject of Ruchira Banerjee's essay. And Muzaffar Alam and Sanjay Subrahmanyam, in a joint essay, study the problem in the context of Arcot.

Bhattacharya and Subramanian in their essays argue against two of the most overarching generalizations made about the eighteenth century. Bhattacharya shows that in the Coromandel coast the impact of political instability and warfare on trade was no where as devastating as is often made out to be. Masulipatnam, the most important port of the region in the seventeenth century, declined in the eighteenth, so did its trade with Hyderabad. But other trade routes developed and 'some of the earlier trade continued, albeit through a different route and directed to a different destination.' In the southern part of the Coromandel coast new towns like Hindupur and Walajahpet emerged as centres of transpeninsular trade. One conclusion suggests itself: the impact of instability was disaggregated and localized. Despite the political disruption, 'there were extensive networks of commodity production, trade and marketing connecting centres of production and trade across the peninsula, extending the hinterland of the Coromandel coast almost upto the western coast.' Bhattacharya's conclusions modify the argument put forward by Das Gupta in his very influential essay 'Trade and Politics in 18th Century India'.

If the picture of overall decline has dominated the understanding of the eighteenth century, another hardy perennial has been the swift and smooth subordination of Indian merchants and artisans by the English East India Company. Subramanian shows that the subordination of the merchants and manufacturers in Surat was a long drawn-out process. Artisans and merchants maintained their autonomy and struck stronger terms in their negotiations with the Company. This strength of the weavers was evident even in 1800 when the dominance of the Company was firmly in place. Merchants gained from the revival of the Arab trade and the reintegration of the Arab and the East African markets. Thus, *vis-à-vis* the growing importance of the Company, the merchants and the manufacturers of Gujarat succeeded in clinging to their independence in the eighteenth century. This was in sharp contrast to the experiences of their counterparts in the eastern seaboard. The reasons for this difference are not far to seek. As Subramanian points out, full British annexation of the west coast did not take place till 1818. Before that the power of the Company was hamstrung by financial constraints and its sway was threatened by the presence of the Marathas.

Banerjee chooses a grand wedding feast as the site from which to explore the commercial rivalry between the Ali Rajas, the Mappila chieftains of Cannanore and important maritime merchants of Malabar, and the English factory in northern Malabar in the eighteenth century. The wedding in question—between the niece of Ali Raja Kunhi Amsi and a rich businessman of Calicut—took place in 1771. That year marked the end of five decades of hostility between the Mappila chieftain and the English factory in Tellicherry. Kunhi Amsi had countered persistent English attempts to undermine his family's economic and political importance by entering into a military alliance with Haidar Ali and by helping him to conquer Malabar in 1766. But this rise to prominence of the Ali Rajas aroused the animosity not only of the English but also of the defeated Nair rulers. They struck back. The ostentatious display of the wedding could not hide the fact that the influence of the Ali Rajas was declining. The future belonged to a British-backed lobby of merchants. Banerjee studies changes in the fortunes of merchants and the nature of trade in the context of a political configuration—the Anglo-Mysore wars of the late eighteenth century.

Subrahmanyam and Alam set up for themselves the challenging task of breaking down what they describe as 'the disciplinary Berlin Wall erected in the 1960s'. This wall separated maritime historians who worked on the basis of European records and reconstructed the histories of port cities and their trade from 'the land lubbers' who worked on indigenous sources and concerned themselves with agrarian production, peasants, prebendholders and inland cities. These two domains were completely separate and they met only when the world of inland politics was invoked as a crucial factor to explain the rise and fall of trading systems. A number of studies are now questioning this division and the assumptions which underpinned it. 'It is now possible', write Alam and Subrahmanyam, 'to pose even the history of inland regions in relation to the problem of trade routes and the control over them, rather than simply assume that the agrarian overlords who controlled such regions regarded trade with disdain for reasons of caste, ideology, steppe mentality, or whatever else.' Their essay deliberately juxtaposes the two perspectives. In their view, there are good reasons to modify the view that the years between 1680 and 1740 were a period of gloom for Karnatak Payanghat. In fact, the region was efficiently administered by Saadatullah Khan. An inevitable fallout of this centralization and consolidation was the drive to control the ports. This brought conflict and competition with the Europeans who were already entrenched along the coast line. Those who could succeed in this competition had a well-defined trading niche. The consequences of this shift in the balance of commercial and political power were felt in the middle of the century when a new political dispensation under English patronage was installed in Arcot. Alam and Subrahmanyam thus question on the basis of new documentation the idea of an overall decline in early eighteenth-century India; moreover, the indigenous rulers were not as uninterested in trade as is made out in an older historiography, nor was the eventual triumph of the English in Arcot altogether smooth and uncontested.

Om Prakash's essay acts as a bridge between the two broad themes explored in this volume. He begins by establishing the central position that India occupied in both the Euro-Asian as well as the intra-Asian trading networks of the Europeans. This critical role played by India was related to her capacity 'to provide cost competitive manufactured goods—predominantly cotton and other textiles—in the case of the Europeans engaged in intra-Asian trade.' The political and economic environments in which the Europeans had to operate in different parts of Asia like the Indonesian archipelago, Japan and India are analysed. In India this context alters radically in the second half of the eighteenth century when the English East India Company acquired political power in Bengal. The English Company was now placed 'in a position of substantial differential advantage *vis-à-vis* both the rival

European companies as well as the intermediary merchants and artisans. The terms and conditions the Company imposed on those doing business with it were no longer determined by the market... Using its political power, the Company enforced unilaterally determined below-market terms on the producers and the dealers in commodities like opium and textiles. This robbed producers and merchants of a good part of what was legitimately their due. It also must have adversely affected the incentive structure in the manufacturing sector of the economy. Om Prakash argues that this, combined with the English traders' monopolies in salt and opium, must have brought about a decline in the value of the total output in the province. These are familiar themes of Indian nationalist historiography and they cannot be ignored in the pursuit of revisionism.

Om Prakash's essay also turns the attention back to the ocean and thereby marks the passage to the second cluster of essays in this volume. These essays are about the sea and its trade rather than on the relationship between trade and politics.

Kenneth McPherson takes on the big canvas and looks at changes in maritime trade in the Bay of Bengal from the fifteenth to the nineteenth century. What was a 'traditional' maritime trading system with an Asian network was intruded upon by Europeans who until the late eighteenth century made their fortunes with the help of indigenous partners and used the traditional system to their advantage. They opened up that system to influences and demands originating in Europe. The operations of the Europeans introduced new types of commercial practices in the region. There was a decline in the dependence on indigenous partners. The substantial change in the nature of trade came around the close of the eighteenth century when not only were indigenous partners dispensed with, but British maritime interest also moved eastward across the Bay of Bengal from India to Southeast Asia.

S. Arasaratnam studies the eastward trade of India in the eighteenth century. In the seventeenth century, he writes, 'India's Asian trade flowed eastwards and westwards in roughly equal proportions.' But this changed in the eighteenth century as the eastward trade of India was influenced by a variety of factors. The first three decades were difficult as there were problems affecting both ends of the trade. In the middle decades the eastward trade experienced a sharp decline because of political instability. But this was compensated by the massive eastward drive of English–Asian commerce. The impact of the expansion of English exports from China was felt in the Asian maritime world, especially the India–Southeast Asia trade. But this, Arasaratnam warns, was a mixed blessing.

M.N. Pearson explores the contacts between western India and the Swahili coast in the early modern period. His conclusions caution against exaggerating the importance of Indians in East Africa. Indians were certainly not in a position of dominance and the impact of their activities was limited. Indian goods, however, were the main imports of the region and Indians—Hindus and Muslims—were active in trade on the coast. Despite problems of poor documentation, Pearson suggests that this trade continued both within and without the Portuguese monopoly system. This trade was coastal and in the case of the Canarins, far inland also. The other group which matched the activities of the Canarins were the *banias* who, as was their wont, played a large role in finance, trade and commerce.

The essay which does not fit into either of the two broad themes delineated above is by Peter Marshall on 'Edmund Burke and India: The Vicissitudes of a Reputation'. There are two reasons for including it in this volume. One is the fact that Das Gupta has had a lifelong interest in Burke. The other is the deep friendship between Marshall and Das Gupta. We believe that no *festschrift* to Das Gupta can be complete without an essay from Marshall. Here Marshall evokes Burke's grand vision of 'peoples united through God's providence in a bond of protection and mutual benefit'. This is a vision, we feel, with which Das Gupta would have no quarrel. On the contrary, he would perhaps share it only with some minor modifications.

2

Ashin Das Gupta: Some Memories and Reflections

RUDRANGSHU MUKHERJEE

There are men who, when they go back to Presidency College, feel their youth beckon to them from its badly painted walls, its steep staircase with the gong at the end and its dark and dank classrooms. When I enter the portals of my old college, there is no such emotion. My feelings, more often than not, tend to revolve around my teacher Ashin Das Gupta.

The late sixties and early seventies, when I went to Presidency, were turbulent years for the College. Those who decided to go there as undergraduates did so with a number of risks in mind. The risk to have their classes disrupted, the horror of seeing books and laboratories burnt and the danger of being caught in a pitched battle between gun-toting policemen and bomb-throwing students. But for those who took the decision and chose to study History there was a grand compensation. This was being taught by Ashin Das Gupta who was then professor and head of the History department.

Within the college, Das Gupta had a quiet presence which was often mistaken for aloofness. The first encounter could be intimidating as bright penetrating eyes summed up a nervous student. It was only later, as one got to know him better, that the eyes danced with humour, mischief and affection.

Those who were his students will never forget that first low-keyed announcement: 'This is Ashin Das Gupta. I will read the history of eighteenth-century India with you.' The choice of the verb 'read', I always felt, was deliberate and it set him apart from all other teachers. It was also an indication of his pedagogic method. That he did not talk down to his students seemed to be symbolized by the fact that he never stood on the dais. Teaching for him was a learning process. This was evident from the enormous care he took to prepare for his classes. His lectures were well thought out and beautifully structured. He did not lecture with fanfare; he spoke quietly and slowly as he explained the logic of eighteenth-century Indian politics. He did not expect you to take down all that he said but to understand everything he explained. The emphasis was on the logic and the method of unravelling the logic inherent in historical events. He taught his students to think about problems.

But undergraduates, as is their wont the world over, hung on to every word he said. This was partly out of hero-worship and partly out of habit. This attitude bothered Das Gupta and he would impishly try and trip the students. On one memorable occasion he said: 'Then Baji Rao did something he had never done before—(pause, as students dutifully wrote this down)—he died.'

Lookng back at Das Gupta's teaching, I think I can discern two distinct levels. One was within the classroom where the analytical structure of a topic was laid bare and a basic reading list provided. The relentless logic of this exposition did convey the impression that history was very neat without any rough edges. He was not unaware of this danger. Those who had tutorials with him or those who took the trouble to see him outside the classroom had their eyes opened to a different and deeper level. Here history was about controversies and discussions revolved around historiographical issues and gaps or unsolved problems in the present state of research. Das Gupta fed students with books and articles. This was a challenging encounter for he had no time for those who did not respond or were unable to keep pace or pestered him about how to answer this or that question which could be set in the exam paper. He could take enormous trouble to nurture a student's intellectual curiosity. I remember on one occasion when I was looking for an article by Barun De which had appeared in an obscure anthology, Das Gupta actually went to a bookshop and bought the book for me.

For those who took the trouble to get close to him, Das Gupta's elegant drawing-room in his south Calcutta flat became an extension of the classroom and much more. On Sunday mornings, friends, former students and present students would drop in and many things would be debated and discussed over cups of coffee. I remember it was in his drawing-room that I first met Eric Stokes. I was then a very precocious undergraduate whom Das Gupta indulged and I had no idea then that Eric's work would have profound impact on my own research and that he would eventually examine my D.Phil dissertation. In his characteristically undemonstrative way, Das Gupta saw to it that I met Eric, assuming that as a student of history I should get to know one of the leading historians of modern India.

Those *adda* sessions had an air of informality about them but at the same time they were intellectually demanding. It was taken as a matter of course that you had read and were familiar with some books and certain topics. Discussion moved from history to fiction to Sombhu Mitra's latest plays. Politics was never a principal concern, though Das Gupta's distaste for the violence which then stalked the streets of Calcutta was all too evident. I have spoken of his indulgence. I recall to my eternal shame once holding forth with a zeal given only to the young on the biblical allegory in John Steinbeck's *The Grapes of Wrath*. My teacher listened with rapt attention and then proceeded to knock a few holes into my starry-eyed adulation of Steinbeck's novel.

Das Gupta left Presidency College to teach at Heidelberg in 1972. When he returned a year or so later he learnt that some of his best students had done badly in their BA examination. He had no explanation or consolation for them. He put it down to the complete chaos which then reigned in Calcutta University. But I can still recall the look first of anger and then concern which passed over his face when he learnt of the results.

As I grew up and began pursuing my own research and other interests, Das Gupta kept a watchful eye over my development. As indeed he did over the career of some of his other students. Whenever we met, he would listen to what I was doing, to what I was reading. But everytime, and this is true even after knowing him for over twenty-five years, I come away from seeing him with an ineffable glow of warmth. He never fails to strike a special chord—a word of praise casually passed on, a special insight into a book or article which we discussed or sometimes the look of sheer affection at the sight of an old student. There are too many moments to be cherished than can be written about.

I have said that there were two levels to Das Gupta's teaching. I would suggest that Das Gupta operated on two different but interrelated registers as an historian. At one level, he was a story-teller. In conversation he always emphasized the story element in history. He once told me in self-deprecating irony that his biographer would have to reckon with the fact that the two major intellectual influences on him had been Agatha Christie and P.G. Wodehouse. I suspect this was said half in jest. In the serious half of it, Das Gupta wanted to draw attention to the art of crafting a narrative. At the second level, came the analysis where Das Gupta endowed meaning and significance to the historical events his narrative had plotted. Das Gupta would agree with Peter Gay's injunction that 'Historical narration without analysis is trivial, historical analysis without narration is incomplete.'[1]

The story-telling aspects of Das Gupta's historical idiom is best displayed in his first book.[2] The various elements of the story are introduced in the first chapter: the turning of the Northern trade following the collapse of the Safavid dynasty in Persia and the consequent dislocation of trade in the Persian Gulf; the ensuing spectacular revival of Calicut; the rise, expansionism and interventionism of Travancore under Martanda Varma (1729–58) and Rama Varma (1758–98); the decline of the Dutch Company; and the collapse of the independent merchant community in the Malabar coast.

In the very setting out of the elements, the progress of the plot is clear. The rise of Travancore contains within it the seeds of a conflict with the Jan Company and the resolution of the conflict takes the tale to its denouement in which medieval Asian trade in Malabar disappears at the end of the century. Das Gupta deals with these aspects in separate chapters and gives to historical events a coherence and interrelationship which were obviously not in the minds of contemporaries. He also applies to his narrative a closure marked by a remarkable last sentence: 'Medieval Asian trade along the coast called Malabar had sounded its last retreat.'[3] This is how Das Gupta brings out the 'storiness' in his history.

Already in this very early statement of his research interests two major themes of Das Gupta's work are set out: the fate of the Indian merchant and the intimate links between the unmaking of empires and decline of Indian trade in the Indian Ocean in the eighteenth century. The latter dimension which Das Gupta would explore in greater analytical depth in his subsequent work, serves the purpose in his first book of providing a moral to the Malabar story.

Travancore under Martanda Varma, after the victory over the Dutch at Colachel in August 1741, destroyed the dreams of a revived Dutch monopoly. Martanda Varma began a policy of expansion along the coast. To finance this, he set up a commercial department 'which began by establishing strict monopoly in the trade in pepper and then engrossed other commodities as well.' Merchants of Travancore were thus made into servants of the state or made dependent on it. The merchants of the principalities between Travancore and Calicut also lost their business. The powerful merchants of Cochin had to give up their trade in pepper.[4] There was thus a close linkage between politics—Martanda Varma's expansionism and his consequent need for money—and trade. The monopoly of Travancore determined the fate of trade and business in Malabar.

Implicit in Das Gupta's exposition was a critique of the position that the intervention of the European companies had resulted in the squeezing out of the Indian merchant in the eighteenth century. Both the Dutch company and the medieval Indian merchant were victims of the political regime inaugurated by Martanda Varma. The complete withdrawal of the Dutch came in the 1790s. If it had come earlier in the century, Das Gupta wrote, it 'would undoubtedly have been welcomed by the merchants of the coast'.[5] They would have been freed of the irksome monopoly of the Netherlands East India Company. In fact, the merchants of Cochin 'tried to work out a new business arrangement with the Dutch'[6], but the latter's withdrawal sealed their fate. In the north, Calicut went under the onslaught of the armies of Haidar Ali and Tipu Sultan. By the close of the century both Cochin and Calicut were stagnating.

Trade in the eighteenth century was dependent on politics. The Mughals were not interested in maritime trade and intervened in overseas trade only in an emergency and at that very sporadically.[7] But Mughal peace and Mughal law and order were absolutely essential for the smooth functioning of the ports, maritime trade, the flow of commodities along arteries of internal trade which fed the ports and the network of credit which supported the world of trade and commerce. Without this infrastructure trade would be impossible. The importance of the infrastructure became obvious only when it began to collapse. The disintegration of empire meant the decline of trade. In a masterly *tour de horizon*, Das Gupta analysed this interrelationship.[8]

The crisis of the Mughal empire, known variously as the *jagirdari* or the *mansabdari* crisis, was essentially a crisis concerning declining revenues. Faced with a scarcity of *jagirs* and a decline in the number of paying ones, the Mughal nobles became more oppressive and rapacious. On the one hand, as Irfan Habib has shown, this led to *zamindar*-led peasant uprisings which broke down the system of law and order.[9] On the other hand, Mughal nobles, strapped for money but threatened by the Marathas, 'turned to the revenue to be extracted from trade and this process soon took on the aspects of a barely concealed plunder of the merchants of Gujarat.'[10] Gujarat, the chief trading area of the Mughal empire, and its chief port Surat were thus cut off from the centres of production in north and central India and the Gujarat merchants lost these markets. The long term impact of all these factors upon Surat was devastating. The merchants were caught in a vicious cycle of oppressive administration, declining law and order, continuous quest for revenue and shrinking markets. They went under one by one. 'Thus,' in the words of Das Gupta, 'in course of the first fifty years of the eighteenth century India lost much of her trade in textiles and indigo which used to be channelled through the ports of Gujarat, principally to the Red Sea. The commercial fleet, comprising about sixty sails in all, which had spanned the Arabian Sea every year, virtually disappeared. The strong links with Western Asia which had been maintained through the port of Surat were gravely weakened. The shipowners of Surat, who had been almost exclusively Muslim, were virtually wiped out.'[11] To the Surat story, Das Gupta would return in greater and richer detail to show that the decline of Surat was also related to the weakening and collapse of two other empires: the Safavid empire in Persia and the control of the Ottomans over the Red Sea area.[12]

The dislocation of trade consequent upon the decline of the Mughals in the first three decades of the eighteenth century coincided with the overthrow of the Safavids in Persia. The merchants of Surat found it increasingly difficult to make profits from the Persian markets. The Red Sea trade, once flourishing, also began to languish with the onset of a protracted civil war amongst the Zaidis in Yemen.[13] The contraction of its markets brought to grief 'the blessed port of the Mughals'.

His next port of call in his survey of trade and politics was Hughli. Bengal, because it was under a stronger administration thanks to Murshid Quli Khan and his successor, did not feel the impact of the imperial political collapse quite in the same way as Gujarat did. But by the 1740s, Bengal was threatened by Maratha *bargi* raids and Hughli itself was once overrun. The merchants also felt the impact of exactions of local officials and of the decline of other areas, especially Gujarat with which Bengal had close trading connections.[14] Trade in Bengal declined by the 1730s and revived again, as Peter Marshall has shown, in the 1770s.[15] But this was a trade directed towards China, controlled by the British with different priorities and orientations.

In what Das Gupta himself described as the 'standard text' for seventeenth-century Coromandel, Tapan Raychaudhuri had suggested that the decline of trade in that area was due to the inability of the merchants to cope with the competition from a well-organized body like the English East India Company.[16] But Das Gupta with equal tentativeness probed a different line of enquiry in line with his overall hypothesis about political collapse leading to decline in trade. Coromandel had experienced political weakness from at least a hundred years before the eighteenth century. This weakness, Das Gupta said, 'broke down into total anarchy in the eighteenth century'.[17]

Three major conflicts engulfed the region from around the 1730s: (i) Muslim power from the north of Coromandel descended to the south to attack the Hindu principality; (ii) the Mughal–Maratha conflict touched the coast in the 1740s; (iii) the French and the English intervened in local conflicts to make the entire area embattled. Coromandel thus confirmed Das Gupta's general conclusion about the close links between political collapse and decline of trade and the merchant class.

But Das Gupta's historical imagination could not be satisfied with this kind of faceless generalization. Despite the difficulties of the documentation,[18] Das Gupta wanted to capture the human faces—the reactions of the merchants as they faced the deepening crisis of declining trade and fortunes. In the introduction to his book on Surat, where in an unusual departure from his story-telling mode, Das Gupta revealed to his readers the major conclusions of his study. He wrote,

> In this essay I have tried to approach as close as to the Indian merchants as the sources, under some duress, would allow, to see them as human beings in concrete situations, sizing up problems, making decisions, forming factions, and in general working out their own salvation according to their own light...This essay is an attempt to break up the large aggregates and, particularly an attempt to see the different elements among the merchants in their cooperation and in their conflict. By and large these were men who were losing, and they were losing ground against the Europeans in particular, but some among them were losing more than others.[19]

The merchant who emerges pre-eminent in Das Gupta's story is Mulla Abdul Ghafur. The decline of his house is the story of Surat's decline. Towards the end of the seventeenth century when we first encounter him in Das Gupta's pages 'he was already among the richest shipowner–merchants of Surat'.[20] By 1700 he owned seventeen sea-going vessels with a total dead weight carrying capacity of well over 5000 tons. The scale of his operations can be guaged from the fact that his nearest rival in Surat owned only five ships. When he died in 1718 he left behind a property of Rs 8.5 million, substantial real estate and a running business.[21] Ghafur's business network could easily be compared to that of the European companies at Surat. His ships moved across the Indian Ocean from Manila to Mocha. Ghafur ran a tight ship: the *nakhudas* on his ships were either his own relatives or important businessmen of Surat connected with him. They had strict instructions regarding sailing and trading and they seldom, if ever, deviated from these directions which they received before they left Surat.[22]

Ghafur was a Bohra and had very little social prestige when compared to Arab, Persian or Turkish merchants.[23] His success created enemies among his competitors, the Turks and the Arabs who also did the Red Sea run. But more than power and social prestige, Ghafur cared for money and the continuity of trade. He knew the politics of his time and could play the game when it suited his interests. He was, however,—and Das Gupta is emphatic on this point,—'primarily a merchant'.[24] The high point of his career was his campaign against the Europeans.

At the end of the seventeenth century the principal threat to the Indian merchant on the high seas was piracy organized by Europeans. Ghafur decided that Europeans should be forced to provide compensation for the losses the Indians suffered. This was a piece of enlightened altruism on his part since as the richest merchant in the Red Sea trade he stood most to lose by the piracy. Things came to a head in September 1692, when news came that four vessels, (of these two belonged to Ghafur) had been plundered. The piracy continued and in 1695 the system of convoy to the Red Sea was introduced. Dutch ships were to escort the convoy. This system worked, with minor hiccups, for the next three years. But in 1698, Hasan Hamdani, an influential merchant with good connections in the Mughal court, lost one of his ships to William Kidd. Hamdani's lobbying resulted in new regulations for the Red Sea convoy. The Mughal emperor decreed that Europeans should pay compensation to Hamdani and to others who suffered similar losses in the future. The European factors were to sign a *muchalka* to compensate the merchants of Surat for piracies by *topiwallahs*, as all Europeans were then called. This brought unbounded joy to the Surat merchants who sent out large number of ships, disregarded the convoy and did not even take passes. Ghafur had a crucial role in all this. Das Gupta writes,

> He continuously assured the citizens that they need fear no reprisals from the Dutch for having extorted the muchalka from them, as they would never give up their lucrative trade in Hindustan. Ghafur was also taking the lead in the carefree sending out of ships and several of his vessels sailed without any European passport. The idea now was that the convoy was not necessary for the Indian merchants, but it was necessary to protect the interest of the Dutch, as they were bound to compensate the merchants for any loss. That is why the merchants of Surat did not feel they were bound to pay for the convoy any more. Similarly passes were no longer obligatory as, with or without them, compensation would be due.[25]

The situation, as the Dutch realized, was heavily loaded against them. They had no intention of honouring the blank cheque which Ghafur had thrust on them. When during the 1701 season, three ships, two belonging to Ghafur and one to his friend, Mia Muhammad, were plundered after passing the Bab el Mandeb, Ghafur demanded compensation. When the Dutch refused, Ghafur worked overtime to achieve an understanding among all the merchants to suspend all trading till the Dutch coughed up. Ghafur gave a religious twist to the situation by declairing an Islamic crusade against the *firangis.* The fact that pilgrim ships also suffered at the hands of the pirates helped Ghafur's cause. The Arabs, the Persians and the Turks responded positively to Ghafur's campaign. Ghafur's righteous anger had material underpinnings. He had built up substantial stocks at Mocha and when because of his campaign no goods from India reached the Red Sea ports, Ghafur made a killing. He also successfully bought up at about half price the goods which the smaller merchants had gathered as their ware. Under these circumstances, it was not surprising that Ghafur failed to hold on to his united front, especially after the Dutch paid the compensation. The Persians with no interest in the Red Sea trade broke away first and the Arabs and the Turks realizing that they were only helping Ghafur decided to settle there. But the payment by the Dutch was only a temporary reprieve. It did not solve the problem of piracy on the high seas and it did not mean the cancellation of the muchalka, the Dutch so resented. It was the muchalka which became the bone of contention. The Dutch with the connivance of the governor of Surat tried to have it withdrawn. The merchants under the leadership of Ghafur moved to keep it in force. The seas remained under Dutch control and they blockaded Surat but the city remained with Ghafur. Ghafur won in the end since after three seasons, the Dutch lifted the blockade and the city came back to normal. Mulla Abdul Ghafur had taken on the Dutch and won. He had the staying power, the ability to carry large sections of the merchants with him and he could play power games with the governor. Our author justifiably labelled him a 'phenomenon'.[26]

The figure of Ghafur gave Das Gupta the opening to engage with Jacob Van Leur. In his very influential *Indonesian Trade and Society* (The Hague, 1955), Van Leur pioneered the attempt to reduce the weight given to the European factor in the trade of Asia till the nineteenth century. He wanted to see Asian trade and the Asian merchant in their own terms, free from any European models. This produced what Das Gupta rightly called 'paradoxical results'.[27] He characterized Asian trade as a trade in luxuries and the Asian merchant as a pedlar. Nobody now takes seriously the idea that Asian trade was confined to luxuries.[28] But the pedlar thesis is more complicated and more difficult to dismiss. The first idea that Das Gupta gets out of the way is the one which associates peddling trade with a simple and primitive commercial structure. The money market, the credit network and insurance were all of a very sophisticated level in the seventeenth century in India.[29]

Das Gupta has no problems with seeing the Asian trading world peopled by small merchants plying the Red Sea route with their wares. He writes:

> I find no difficulty in accepting the position that India's oceanic trade was carried very largely by small merchants who travelled the maritime routes with their bundle or two of coarse cloths. On any Indian ship the majority of passengers were of this kind and their ranks were swelled by the common sailors with their headmen, all of whom engaged in petty trading to supplement their meagre wages. If the Mughal port of Surat at the close of the seventeenth century was the home of about thirty thousand merchants, only a few hundred at the most of this total could be called affluent traders. Of the small men some travelled as factors of the wealthier businessmen and in the strict sense of the term these were the pedlars of the Indian Ocean. Mostly however such men owned what they sold or traded on respondentia loans which left a substantial part of the profit with them. In selling their wares, it is true, they sold in retail and even substantial merchants often sold their stock in small lots because of the uncertainties of the market. If peddling means the existence of small merchants and sale in retail, then Indian maritime trade was by and large a peddling trade.[30]

The small merchant, however, coexisted with men like Mulla Abdul Ghafur, who were fabulously wealthy and who were driven by the desire to maximize profits. But Ghafur's was a fringe existence perpetually threatened by the uncertainty of volatile markets. He also had little control over his sources of supply. Men like Ghafur lived out a paradox:

> He was powerful and he was weak; he was rich but his money bought him some things, not others. Finally he could never get the better of the pedlars. He tried often and he tried hard to run the small merchant out of the Red Sea trade where he craved a monopoly. He ruined several of the small fry but the myriad of travellers from whose ranks Ghafur himself had almost certainly risen, were there to stay. They invested little and for the most part they wanted little. There was not much that Ghafur could do to them. In fact as the giants of the Indian Ocean trade gradually faded from the scene during the eighteenth century, the pedlar inherited the world.[31]

Medieval Indian trade had space for both the pedlar and the merchant prince.

The most important lesson that Das Gupta took from Van Leur was that a Eurocentric vision distorted the reality of the medieval Indian maritime world. At one level, by looking closely at Indian merchants, their trade, their problems and their fortunes, Das Gupta brought to light a history which was separate and distinct from that of the European companies. But Das Gupta's work contained another challenge. The port, the site from which the Indian maritime merchant operated, needed a larger context. For Surat, he emphasized the setting of the three Islamic empires. But ports are nothing without the ocean. The Indian Ocean, itself, became a field to explore. As Das Gupta put it in an epigram: 'without going out of India one cannot explain India.'[32] The history of the Indian Ocean in the eighteenth century runs parallel to developments in the continent. If India in that century saw a transition from the dominance of indigenous political rulers to the sway of foreign rule, the ocean also experienced a similar transition. The western ocean, with Surat as its most important Indian port, lost its relative importance as the trade to the Red Sea and the Persian Gulf dried up. The Calcutta fleet run by British traders and plying the eastern ocean became pre-eminent. Asian vessels retreated to the roadsteads as European sails took over the ocean.[33] In Calcutta, many important independent merchants became *banians* of the servants of the English East India Company. The relationship of the banian to the Englishman was initially, as Peter Marshall has noted, only nominally one of master–servant. The banian retained a considerable degree of initiative and clout. But as the century wore out, there were clear indications that the age of partnership was coming to a close.[34] In any case, men of the stature of Abdul Ghafur belonged to a different era and a different ocean. The emergence of British political and economic power had forever changed the nature of the trade, the ships which had carried the cargo and the ocean on which the ships had sailed. The currents of trade in the Indian Ocean increasingly moved to winds originating in Europe.

In a symmetry which was the hallmark of his teaching, Das Gupta has moved from the ports to the merchants to the sea. At every stage, he constructed a coherent story which attempted to capture a complex reality in its contrasting richness. But his manner of telling always indicated problems which promised rewarding solutions. He lit up Malabar and Surat, the radiance of that light showed up the details of Ghafur's face and for a transient moment it passed over the anonymous pedlar. The path of that light like the beam from a lighthouse lead irrevocably to the ocean.

For those like me who learnt to navigate in the complex currents of history with Das Gupta as the captain of the ship, and for those who shared the journey with Das Gupta, it has been an enormously enriching experience. Das Gupta has been that magical mariner who never allowed the old ports of call to be misted over and always unerringly picked out unknown coast lines with a new brightness.

NOTES

1. Peter Gay, *Style in History* (New York, 1974), p.189: cited in Hayden White, 'Narrativity in the Representation of Reality'. Hayden White notes that Gay is echoing Immanuel Kant who said historical narratives without analysis are empty, while historical analysis without narrative are blind. See the above article in *The Content of the Form: Narrative Discourse and Historical Representation* (London, 1987), p.5.
2. A.Das Gupta, *Malabar in Asian Trade, 1740–1800* (Cambridge, 1967).
3. Ibid., p.136.
4. Ibid., p.33.
5. Ibid., p.103. Das Gupta reiterated in stronger terms the position that Indian trade had declined before the dominance of the European companies in a later essay. See his 'Indian Merchants in the Age of Partnership, 1500–1800', in D.Tripathi (ed.) *Business Communities of India* (Delhi, 1984), pp.28–39.
6. Ibid.,
7. See A.Das Gupta, 'Indian Merchants in the Indian Ocean', in I.Habib and T.Raychaudhuri (ed.) *The Cambridge Economic History of India, vol.i c.1200–1750* (Cambridge, 1982), pp.421–2.
8. A.Das Gupta, 'Trade and Politics in 18th Century India', in D.S.Richards (ed.) *Islam and the Trade of Asia* (Oxford, 1970), pp.181–214.
9. I.Habib, *The Agrarian System of Mughal India* (Delhi, 1963), pp.330–51.
10. Das Gupta, 'Trade and Politics', p.190.
11. Ibid., p.195.
12. A.Das Gupta, *Indian Merchants and the Decline of Surat c.1700–1750* (Wiesbaden, 1979), repr. 1994, Delhi.
13. Ibid., pp.9 and 155ff.
14. A. Das Gupta, 'Trade and Politics', pp.200–1.
15. P.J.Marshall, *East Indian Fortunes: The British in Bengal in the Eighteenth Century* (Oxford, 1976), pp.76–105. Holden Furber first drew attention to this turning of trade in the Indian Ocean in *John Company at Work* (Harvard, 1948) and called it (p.162) a 'commercial revolution'. Marshall

only slightly modifies Furber's chronology by noting that the rise of the eastward trade was not concomitant with the decline of the westward one. There was, in fact an interval with the decline of one and the rise of the other. Marshall, *East Indian Fortunes,* p.104.

16. Das Gupta made this point about T.Raychaudhuri's *Jan Company in Coromandel* (The Hague, 1962) in 'Trade and Politics', p.213 n.68.

17. Das Gupta, 'Trade and Politics', p.204.

18. Das Gupta's lament about the problems of documentation is expressed in practically everything he has written but most notably in 'Sources for the Study, A Discussion' which forms Appendix B of *Decline of Surat;* and in 'Indian Merchants in the Indian Ocean', *Cambridge Economic History.*

19. *Decline of Surat,* pp. 10 and 16.

20. 'The Maritime Merchant *c* 1500–1800' (Presidential Address to, the Medieval section, 35th session, Jadavpur University, 1974), in *Proceedings of the Indian History Congress,* p.11.

21. *Decline of Surat,* p.13; and 'The Maritime Merchant', p.11.

22. *Decline of Surat,* p.13.

23. 'The Maritime Merchant', p.11.

24. *Decline of Surat,* p.13.

25. Ibid., p.100. Ghafur's campaign against the Europeans is reconstructed in ibid., ch.2.

26. Ibid., p.134.

27. Ibid., p.10.

28. *See* Das Gupta, 'The Maritime Merchant', pp.5–6.

29. *Decline of Surat,* pp.11–12.

30. 'The The Maritime Merchant', p.7.

31. Ibid., p.14.

32. *Decline of Surat,* preface to 1994 reprint.

33. Das Gupta looked at the Indian Ocean in two essays: first in his introduction to A.Das Gupta and M.N.Pearson (eds), *India and the Indian Ocean, 1500–1800* (Delhi, 1987), pp.25–45; and in 'India and the Indian Ocean in the 18th Century' in ibid., pp.131–61.

34. Marshall, *East Indian Fortunes,* pp.45–7.

3

The Hinterland and the Coast: The Pattern of Interaction in Coromandel in the late Eighteenth Century

BHASWATI BHATTACHARYA

The history of India in the eighteenth century has been a much discussed topic among historians. A period of transition as it was, the nature of Indian politics, society and economy during the period has raised debates from time to time. Some have argued that the decline of the Mughal empire in the eighteenth century caused, and coincided with an overall decline of merchants, trade and commerce. But this hypothesis has been seriously challenged in recent years by others who argue that to think that the decline of the imperial Mughals brought about an all-pervading disaster in Indian life would be to over emphasize the role of the Mughal empire. It is true that the power of the Mughals was thoroughly weakened; but this, according to these historians, did not lead to anarchy. The successor states that emerged in the eighteenth century took up many of the traits of the Mughal empire and maintained the continuity by providing opportunities of peace, political stability and economic prosperity at a regional level. An attempt will be made in this essay to understand the developments in the political life in the hinterland of the Coromandel coast and their implications on trade and commerce in the region. The region was known for its buoyant agrarian and commercial economy supported by the networks of trade. Textiles of numerous varieties, the most important commercial manufacture produced far and near in the 'rurban' centres of the hinterland, had to be transported to the ports on the coast for transshipment for coastal and overseas trade.[1] In the eighteenth century, when the demand for textiles increased by leaps and bounds, much of the cotton required for the textile industry of the coast came from the cotton producing areas deep in the hinterland. Commodities like pepper and areca nuts, produced in the western part of the coast, were gathered at the markets there and then relayed through different market-towns to the markets on Coromandel.[2] Textiles produced in the weaving villages near the coast, together with goods imported through the overseas trade were carried overland to market-towns and centres of consumption on the western part of the peninsula. A number of factors emerge from the study of the records of the Dutch and English East India companies in the middle and late decades of the eighteenth century. The disruption in the indigenous political structure and the emergence of the English as the predominant political power was the most important development of the time. The ruling houses of the region were mostly preoccupied with internecine rivalry and warfare, often fighting over resources which were already scarce. Apart from extortion of money from European companies and merchants settled at the port settlements, heavy imposts on goods carried inland for trade worked as a serious impediment to the normal functioning of trade in some areas. Secondly, the political disruptions caused first by the Maratha depredations and then by the Carnatic Wars, hit, among other things, the supply of cotton. As a result of these cumulative factors, trade and commerce in some parts of the region was seriously affected during the course of the eighteenth century. Some trade-routes lost their historic importance; some branches of trade were thoroughly disrupted. This however, is not to say that there was a complete cessation of all economic activites or that there was an overall decline of trade throughout the coast. On the contrary, there were areas, even in the later half of the century, where commerical manufacture went on undisturbed. New market-towns and commercial centres came up both on the coast and in the hinterland ensuring that the networks of commodity production and trade across the peninsula continued to function. But before going into the details regarding the trade in Coromandel, I shall brieflly touch on the debate I have referred to earlier.

Historians working on eighteenth-century India have looked at the problems of the period from different points of view. On the one hand there are scholars like Irfan Habib, Athar Ali and others working on problems related to the Mughal empire. Working on the agrarian relations in Mughal India, Irfan Habib noted that the decline of the Mughal empire in the first half of the eighteenth century and the economic breakdown of India at the end of the seventeenth century were interrelated.[3] The close link between political instability and decline of trade has been established by Das Gupta. While discussing the maritime trade of the Mughal port of Surat in the first half of the eighteenth century, he has shown that the political turmoil in the hinterland of the port was one of the reasons for the decline of trade and merchants of that port—the other reasons being political disorder in Persia and civil war in Yemen, disrupting the trade of Surat with those two regions.[4] Arasaratnam, in his recent studies of the Coromandel coast, has reflected on the close relationship between political stability and trade. The most important port on the coast in the seventeenth century was Masulipatnam which flourished under the patronage of the state of Golconda. The existing relationships between the port and its hinterland built up by its merchants were totally upset following the establishment of Mughal rule in the region in the late 1680s.[5] Richards has shown how due to his erroneous policy Aurangzeb failed to reorganize the wealth of Bijapur and Golconda for the benefit of the empire and how Mughal rule in Golconda became ineffective.[6] In his study of the central Coromandel in the eighteenth century, Basu has pointed to the '...breakdown in the traditional structure in society and government which alone could hold the existing production network intact'.[7] Establishment of Mughal rule in the region did not bring about stability. Mughal officials, as they were frequently transferred from one place to another, did not have any long-term interest in the country, with the result that the irrigation system which was developed in an earlier period was utterly neglected while land-revenue demand underwent a remarkable increase. Agricultural production fell. Cost price of foodgrains, cotton and textiles showed an upward trend. Thus, the 'anarchy and lawlessness' in the hinterland of central Coromandel was followed by an economic crisis in the region.[8]

Recent studies of different regional states—specially of north India in the eighteenth century have brought forward a totally different line of argument challenging the old concept of lawlessness and decline during that period. C.A. Bayly is the pioneer among historians who are trying to interpret eighteenth-century Indian history in an optimistic way. According to Bayly, in some areas of north India like Awadh and Benares, the decentralization of imperial power in course of the eighteenth century 'encouraged the further growth of a rooted service gentry and a homogeneous merchant class operating around small town centres'. Bayly thus argues that despite the decline of the Mughals at the centre and the emergence of the British as the supreme political power in some regions, there was a continuity noted in many other parts of the subcontinent, to be disrupted ultimately only in the nineteenth century, in the wake of the colonial rule.[9] Frank Perlin, working on Maharashtra, sympathizes with Bayly and refuses to give the Mughal empire a central position in any discussion on Indian society and economy in the eighteenth century. He goes on to disapprove of such writings, and terms the attempt to see the economic developments of the eighteenth century through the failure of the Mughals or Marathas as 'Mughal and Maratha centric treatments of economic history' and stresses the necessity of concentrating on 'other aspects of society and state formation' than 'such system making' in order to avoid generalization of a particular development which might have taken place under particular circumstances that varied from region to region.[10] Other scholars also have argued that the decline of the empire in some areas was not an indication of the decline of the empire as a whole.[11]

A recent study of the medieval Deccan and Maharashtra has again emphasized the link between political stability and the extension of cultivation and the ability of people to bear the burden of revenue. For most of the eighteenth century the region witnessed a stable government that encouraged the cultivation of wasteland. Consequently, the number of landholders increased during this period. This number showed a declining trend as the political stability was disturbed towards the end of the eighteenth century.[12]

But if peace and security in the western Deccan were disturbed at the end of the eighteenth century, stability was disrupted in the eastern part of the peninsula from a much earlier period as political fragmentation had started in the region at least a century before. The hinterland of the northern part of the coast was first to witness political disruptions resulting from the Mughal annexation of Golconda. Earlier, local administration in the region was in the hands of chiefs of various Telugu warrior clans under the authority of *sarlashkar,* or provincial governor appointed by the Qutb Shahi rulers for the province of Sicacole. The service of Telugu warriors was indispensable for the collection of revenue and maintenance of law and order. In the Sicacole district the *sardars*—like the Pusapati Razus—served as troop commanders holding lands on military tenure. In Elluru, the Vauchevoy Razus of Peddapuram and in Rajamundry the Koldinder Razus of Mogulturru acted as *deshmukhs*—assisting the collectors sent from Hyderabad in collecting taxes from the villages in a *pargana* and in return enjoying tax-free land, an allowance on the taxes collected and assurance of power and status in the locality. *Muniwars* were usually in charge of law and order in market towns, overland routes and ports in a few parganas or a district. The three Razu houses mentioned above were the most important intermediaries in the region. Increased demand for tax and the conversion of fertile tracts into *khalsa* land following the Mughal conquest initially alienated these intermediaries. But the weakness of Mughal rule became clear as soon as these intermediary *zamindars* revolted against the representatives of the Mughals. As most of their uprisings were successful, the Razu leaders exploited the weakness of the Imperial rule to develop their own power. Unable to suppress them, the Mughal officials came to terms with them by offering them various concessions.[13] The period that followed saw the emergence of these Telugu chiefs who were constantly engaged in contesting Mughal authority.

Arasaratnam's position is that as a consequence of this shift in the balance of political power, the processes of textile manufacture and trade in the northern Coromandel region suffered and the European Companies settled on the coast concentrated their attention on the southern part of the coast where peace prevailed and provisions were cheaper in comparison with those in the north.[14] But the situation in the north seems to have turned for the better for a brief period in the early eighteenth century, specially after the Nizam Asaf Jah assumed the governorship of Hyderabad.[15] The English, who had stopped trading at Masulipatnam, resumed their operations at that place in 1723. Letters from Fort St. George reported a good investment in the northern settlements of Ingeram, Madapollam and Vizagapatnam where cost of provisions and textiles was cheap.[16] Though the Dutch continued to concentrate in the southern part of the coast, at least till the 1750s textiles in general were bought by the Dutch in the northern part of the coast at a rate cheaper than that in the southern part.[17] They had withdrawn from a few of the settlements in the interior but were on the lookout for others and at least one such place was found in the port of Jagannathpuram. In 1735 they resumed their operations at Pallicol which they had deserted in 1729, and continued to trade from Masulipatnam and Bimlipatnam, while the trade of the French and English was growing from Yanam and the settlements of Madapollam, Ingeram and Vizagapatnam respectively. Occasional disruptions of trade, however, continued due mostly to what was described as extortion by those in power. As a report written in 1738–39 noted:

> ...Painters [of chintz] from the Masulipatnam region have deserted that place due to the illtreatment received from a *daroga* appointed since two years by Nasir Jang who had ordered the manufacture of a large quantity of painted goods but did not pay the making charge to those people. As for the painters who are still here are overworked as they are employed by the Armenians and the son-in-law of the late famous Muslim merchant Awas Beg for the said Nasir Jang.[18]

Similarly, another report noted that the process of investment was seriously impeded for four to five months at a stretch due to the wars between Omar Quli Khan, the Nawab of Elluru and Rajamundry and the revenue farmers of Pittapuram and Peddapuram. No sooner than peace was made, the Dutch were requested that the customary annual present be sent to him immediately along with the tolls. Then very unexpectedly he sent some cavalry soldiers to those residencies with the order to put the Company's merchants there under arrest. The idea was to force these merchants to pay a considerable amount of money in exchange for some woodwork. The soldiers extorted 500 [? rupees] from the interpreters under the threat that otherwise they would appropriate the revenue of the Company's villages which would hamper the latter's trade. Armed with a *parwana* from the Nawab, the horsemen forced themselves into the factories, turned everything upside down and demanded 500 rupees from each of the factories. It was only after a serious threat from Hooreman, the chief at Masulipatnam, that the horsemen were recalled.[19]

One comes across this kind of information more frequently after the death of Asaf Jah, the Nizamul-mulk in 1748 when a struggle for power started at Hyderabad between his son Nasir Jang and the latter's nephew Muzaffar Jang. This brought in its train the involvement of the Europeans in this struggle which finally prepared the ground for the foundation of colonial rule in India. During this period commercial activity in the north seems to have received a check as local rulers like the leaders of the Razu houses, other zamindars and Mughal officials posted in the region had entered into a race for enriching themselves and developing their power, with the result that rival interest-groups were engaged in an internecine warfare. Trade, merchants and European settlements were easy targets of a local ruler in need of money. Specially affected was the overland trade linking the coast with Hyderabad and the western part of the Deccan. It is evident from Dutch and English records that the high rate of imposts on goods moving along the Hyderabad–Masulipatnam route coupled with political disruptions and frequent plunders and extortions by intermediaries at different levels hampered normal commercial activity in the region.[20]

Still, till about the middle of the century, Masulipatnam, the major port in the northern part of the coast with links in the hinterland, had retained some of its trade. An account written around the year 1753 noted that the port was a big one but not fortified at all. It was densely populated though the trade flowing from the port had become insignificant. There were 'Moors', Hindus, Pathans, Armenians and Portuguese living in Masulipatnam. Every year ten to twelve ships were fitted out on behalf of the Pathan merchants of the port for Bengal. This line of trade now formed the most important branch of Masulipatnam's trade. Numerous smaller vessels engaged in coastal trade were also found in the roadstead.[21] Some idea about the nature of the trade carried on at Masulipatnam can be formed on the basis of the information available on the shipping at that port during 1729–1740.[22] The shipping lists of Masulipatnam are not very clear in the sense that they noted the total number of ships and vessels coming from a region without referring to the owner or the date of arrival. In case of a European ship the nationality was mentioned. So far as the exports and imports were concerned, the total quantity of a commodity brought by all the vessels coming from a region in a particular year or to be taken back to that region was mentioned. It is true that the trade of the port was now limited in nature as it had lost most of its overseas connections. Still, one to four vessels came from the Maldives during the recorded years with cauri, coir, sandalwood, coconut, round pepper, areca, tortoise shell, and other goods varying from year to year. The return cargo on this run consisted of some printed and painted cloth, rice, steel, sesame seeds, tobacco, butter, sugar and cotton. Among the ports on the other side of the Bay of Bengal, Masulipatnam had regular contact with Tenasserim while occasionally one ship would also come from Pegu or Siam. It is not clear if the port had some trade with ports in the western Indian Ocean. Ships coming from Surat sometimes touched Masulipatnam but these were perhaps ships operating between Surat and Bengal. The Mughal officials in Coromandel in the early eighteenth century did take part in the trade with Surat and ports in Arabia and the Gulf of Persia. But often their ships were sailing from ports like San Thome and Porto Novo.[23] Masulipatnam in this period seems to have been a busy centre of coastal trade through which a wide range of goods were circulated. It appears from the shipping lists that the nature of the coastal trade flowing from Masulipatnam retained the same character as in the previous centuries.[24] The greater part of Masulipatnam's coastal trade was directed to ports in the north. Most of the vessels visiting the port came from the ports on the Gingelly coast. The number of vessels coming annually from these ports varied between eighty-five to one hundred and ninety-five.[25] The bulk of the import from these ports consisted of cereals, specially rice and paddy but also wheat. Different kinds of beans, seeds, edible oil, spices like cumin, turmeric (also noted as borro borri or indigenous saffron), some sugar, dried coconuts, opium, ginger and other medicinal roots, indigo, dye-roots, hemp, coir, wax, soap, planks, brimstone, gunnycloth, resin, iron bars and nails also formed part of the cargo brought from these ports. The return cargo included spices, pepper, copper, cotton, indigenous iron and steel, long pepper, areca nuts, tin, pewter, asafoetida and tobacco. Many of the commodities, for example sugar, resin, tobacco and rice mentioned in the lists of imports also appear on the lists of exports. It is not clear if the different varieties of the same goods were exchanged between the two regions through this trade or the unsold imported items were taken back for sale elsewhere.

The number of vessels sailing between Bengal and Masulipatnam varied between sixteen and twenty-eight during the recorded years. It has been mentioned above that there was a group of Pathans living in Masulipatnam. Arasaratnam's position is that Pathan merchants had played an important role in the trade of Masulipatnam in the seventeenth century. After the decline of Masulipatnam towards the end of that century these merchants dispersed to San Thome, Porto Novo, Covelong and ports in the Gingelly coast.[26] Arasaratnam is not very clear about who these Pathans actually were. Pathans belonged to the Indo-Afghan tribes who had migrated to India in the earlier centuries in search of fortune. Many of these Pathans had settled in different parts of India. They had a strong influence in Bijapur. Around the middle of the seventeenth century half of the Bijapuri army was composed of Pathans. Pathans played an important role in the politics of the states of Savanur, Cuddapah and Karnul.[27] Daud Khan Panni, the well-known Pathan deputy governor and commander of Hyderabad at the beginning of the eighteenth century seems to have been interested in overseas trade.[28] It is likely that some of the Pathans had settled at Masulipatnam where they took part in the flourishing trade of that port. It is true that in the beginning of the eighteenth century many of these Pathans had concentrated at ports like St. Thome, Alambaram and Covelong. The employees of the English East India Company at Fort St. George noted in the 1730s that the grantees of the ports of Alambaram and Covelong employed Pathans to carry on trade at their ports. Pathan merchants were noted to have entered into contracts with these grantees who supplied them with the capital required for trade. The Pathans enjoyed one-third of the profit coming from these voyages for the troubles they undertook and the expenses they incurred whereas the remaining two-third went to the grantees.[29] But some of these Pathans were still to be found at Masulipatnam in the fourth and fifth decades of the eighteenth century. A large part of Masulipatnam's trade with Bengal was in the hands of Pathan merchants as every year they fitted out ten to twelve ships at Masulipatnam for Bengal.[30] These vessels usually came back in the following spring with products of Bengal, mainly rice, raw silk, silk cloths and muslin. But their good old days must have been over with the decline of the port. A wide range of goods was imported from Bengal including foodstuff, textiles, gunpowder and saltpetre.[31] It is important to note that raw silk and muslin from Bengal continued to be brought to Masulipatnam which fed Hyderabad and other markets in the interior. Compared to the import, the range of the return cargo was rather small: some painted and printed textiles, cotton, spices, pepper, brimstone and wax.

Among the ports in the south, Masulipatnam had a regular trade with Madras and Pondicherry. Nine to twenty-five vessels sailed from Madras to Masulipatnam in a year. The imports from Madras were mainly goods coming to that port from overseas ports.[32] It is interesting to note that the imports in 1736 included 9 pieces of cannon for the Nizam-ul-mulk. The returns from Masulipatnam were usually painted, printed and white textiles, cooking oil, coir, ginger, long pepper, coriander and cummin seeds, tamarind, some rice and iron. French vessels coming from their factory in Bengal and Pondicherry were noted together. The number of French company and private vessels touching Masulipatnam were two to eight between 1729 and 1739 and eighteen in 1740. The imports on this run consisted of rice and paddy (in all probability from Bengal), jaggery, white textiles, porcelain, lacquer, pewter, China radix, looking glass, anchors, silver cash boxes, martaban jars, teak beams for construction, cannons, guns and pistols, wax and coir while the return cargo included mainly printed textiles, brimstone, butter, rice and wheat. As the vessels belonging to the Europeans are mentioned separately, it seems that most of the numerous small coasting vessels trading at Masulipatnam belonged to indigenous people engaged in the port to port trade. Masulipatnam was still the main point of Hyderabad's trade on the east coast. The articles of trade that found their way to the hinterland from Masulipatnam were spices, copper, salt, chintz, chay, coloured cloths of all kinds, silk thread of different colours, muslin and silk from Bengal. Also taken were looking glasses, carpets, rose water and other imported goods which now found their way to Masulipatnam through the port's coastal trade. In return, the coast received cotton, wheat produced in western Hyderabad, horses, camels, hardwares of Bidar, swords, arms, and a variety of other articles. It continued to be an important centre for procurement of textiles. Till 1750 it was the headquarters of the Dutch on the northern part of the coast and a centre for redistribution of the imported spices, copper and other goods to other ports in the north and the markets in the hinterland. Around the mid-eighteenth century, specially after the fall of Masulipatnam to the French, the Dutch were trying to develop Jagannathpuram as a centre for redistribution of imported goods. Upcountry merchants were coming to Jagannathpuram, and also to Bimlipatnam. We have some information on Masulipatnam's trade with Hyderabad to show that political instability and exaction of heavy duties on goods in transit affected this trade in the second half of the eighteenth century.

Among the commodities brought from the hinterland to the coast, cotton is of special importance because though some cotton was produced in the textile producing regions of Coromandel, the coast was dependent on cotton imported from elsewhere for the thriving textile industry and trade. In the fifteenth and sixteenth centuries cotton was grown over extensive areas in the Godavari delta and in the Palnad and Vinukonda taluks of the Guntur district.[33] But imported cotton started assuming a major role in the expanding textile industry of the region since 1630 when there was the beginning of large scale import of cotton from central Deccan by the *banjara* community.[34] It will be in order here to remind ourselves once more that unlike in northern India where inland waterways formed an important channel of trade, the means of transport in greater part of the southern peninsula were pack-oxen and buffaloes.[35] It was noted towards the end of the seventeenth century that cotton required for the textiles manufactured at Masulipatnam and the surrounding weaving villages was brought from the up-country of Golconda, Bijapur and Hindusthan.[36] In the eighteenth century, northern Coromandel continued to get its supply of cotton from the upper part of the Deccan. Raichur and Bidar in the Gulbarga division of the Hyderabad state had black cotton soil and were centres of cotton trade. Adoni, in the Bellary district also had fertile black cotton soil and was a chief centre of cotton trade in the district.[37] An ample supply of cotton came from the districts of Adoni, Raichur and the western parts of the doab and found a ready and profitable sale in the manufacturing towns near the coast.[38] The Maratha districts of Pune, Satara and Nagpur also furnished the essential staple cotton required for the textile industry.[39] The banjaras bought the cotton at its source at a minimal cost. Laden on pack bullocks, the cotton would then be transported by them to the markets on the coast. The banjaras would usually sell the cotton to the chief merchants in the weaving villages on the coast with profit stretched to the utmost. The merchants again sold the cotton to low-caste people and poor women who spun the cotton into yarn and brought it to the market for sale. The weaver would buy the cotton in the market according to his need and capability.[40] The banjaras took back mainly salt but also some copper, and cash.

The trade carried on by the banjaras received special attention of the French and then the English when they gained control over the Northern Circars, not only because they imported cotton to the coast but also because they took back salt, which was an important source of income at Masulipatnam, to the interior. Masulipatnam and the neighbouring region produced a huge quantity of salt. Salt had been a state monopoly at least since the seventeenth century. Right to the salt-pans was farmed out and it was noted towards the end of the seventeenth century that during the years 1684 and 1685 the *havaldar's* income from the salt-pans under his jurisdiction was 180,000 ducats.[41] Leon Moracin, who was appointed the chief of Masulipatnam by de Bussy after Masulipatnam and its dependencies were ceded to the French in 1752, noted that production of salt formed a principal source of income at Masulipatnam. 'One can regard the salt-pans [Moracin wrote] as silver mines; ...one does not have to be afraid that one has too much salt...the more salt one has, the more buyers he will get...[42] Evidently there was a great demand for this 'annual tribute from the sea'. Some of this salt was carried to Bengal and Orissa by vessels engaged in coastal trade while Moracin noted that 30,000 to 40,000 pack bullocks were employed every year by the banjaras to carry salt inland. There was an extensive production of salt in the salt-pans at Masulipatnam, Nizampatnam, and the parganas of Tumdurru and Bomdada among other places. Salt was produced by low-caste agricultural labourers from time to time during the months from January to May.[43] During the year 1752–53 the French had employed 600 labourers in the salt-pans of Masulipatnam. The quantity that was produced was sold within two weeks and it yielded them a net profit of 60,000 rupees. Moracin noted that the French company could easily have sold double or triple the quantity, if only the supply was more. The salt-pans at Nizampatnam were expected to yield a profit of 50,000 rupees and those at Tumduru and Bomdada another 8000 rupees. Moracin's enthusiasm about the salt trade is worth noting since he was otherwise rather disappointed with the situation at Masulipatnam. Though he noted that the trade of the banjaras was affected due to the extortion of the ruling élites, he also noted that a large number of banjaras were coming to the coast and taking salt inland. There was a high demand for salt against which the supply was not enough and consequently the farmers of salt-pans could make huge profits from the sale of salt. He pointed out that the poligar of Ongole had obtained the farm of the salt-pans in the province of Kondavidu from the *faujdar* of that place for 6000 rupees, whereas his profit from the production of salt amounted to 60,000 rupees a year. Moracin was sure that with the help of a well-supported system of sale the company could easily earn 250,000–300,000 rupees a year, if not more.

What happened to this branch of trade in the late eighteenth century? In a report to the Board of Revenue, Madras, the Collector of the district of Sicacole stated that the trade in salt 'the manufacture of which might be extended to almost any quantity', had considerably declined due to reasons not known. Around 1780 a large stock of salt was found unsold for several years at Masulipatnam. Upon enquiry the collector came to know that the high rate of customs charged on salt and other articles of inland trade both in the company's territory and the country under the nizam was a source of great impediment to this trade.[44]

There is evidence to show that the Hyderabad–Masulipatnam trade which 'was at one time no doubt extremely flourishing', was suffering a set-back already by the 1760s, due mostly to political instability in the region and the excessive duties charged on goods meant for inland trade. After the English came in possession of the Northern Circars following the defeat of the French, they noted a considerable increase in the duties imposed on traders at Masulipatnam. Under the indigenous administrators, it was noted, all traders from Bengal, if they produced certificates, paid for instance four annas for 2 1/4 maunds of raw silk mugadootis and other piece-goods and two annas for sugar and pepper of the same quantity. In case they did not possess the certificate, Muslim merchants were to pay 2 1/4 per cent on all goods while Hindu merchants were to pay 5 per cent. Under the French, on production of the certificate, the merchants paid six rupees for 2 1/4 maunds of raw silk (4 rupees if the silk was coarse), one rupee for a maund of mugadooti, one rupee for two maunds of pepper, four annas for 2 maunds of sugar. If no certificate was produced, then Muslims and Hindus paid 2 1/2 per cent and five per cent respectively on all goods. The English followed the pattern when they took over the region from the French. John Andrews, the resident of the English East India Company at Masulipatnam wanted to know if this pattern was to be continued 'on account of these traders having paid customs in Bengal and the great charge they are at in carrying their goods to Idrabad'.[45]

This notes a remarkable increase in the customs duty payable at Masulipatnam on goods imported from Bengal, which was the most important trading partner of Masulipatnam in the early eighteenth century. The duty payable at the gates of Hyderabad also had gone up considerably. For a bale of Bengal silk sent from Masulipatnam the merchant in the early eighteenth century paid fourteen annas as duty at Hyderabad. The charge payable in the late eighteenth century increased to fifteen rupees for the same quantity. It was noted that the customs of the city of Hyderabad were rented yearly. The government supported the renter's collection in order to enable the latter to pay a large sum.[46]

What made it more difficult for the merchants was that there was no fixed standard for the collection of rent by the zamindars and consequently the expediency of the adventure also was uncertain. This was thought to be the main reason for Bengal silk not being brought to the markets in the Deccan through Masulipatnam anymore in the late eighteenth century.

The unreasonable and unrestrained exactions by the zamindars also affected the farms at Masulipatnam. As noted above, various farms in the town were offered for a certain period to the highest bidders who invested the sum in the shape of farm money in the hope of getting it back, along with some profit, from the sale of the commodity concerned. The salt farm, among others, suffered due 'to the unreasonable exactions of the zamedars for duties on the salt passing thro' their territories.'[47] This in turn affected the trade of the banjaras.

Due to the exorbitant customs extracted from the banjaras by the zamindars *en-route,* there was a fall in the demand for salt usually taken by the former to the up-country.[48] The high rates of duty charged in the Company's territories also hampered their trade. In theory the customs on most staple articles were fixed. But in practice the duties were heavy.[49] It was reported in 1765 that the previous farmers [of salt] Mir Sayyeed Hussain and Rustam Ali Khan could not pay the contracted money to the East India Company on account of the exorbitant fees demanded from them by the zamindars.[50] The farmers at Masulipatnam were trying to make good the loss by increasing the rate of customs payable at that place. In 1764 John Pybus, the Resident of Masulipatnam, gave an account of the growing impositions made by the farmers of salt at that place during the previous few years:

Duty collected on every 200 gunnybags of salt

By	Under the French	1761	1762 and 1763	1764
Appa Row	8	8	16	24
Collowa Collue	1:8	1:8	6	6
Sooranamy Pottanah	1:8	1:8	6	6
Sooriah & Paupiah	...	...	...	5

(*Source:* L to FSG, v.43, pp.97–8).

As the rate of duties increased, farmers usually were left with a large stock of salt unsold. Pybus maintained that it would not be possible to carry on the business of farming salt any longer 'unless some effectual means can be taken for putting a stop to these unwarrantable impositions'.[51]

That the trade carried on by the banjaras was of great importance to the English at Masulipatnam is clear from the fact that in 1764 Pybus had, in view of the extraction of money by the zamindars from the banjaras, sent a few sepoys to escort some banjaras coming down to Masulipatnam in order to purchase salt. The sepoys joined the banjaras about fifty miles on the other side of the Besora Pass. According to the report Pybus sent to Robert Palk, the Governor at Madras:

> . . . They [the banjaras] consisted of two different tribes and had been engaged in disputes with each other to such a length that many people of both sides are killed. The zamindar, in whose districts they then were, taking advantage of this, pretended they had done considerable damage to his country and robbed some of his people, demanding from them a considerable sum of money . . . which they not having to pay, he seized on their cattle and such merchandise as they were bringing with them from the country to exchange for salt and then endeavoured to drive them out of his limits by force of arms. In this situation they were when our sepoys joined them . . . .[52]

The decline in the trade carried on by the banjaras was noted by others too. In 1767 Pieter Haksteen, the Dutch governor of Coromandel, reported in connection with the sale of grains and salt at Bimlipatnam that before the Vizianagaram princes had conquered the provinces of their neighbours, specially that of Bobbeli, there had been a considerable sale at Bimlipatnam, mostly to the Lambadies who used to come to that place through Bobbeli. They stopped coming since the province was conquered by the princes as every time they were victims of the greed of the princes and their troops.[53] As they were the principal carriers of cotton from the Maratha districts to the port towns, naturally that trade was also affected.[54] This branch of trade carried on by the banjaras further declined in the later years of the eighteenth century.[55]

In sum then, following the transfer of the coastal region to the French and the English the trade of Masulipatnam further deteriorated. This was reflected in the disrupted contact of Masulipatnam with its hinterland. While the port ceased to get its supply of Bengal silk, among other trade goods, which found their way from that place to Hyderabad, it also impeded the import of cotton from the interior to the coast. The salt trade carried on by the banjaras also was affected.

But does it imply that all trade came to a standstill in the second half of the eighteenth century? To put it differently, did the trade in Bengal silk and cotton from the western Deccan also witness a similar decline in the late eighteenth century? The answer is, obviously, no. It has been shown that with the growth of textile trade of Bengal in the late eighteenth century, cotton required for the industry was being imported to that region overland from Maharashtra.[56] The route linking Bengal with the Deccan via Mirzapur was very important in this connection in the last quarter of the eighteenth century. While raw cotton required for export to China and the textile industry in Bengal dominated the eastward trade, muslin and silk carried for the consumption of the Maratha élites, and sugar were prominent in the trade moving westward. By 1800, the direct road from Nagpur to Mirzapur through the territories of the raja of Rewa, the only one for carrying cotton eastward, was the most frequented among all the routes between the Ganges valley and the capital of Berar.[57] The same source which noted that muslin, shawl and silk were not being distributed to the Deccan through Hyderabad in this period any more, noted that the western part of the Deccan was being supplied with those products via another route, that is the route linking Nagpur with Bengal.[58]

It can be argued then, on the basis of this evidence, that confusion in the political life in India in the eighteenth century disrupted some routes of trade, trading towns and ports. Masulipatnam lost its overseas trade and also the trade which connected the port with its hinterland. But at the same time, there is indication that there was some re-routing of trade linking different regions which meant at least some of this trade continued, though carried on by different merchants and through new towns and routes to different destinations.

Moving southwards, we find that the experience of the middle decades of the eighteenth century was not much different. Here, the Vijayanagara period had witnessed the gradual emergence of Telugu *nayakas* or warrior-leaders from the northern countries who established their rule in many parts of a predominantly Tamil region in the south. In the wake of the weakening of the Vijayanagara empire, the nayakas of Madurai and Tanjore asserted their independence. The region attracted many supra-local powers in the second half of the seventeenth century. First there was a struggle between Mysore, Tanjore and Madurai for political supremacy in the region. Coimbatore and Salem, the north-western provinces of Madurai, passed under the control of Mysore by 1670. Later on Ekoji, Shivaji's half brother, occupied Tanjore from the nayakas. He would be followed by Shivaji who invaded the Carnatic in 1676, occupied Jinji from Bijapur, marched to Tanjore and confirmed Maratha rule at that place. Rustam Dil Khan, a Muslim adventurer, made an attempt to establish his authority at Tiruchirapalli by expelling Chokkanatha Nayaka, the ruler of that place. He, however, was defeated and killed and the nayaka was restored to power. Finally Aurangzeb, following the conquest and annexation of Bijapur and Golconda during 1686–87, appointed Zulfiqar Ali Khan as the Nawab of the Carnatic with his capital at Arcot. In his bid to make the nayakas and poligars submit to the Mughal rule, Zulfiqar marched southwards and exacted contributions from the ruler of Madurai. The king of Tanjore acknowledged Mughal sovereignty. The Mughals captured Jinji in 1698. This marked the beginning of a bitter rivalry between the Mughals and the Marathas in the region which would continue till the middle decades of the eighteenth century. While the Nawab of Carnatic represented Mughal authority, Maratha claim to overlordship was reflected in the periodic Maratha incursions demanding allegience and exaction of payment from the rulers in the region.

An imminent outcome of the breakdown of the traditional ruling structure was the decline of the indigenous irrigation system. Since land revenue was the most important source of their income, the rulers in earlier times would, in their own interest, keep up the banks of the tanks or water reservoirs and water channels at their own expense. This was the mainstay of the indigenous irrigation system and had been taken care of by both the central and local administrative authorities during the Vijayanagara period. The system was utterly neglected in the wake of the weakening of the Vijayanagara empire and the establishment of Mughal rule in the region. The latter did not take its roots deep into the soil. After the death of Aurangzeb, Sadatullah Khan of the Navayet lineage had made the Carnatic virtually independent of the Mughals. His attempts in organizing an efficient administration restored some stability in the region. The situation seems to have turned for the worse after 1725 when the Nizam-ul-mulk sent Iwaz Khan to drive the Marathas out of the Carnatic. The conflict that ensued had some disruptive effect on the society and life in the hinterland. Mughal officials did not have a permanent interest in the region. The system of frequent transfer of the officials had its effect in that all wanted to extract as much revenue as possible while in office.[59] To top all this, the dynastic struggles centring the thrones of Arcot and Hyderabad engulfed the region in the 1740s and 1750s.

As a result of these multiple factors, land revenue demand increased by leaps and bounds.[60] This in turn affected agricultural production. Foodgrains and cotton became scarce and dear. The droughts and near famine situations occuring in the 1720s and 1730s further aggravated the condition.[61] '. . . Paddy at 25 pagodas a Garce is now thought cheap (wrote Fort St. George sometimes in 1733–34) whereas 20 years ago, at that price, it was reckoned a Famine . . . now it sells for 40 pagodas a Garce.'[62] Within a span of four years, the price of rice was reported to have further increased from 90 to 100 pagodas a garce 'and much more in the country', while the cost price of cotton went up from 18–20 pagodas to 30–32 pagodas a candy.[63]

As in the case of northern Coromandel, one important feature of the political disruption in the hinterland of southern Coromandel also was the disruption of many established networks of trade. But here it seems that certain important market-places and weavers' villages near the coast were ruined while others continued to function. In addition, new market towns came up with links stretching far into the interior of the peninsula. As the textile trade was initially the most important concern of the Europeans, naturally they focussed on the trade in cotton and the areas manufacturing textiles.

Writing in the early 1730s, the Council of Fort St. George noted that cotton required for the manufacture of textiles was not usually grown on the coast. The English used to make contracts for cotton with the inhabitants of Nyenda Petta, a town about 100 miles from Madras, Cotton was grown in the region about 230 miles north-west of Madras from where it was brought to Nyenda Petta and then sent to the ports lying between Armagon and Carera ports in the Nellore district. This variety was usually sent to Bengal. The kind of cotton yarn used for manufacture on the coast came mostly from the region which was about thirty days journey south-west from Madras. This was the region which also provided most of the cloth procured by the English on the coast. A large quantity of cotton found its way from that region to the market centre of Lalapet, a town about sixty miles from Madras. Cotton yarn amounting usually from 1,20,000 to 1,50,000 pagodas was sold annually at Lalapet from where it was distributed to all the weaving centres on the coast. 'Of late years and particularly these 3 years past (the Council continued) those Inland Provinces have been miserably Ravaged by the Marathas . . . The Cotton Plantations have therefore been neglected and of course the quantity of Cotton Yarn at the Fair at Laulapetta has been trifling and inconsiderable.'[64]

As war continued, it not only created great confusion in the cloth producing countries, but also hindered the communication between several parts of the country preventing the usual supply of cotton and grain.[65] It became hazardous for the indigenous merchants in European towns on the coast either to invest money in the country or to bring their goods, specially cotton and yarn from distant inland provinces.[66]

It was noted in 1741 that at Ulandorepettai, where every month cotton yarn was brought and sold to the amount of 12 to 15,000 pagodas, none had been brought for some months at a stretch.[67] This kind of disturbance was noted particularly during the years when the Marathas fell upon the coast causing insecurity on the road. There was no guarantee that the cotton yarn or textiles despatched from the hinterland would reach their destination on the coast safely, or a merchant coming to the coast for buying imported goods would go back with the goods he intended to purchase. Thus, it was noted in 1745 that the Marathas, while plundering the inland provinces providing cotton and yarn, captured and set 1000 oxloads of cotton and thread on fire.[68] Similarly, on another occasion, 'they [the Marathas] seized a caravan of goods of 2,00,000 pagodas value going into the Kanara country by which some of the Madras merchants suffered.'[69] The spices, copper and other goods imported by the Dutch company to Paliacatta and Sadraspatnam found their way to the inland markets at Arcot, Kanchipuram and Lalapet which served as centres for exchange of goods coming from the ports on the east coast and markets in the western part of south India. Kanari merchants came to Lalapet and Sadraspatnam for buying spices and copper.[70] Merchants coming from the interior were often victims of plunder and extortion. It was reported in 1748 that the up-country merchants coming from Lalapet and Kanchipuram could not come to the coast because of an engagement between them and the farmers of land revenue in the lowlands of the Carnatic, as the latter claimed that the former must pay them in order to make up the shortfall in the farm money as returns from those regions had been insignificant.[71]

Procurement at the famous weaving mart, Udaiyarpalayam, suffered greatly for this very reason. Muhammad Ali, the Nawab of Carnatic, had farmed out the region to the old zamindar of the place for a large sum of money. The zamindar started extracting money from all the weavers, merchants and other inhabitants which induced all the people to desert that region.[72] This greatly impeded the course of procurement of textiles by the European companies. As many of the weaving centres and markets for collecting textiles were situated deep inland, it became almost impossible to carry on investment as before. 'Trusting money in the country at any distance', wrote the Council of Fort St. George, 'is very hazardous. The merchants take but little money . . . since the troubles send none so far south as Salem suspecting the Marathas will visit those parts.'[73] Due to disturbances in the hinterland, price of ordinary textiles at Salem, Chennamanaikpalayam and Udaiyarpalayam had very much increased in the early 1740s. 'The ordinary sorts of cloth chiefly made in those places (wrote the Council in September 1741) came out dear—the difference is too considerable not to be taken notice of.' For this reason the English, specially since 1740, asked their merchants not to send the *gumashtahs* to those places and decided to confine their merchants to the region around Madras.[74] It was for the same reason that out of the 58,000 pieces of textiles ordered at Cuddalore for the year 1762, only 7510 pieces could be collected by November of that year from Salem, Shialy, Udaiyarpalayam, and Chennamanaikpalayam. It was reported that due to the troubles in the region during the preceding few years, weavers had left their villages for other places seeking protection.[75]

Thus, the uncertainty resulting from the political instability in the hinterland affected the textile trade at some places on the southern part of the Coromandel coast. Important weaving centres and market towns were subjected to frequent plunder and devastation. Arcot, Ramapet, Lalapet, Kanchipuram, Salem and Udaiyarpalayam were often plundered.[76] It was noted that in the wake of Haidar Ali's campaigns most of the civilian population of the Carnatic had fled their homes, fields, shops and towns. The only inhabitants were the garrisons of the forts, the British and Mysore armies.[77]

It would appear from these accounts that trade and manufacture were seriously hindered at some places in the southern part of the coast. But as we have noted before, the effect of the dislocation in the political life seems to have been local. As some of the market-places and weavers' villages were plundered and ruined, there were others where manufacture went on undisturbed. This can be argued on the basis of evidence available in the records of the Dutch company. This is interesting because the servants of the company who collected their information sitting at the port towns usually spoke of overall decline and decay. Perhaps this was done partly in order to prove the incapability of the indigenous rulers while at the same time the officials of the company tried to justify their own inability to supply the required quota of textiles. It is noticeable that when they were speaking about the difficulties in procuring textiles, or the competition from other traders, for most of the period the Dutch officials on the coast made no enquiry in the weaving villages. The only time such a survey was made during 1740–80 was in 1771, and the brief report outcome of this survey showed that at least in some areas manufacture of textiles went on undisturbed. But there was definitely a decline in the demand for textiles for long distance trade, specially the trade of the Dutch East India Company. It will be interesting to consult this report in some detail as this kind of document is rare.

I have shown elsewhere that the textile trade of the Dutch was not very promising in the 1760s any more.[78] Dissatisfaction on part of the Directors of the company and the government at Batavia expressed regularly in their letters had failed to achieve any success in this respect. Things were in a mess specially during the tenure of Christiaan van Teijlingen (1758–65). Peter Haksteen, the next governor, took a few positive measures with regard to the textile trade on the coast.[79] It was perhaps at Haksteen's insistence that a *brahminee* (interpreter) was sent to some weavers' villages near Sadraspatnam. The reason for sending the interpreter was to enquire about the demand of textiles on behalf of the European companies and the price paid by their merchants to the weavers in those villages. It is not known if similar attempts were made at other factories of the company. Since textiles coming from the region around Sadras were much wanted in Europe, and it was one of the areas where the pressure of English presence was quite heavy, it is possible that Haksteen wanted to make a sample survey of the region as there were quite a few notable weavers' villages in the immediate hinterland of that port.

The brahmin, Achi Appa went to several villages and talked to the head weavers. The report he submitted does not go into the details of how the weavers worked, but it shows the number of looms in the villages and the kind of textiles manufactured there. Thus we are told at Tirukodikondam, for instance, there were hundred looms, at Arkadupettai and two neighbouring villages two hundred looms, at Manamadura and the surrounding villages of Chinnapakkam,

Acharapakkam, Agaram, Kannigapettai, Ammapettai, Karanai and two other villages a total of five hundred looms, and at Karunguli and Palanjur fifty looms each were employed for manufacturing *guinees, salempores* and *muris.* The European companies were represented here through their merchants. Thus, the indigenous supply-merchants working for the Dutch placed the demand for the company with the weavers and their colleagues from Madras, for instance, did the same for the English. The demand of the Dutch and the French companies had declined, but the weavers still counted on the demand from Madras. Merchants were required to make some advance payment either in cash or in yarn. If they were given the cost price of the piecegoods they wanted, the weavers were willing to manufacture for any buyer whosoever. More important, as the demand from the European sector was not big, the weavers were manufacturing for the *bazaars*. It is difficult to make generalizations on the basis of such a document. But this report indicates that in areas outside the control of the Europeans, the English in particular, the weavers still enjoyed the freedom to choose their employer—in other words, merchants did not have absolute control over producers and the methods of production. Unfortunately, we do not know the final destination of the textiles which found their way to the local markets, but this contradicts the frequently repeated information on decline and destruction. It should, however, be noted that we have evidence to suggest that at least some of the trans-peninsular trade continued in the late eighteenth century. Specially in the second half of the century new towns and market-places came up in different parts of southern India linking the east and west coast of the peninsula.

One such place on the Coromandel coast was Walajahpet or Walajanagar.[80] This town was founded by Rayoji, a minister of the nawab Muhammad Ali Walajah and was named after him. The town was located sixty-eight miles from Madras and three miles north of the Palar river. There were eighteen *pettahs* or squares containing convenient shops surrounding a small temple at the centre of the town. At the close of the nineteenth century, there were twenty-one drinking water tanks and about hundred public wells scattered about the place, all attributed to the said minister of Muhammad Ali. In order to tempt merchants from other places, Rayoji was said to have exempted the traders of the new town from taxation which led the rich Kanari merchants of Lalapet, the well-known market town six miles away from Walajahpet, to leave *en masse* for the latter place. Soon afterwards it fell into the hands of Haidar Ali. On the restoration of peace, Muhammad Ali placed his favourites in charge of the new town and with the benefits coming from the court, the town soon rose to a great size. Within a short time Walajahpet became one of the busiest marts in southern India where goods of various assortment could be procured. It carried on a large trade, mainly in grains and cotton, with Madras, Mysore and the ceded districts. Buchanan noted that almost all the trade between the country above the ghats and the sea coasts centred at Walajahpet. Provisions here were cheap and plenty. A larger assortment of goods could be procured at Walajahpet than in any other town of the peninsula, including Madras.[81]

It is interesting to follow the trade of Walajahpet because the growth of this place as a centre of transpeninsular trade was to some extent dependent on developments in the state of Mysore, and much of its trade was directed to the western part of the peninsula. It is known that the state of Mysore, with its extensive territories and rich resources, became a formidable power under Haidar Ali and Tipu Sultan in the late eighteenth century.[82] One of the places in Mysore with which Walajahpet had thriving trade was Nagar in Shimoga district in present Karnataka. Situated at 13°50/ N. lat. 75°6/ E long., Nagar was originally a small village called Bidaruhalli or Bamboo village. Virabhadra Nayaka, (1629–45) who succeeded to the nayakaship of Ikkeri after the death of his grandfather Venkatappa Nayaka (1586–1629), transferred his capital from Ikkeri to this place in 1639 when it became their capital under the name of Bidarur or Bidanur, popularly known as Bednur.[83] The town was enlarged during the rule of Sivappa Nayaka (1645–60). Lying on the direct trade route by the Hosangadighat, Bednur was favourably situated for trade as many important trade routes connecting the port town of Mangalore and the ghats converged here. The town grew so rapidly in size that it was said to have contained about 100,000 houses which led to the renaming of the place as Nagara. Bednur remained under the Keladi dynasty till 1763 when Haidar Ali fell upon and captured the fort of Bednur after he had conquered northern Mysore. The ruling queen, Virammaji tried to make a compromise by offering Haidar a large sum of money. She even proposed to pay Haidar an annual tribute of a lakh of pagodas and a share in the pepper, areca nut, sandalwood and other produces of the country. As Haidar rejected the offers, the queen took flight after offering some resistance.[84] Haidar stormed the palace and captured the city and renamed it Haidarnagar. With his intention to make this place a city and increase its trade, he established his principal arsenal here. Many people were employed in the manufacture of arms and ammunition. Haidar also established a mint where Haidari pagodas and many other coins were issued in his name. All these measures encouraged merchants from other places to settle in Nagar. The prosperity of the town suffered much during the wars with Tipu Sultan. It was captured by the British in 1783, but was recovered by Tipu. Nagar was a place of considerable trade at the turn of the nineteenth century.

The trade between Nagar and Walajahpet was channelized through Hindupur. The latter was the headquarters of the *taluk* bearing the same name in Anantapur district. This taluk forms a part of the Mysore plateau and shares its higher elevation and cooler climate. Together with Madakasira, Hindupur receives more rain than other places in the neighbourhood and in contrast to the more arid central division of the district, supports a considerable amount of vegetation. The soil here is fertile. Both the taluk were noted to have a higher percentage of land under tanks than any other taluk and grew more paddy than others, though ragi and horsegrams were the chief crops. They were also the most densely populated taluks in the district.

The region remained a bone of contention between the Marathas and Haidar Ali. Around the year 1746, Murari Rao Ghorpade had established a fort at Gooty where he had his permanent residence since 1754. In 1762, Haidar's army swept over the entire region when Hindupur, Kodikonda, Penukonda, Madakasira, Tadpatri and other places were captured by Haidar Ali. Murari Rao recaptured Kodikonda and Madakasira in 1766 but a few years later they again fell to Haidar. Hindupur was the largest commercial centre in Anantapur district towards the end of the eighteenth century. According to local belief the town was founded by Siddoji, the father of Murari Rao. Till the 1779–80 it was a small place. In that year Jungamkotta Krishnappa, the *amaldar* of Penuconda and Kodikonda, obtained from Haidar Ali the permission to establish a market and petta at that place. In order to encourage merchants from neighbouring areas to settle here, Haidar exempted merchants at this place from the payment of all duties and taxes for a period of three years. Consequently, the place became populous and a fair was started here since that time. When Tipu Sultan marched with his army against the fort of Adoni in 1787–88, he halted at Vapachee, a place about six miles east of Hindupur. With the view to make the petta of Hindupur more flourishing than before, Rangappa, the then amaldar of Kodikonda, addressed the sultan and obtained his *cowle* to the merchants exempting their commerce from all kinds of payment for another three years. Rangappa also extended the petta and encouraged a number of rich merchants from neighbouring areas and denominated the place Sultanpetta. This place being at the centre of several roads, different kinds of commodities were imported here both from the east and the west. As it lay half way between Nagar in Mysore and Walajahpet, it soon became a commercial centre of importance. Areca nuts were one of the major items carried from the west to the east in this transpeninsular trade.

Bullocks were usually used for transporting goods, each bullock load containing eight maunds. If the entire lot of areca brought from the west was sold at Hindupur, a duty of ten Kanthirai pagodas per hundred bullock loads was paid at that place and the nuts were disposed of at that place at two pagodas a maund. Cotton imported from Adoni was sold at nine to ten *fanams* per maund at Hindupur and was also exported to Kolar and Tumkur among other places. Coconuts came from the Gubi taluk and were sent to Dharmavaram, Cuddapah and Siddavattam. Bought at three to four fanams a maund at Gubi taluk, these were sold at six to seven fanams at Hindupur and ten to twelve fanams at Cuddapah. Finer kinds of cloth were brought from Dharmavaram, Gooty, Bellary and Tadpatri and were sent to Putnam and other places of commerce via Hindupur. In addition to the expenses of three fanams on road, a land custom of five fanams had to be paid at Hindupur for each load of cloth. Ghee, oil, tobacco were also imported from Dharmavaram, Tirumany and other places to Hindupur. The trade between Nagar and Walajahpet seems to have been carried on mostly by the Kanari merchants, who had their agents at the latter place. They purchased areca nuts and pepper at Nagar and other places which they carried eastward to Hindupur and then to Walajahpet. A maund of areca nuts purchased at eight gatty fanams at Nagar would be sold at nine to fifteen gatty fanams at Hindupur. Goods bought at one pagoda a maund at Nagar would usually be sold at two pagodas the same amount at Walajahpet. But if the entire lot of areca brought from the west was sold at Hindupur, a duty of ten Kanthirai pagodas was paid per bullock load and the areca was sold at two pagodas per maund. From Walajahpet they would take back silk and woollen cloths, indigo, camphor, lead, copper and spices like clove, nutmeg and mace. The trade between Walajahpet and Nagar is important because it shows that in spite of Tipu's ban on trade with the dominions of the nawab of Arcot, such trade did take place. When Buchanan was travelling through Mysore, he was told that Tipu's regulations prohibiting trade with places under the jurisdiction of the nawab of Arcot were not strictly observed. Principal officers at Bangalore privately issued passports to traders for trade with the nawab's country.[85] The trade between Walajahpet and Bangalore was conducted at the former place again chiefly by Kanari merchants who had their agents there.[86] The duties payable to the nawab on this trade were bearable and the merchants did not complain about the duties.[87] Merchants from Walajahpet also traded at Waluru in the Mysore dominions. Cotton cloth, both for local use and for export, was the most important manufacture of this place where a weekly market was held. Because the cloth manufactured here was cheap, much of it was smuggled out of the country. Merchants from Walajahpet sent some spices, European goods and other commodities to Waluru and took back cloths which were sold at Madras.[88] Merchants of Tanjore carried on some trade at Bangalore. Palghat was another market town where merchants from Tirunelveli, Madura, Tanjore, Madras Coimbatore and Salem met merchants coming from Calicut, Cochin and other places in the west.[89] Pepper, grown extensively in Malabar, was an important commodity carried overland to Coromandel. This trade was a monopoly of the Tamil brahmins settled mainly in the regions around Palghat. They brought pepper from the west and sent back coarse cloth from the Coromandel coast. Much to the annoyance of the Dutch East India Company, this trade enjoyed the protection of the indigenous rulers.[90] Much to their annoyance the Dutch at Nagapatnam noted that pepper from Malabar was first brought to Tirunelveli, from where it was transported overland to Muttupet which a lay a few miles south of Nagapatnam. From Muttupet it was finally sent to Nagore, a port under the jurisdiction of the king of Tanjore, where it was disposed of at a rate cheaper than the Dutch could afford to offer.[91]

The above discussion has tried to show that different parts of Coromandel went through different experiences in the mid and late eighteenth century. In the north, the internecine rivalry among the local rulers, and following the Mughal conquest of Golconda, the hostility between the old Hindu ruling houses and the Muslim officials appointed by Hyderabad, had led to the decline of trade and industry. But there seems to have been some recovery of the trade in the region in the first half of the eighteenth century. This was reflected in the attempts of the Europeans to establish new settlements in the region. They were investing in the textile trade in the north where the cost of provisions and textiles were noted to have been cheap. Though the existence of many ports was a feature of the Coromandel coast, in the north, Masulipatnam had been the most important port in the seventeenth century. This port lost much of its sea-borne trade and its contact with the hinterland was jeopardized in the course of the eighteenth century as a result of instability in the political life. But Pathan merchants of that port still carried on a considerable trade with Bengal. The cotton required for the textile industry in the coast and its immediate hinterland came from up-country. The warfare that started centring the thrones of Hyderabad and Arcot brought many regional and extraregional elements on the scene, all trying to gain control over the resources. The confusion that resulted from this unstable situation had an adverse impact on the production of and trade in textiles in the region. The grant of the Northern Circars first to the French and then to the English added to the confusion. The French, when they took possession of the Northern Circars, criticized the preceding indigenous government for having ruined the region.[92] But if one takes into consideration the dues which, according to the English, had been imposed by the French on merchants and farmers at Masulipatnam, one does not get the impression that the French were trying to revive the prosperity of that port. Soon, however, the region passed under the control of the English. The heavy duties imposed on transit trade both in the territories under the Nizam-ul-mulk and the French were continued during the early years of English rule. This further affected for instance Masulipatnam's trade with its hinterland on one hand and with Bengal on the other. In sum then, northern Coromandel in the eighteenth century witnessed forces that worked as a constraint to further growth of trade and commerce in the region.

The situation in some areas of the southern part of the coast was similar in the 1740s and the 1750s. Here, the supply of cotton, yarn and textiles from places like Salem, Coimbatore and Lalapet was severly disrupted, first due to the Maratha depredations and then the Carnatic Wars. While this was the picture in the middle decades of the century, documents dating from the later part of the century are comparatively more positive and show that though there was a decline in the demand for the trade of the European companies, textile weavers continued to cater to the demand of the market. New towns were founded which also served as market towns linking the western and the eastern parts of the peninsula. It is likely that most of the trade that took place at Walajahpet was carried on under the aegis of the English. But the pattern of this trade seems to have remained unchanged till the end of the eighteenth century. Goods imported through coastal and overseas trade together with the products of the coast found their way into the interior while pepper and betelnuts remained the chief items taken eastward. Kanari merchants, like in the earlier part of the century, continued to dominate this overland trade linking the coast with the interior.

I started with the debate on the eighteenth century. The above discussion on trade in Coromandel in the late eighteenth century has tried to show that even in a region like Coromandel there were areas of growth and decline during the course of the eighteenth century. Masulipatnam declined and much of the trade that went to Hyderabad from that port also declined. But it is also evident that though some branches of trade underwent a decline, some other trade routes came up indicating that at least some of the earlier trade continued, albeit through a different route and directed to a different destination. In the case of the northern part of the coast such developments took place outside the region. Moving southwards, one notices the new towns like Hindupur and Walajahpet as centres of transpeninsular trade. In spite of the fact that the account of trade at these places is not exhaustive, it can be said that the theory of possible link between political decline and decline in trade and economy is not valid because instability in political life did not play the central role it was supposed to have.[93] Effect of political decline on the economy was localized. Whereas some centres of power witnessed decline, many regional states came up where initiatives were taken to foster trade and commerce. Consequently, there were extensive networks of commodity-production, trade and marketing connecting centres of production and trade across the peninsula, extending the hinterland of the Coromandel coast almost upto the western coast.

NOTES

[1] *See* F. Perlin, 'Proto-industrialization and pre-colonial South-Asia', in *Past and Present,* no. 98, February 1983, pp.430–95 for the phrase 'rurban'.

[2] For an excellent survey of the coastal, overland and the overseas trade of South India *see* S. Subrahmanyam, *The Political Economy of Commerce, Southern India 1500–1650,* Cambridge, 1990, specially ch.2. *Also see* S. Arasaratham, *Merchants, Companies and Commerce on the Coromandel Coast, 1650–1740,* Delhi, 1986, ch.2 for markets and trade-routes in the hinterland of the coast.

[3] I. Habib, *The Agrarian System of Mughal India, 1565–1707,* London/ Bombay, 1963. M. Athar Ali has summed up the position of Irfan Habib and the views of other historians on eighteenth-century India. *See* 'Recent theories of eighteenth century India', *Indian Historical Review,* 1986–7, XIII, 1–2, pp.102–10, and 'The Mughal polity—a critique of Revisionist Approaches',

Modern Asian Studies, 27,(4), 1993 pp.699–710.

[4] A. Das Gupta, *Indian Merchants and the Decline of Surat c.1700–1750*, Wiesbaden, 1979, first Indian reprint Delhi, 1994.

[5] S. Arasaratnam, *Merchants, Companies...*, pp.159–60; S. Arasaratnam and A. Ray, *Masulipatnam and Cambay: a History of two Port-towns, 1500–1800*, Delhi, 1994.

[6] J.F. Richards, *Mughal Administration in Golconda 1687–1727*, Oxford, 1975.

[7] B.J. Basu, 'Central Coromandel in the eighteenth century', unpublished Ph.D. thesis submitted to the Visva Bharati University, 1988, p.16.

[8] ibid.

[9] C.A. Bayly, *Rulers, Townsmen and Bazaars, North Indian Society in the Age of British Expansion, 1770–1870*, Cambridge, 1983, p.8.

[10] F. Perlin, 'State formation reconsidered', part II, *Modern Asian Studies*, 19, 3 (1985), p.429. This and a few other essays by Perlin have been revised and put together in *The Invisible City: Monetary, Administrative and Popular Infrastructures in Asia and Europe, 1500–1900*, Hampshire, 1993.

[11] These scholars are, for the Deccan M.A. Nayeem, *Mughal Administration of Deccan, under Nizam-ul-mulk Asaf Jah (1720–48 A.D.)*, Bombay 1985, pp.7, 230; for the Punjab and Awadh Muzaffar Alam, *The Crisis of Empire in Mughal North India, Awadh and the Punjab, 1707–48*, New Delhi, 1986, specially pp.9, 12; for Maharashtra Andre Wink, *Land and Sovereignty in India: Agrarian Society and Politics under the Eighteenth Century Maratha Svarajya*, London, 1986; for South India David Washbrook, 'Progress and Problems: South Asian Economic and Social History, c.1720–1860', *Modern Asian Studies*, 22 (1), 1988, pp.57–96; Burton Stein 'Eighteenth century India: another view', *Studies in History*, 5, (1), 1989, pp.1–26.

[12] H. Fukazawa, 'The Medieval Deccan and Maharashtra', in Tapan Raychaudhuri and Irfan Habib ed., *Cambridge Economic History of India, v.1, c.1200–c.1750*, Indian reprint, Delhi, 1984, pp.193–203.

[13] The process of administration of the Andhra coastlands has been studied in detail by J.F. Richards in his *Mughal Administration...*

[14] *See* S. Arasaratnam, *Merchants, Companies...*, chapter 2. Recently he has noted that 'there are signs of some picking up from the low position to which trade had sunk in the last decade of the seventeenth century and the first decade of the eighteenth'. *See Masulipatnam...*, p.87.

[15] *See* J.F. Richards, *Mughal Administration...*, pp.304–5 and B.J. Basu, 'Central Coromandel' for a similar position.

[16] Records of Fort St. George (RFSG), Despatches to England (D/E), v.11, 31 August / 2 September 1734, p.42; 1 October 1733, p.6. Valentijn noted that cotton and provisions were much cheaper at Bimlipatnam where many types of cloth were available. The quality of the cloth here was better and the cost price lower than elsewhere in Coromandel. F. Valentijn, *Oud en Nieuw Oost-Indien*, Amsterdam 1724, v.5, p.42.

[17] For details regarding the textile trade of the Dutch company on the coast during this period *see* B. Bhattacharya, 'Some aspects of the textile

trade of the Dutch East India Company on the Coromandel Coast, 1730–1780', in *The International Institute of Asian Studies Yearbook,* 1994, pp.169–82.

[18] Algemeen Rijksarchief (henceforth ARA) The Hague, Nagapatnam–Batavia, December 1741 VOC 2539, pp.2725–6; *also see* VOC 2702, p.584; VOC 2744, pp.159–60; VOC 2784, pp.607–8 for similar evidence.

[19] ARA, Nagapatnam–Batavia, 22 July 1745, VOC 2652, p.242; *also see* VOC 2702, p.584; VOC 2744, pp.159–60, 515–16; VOC 2784, pp.607–8 for similar information.

[20] The unpublished manuscript written by Adrianus Canter Visscher who was a junior merchant and fiscaal at Masulipatnam before he left the coast in 1744. (private collection).

[22] *See* lists of ships and vessels arriving at and departing from Masulipatnam, ARA, VOC nos. 2135, pp.119–25; 2197, pp.691–6, 1920–6; 2244, pp.185–91; 2318, pp.2576–80; 2351, pp.3780–5; 2387, pp.1617–19; 2443, pp.2964–71; 2471, pp.802–12; 2538, pp.1185–94.

[23] In 1721 Khojaji Ibrahim, the then faujdar of Masulipatnam in a letter to Hendrik Zwaardecroon, the Dutch governor of Ceylon mentioned that his ship *Fate Murad* had an accident between Colombo and Galle on its way back from Surat. There were fourteen Muslim merchants on board who were able to save the cargo of the ship (both goods and cash) amounting to little more than 25,000 rupees. The cargo was later looted by the officials of the Dutch East India Company at Colombo. ARA, translation of a letter from Khojaji Ibrahim, the governor of Masulipatnam, to H. Zwaardecroon, 23 March 1721, VOC 1962, pp.437–9. For Coromandel's trade with ports in the western Indian Ocean *see* B. Bhattacharya, 'Porto Novo and the trade in the Bay of Bengal in the mid-eighteenth century', paper presented to the International Conference on Factories, Shipping, and Colonisation, Brussels, 28–30 November, 1994 (forthcoming).

[24] For the trade of Masulipatnam in the earlier period *see* S. Subrahmanyam, *The Political Economy...*, pp.50–1, S. Arasaratnam and A. Ray, *Masulipatnam...*, specially pp.90–6.

[25] 749 thonies noted in the document for the year 1730 (in addition to 45 grubs and 1 sloop) seems to have been a mistake. A comparison of the number of vessels coming in the other years suggests that 149 thonies were likely to have come to Masulipatnam from the ports in the north in that year. ARA, OBP. VOC 2197, pp.691–6.

[26] S. Arasaratnam, *Merchants, Companies...*, pp.166, 169–71.

[27] B. Bhattacharya, 'The Dutch East India Company and the Coromandel Coast, 1740–1780', unpublished Ph.D. dissertation, Visva Bharati University, 1993, ch.3.

[28] S. Arasaratnam, in S. Arasaratnam and A. Ray, *Masulipatnam...*, p.79.

[29] B. Bhattacharya, 'Porto Novo and the trade...'.

[30] The memoir of Adrianus Canter Visscher... .

[31] These goods were rice, wheat, beans, sugar, long pepper, opium, honey, almond, ginger, sugar, cummin, dry fruits, rosewater, dye-roots, fragrant oil, hemp, mats, bows and arrows, saltpetre, gunpowder, and some cotton and

silk textiles together with silk yarn.

[32] Some of these commodities were copper, fragrant resin, dates, various kinds of nuts, sugar, tea, cummin, dye-roots, long pepper, asafoetida, saffron, borax, lead, tin, coral, ivory, tortoise-shell, vermilion, quick silver, mirrors, spectacles, paternosters, gunpowder, chinaware, etc.

[33] S. Subrahmanyam, 'Rural industry and commerical agriculture in the late seventeenth century south-eastern India', *Past and Present,* no. 126, pp.76–114.

[34] J.J. Brennig, 'Textile producers and production in late seventeenth century Coromandel', *The Indian Economic and Social History Review* (henceforth *IESHR*), XXIII (1986), pp.66–89; For the role of the banjaras in pre-colonial Indian commerce *see* I. Habib, 'Merchant communities in pre-colonial India', in J.D. Tracy (ed.) *The Rise of Merchant Empires: Long-Distance Trade in the Early Modern World, 1350–1750,* Cambridge, 1990, pp.371–99.

[35] *See* J. Deloche, *La Circulation en Inde avant la revolution des transports,* 2 vols, Paris 1980.

[36] Daniel Havart, *Op en ondergang van Coromandel,* Amsterdam, 1693, Book I, p.148; Pieter van Dam, *Beschrijvinge van de OostIndische Compagnie,* 7 vols, eds F.W. Stapel and C.W. Th. van Boetzelaer, The Hague 1927–54, Book II, part II, p.148.

[37] *Imperial Gazetteer of India,* reprint edition, different volumes.

[38] India Office Library and Records (IOL), London. Board's Collections F/4/80/1771, John Read, Collector at Masulipatnam to Board of Revenue, Madras, 14 November 1799.

[39] ARA, Nagapatnam–Batavia, 3 August 1768, VOC 3229, p.466; *also see* A. Guha, 'Raw cotton of Western India 1750–1850', *IESHR,* IX, 1972, no.1, pp.1–42.

[40] Pieter van Dam, *Beschrijvinge...,* p.148.

[41] D. Havart, *Op-en ondergang...,* Amsterdam, 1693, I, pp.225–6.

[42] J. Deloche, 'Le memoir de Moracin sur Masulipatnam', in *Bulletin de l'École Française d'Extrême Orient,* LXII, 1975, pp.125–49.

[43] An account of the process of manufacture of salt can be found in Francis Hamilton Buchanan, *Journey from Madras through Mysore, Canara and Malabar,* (3 vols, London, 1807), v.1, p.35.

[44] IOL, Board's Collections, District Collector of Chicacole to Board of Revenue, Madras, 5 November 1799.

[45] RFSG, L to FSG, v.41, no.55, Masulipatnam to Fort St George, 22 July 1761, pp.49–50; also v.42, no.56, Masulipatnam to Fort St George, 3 May 1762, p.41.

[46] IOL, Board of Trade, F/4/80, 1771, Extracts of Public Consultations, Fort St George, 14 March, 1800; letter from the Board of Trade to the Council of Fort St George, pp.53–7.

[47] RFSG, L from FSG, v.38, no. 129: to Masulipatnam, 1 November 1764, p.102.

[48] RFSG, L to FSG, v.43, no. 102, Masulipatnam to Fort St George, 14 September 1764, pp.97–8.

[49] IOL, Board of Trade, Madras to Lord Clive.

[50] RFSG, L to FSG, v.45, no. 86, Masulipatnam to Fort St George, 22 April 1765, p.82.

[51] Ibid.

[52] RFSG, L to FSG, v.44, no. 123, Masulipatnam to Fort St George, 29 November 1764, p.123. It was not unusual that different groups of the banjaras would fight each other for the possession of salt; *see* the memoir of Moracin.

[53] Nagapatnam–Batavia, 21 December 1767, VOC 3197, p.370. Visia Rama Razu, who could not subjugate Ranga Rao of Bobbei due to want of armaments, insisted de Bussy to remove his enemy. For details *see* R. Orme, *A History of the Military Transactions of the British Nation in Indostan, from the Year MDCCXLV,* London, 1763–78, v.2. part I, pp.253–61.

[54] ARA, Nagapatnam–Batavia, 3 August 1768, VOC 3229, p.466.

[55] IOL, Board's Collections, Collector of Vizagapatnam to Board of Revenue, Madras, 13 December 1799. But the banjaras continued to take salt to the Nizam's dominions even in the late nineteenth century. Salt manufactured in the Kistna district was first taken by local merchants to the market at Jaggayyapet from where the banjaras took it inland. About 120,000 maunds of salt was taken to Jaggayyapet every year. G. Mackenzie, *A Manual of the Kistna District on the Presidency of Madras,* Madras, 1883, p.369.

[56] A. Guha, 'Raw cotton...'.

[57] British Museum, Additional Mss. 13,588, Narrative of a journey from Mirzapur to Nagpur in the year 1799. *Also see* C.A. Bayly, *Rulers, Townsmen...,* pp.234–9, 242–52 for trade in cotton through Mirzapur in the last quarter of the eighteenth and the first quarter of the nineteenth century and pp.268–9 for the decline in the elite consumption of fine products like muslin, shawl and kinkhab in the Maratha courts after 1825.

[58] 'This evil [i.e. the numerous duties on transit trade] helped not a little to make the Bengal silks find their way to the markets of the Deccan by the route of Nagpour...' IOL, Board's Collections, F/4/80, 1771, extracts of Public Consultations of Fort St George.

[59] For the avaricious and extortionate nature of the faujdars of Porto Novo for example, see Nagapatnam–Batavia, 30 October 1747, VOC 2702, p.587; Nagapatnam–Batavia, 23 November 1748, VOC 2711, pp.204–5. In 1751 the Dutch Chief of Paliacatta noted that in six days the Mughal governor of that port was changed as many as four times. ARA, Political Meeting at Nagapatnam, 1 October 1751, VOC 2784, p.902.

[60] A.S. Raju, *Economic Conditions in the Madras Presidency 1800–1850,* Madras, 1941, pp.4–5.

[61] RFSG, D/E, v.8–9, 12 October 1729, p.58; v.12, 29 January 1737, p.25; 5 October 1737, pp.74–5.

[62] RFSG, D/E, v.10–11, 1733–5 not dated, pp.20–1.

[63] RFSG, D/E, v.12, 5 October 1737, pp.74–5.

[64] RFSG, D/E, v.10–11, (1733–5) not dated, pp.20–1; *also see* Consultations of Fort St George, P/240/4, pp.148, 159 and 383–4 for information on Maratha troops plundering Arcot and Lalapet.

[65] RFSG, D/E, v.12, 1 October 1736, p.12.

[66] RFSG, D/E, v.12, 12 October 1740, p.116; v.12, 26 September 1741, p.39.

[67] Ibid.

[68] RFSG, D/E, v.1315, 24 September 1745, p.78.

[69] RFSG, D/E, v.12, 29 August 1738, p.88.

[70] ARA, Sadrapatnam–Nagapatnam, 25 April 1742, VOC 2575, pp.14578, 1515; Nagapatnam–Batavia, 14 October 1766, VOC 3164.

[71] ARA, Nagapatnam–Batavia, 5 October 1748, VOC 2720, p.402; *also see* A.S. Raju, *Economic Conditions...*, pp.4–5 for the revenue administration under the Nawab of Carnatic. S.C. Hill, in *Yusuf Khan: the Rebel Commandant* (London, 1914) has portrayed this confusion in the political life in the territories of Madura and Tinnevelly. Land was being farmed out to the highest bidder resulting in the non-payment of rent. Poligars, amaldars, faujdars all tried to take advantage of a corrupt system.

[72] ARA, Copy, Nagapatnam–Batavia, 17 January 1778, VOC 3482, pp.263–6.

[73] RFSG, D/E, v.12, 12 October 1740, p.116.

[74] RFSG, D/E, v.13, 26 September 1741, p.10.

[75] RFSG, L to FSG, v.42, no.48, from Charles Turner at Cuddalore, 2 November 1762, p.131; L from FSG, v.37, no.113, to the President, and Governor and Council, Fort William, 16 October 1762.

[76] *See,* e.g., ARA, VOC 2505, pp.1477, 1916–18, 1925; VOC 2652, p.248; VOC 2801, p.47; VOC 3136, p.361; VOC 3229, pp.424, 459; rfsg, d/cb 1744, p.80.

[77] B. Stein, *Thomas Munro: the Origins of the Colonial State and His Vision of Empire,* Delhi, 1989. For decline in the production of textiles in the south as a result of the wars between Haidar and the British *see* O. Feldbaek, *India Trade under Danish Flag,* pp.50–1.

[78] B. Bhattacharya, 'Some aspects of the textile trade...'.

[79] *See* B. Bhattacharya, 'The Dutch East India Company and the Coromandel Coast, 1740–1780', unpublished Ph.D. thesis, Visva Bharati University, 1993, for details.

[80] The account of the trade of Walajahpet with Hindupur and Nagar is based on IOL, Mackenzie Collections, General, no. 11.

[81] F.H. Buchanan, *A Journey...,* v.III, pp.464–5.

[82] An account of the measures taken by Haidar Ali and Tipu Sultan in order to develop the economic resources of the state of Mysore can be found in N. Guha, *Pre-British State System in South India, Mysore 1761–1799,* Calcutta, 1985.

[83] K.D. Swaminathan, *The Nayakas of Ikkeri,* Madras, 1957, pp.82–3. For an account of Nagar see IOL, Mackenzie Collections, General, nos. 6 and 45 and Home Miscellaneous 377; also F.H. Buchanan, *A Journey...,* v.III, pp.261–2, 268.

[84] K.D. Swaminathan, *The Nayaks of Ikkeri,* pp.156–60.

[85] F.H. Buchanan, *A Journey....,* v.1, p.49. Despite his religious policy and the measures he took for the protection of internal trade including the ban

on trade with places in the lower Carnatic, Tipu had established *kothis* or trade-centres at Madras and Pondicherry among other places on the Coromandel coast. Burton Stein, *Thomas Munro...*, p.34.

[86] For goods involved in this trade *see* F.H. Buchanan, *A Journey...*, v.1, pp.199–200; *see also* Guha, *Pre-British State-system...*, pp.40–1.

[87] F.H. Buchanan, *A Journey....*, v.1, pp.199–200

[88] Ibid., pp. 38–40; p.326 for Walajahpet's trade with Silagutta in Mysore; for Walajahpet–Gubi trade, v.II p.32.

[89] Ibid., v.I, p.200, v.II, pp.359–60.

[90] M. Vink, 'The Dutch East India Company and the Pepper Trade between Kerala and Tamilnad, 1663–1795: a Geo-historical Analysis', in K.S. Mathew (ed.) *Mariners, Merchants and Oceans: Studies in Maritime History,* Delhi, 1995, pp.273–300.

[91] B. Bhattacharya, 'The Dutch East India Company, ch. 5.

[92] J. Deloche, 'Le memoir de Moracin...'.

[93] Though many of the indigenous merchant groups taking part in the overseas trade of the coast had undergone a decline in the course of the eighteenth century, the Chulia or Marakkayar merchants of southern Coromandel continued to trade in the late eighteenth century. *See* B. Bhattacharya 'The Dutch East India Company and the Trade of the Chulias in the Bay of Bengal in the late eighteenth century', in K.S. Mathew (ed.) *Mariners...*, pp.347–61.

4

Power and the Weave: Weavers, Merchants and Rulers in Eighteenth-century Surat

LAKSHMI SUBRAMANIAN

The warp and woof of power were inextricably woven into Indian textiles and politics in the eighteenth century. It extended downwards from the ramparts of the Red Fort at Shahjahanabad to the *durbar* of the emperor's *mutasaddi* at Surat where the English East India Company had its flag in 1759.[1] As one moved out from the court and the castle into the streets of Surat, further levels of power and protest, not always formally articulated, became visible to the discerning observer. The play of power at whatever level directly derived from the compulsions of transitional politics—the transfer of power from the court to the castle—a process that strained existing social and economic relationships which had so long held the city together. The threat of dislocation and ruin was a very real one, shared widely among a miscellany of commercial and artisanal groups who, in turn, sought to negotiate for survival in an increasingly difficult situation. Their politics was, therefore, necessarily marked by a sense of urgency and alternated between compromise and conflict. Political communication and persuasion acted both as a substitute and a supplement to violent action expressed either through everyday forms of protest or through full fledged rioting, as was the case in 1788 and 1795.

This essay focuses specifically on the Surat weavers and their resistance in the second half of the eighteenth century as they sought to grapple with the twists and turns of transitional politics and salvage what remained of their bargaining strength. It was thus not entirely fortuitous that the Surat riots of 1788 and 1795 were primarily weavers' riots directed against purchasers and procurers of cloth, particularly those who did business with the alien power, the English East India Company.

The English East India Company was one of the many components in the dissolving power structure of Surat. The dissension within the Durbar, the movements of the Maratha *chauteas* (revenue collectors) constantly hovering on the city's outskirts and the collapse of the public order heightened the sense of isolation among Surat's beleagured residents. It was a troubled and turbulent world, where it was no easy matter to locate risks, identify adversaries or seize opportunities. The result was a kaleidoscopic range of alignments and ruptures: weavers combining against weavers, weavers combining against the durbar and most obviously weavers combining against the Company. The games of power that weavers played in their localities were connected with the political contests in the subcontinent and the shifting balance of power between the various contenders for supremacy. Exploring these linkages and connections between the larger subcontinental rivalries and localized weavers' resistance is important in that it underscores the organic solidarity of the Mughal order that had for two centuries spawned a complex web of relationships of patronage and dependence.

That the accretion of power by the English East India Company was a critical determinant in the remoulding of production structures is reasonably well known. This was particularly evident in the coastal enclaves of Calcutta, Madras and Bombay, each of which symbolized the growth of Company power in centres away from the Mughal heartland. The expanding requirements of the Company's textile trade in Bengal in the eighteenth century provided the authorities the rationale for developing alternate and more efficient systems of procurement of calicoes directly from the weavers. These were essentially intended to bypass the strong vertical link that existed between marketing and industrial production in the seventeenth and eighteenth century.[2] The politics of the Company's Bengal trade guaranteed a greater and more intrusive degree of control over the organization of the textile business and its procurement—the process dating from 1753–4 with the disbanding of the *dadni* system, quickening after Plassey when controls became more pervasive and rigorous and culminating in the coercive Regulations of 1775 and 1782. Subsequent legislation ironed out residual anomalies and matters of minor detail and ambiguity as the Bengal weaver lost all autonomy and subjected himself to a redefinition of his legal status.[3] In Madras, too, it was political control that enabled the Company to control weavers and set up controls on a scale that was unprecedented. The change was first visible in the small enclave of Cuddalore, where the Company acquired in 1762 two weaving villages of Chinnamanaikpollam and Naduvirapattu as *jagir* villages. Direct contacts with weavers were encouraged resulting in the eradication of middlemen and merchants by the 1770s.[4]

In western India, however, intervention came decidedly later and was on the whole more cautious and circumscribed. K.N. Chaudhuri suggests in this connection that as Surat in the first half of the eighteenth century became more and more of a Mughal enclave surrounded by the hostile military power of the Marathas, the stability of the Company's investment paradoxically enough improved. This, according to him was because of the increasing influx of weavers and merchants from Ahmedabad and its environs, Cambay, Broach and Baroda to the city of Surat that made it possible for the Company to procure their calicoes in the Bandar Mubarak itself.[5] While there is little reason to contest the fact that Surat did emerge in the later decades of the eighteenth century as an important centre of textile manufacture, it nevertheless appears far fetched to suggest that the Company's investment situation was satisfactory. Despite the assumption of political office as *Qiladars* of Surat in 1759, the Company was hardly in a position to institute restrictive and coercive mechanisms of procurement. This derived as much from the inherently fragile and fractured nature of the Company's political authority in western India, as from the inherently dynamic and autonomous traditions of mercantile and manufacturing activity in the region. The relationship between merchants, rulers and weavers was a changing one and in constant flux; its myriad expressions revealing only too clearly the search for options in a fast deteriorating situation. The relatively greater flexibility that indigenous client groups as merchants and manufacturers were able to demonstrate in their negotiations with the Company had an immediate political context. The English East India Company was only one of the many political contenders to reckon with, and not the most resolute or articulate of them either. As the century progressed, the very business of cloth purchase by rival buyers in Surat, or for that matter in the Coromandel or Bengal, became a matter of competing authority and reflected a complex interlocking of power relationships—local, regional and continental. Cloth, its production and purchase was very much a matter of politics, not simply a commercial transaction.

The Changing Balance of Power in Surat

The Castle Revolution of 1759 in Surat introduced the English East India Company as joint rulers of the port city.[6] Backed by a substantial section of the city's commercial population, the English Company's authorities assumed the office of Qiladar, an office that invested them with substantial powers of arbitration and appointment of senior officials and bureaucrats. The induction of the English East India Company into the city's political structure was envisaged by their clients as an effective counterpoise to the aspirations of the Marathas who had staked their claims in the early decades of the eighteenth century, when they moved in to occupy the Athavisi or adjacent twenty-eight villages of Surat. Thereafter, they organized annual excursions to the city in search of revenues, which the ruling mutasaddi of Surat was quite unable to provide. The stationing of the Maratha revenue collectors or chauteas in Surat to 'persuade' the administration to regularize revenue payments did not help. The upshot of all this was mounting pressure on the city's fragile revenue structure and on its residents who groped uncertainly towards an alternative. The city's *bania* community preferred to work through the English East India Company that had in the 1740s and 1750s effectively protected its protégé merchants against all arbitrary demands from the ruling Mughal administration as well as the Marathas.

The English take over of the Castle allayed the fears of this community, but did not, in the long run, deflect the course of decline that began in the city's public order. The Company showed itself singularly reluctant to assume any responsibility for government so long as its position in the city's political structure was secure. The benefits of the newly acquired office were not immediately apparent in so far as the Company's textile investment was concerned. Admittedly, the value of the Company's investment was not considerable, and until the 1780s averaged between Rs 350,000 and Rs 500,000. The investments for the most part consisted typically of *Necanees* (long and small), *Tapseils* (large), *Bejutapauts* (blue), Brawls, *Guinea* (red and blue), *Byrampauts* (blue), *Chelloes* (red and blue). To this list were added further varieties and assortments in the succeeding decades. Until the late 1780s, these supplies were procured from a number of Gujarati towns—Cambay, Broach, Baroda, Navsari and Surat. Supplies were, however, erratic throughout the 50s, 60s and 70s and the disruptions more often than not occasioned by Maratha military excursions in Gujarat. Instances of drought and floods that caused a high incidence of mortality among weavers, rising prices of yarn and the reluctance of weavers to work on the Company's investment before they had completed their engagements for the Gulf markets were also important factors that frequently impeded the Company's investment.

In 1753, we come across a lengthy representation of the Surat factors who set out somewhat plaintively the difficulties their contract merchants had encountered in getting the investment together.[7] 'The heaviness of lst years's rains, the loss of their goods taken by the Cooleys and the late troubles in Gujarat when the Ghenims took Amdavad and the Government's frequent oppressions of the workmen particularly when the general tax was intended to have been laid on the town, all business was for a considerable time at a standstill.'[8] Their superiors in the Bombay Council did not take these excuses very seriously and dismissed them as frivolous. They pointed out that the heaviness of the rains could not be a serious impediment considering that weavers at that season were 'most disengaged from all other business, the several investment of piece-goods for the gulf of Persia and the Red Sea being then completed.'[9] Complaints and accusations were, in fact, a common feature in the Company's dialogue with the contract merchants who were generally able to wheedle their way out of any penalty the Company authorities wished to enforce on non-performance. On the whole, it appears that the Company authorities in Surat enjoyed access to the requisite number of goods that made up their annual investment. There were occasions, however, when a number of pieces manufactured were actually rejected for having failed to conform to specifications of dimension and quality, but these did not seriously affect the Company's business.

It was in the 1780s that the situation showed signs of instability. The expanding requirements of the English East India Company for piece goods coincided with the growing trade of the Portuguese as well as the Dutch and French Companies for piece goods of an inferior variety. The latter were prepared to pay high prices for the coarse and inferior calicoes with the result that the weavers found material benefits in turning out substandard cloth and selling it at a higher price to the 'foreigners'. By this time, i.e. the 1780s, Surat was emerging as an important centre of manufacture—a development that should have suited the English East India Company in view of the privileges they enjoyed as the city's Qiladars. In fact, however, the apparent benefits of political office could not attenuate the basic constraints of the Company's position in western India. Acute financial stringency necessitated at one level, the initiation of limited financial cooperation with local monied groups and at another, the articulation of a restricted political agenda. Under the circumstance, the Company authorities showed little inclination in overhauling the existing system of textile procurement, or of stepping up controls over merchants and manufacturers. Until the 1780s, and even thereafter, the Company authorities operated through the agency of the contract merchants who in turn worked through under-contractors, the principal mediating link between the weavers and the merchants. The advantages of the system were evident in a situation where the investment had to be carefully and closely planned and set in motion at different times of the year depending on the items in question (see Table I). The system was not without disadvantages, particularly at a time when excessive competition and large-scale evasion by the weavers combined to undermine the stability of the Company's investment.

That brings us to the existing system of purchase and procurement and to the organization of the textile industry in Surat. The system of procurement, notwithstanding regional difference was fundamentally the same for all areas of the Company's trade in India. Its basis was a contractual agreement between the merchants and the Company. The former undertook to supply at the port of shipment a specified number of textiles by a certain date. The Company in return paid them a certain proportion of the total value of the goods in advance, the rest being paid on delivery. The system had one obvious merit in that it drew on the immense commercial experience and resources of the local merchants and thus economized on transaction costs.

The contracting merchant in Surat, in accordance with local and customary practice, employed a number of town merchants (about 300 of them are mentioned) of the Bania, Bohra and Parsi community who generally retained in their employ a number of weavers belonging to Surat and its adjacent areas. These under-contractors are almost always described as men of little property with an unsavoury reputation of absconding with cash advances. Their services were nonetheless crucial, for it was through them that the labours of the weaver could be collected, 'the weavers finding a regular subsistence by acknowledging subordination to a people who pay them regularly for their work as it comes from the looms besides occasionally assisting their exigencies and supplying them in sickness'.[10] The under-contractors also acted as bankers to the weavers advancing them sums as and when required and thereby assuring their services on a regular basis.

The weavers themselves were organized on caste lines around their headmen known alternately as the *patel* or *muqaddam*, who in fact negotiated for contracts on behalf of the community. There were individual weavers as well; Ashin Dasgupta refers to the dealings of Lakshmidas Bania who was obliged to maintain in his rolls eighteen headweavers besides 101 particular weavers, all of Surat.[11] Weaving was a specialized occupation with each caste assiduously guarding its skill and permitting no encroachment.

The Organization of Textile Production and the Weavers of Surat

The manufacture of piece goods was a highly specialized business characterized by an unusual degree of specialization and division of labour. A miscellany of castes drawn from Hindu, Muslim and Parsi communities were involved in the actual manufacture of textiles and were known to guard their preserve quite fiercely. The Surat factors had, on more than one occcasion, to remind their superiors both in London and Bombay that 'each branch of the manufactures of this place is confined to one set of people who by tradition and religious custom can never be persuaded to change their occupation.'[12] The Khatri weavers of Surat were particularly recalcitrant and resisted any violation of their exclusive privileges and prerogatives particularly that of manufacturing gummed silk and red calicoes.

The manufacturing process began not in the loom but in the cotton marts, where raw cotton was first cleaned.[13] This was done by the *pirijarrahs* referred to as an indigent and depressed group who purchased the cotton in small lots and frequently on credit from merchants paying a price generally twenty per cent higher than the market price. The cotton bales once cleaned were purchased by the spinners, mostly women (our documentation says) who sold the spun thread at the town gates to the *sootreahs* or dealers in cotton yarn. The yarn was twisted and divided into thread of the requisite length and dimensions (vees and choke are mentioned as units) by workers of the Deerah caste and subsequently sent out for dyeing. This was done at the rate of Rs 7 per maund if the colour specified was blue and at Rs 10 if the colour specified was red. Pasting of threads or *tahnee* followed, making it finally ready for the loom. The looms employed in Surat totalled 15,777 and turned out an impressive array of goods (see Table II).

It may be noted that out of the total number of looms worked in Surat, only 5451 looms were engaged in the manufacture of piece goods that entered the investment of the European Companies. The output of the remaining looms was largely exported to Malabar, Muscat, Poona, Bombay and other parts of India besides being absorbed by the city residents themselves. The manufacture of piece goods both in the city and its suburbs was subject to a number of taxes labelled as *mokats* or town duties by the ruling administration in the 1750s. Mokats were issued on goods brought into town as well. For instance, there was a mokat on cotton that was annually brought into Surat for consumption in the city at the rate of half a rupee per maund. The sootreahs or dealers in yarn had to pay an additional *nazrana* from two quarters of a rupee to a rupee annually to the durbar. The mokat on piece goods manufactured in Surat was paid by the under-dealers at the rate of one and a half per cent on every hundred rupee. Merchants bringing dooties to Surat from Broach, Baroda, Jambuser and Dabhol were exempted from the mokats but were obliged to pay an annual nazarana to the Nawab from Rs 10 to Rs 15 according to the gross quantity they imported from this district. Goods imported from the southern districts such as Navsari, Versal and Gundavie paid the Nawab a mokat of one and a half percentage.[14]

The mokat seems to have originated in 1759, the year of the Castle Revolution and the beginning of Dyarchy when the Nawabi administration attempted to improve its finances by imposing taxes on piece goods manufacture.[15] The measure was clearly one of the many efforts of the local administration to generate additional revenues and stave off bankruptcy at a time when claimants for revenue were increasing. The imposition could not but have rested heavily on the weavers, the generality of whom were poor and indigent. The declining demand from the Gulf markets, the lifeline of the Surat manufacturers, combined with rising prices of food and raw materials such as yarn and indigo put pressure on the weavers. The Company's annual investment in the 1750s and 60s did not materially improve prospects for the manufacturers most of who continued to work on Gulf goods from September to February. They were reluctant to enter into any other business, making it excessively difficult for the Company authorities to detach them and tie them exclusively to the Company's annual investment. The weavers, however, were neither impervious to the changing balance of power in the city nor to the idea of employing their bargaining skills to extract what little leverage they could from the ruling administration. The more affluent and articulate among them like the Khatris, who claimed the exclusive privilege of working piece goods called Oeryaye and Red Calicoes negotiated with the Nawabi administration to secure remission of the mokat.[16] Instead, they undertook to pay an annual contribution of Rs 5 to the mokat farmer and Rs 50 to the Nawab and to supply the durbar and its dependants with coloured threads and other trifling articles when required. Their traditional rivals, the Kumbis, went a step further and actually persuaded the Nawabi administration to give them permission to work 401 looms in the manufacture of silk gummed goods, over which the Khatris had so long maintained absolute control.[17] This became a major bone of contention between the two communities, each looking for an opportunity to deprive the other of the manufacture of the prized

'Red' goods. In the end, the Khatris succeeded in exerting their influence over the Durbar and the Castle which in 1804 revoked the license earlier issued to the Kumbis.[18]

The Expanding Textile Trade of the English East India Company and Problems of Procurement

The investment requirements of the English East India Company in the 60s and 70s did not warrant any major rehauling of the existing system. For the most part, the Company authorities conceded to the demands made by their contract merchants and did not seriously enforce the penalty of non-performance. The contract merchants for the Company were generally Bania or Parsi and periodically came up with their proposals. They bound themselves by contract to deliver goods to a specified amount by the end of December of the calendar year, and in case of failure agreed to a penalty of nine per cent. The remaining amount was to be made good by October, and in case of further default, the risk of an additional penalty of nine per cent was incurred.[19] The penalty was not strictly enforced; the merchants on most occasions were able to justify their performance to the English Chief and Council at Surat, although the Bombay Council did not always take a kindly view of the proceedings. The contractors complained against the tardiness of the Company to make good the cash advances on time, and even tried occasionally to dictate their own terms in framing the annual contract. The Surat factors in their letter dated 7 June 1752 mentioned that while their contractor Baboojee had agreed to submit to a penalty of nine per cent on such goods as were delivered short of three lakhs of rupees within sixteen months, he also suggested that 'it might be an article in the contract that no new investment should be set on foot till after sixteen months as it would greatly impede him in fulfilling his contract and that whatever goods were received at Cambay should be reckoned as so much delivered in Surat, and that no abatement should be made here on the goods after once being accepted there.'[20]

The Bombay Council refused to consider these suggestions. By July 1752, the Surat factors had persuaded the contractor to submit to a penalty of nine per cent[21], but they ruefully admitted that they had failed to prevail on him regarding the commencement of a new contract.[22] Regarding performance, the contractors seem on the whole to have been successful in fulfilling their obligations in the succeeding years. The provision of the Red Goods, the produce of the Khatris, however, remained unsatisfactory. In 1764, in a letter dated 21 September, the Surat factors pointed out that their contract merchants were finding it difficult to complete the Company's investment because only a few Khatris were willing to negotiate.[23] At the same time, the factors noted with increasing anxiety the deterioration in the quality of manufacture as well as its rising prices. The contractors, on interrogation, argued that they could do little to reverse this trend. The weavers were being forced to compromise on quality in order to be able to supply at the prices the Company dictated. They also pointed out that the Dutch and the Portuguese of late had volunteered to give better prices for the rejected goods.[24] The merchants, however, resisted any attempt by the Company to allow a stamp being affixed to such goods of the investment that did not pass muster.[25] The Company on its part did not press the issue. Obviously, this was no simple market transaction. The Company insisted on obtaining the pick of the lot. It would not allow the contractors and weavers to sell the rejected piece goods to other customers at higher prices because that would undermine its businesss. But the contractors would not accept such a monopolistic English ascendancy in the market, at least not yet. This was very much a game of power. Since the Company was not supreme as yet, the contractors gathered up the rejected goods and took them away without the mark of reject being stamped upon the goods.

Controls and Resistance

It was in the 1780s that the system of procurement came under pressure compelling the Company authorities to tentatively consider changes. The pressures related primarily to the growing demand for piece goods by the European traders and Companies and to the resistance of the weavers in conforming to specifications. Both of these prevented the contract merchants from adhering to their agreements. Deficiencies in quality and quantity became a major and recurrent problem in the 80s and 90s forcing the contract merchants to put pressure on the weavers, forcibly collecting their goods and maintaining a tight control over the advances. The weavers were not impervious to the changing situation with its multiple pressures that threatened to undermine their bargaining position. They responded in their characteristic fashion of turning out defective goods particularly in terms of dimensions and texture and marketing them at a higher price to the Portuguese private traders who drove a vigorous trade in Indian calicoes with West Africa. As a preventive measure, the Company worked through contract merchants and even under-brokers to put pressure on the weavers and intercept any clandestine transaction. Use of force and coercion increased with the inevitable result that the Muslim weavers of the city like the Bhandarrahs and Momnas resorted to violence whenever the opportunity so presented. Predictably, their antagonism focused on the Parsi/Bania contract merchant who worked for the Company.

The violence of the weavers' resistance was particularly marked in 1788 when a riot broke out between Muslims and Parsis in Surat city.[26] The riot itself was occasioned by a case of theft and assault which snowballed into a major communal conflagration involving Muslim lower orders, among which weavers constituted a sizeable segment. Most of the victims were cloth dealers and contract merchants, all of whom unanimously claimed that the rioters were aided and abetted by the Nawab's sepoys. Rustamjee Monakjee, a dealer in cloth and a resident of Syedpura, the city's commercial quarter, stated in his deposition that he actually saw Abdur Rahim, the Bakshi's servant walk into the residence of a weaver where three Parsi merchants were present. All of them—Shapoorjee Burjorjee, Framjee Shapoorjee and Nasserwanjee Shapoorjee were dragged out and beaten.[27] Nathu Gasjee Muselman, a weaver, confessed that the rioters were mostly Muslim weavers protesting against Parsis, and that he himself had abstained from participating in the violence by pleading that 'he earned his subsistence by working for Parsis'.[28] Clearly, the indigent weavers had decided to give vent to their sense of pressure by directing their anger against the Parsi contract merchants who in pursuit of their own business had stepped up controls over the weavers. This assumed multiple forms: the most obvious one was to reduce and control the amount of advance, others involved very close monitoring of the activities of the weavers and prevention of any clandestine sales the weavers might indulge in. Rustamjee Monakjee himself mentioned that he was in the process of checking on the produce of one of the Syedpura weavers when the conflagration actually occurred.[29] Sciad Yaseen, deputed by the Nawab to look into the dispute mentioned that on the day preceding the riot, a number of Parsis ill-treated a young Muslim weaver and his brother and actually beat them.[30] For the subordinate officials and sepoys of the ruling administration, the occasion was appropriate for articulating their own sense of displacement and animosity against the growing political control of the English Company and the prosperity of their clients, the Parsis and the Banias.[31] For the weavers, the issue was more immediate and tangible—one of controls and coercion. The riot was thus the first visible expression of resistance by manufacturers against a crisis situation. Admittedly, the Company had not instituted control mechanisms, but the situation was by no means conducive.

The resistance of the weavers became more pronounced in the

90s even as pressures on them mounted. The paucity of advances, the growing rigidity of company specifications, the tightening of controls relating to sales at a time of growing European demand for Surat piece goods combined to strain both the weaver and the contractor. The Company's contract merchant, Mayaram Atmaram bitterly complained that he was encountering innumerable obstacles principally occasioned by the dilatoriness of the Company advances. He also bitterly complained that the Company authorities had needlessly rejected goods worth Rs 15,000, although most of them had been near equal to muster as far as 'was possible to procure them from so many hundred different workmen, some of whom will naturally be inferior to others.'[32] Further, he pointed out that goods delivered during the dry winds could not be equal to those made in the rains. Besides, the Company's last minute alterations regarding the fineness of the Byrampauts were irksome considering a lot of time was lost in 'taking off the workmen from looms already prepared'.[33] Worse still, the pieces rejected had been quickly bought up by other purchasers, the number of whom in Surat was equal to that of workmen. The Company, Atmaram pointed out, could hardly be ignorant of the positive encouragement that rival buyers gave to the workmen by offering them higher prices for goods that the Company adjudged as inferior in terms of both quality and measurement.[34] Atmaram also referred to Maratha obstruction in Baroda and Navsary, and accused the brokers of the Portuguese factory who insisted on their goods being dyed first. The Surat factors acknowledged the validity of Atmaram's defence and let the matter pass. Clearly, they did not feel confident about pursuing a matter that they claimed was unpredictable, related as it was to the larger issue of Maratha presence in Gujarat.

In 1791, Atmaram was once again appointed to secure the provision of the Company's piece goods investment. Supplies took long in coming and once more, Atmaram came up with a lengthy representation detailing the problems he faced.[35] He pointed out that the cotton crop itself had suffered several years of continuous failure and which subsequently had inflated cotton prices. Cotton yarn and indigo were not procurable at any price and the mortality that had raged had taken a severe toll on the weavers in particular—in the contractor's moderate computation,'ten to twelve daily'.[36] Poverty also forced many of the survivors to abscond with their cash advances.

This time, Atmaram's impassioned defence did not go down very well either with the Surat Council or the Bombay Government.[37] A committee was instituted to look into the failure of the investment and the Surat factors were directed to investigate the measures the Dutch and other foreigners adopted to procure their supplies.[38] The Surat factors found it difficult to ferret out information from the Dutch who observed very great secrecy in their commercial transactions.[39] But on closer scrutiny the factors discovered that 'not more than one third of the goods therein mentioned are proper for the Europe market and manufactured at Surat, the remainder being for Ceylon and the Batavia markets'.[40]

Pursuing the matter, John Griffith, the Chief of the Surat Council came up with a report dated 14 April 1792, in which he pointed out that the Dutch, French and Portuguese Companies as well as private traders did purchase considerable quantities of goods (though not of the same quality as those of the Company) for the African markets and employed for this purpose a great number of weavers.[41] On account of the English Company's rigid specifications, practically one third of the goods were rejected and these rejects were immediately bought up by brokers of foreign factories or individuals at a higher price than what the Company allowed for. This naturally provided the incentive for weavers to manufacture 'inferior goods'. Griffith pointed out that it was impossible to persuade the manufacturers at Surat to change their occupation and produce goods for the Company considering that 'each branch of the manufacture was confined to one set of people', and that the trade of Hindustan to the Gulfs of Arabia and Persia constituted the most important line of business.'[42]

Griffith's report also suggested for the first time a more comprehensive solution to deal with the problem. He pointed out that the only option for the Company was to insist on preference being given to the Company's concerns and that the necessary number of weavers had to be compelled to work for the Company. Griffith, however, added that the Company would also have to come up with good if not better prices than the foreigners.[43] Meanwhile, the Enquiry Committee gave it as their opinion that no blame could be attached to the contracting merchant, and that while the quantity of piece-goods exported by foreigners might be legitimately held by the Court of Directors to question the so called mortality among weavers, nevertheless it was important to remember that 'in the number of weavers of the various manufactures of this part of the country, those who can work the Company goods have a very small proportion and that any loss of them must have been severely felt. Weaving has its degrees of skill and a weaver of coarse goods cannot at command or choice weave fine, every caste has its particular work and no impingement may be allowed'.[44]

The situation showed no signs of improvement in the following year. Deficiencies continued to plague the Company as weavers dishonoured their obligations. The Chief of the Surat Council expressed his anxiety in no uncertain terms and commented that the deficiencies were 'extraordinary and depressing', particularly at a time when both from general circumstance and repeated advances, there was no just reason to suppose that there would be any deficiency.[45] Neither the French nor the Portuguese were making their investments while the Dutch had stopped operations in July. The Company had, moreover, agreed to accept goods commonly called Cambay Goods (but manufactured at Jambuser) in the hope of increasing the quantity of goods for the ships waiting for despatch.[46] None of these measures had helped, and for the first time the Chief of the Surat Council put the blame squarely on the system rather than on the individual. The Company had not formalized its controls over the weavers but the latter were clearly under pressure, a fact that was borne out by the August Riots of 1795 with the Bhandarrah weavers rioting in large numbers.[47] Their mounting resentment against the restrictive nature of Company control articulated through the agency of the Bania contract merchants who were sparing with their advances surfaced in the course of the riots as weavers joined hands with the sepoys and servants of the ruling administration to protest against the displacement of the traditional Mughal order. The aftermath of the riots prompted the Company to consider the enforcement of more formalized controls. The Court of Directors directed the Surat and Bombay Council to introduce a more viable system which would ensure the efficient provisioning of the annual investment.

The New System and the Weavers of Surat

As a preliminary measure, the Surat Council decided to buy up a considerable proportion of the rejected goods on private account, thereby neutralizing Dutch and Portuguese competition.[48] Mr Cherry was appointed for this transaction.[49] At the same time, an attempt was made to persuade the Khatri weavers, who by their special skills were ideally equipped to deal with the Company's investment. The weavers were approached and an agreement was held out to them that if they consented to work for the Company, they would receive protection and patronage, and that they would be allowed to work their silk business without any impediments. This was in fact an allusion to the Khatri–Kumbi dispute that the Company showed itself willing to resolve in favour of the Khatris. On 5 October 1795, the muqaddam of the Khatris presented an *arzee* stating their consent to work for the Company exclusively till their business was finished.[50]

The success of the negotiations bolstered the Company's hopes of tying the weavers to their contractual obligations and of approaching other weavers to consider similar obligations. The Nawab's protests were brushed aside as the Chief insisted that 'measures had been taken to secure the labour of the Surat weavers with their own free will and consent, which if once obtained would certainly be held to the performance of their agreements.'[51] By 27 October 1795, guidelines were discussed for the establishment of a Commercial Board in Surat under a Commercial Resident who would supervise the provisioning of the annual investment.[52]

In 1796, these discussions were renewed as the contracting system came under close scrutiny. The Court of Directors explicitly suggested disbanding the existing procurement system. They argued that the leading cause of all complaints regarding the languid state of their investment derived from the system in practice 'of having a contractor who has himself immediate connection with the weavers but engages in subordinate contracts with large numbers of native merchants of little property.'[53] The Commercial Resident, John Cherry, however, advised against abolition of the system which he warned would be hazardous. For one, control of numerous workmen could not be managed by Company servants unless they were immediate subjects of the government, or like those in Bengal and elsewhere were collected in *aurangs* and working in one body. In western India, the situation was strikingly different—weavers were in general independent of the Nawab's authority and scattered not only in Surat, but throughout Gujarat and the Maratha country, which meant that the assistance of a native medium became indispensable both at the level of the contractor as well as that of the under-contractor.[54] The observation was telling. It amounted to an unilateral admission on the Company's part that uncertain and partial political control precluded the enforcement of coercive mechanisms for textile procurement. The Maratha factor was not to be lightly treated and even in Surat, where the Company was the *de facto* master, the scope for intervention seemed uncertain. Under the circumstances, a soft option was presented by Mr Cherry who suggested that the abolition of the mokats might be considered as an incentive to work for the Company. Conciliation rather than coercion appeared to be the Company's official watchword. In practice, however, controls were tightened over both the merchant as well as the manufacturer. This was evident from the increasing use of force: armed peons compelling the weavers to turn over their produce as well as by the enforcement of the penalty for non-performance by the contracting merchant.

In a subsequent meeting, Cherry also discussed the possibility of other options for providing the investment: (a) by the contractor as at present (b) by the junction of several merchants under one term (c) by employing a person of credit and responsibility under the appellation of broker who would provide goods by order of the Commercial Resident alone.[55] These options were discussed at length. Recommendations for abolishing mokats and loom taxes were approved, while it was proposed that the Commercial Board should receive proposals from merchants jointly for the whole investment, and that the contractors were obliged to give security for money advances and submit to an enhanced penalty of fifteen per cent. Rejected goods were to be purchased at the market price by the Commercial Resident and directly paid to the contractors without having any connection with money advances for the contract.[56]

The Surat Council went a step further. The President renewed discussions on the subject and argued that the most likely means of arriving at a just medium between the Contract and Agency system was to adopt the latter mode, that is by the agency of the Commercial Resident in so far as the influence of the Company's government prevailed throughout Surat and its adjacent villages. So far as the investment from the Maratha districts of Gujarat were concerned, contracts had to be continued with full security for performance and proportionate penalties for failure in breach of engagements, the amount and detail of which had to be settled by the Chief and Commercial Board.[57] Bombay approved of these suggestions and orders were accordingly issued in March 1796 to the Commercial Board to appoint Nagardas Cursondas and Vrzbhucandas Ramdas as Brokers under the Commercial Resident.[58]

Meanwhile, the mokats were taken off by the Nawab who, however, pointed out that it was a purely temporary measure. The Surat factors were confident that the Nawab could be persuaded to make it a permanent arrangement which would thereby give the 'Company a decided preference over all other competitors'.[59] The Commercial Resident entrusted the provisioning of the Standard Investment as well as the Subordinate Investment with the same broker. At the same time, he adopted the mode of regular agreement rather than occasional purchases of inferior goods arguing that without positive assurance of these goods being purchased, his brokers could not venture to prevent foreigners or their agents from investing them or weavers carrying away goods that were rejected.[60]

The Surat Council approved of these arrangements, the efficacy of which, however, remained in doubt. The arrival of the Portuguese ships in August 1796 created consternation as the Commercial Resident busied himself in persuading the Nawab to insist on strict preference being given to the Company in all the manufactures of Surat but 'particularly in the article of piece-goods as they give liberal price and make most extensive advances of money'.[61] The Portuguese Resident immediately protested against these measures and complained to the Governor and Council in Bombay against the embargo that had been laid down by the Nawab. He referred to instances of harassment that his servants had undergone when they had been hindered from going to the houses of weavers to receive goods and for which advances had already been made. The Surat factors, when questioned, disclaimed all responsibility for the embargo arguing in their advices of 26 August 1796, that the act was solely of the Nawab and that his 'Highness may have exceeded our wishes'. But they cautioned against the removal of the restraints particularly because the Portuguese were actually offering twenty per cent more for the goods and were negotiating with ready cash. They anticipated that without some form of protection, their brokers would be ruined.[62] On 20 October 1796, the Company's brokers themselves solicited English protection and asked for sepoys to be stationed in public streets and intersections. The British and the Banias alike underscored the appreciation of the fact that the Portuguese attempt at cash and carry was itself a flaw in the game of power. Battle lines were clearly being drawn: the Company making no attempts to obscure their real intentions of coercing the manufacturers to sell their goods exclusively to the Company at prices which were below the market ones. The Commercial Resident was among the most articulate spokesman of the Company's new policies in so far as it related to textiles and their procurement and insisted that the new system proposed be tried out. He described the system as being moderately restrictive, not coercive (as his superiors at Bombay thought) and that it combined the advantage of the native medium and security for Company advances with that of more immediate control over under-brokers and dealers, and protection of manufacturers in general from the rapacity of both, as well as the interference of native government.[63] He also declared that no part of the measures so far enforced went further than the use of the Company's political influence throughout the adjacent country in securing a preference to their concerns and compelling those who contract to supply goods for them to abide by their engagements.[64]

The introduction of the new system did not improve the Company's prospects overnight. Deficiencies continued to baffle the Commercial Board. This was particularly serious in the case of the Khatri manufacturers, 'an obstinate set of people who never work unless compelled by want, they cannot in the least be depended upon'.[65] Interference was however, not without risk. Cherry in fact admitted that it was exceedingly difficult to persuade other workmen (like those who manufactured the blue chelloes) to increase the number of looms. There was thus no question of dealing directly with the weavers as yet, and the business had to be conducted through the designated brokers. At the same time, the Chief of the Surat Council, Daniel Seton admitted his inability to force the mokat issue with the Nawab and secure a permanent abolition of the tax.[66]

In November 1797, for the first time, the question of controls over weavers came up for a detailed discussion in the meeting of the Surat Council. A number of regulations were considered for engaging the produce of the weavers to the Company's investment.

1. Weavers not indebted nor under engagement to the Company shall not be compelled to enter into their employ. Weavers indebted or under engagement to the Company on duly discharging such debts shall not be compelled to enter into fresh agreements.

2. Weavers or merchants who may engage for provision of any part of the investment were:

(a) to enter all engagements in writing, duly attested by two creditable witnesses. If they did not intend to have further advances, they were expected to give a fortnight's notice of their intentions. Those of them who were indebted to the Company, or in receipt of the Company advances had to deliver cloths according to their agreement and on no account were to dispose of it to any buyer.

(b) In case of weavers failing to deliver by the stipulated period the cloths which he had been engaged for, the Commercial Resident was at liberty to place peons upon him to expedite his deliveries.

(c) If weavers were found selling cloths to other merchants, dealers or agents of whatever description while remaining deficient in their stipulated deliveries to the Company, they were liable to prosecution and upon sufficient proof would be compelled to forfeit all the produce of all the cloths they sold.

(d) Weavers or other merchants possessing more than one loom and entertaining one or more workmen would be subject to penalty of thirty-five per cent on the stipulated price of every piece of cloth that they failed to deliver in accordance with the written agreement they had executed.

3. The authority of the Commercial resident was to be strengthened.

A register of weavers and merchants employed in the provision of the Company's investment was to be maintained.[67]

Taken together, these regulations constituted the first definitive means of control over the manufacturers in western India. Alongside, a consensus emerged on the validity of breaking the investment into distinct categories with separate contracts for each of them, and of leaving one branch under the immediate charge of the Commercial Resident, 'thereby furnishing him an ample field for the exercise of his best abilities and the consequent improvement of this knowledge while by being placed in a predicament of honest rivalry with contractors, the most efficient preventive is established against those evils that might ensue from being vested with the whole.'[68] It is no accident that these new commercial proposals were framed in the altered context of British expansion in India. The extension of English power over the princes of India emboldened the Company to extend their controls over the merchants and weavers of the land.

Advertisements were accordingly issued inviting proposals for the various contracts for the following year's investment. Not many were forthcoming—in fact only four proposals were tendered for Chints and Byrampauts. None of them were related to the provision of the red or blue goods—varieties that were particularly difficult to have access to. The Commercial Resident fell back upon the services of the previous year's contractors.[69] They refused to undertake the assignment unless they were given the whole investment. The President of the Surat Council found this demand inadmissible besides being expensive—their brokerage services would involve payment of Rs 20,000 per annum.[70] Eventually, as it transpired, the Company had to concede and negotiate with the contracting brokers Nagardas Cursondas and Ramdas Vrzbhucandas for the standard investment.[71] Until the political and economic realities in western India were drastically altered, the Company's march through the market was impeded by the entrenched indigenous relationships.

Control of weavers too was not as smooth as anticipated. The brokers explaining the deficiency in the amount of the standard goods to the amount of Rs 46,529 pointed out that in addition to the high prices of cotton and scarcity of thread, the obstinacy of the Khatris was proving to be a major impediment. The application made by the Chief to the Nawab of Surat had been of little consequence. On closer scrutiny, it appeared that the Khatris had renewed their disputes with the Kumbis. The Company also found it difficult to exert their influence in Broach where the Sindhia's banker Prabhudas was personally involved in the Portuguese investment, and who made in this connection large advances of money to the weavers.[72] The competing interests of the principal contenders for power—the Company, the Marathas and the ruling Mughal administration—were interlocked in every facet of commercial activity of the region, particularly in the business of textile manufacture and procurement. The multiplicity of claims and counter claims only intensified the pressures that the weavers underwent even as they took recourse to clandestine sales and boycott of the Company's investment.

In September 1793, instructions were issued to the Commercial Board directing them to continue with the investment as earlier planned, but to persuade the contracting brokers to make use of the English Company's bonds and raise funds thereby. This was found to be an impossible condition to pursue. The Board also made it clear to their superiors that it was not possible to limit the investment whatever the financial constraints on the Company.[73] Since the contracting brokers were bound under penalty to complete their investments in twelve months from the date of the contract, charges of deficiency could not be levelled against them.[74] The brokers themselves complained of the Company's inconsistent and ambivalent stand on the investment, arguing that they had already made their advances to manufacturers. The abrupt suspension of the investment would, therefore, be attended with great difficulty for they would not be able to sell their goods that remained to others at a fair price. 'Everyone desirous of buying will say that the Company has no money they must sell them cheap and we will then buy what we want.'[75] In yet another representation, they proposed that as they had already sent in cash and goods to the amount of Rs 620,000 they should be permitted to continue delivering supplies of piece goods as specified. In return, they agreed to receive Company bonds against whatever balances outstanding to them over and above Rs 620,000.[76] These suggestions were accepted by the Commercial Board whose members in fact, apologized for their conduct saying that 'nothing but the pressure of times could have induced the smallest deviation in contract.'[77]

The following year's proposal set out at the very outset, the inclusion of Company bonds as a means of advance. On 10 May 1799, the Surat Council proposed that the contract was to be handled by the previous year's broker but with a couple of alterations. These were (1) two-eighths of the amount of the contract was to be paid in cash, (2) three-eighths of the amount to be paid in European articles of merchandise as may be selected, and the remaining three-eighths to be paid in ten or twelve per cent bonds at the option of the contracting parties on the same conditions as those of last year and suitable at such times as may be agreed upon between parties.[78]

The contracting brokers did not appear too happy with these conditions and haggled over cash advances. They contended that it was absolutely essential for the Company to make more cash available, the failure of which would involve renewal of the injurious competition of the Portuguese who spread their advances precisely when piece-goods were being provided for the Company.[79] The Commercial Board consented to these proposals and also allowed a brokerage fee of one per cent on the full amount of goods they undertook to provide. The penalty, however, of eighteen per cent in case of failure was to be enforced more strictly, while part of the advance was to be arranged by means of the Company paper.[80] Thus by 1799, important if not fundamental alterations had been initiated in the organization of textile procurement. The contracting merchants had been replaced by brokers under the Commercial Resident, while the penalty for non-performance had been substantially enhanced. Weavers under engagement to the company were bound to turn over their produce to the Company, the failure of which made them liable to penalty and forfeit. The use of armed sepoys was admissible while the total stock of cash advances that remained in the hands of the local brokers was reduced by the use of Company paper which was given greater currency. In terms of actual practice, however, these alterations do not seem to have gone very far in guaranteeing the Company access to supplies. Nor did these immediately erode the independence of the weavers who combined to evade the Company's controls and conduct business with other buyers.

In 1800, the Commercial Board once more drew attention to the increasing competition of the Portuguese for piece-goods as well as the activities of the local agents of the Bombay merchants who were impeding the business of their contracting brokers. They identified Vamalchand as the ringleader in the business. The brokers themselves represented their difficulties elaborately, stating that the Portuguese offered very high prices for even the inferior quality Necanees (Rs 80 per corge as against Rs 67 offered by the Company). They maintained that the only way to quell this competition was to solicit the active interference of Government.[81] The problem of clandestine purchases was insurmountable particularly as Surat was so large a city that even 500 peons could not intercept people engaged in this traffic. They described the strategy that was adopted: eight or nine people went together with four or five of them fastening a piece of cloth around each leg and the others fastening a price list around their waists. They were escorted by a small party of Parsis armed with sticks. They sang and danced thereby drawing public attention and eluding the Company peons in the bargain.[82]

Resistance was not the only hallmark of the actions of the weavers who chafed against Company controls and tried to come to terms with a crisis situation. The situation encouraged weaving groups to use Company patronage to extract benefits and resolve traditional rivalries. In April 1800, the Khatri-Kumbi dispute once more surfaced. Earlier, on 15 February 1800, a petition had been forwarded by the Patel of the Kumbis (Jaga Bula Patel) complaining against the Khatris who had persuaded the Nawab to revoke his earlier licence that he had awarded the Kumbis for manufacturing silk cloth employing 401 looms for the purpose.[83] The Commercial Resident took up the matter and informed their superiors at Bombay that in order to put an end to the Khatri–Kumbi dispute which was adversely affecting the Company's engagements, the Surat Chief had entered into a negotiation with the Nawab persuading him to withdraw the licence he had earlier issued to the Kumbis. The Surat authorities, including the Resident confessed that this had been unavoidable considering the fact that the Red goods could not be provided for without the Khatris, that no other caste of weavers could work them for fear of the Khatris and that the Khatris themselves would not work them unless their exclusive privileges were restored on paper officially.[84] This was accordingly done by the Nawab restoring the monopoly of the Red goods manufacture to the Khatris.[85]

Meanwhile, the difficulties relating to the investment multiplied. In April 1800, the rise in cotton prices and excessive competition were cited as major impediments by the contracting brokers who also insisted on greater regularity of cash advances. By September of the year, the deficiency was even nore pronounced. The brokers referred to the heavy rains that delayed deliveries and to the disinclination of the weavers to receive any advances from the Company. The Surat Council, however, rejected these excuses and advised the brokers to compel the refractory Khatris to deliver their engagements and induce them to accept advances.[86] They brought the attention of the factors to the altered political situation which gave the Company greater leverage in their commercial dealings. The death of the Surat Nawab and the assumption of direct administrative control by the Company implied that the new regulations affecting the textile business could be more effectively enforced.

For the moment, however, the impasse continued. The brokers

pointed out in their December notices that despite their efforts, goods were not coming into the warehouse and not more than five corges came everyday whereas 'the produce of the city's manufactures must be from 25 to 30 corges daily.'[87] They also referred to impediments they faced in Jambuser where merchants from Daman and Diu had invested goods to the tune of rupees four lakhs for the African market paying high prices for inferior goods, the consequences of which were serious. 'Our work', they mourned 'is at a stand, the merchants who are engaged to supply us tell our agents this is the time for us to make our profits, we will give you your goods after two months'.[88]

The Company did not take long to call off the stalemate and exercise its newly acquired political authority to eliminate residual opposition from the weavers. The latter came up with a representation stating that while they were glad to work for the Company, they resented the actions of some of their merchants who oppressed poor weavers and prevented them from selling even one or two corges of cloth. They pointed out that 'formerly, the purchases of the Dutch, Portuguese and French amounted to Rs 32 lakhs which we weavers completed and all the principals of the town were pleased and satisfied and now the Company's Investment of nearly Rs 10 lakhs is not fulfilled, that is the reason. The oppressive merchants take cloths from us by force which they sell elsewhere to great advantage while we are extremely distressed.'[89] The representation was telling; the weavers were articulating their sense of displacement produced by the new order in which their activities had been severly circumscribed. The Company, on its part, was unimpressed with these representations. Having achieved a substantial accretion of power, they were confident that their investment business would materially improve. On 28 December 1800, the Commercial Board was empowered to bring all cases of defalcation before the Judge and Magistrate for action. The Resident was, at the same time, entrusted with authority (Regulations V and VII of 1800) to place peons upon weavers failing to deliver by the stipulated time.[90] This was followed by the decision to detach responsible workmen from the community to work for the Company's investment. The Kumbis stepped in agreeing to supply the quota of what might be required by the Company.[91]

The succeeding years saw a reinforcement of the new regulations. There were no prospects of immediate success; the Bombay Council observed quite candidly, 'while we fully rely on the Commercial Resident's exertions of the means vested in him by Article V Section III Regulation VIII for preventing those whose deliveries fall short at the stipulated periods working for new engagements, we cannot but express our apprehensions of their inefficacy when applied to banayan merchants who neither weave nor have looms in their houses and consequently can be placed under no check were peons to be placed over him'.[92] By 1802, the necessity of introducing the Bengal system was emphasized in all circles—as the only visible means of breaking the hold of the Bania agents. The Commercial Resident in a minute dated 16 November 1802 reiterated the fact that unless the combination of the intermediate agents was broken, 'neither could the goods be restored to their former excellence, the investment carried to its extent, nor the weaver be assured full produce of his labour but both he and the Resident must be subject to the caprice of a parcel of grain thirsty Banias and overbearing Musalmans'.[93] The debate had thus turned full cycle, as the Company, confident in its power, moved against the bania contractor and the Muslim weaver reducing them in status and rendering them liable to prosecution in case of proved default.

Conclusion

The subordination of the merchants and manufacturers in Surat had thus been a protracted and prolonged process which was essentially determined by the structure of the Company's political authority in western India. Financial constraints combined with the reality of the Maratha presence had prevented the Company from developing effective political initiatives in the region. This in turn enabled local commercial and weaving groups to retain their autonomy and demonstrate greater bargaining power in the negotiations with the Company. Here, alone of all the early British enclaves, were local manufacturing groups able to coalesce and articulate their protests against the new dispensation of the English East India Company. The riots of 1788 and 1795 were both predominantly led by the Muslim weavers of Surat who protested against both Parsi and bania contractors—the agents of the English East India Company—and the coercive system they operated. Even after 1800, when the hegemony of the Company was no longer in doubt, the weavers were not always persuaded to adhere to the new lines of control. We come across numerous instances of weavers working on cloths for domestic consumption and who strenuously resisted acceptance of Company advances. Further, the importance of the Company's textile investment steadily declined in the nineteenth century making the new regulations largely redundant. On the other hand, the revival of the Arab trade and the reintegration of the Arab and East African markets continued to generate new opportunities for the weavers and merchants of Gujarat. The evolving power equations on the west coast—and especially the fact that full British annexation did not occur until 1818 (more than half a century after the British conquest of Bengal)—ensured the survival of a strong indigenous business and production organization around the Surat–Bombay–Baroda–Ahmedabad axis. The late eighteenth century power relationships in western India had a significant bearing on the market economy of the region in the mid-nineteenth century. The strong Gujarati business tradition which ultimately produced Bombay's indigenous capitalist class would not have been possible if power equations had developed in the west coast in the same manner as in the lower Gangetic valley. The divergent routes by which the Company established its power in Bombay, Coromandel and Bengal made possible a range of contrasting market developments in these three regions. What was common to all these regions, however, was the inextricable weaving of power and market relationships.

NOTES AND REFERENCES

1. Lakshmi Subramanian, *Indigenous Credit and Imperial Expansion: Bombay, Surat and the West Coast,* New Delhi, pp.93–100.

2. Hameeda Hossain, *The Company Weavers of Bengal: The East India Company and the Organization of Textile Production in Bengal 1750–1813,* Delhi, 1988, pp.76–115. *Also see* Hossain, 'The Company's Controls over Textile Production: Implications on its Legal Framework for Weavers 1757 to 1800', *Journal of the Asiatic Society of Bangladesh,* vol.XXVIII, no.I, 1983.

3. Ibid. *Also see* Prasannan Parthasarathi, 'Merchants and the rise of colonialism', in Burton Stein and Sanjay Subrahmanyam (eds), *Institutions and Economic Change in South Asia,* Delhi, 1996.

4. Sinappah Arasaratnam, 'Weavers, Merchants and Company: The Handloom Industry in South East India, 1750–1790', *Indian Economic and Social History Review,* vol.XVII, no.3, 1980, pp.257–87. *Also see* 'Trade and Political Dominion in South India 1750–1790: Changing British Indian Relationships', *Modern Asian Studies,* vol.13, no. I, 1977, pp.42–53.

5. K.N. Chaudhuri, *The Trading World of Asia and the English East India Company 1600–1760,* Cambridge, 1978, pp.310–11.

6. Lakshmi Subramanian, *Indigenous Credit and Imperial Expansion.*

7. Public Department Diary of the Bombay Government (hereafter PDD) No.26 (II) of 1753, pp.223–4. Letter from Surat dated 28 June and considered by the Bombay Council on 10 July 1753.

8. Ibid.

9. Ibid., pp.225–6. Consultation of the Bombay Government, 11 July 1753.

10. Commercial Department Diary of the Bombay Government (hereafter CDD) No.9 of 1794, p.132ff. Report of the Committee appointed to enquire

into the failure of the provision of piece-goods of the Surat investment read on 18 March 1794.

11. Ashin Das Gupta, *Indian Merchants and the Decline of Surat 1700–1750,* Manohar 1994 (Reprint), pp.36–7.

12. CDD No.7 of 1792, pp.92–3ff. Report of John Griffith dated 14 April 1792.

13. CDD No. 12 of 1796, p.17ff. Report of the Committee set up to visit the manufacturing towns dated 24 December 1795 read by the Board on 2 January 1796.

14. Ibid. *See also* PDD No.120 of 1796, pp.2232ff. *See* 'Estimate of His Highness the Nawab of the losses sustained by a remission of the Mokats on the probable investment'.

15. Ibid.

16. PDD No.147 of 1800, p.627ff.

17. Ibid.

18. PDD No.147 of 1800, p.627ff.

19. For the terms of the annual contract entered into by the English East India Company in the 50s, *see* PDD No.26 (II) of 1753, p.301ff for Articles of agreement between Richard Bourchier and Nasserwanji Bomanji and Munchurji Bomonji dated 11 September 1753.

20. PDD of 1752, p.212. Letter from Surat dated 7 June 1752 and read by the Bombay Government on 12 June 1752.

21. Ibid., p.214. Letter despatched to Surat on 15 June 1752.

22. Ibid., p.226. Letter from Surat dated 22 June 1752 and considered by the Bombay Council on 5 July 1752.

23. PDD of 1764. Letter from the Surat factors dated 21 September 1764.

24. PDD of 1766. Letter from Surat dated 18 November 1766.

25. Ibid.

26. Lakshmi Subramanian, *Indigenous Credit and Imperial Expansion,* pp.215–21.

27. Surat Factory Diary (hereafter SFD) No.680 of 1788. pp.431. Representation of Rustamjee Monakjee.

28. Ibid., p.456.

29. Ibid., p.431.

30. Ibid., p.460.

31. Lakshmi Subramanian, *Indigenous Capital and Imperial Expansion,* pp.221–38.

32. CDD No.5 of 1790, p.97ff. Letter from Mayaram Atmaram dated 15 April 1790.

33. Ibid.

34. Ibid.

35. CDD No.6 of 1791, p.268ff. Petition of Mayaram Atmaram.

36. Ibid.

37. CDD No.7 of 1792, p.66ff. Consultation of 16 March 1792.

38. Ibid.

39. Ibid., p.73 Letter from Surat dated 21 March 1792 considered by the

Bombay Council on 3 April 1792.

40. Ibid.

41. Ibid. John Griffith's Report dated 14 April 1792.

42. Ibid.

43. Ibid.

44. CDD No.9 of 1794, pp.152–6. Report of the Committee dated 28 February 1794.

45. CDD No.11 of 1795, p.1002ff. Minute of the Surat Chief dated 16 December 1795.

46. Ibid.

47. Ibid., p.1008. The Contractor's reply to the Chief's minute dated 16 December 1795.

48. Ibid., p.691. Letter and enclosures from Surat read on 25 September 1795.

49. Ibid.

50. Ibid., pp.778–80ff. Letter and enclosures from Surat read on 27 October 1795.

51. Ibid.

52. Ibid.

53. CDD No.12 of 1796, p.49ff. Mr. Cherry's Minute on the Investment System.

54. Ibid.

55. Ibid., p.53ff.

56. Ibid. pp.237–8. The President's Minute on the Investment System.

57. Ibid.

58. Ibid., p.319ff. Consultation of the Bombay Council, 15 March 1796.

59. CDD No.15 of 1796, pp.491–2. The Nawab's reply to the Chief.

60. Ibid. pp.520–3. Minute of the Commercial Resident.

61. PDD No.119 of 1796, pp.392–3. Letter and enclosures from the Commercial Board at Surat read by the Bombay Council on 12 April 1796. Also pp.479–80 for Representation of the Portuguese Resident.

62. PDD No.120 of 1796, p.2215ff. Letter and enclosures from Surat read by the Bombay Council on 3 September 1796.

63. Ibid., pp.114–5.

64. Ibid.

65. Ibid., p.310ff. Letter and enclosures from the Commercial Board at Surat read on 10 March 1797.

66. Ibid. *See* Minute of the President, Daniel Seton.

67. CDD No. 16 of 1797, p.932ff.

68. Ibid., p.942ff.

69. CDD No.17 (II) of 1798, pp.259–60. Consultation meeting of 28 February 1798.

70. Ibid., p.262. *See* The President's Minute.

71. Ibid., p.313. *Also* CDD No.18 of 1798, pp.37–8. Letter from Commercial Board at Surat reviewed on 3 April 1798.

72. CDD No.18 of 1798, pp.339–40. Letter and enclosures from Commercial

Board at Surat reviewed on 11 May 1798.

73. CDD No.19 of 1798, pp.76–7ff. Letter and enclosures from the Commercial Board at Surat reviewed on 13 September 1798.

74. Ibid., pp.2214–5ff. Letter and enclosures from the Commercial Board at Surat reviewed on 2 November 1795.

75. Ibid., pp.230–5. Representation of the Contracting Brokers to the Commercial Resident, 27 October 1798.

76. Ibid., p.235.

77. Ibid., p.236.

78. CDD No.23 of 1799, p.514. Council meeting, 10 May 1799.

79. Ibid., p.666. Representation from the Contracting Brokers.

80. Ibid., p.735. Meeting of 2 July 1799.

81. CDD No.25 of 1800, pp.125–6ff. Letter and enclosures from the Commercial Board at Surat reviewed on 28 January 1800.

82. Ibid., pp.150–1. Representation from the Contracting Brokers dated 10 November 1799.

83. PDD No. 146 of 1800, pp.345–6.

84. PDD No.147 of 1800, p.627ff. Letter and enclosures from Surat reviewed on 2 April 1800.

85. Ibid.

86. CDD No.27 of 1800, p.203ff. Letter to the Contracting Brokers dated 19 September 1800.

87. Ibid., pp.504–5ff. Petition of the Contracting Brokers.

88. Ibid., p.510ff.

89. Ibid., pp.549–50ff. Representation from the Mohemmedan Weavers of Blue Cloths, etc.

90. Ibid., pp.558–63. Letter to the Commercial Board at Surat dated 26 December 1800.

91. CDD No.35 of 1802, pp.1096–1100. Letter from Commercial Board at Surat reviewed on 26 September 1802.

92. Ibid., pp.1196–7.

93. Ibid., pp.1284–7. Minute of the Commercial Resident dated 16 November 1802.

Table I

Species of Goods	Place of Manufacture	Time when best made
Nacanees (Large)	Gujarat, best ones manufactured in Surat	These goods are best worked early in the year when they are closer or finer in every respect and wholly finished before the dry winds set in November.
Necanees (Small)	ditto	February–October. The Company's orders must be placed no later than April, especially if the demand is considerable.
Necanees (Coarse)	ditto	
Tapseils (Large)	Made solely in Surat	
Tapseils (Small)	ditto	
Bejutapauts (Blue)	Best kind available at Surat and Baroda.	Before the onset of the dry winds.
Bejutapauts (Red)	ditto	ditto
Chelloes (Blue) Large	Surat and Cambay	During the prevalence of damp winds and rainy season, but as these goods are finer than the generality of piece-goods and those for the Company are of greater length and breadth than those purchased by all the European nations, the manufacturers are loath to work them and will not undertake any large quantity as the red threads used in these goods are best coloured in the hot weather in April, they ought always to be ordered in time to allow threads to be prepared that month.
Chelloes (Blue) Small	ditto	
Chelloes (Red) Large	ditto	
Chelloes Red with Checks	ditto	
Byrampauts (Blue) Large Byrampauts (White) Large	Those at Broach better but prices exorbitant. These cloths coloured and calendared in Surat.	Goods to be contracted early in the year, and being received in course of the period between February and October will be excellent.

contd...

Species of Goods	Place of Manufacture	Time when best made
Neganepauts (Large) Neganepauts (New Muster)	Best in Surat.	At the same time with the Necanees and ought to be put in hand early in the year.
Chints of sorts	Dooties (Navsari) Chints (Surat)	Best time for contracting is the rains, for by March–April, the Chints are completed.
Cambay Goods	Cambay	Same as that for Necanees and Bejutapauts.
Lungees	Cambay	ditto
Goods of Cambay	Surat	ditto
Chader Madowjee	ditto	
Chader Magreb	ditto	
Chelloes Blue	ditto	
Chader for Neganepauts	ditto	
Lungee No.74 for Bejutapauts Red	ditto	
Nasar No.2 for Necanees	ditto	
Dooties (White)	Broach	During the rains.

Source: Commercial Department Diary of the Bombay Government. No.7 of 1792, pp.87–91.

Table II

The Structure of the Weaving Occupation in Surat, 1795 (Looms employed in the manufacture of piece-goods and the weaving castes working on them)

Number of Looms	Piece-goods manufactured	Caste and Religion of Weavers
4086	Necanees—Large, small and coarse	Momna Muslims, Bora and Bhandarees all Muslim castes
	Tapsells—large and small Salotee, Chadar Madowjee, Lungee Madowjee, Chadar Numanee Chelloes Blue, 11 and 9 Vees Bejutapauts Blue	
1865	Neganepauts of four kinds Bejutapauts Red, Chelloes Red of II Vees Chadar Turmallee Chowrangee, Geegum and Cadia	Khatri caste (Hindus)
849	Puchoree, Putkahs, Doria of Sorts, Turbans, Salloes, Seylahs and Dhootias	Bora and Muslim castes
2298	Sarees, Obotiahs, Durreihs, Dootias with silk borders	Khatri caste (Hindu)
1265	Musroo of different kinds	Koolmbee caste of Hindus
2614	Silk goods: Elacha, Ghurbee, Kumbroo, Soosea	Parsees
535	Kincobs	Koolmbees and Muslims
1491	Puchodee, Putkahs Plain, Handkerchiefs Baftas, Dootias, Dupattas	Parsees
171	Hembroos	Koolmbees
135	Potlahs, Chadar with silk borders	Koolmbees and Muslims
115	Dupattas with gold silver border, Patkahs, gold silver Tissue	Koolmbees and Muslims
462	Durrees, Sarees	Koolmbees
391	Baftas, Salloes White Seylas Dungaree, Coarse Patkahs, Coarse Dootias	Malwee and Pancholee, Deerahs
Total: 15776 Looms		

Source: Commercial Department Diary of the Bombay Government No.12 of 1796, pp.17ff.

5

A Wedding Feast or Political Arena?: Commercial Rivalry between the Ali Rajas and the English Factory in Northern Malabar in the 18th Century

RUCHIRA BANERJEE

In a grand ceremony in 1771, Ali Raja Kunhi Amsi,[1] the Mappila chieftain of the Cannanore and a prominent maritime merchant of Malabar celebrated the marriage of his niece with a rich businessman of Calicut. The ostentation that was in evidence, as also the presence of a large number of Mappila merchants during the week-long festivities in Cannanore, attracted the attention of the entire mercantile fraternity of the region. It was apparent even to the most casual observer that the Ali Raja had used the occasion to flaunt his sudden prosperity and his resurgence as a leader of the Mappilas to intimidate his adversaries.[2] This study examines the responses of the different mercantile groups and political agencies to the dramatic rise of the Ali Raja in the trade and politics of the province against the backdrop of old animosities and new alliances in the period between 1722 and the outbreak of the Second Anglo-Mysore War in 1780 in Malabar.

Kunhi Amsi had every reason to celebrate in 1771. After almost half a century of humiliating setbacks, the Mappila chieftain had finally nullified the persistent efforts made by the English factory in nearby Tellicherry to undermine him and his predecessors in maritime and hinterland trade, to isolate them politically and finally to denigrate them socially in the eyes of the Mappila community. Kunhi Amsi had turned the tables on the English officials by entering into a military alliance with Haider Ali and by helping him to conquer Malabar in 1766.[3] By doing so he had not only regained his family's traditional sphere of influence in northern Malabar but also enlarged it at the cost of the English Company and its Nair allies. The wedding feast gave Kunhi Amsi a chance to demonstrate his enormous hold over the Mappila merchants, inhabiting the pepper-rich districts of the Kolattiri kingdom. As the cannons boomed in Cannanore to commemorate the joyous event, the Ali Raja sent out an ominous signal to the existing syndicates of trade in Malabar. He seemed to proclaim that any group which did not acknowledge him as the foremost maritime merchant and supplier of Malabari and Mysorean commodities in the province was in danger of getting completely marginalized. The aim of this study is to find out how real this threat was in 1771.

The wedding feast had caused quite a stir among the contemporary businessmen. The European companies of trade pretended to be unaffected and spoke disparagingly about the elaborate ceremony. According to them, it was nothing but a ploy used by Kunhi Amsi to overawe his detractors and to pressurize the assembled Mappilas into supporting him in the forthcoming trial of strength with his enemies. Notwithstanding the strong bias, there was nevertheless some truth in this viewpoint. The splendour of the marriage ceremony could hardly conceal the chinks in Kunhi Amsi's armour. The fact remained that though the Ali Raja had acquired an edge over the Tellicherry factory and the vanquished Nair rulers, a clinching victory still eluded him. His adversaries were far from reconciled to his elevation within the conventional society and polity of Malabar. It was therefore only a matter of time before they regrouped and struck back. But in spite of his vulnerabilities, Kunhi Amsi could not be offhandedly dismissed either. He had sizeably increased both his resources and his Mappila following and stood a fair chance of winning in the imminent power struggle.

Our study examines this unfinished contest of 1771 in northern Malabar, firstly against the gradual disintegration of the traditional structures of power in the region, caused by the protracted struggle for commercial supremacy between the English East India Company and the Ali Rajas since 1722 and, secondly, in the light of the sudden collapse of the same structures of power due to Haider Ali's victory over the weak Nair Rajas, with the support of Ali Raja Kunhi Amsi in 1766. Finally, while the main emphasis is on the economic implications of this contest, this essay also tries to analyse the compulsions and the general attitude of the Mappila merchants towards the Ali Rajas and their rivals; to understand their specific roles in the conflicts embroiling the Ali Rajas, the English factory, the Nair kings and Haider Ali and, finally, to identify the adjustments that they made in a new era marked by the ebbing influence of the Ali Rajas on one hand and the rising fortunes of a British-backed lobby of merchants, headed by the Choucaras of Tellicherry on the other.

The conflicting roles

The wedding feast of 1771 was a landmark event in the lives of Ali Raja Kunhi Amsi and his adherents. The Mysorean conquest of 1766 had brought unprecedented prosperity and also temporarily resolved the problems arising out of the Ali Rajas playing the conflicting roles of maritime merchants and aristocrats in Malabar.

By virtue of the longest record in maritime trading, the Ali Rajas enjoyed a special status in Malabari society. They were important carriers of pepper, cardamom, timber, coconuts, coir, cowries and rice to far-flung markets in India and abroad since the end of the twelfth century. Besides these exports from Malabar, Mysore and coastal Kanara, they additionally transhipped a whole range of goods that circulated in the Indian Ocean. These activities brought them inevitably and consistently into conflict with the European trading companies which tried by turns, since the early sixteenth century, to control the maritime trade of the region.[4]

As the Europeans resented any kind of competition from the Asian merchants, it was only natural that they should have wanted to dislodge the Ali Rajas from the maritime circuit. But they failed to inflict any lasting damage before the end of the eighteenth century. Unlike many Mappila or Arab merchants who were routinely and irrevocably ruined by the hostility of the Europeans or simply because of unanticipated losses in trade, the Ali Rajas displayed an uncanny knack for surviving the most devastating setbacks. Their regenerative powers emanated from the vast areas of cultivation, markets and trade routes that they controlled in the hinterland as Malabari aristocrats. It was this sphere of influence in northern Malabar that sustained their maritime activities and distinguished them from all other merchants in the region.

The sphere of influence of the Ali Rajas was carved out of the pepper-rich territory between the Nileshwaram and Dharmapatnam rivers. It roughly covered the northern half of what was later known as British Malabar and was ruled, though in name only, by the Kolattiri Raja prior to the establishment of British rule there in 1792. The actual governance of the Kolattiri territory which extended south up to the Kotta river in the late seventeenth and eighteenth centuries was in the hands of the different branches of the Kolattiri house, headed by autonomous Nair rulers and a Muslim chieftain, the Ali Raja of Cannanore. But in spite of his Kolattiri ancestry, the Ali Raja's position in the ruling hierarchy was inferior to that of the other Nair

Rajas.[5] This anomaly was inherent in the original pact between Arayan Kulangara and the Kolattiri sovereign.

The Ali Rajas had descended from Arayan Kulangara, a prince of the Arakkal family in Kolattiri. Kulangara's interest in maritime trade and his closeness to the Muslim merchants from the Red Sea had brought him under the influence of Islam sometime in the eleventh or twelfth century and eventually resulted in his conversion to this faith. After becoming a Muslim, he assumed the name of Mohammad Ali or Mammali. This name was retained by the Arakkal chieftains who subsequentlly also adopted the title of Ali Raja, a corruption of the expression Ada Raja or the Lord of the Sea.[6] The title reflected the Arakkal clan's abiding interest in sea-trade.

Due to their conversion to Islam and their preoccupation with maritime trade, the Arakkal chieftains had been demoted within the hierarchy of political power in Malabar. But they were not, strangely enough, expelled from it. This contradiction had far-reaching implications on their subsequent position in the hinterland, as Muslims, as merchants, and finally as aristocrats. What is noteworthy is that it was the Kolattiri Nairs who had created this role conflict. Later it was they who made it a bone of contention with the Ali Rajas.

Instead of opposing the conversion of Arayan Kulangara, the Kolattiri nobles endorsed it because at that time it helped them to resolve their own predicament. They could not permit him to remain within the folds of the Hindu religion and at the same time play the dual role of Nair aristocrat and maritime merchant. This constituted a blatant violation of the caste laws as it was interpreted in Malabar up to the end of the eighteenth century. The laws of the land forbade the Nambudiris or the priestly caste from either trading or soldiering, the Nairs or the warrior class from performing religious duties or trading and merchants, particularly the Mappilas or the Malayali Muslims from interfering in matters of state or in the management of temple property. Kulangara's position as a Hindu aristocrat had become untenable and yet it was extremely important to allow him to function as a maritime merchant. The impasse was broken by his embracing Islam.

It could of course be argued that the presence of inland traders among certain sub-castes of Nairs and among *Pattar* (Tamil) brahmins meant that the laws were not rigidly observed.[7] But notwithstanding the laxity shown towards the middle echelons of Nairs or towards the non-Malayali brahmins, the caste laws appear to have been more vigorously enforced on the prinicpal *gribams* to which the Kolattiri princes and the Mammalis belonged. As the elite of Kolattiri society, the members of these grihams were required to be role models and adhere to the rules. It was a small price to pay for the sweeping powers that the Hindu nobles otherwise enjoyed as 'protectors' of the prime agricultural land in the region.[8] In a significant departure from established norms, some concessions were also given to the Muslim Mammalis who were permitted to retain some of their secular privileges without giving up their right to trade. They had of course to surrender their earlier prerogative of ascending the Kolattiri throne or of becoming *adhikaris* or custodians of temples. They thereby stood 'demoted' to the rank of chieftain. But this loss of status was offset by the enormous wealth accruing to them from maritime trade.

On the whole Kulangara received a preferential treatment within the caste set-up for freeing the Kolattiri Nairs from the onus of mingling with the 'polluting' classes of overseas merchants and for increasing the maritime trade of the realm. Through their interaction with foreigners, the Ali Rajas gained valuable insight into the mechanism of sea-trade and even managed to build their own fleet to access the maritime markets of the Indian Ocean. Their activities contributed to the general prosperity of the Kolattiri kingdom which flourished because of growing sea-traffic and overland trade with the neighbouring Vijayanagar kingdom. In return, it was only fair that the Mammalis should have continued to enjoy an elevated status within the caste and political hierarchies, even after they had opted out of the folds of the Hindu religion.[9]

The basic anomaly of the Arakkal chieftains playing the dual role of merchant and aristocrat was both advantageous and also a perennial source of trouble for them. While it gave them an edge over other maritime traders in the interior, the dual role also gave rise to serious friction with the Nair princes on the question of jurisdiction in the hinterland. These clashes increased after the arrival of the Europeans. The outsiders made capital of the fact that the Hindu aristocrats had no definite rules for dealing with the Ali Rajas. The Europeans could therefore play up real and supposed acts of transgressions, committed by the Arakkal chieftains and to attack them and their Mappila supporters, in the guise of protecting the weak Nair rulers.

Despite the ambivalence of the Nair aristocrats towards the Ali Rajas, it was clear that they never treated them like common traders. There was a world of difference between the Arakkal clansmen who had descended from a Kolattiri griham and the vast majority of Mappilas who owed their ancestry to common Malayali fisherwomen. These low-caste women had married Arab merchants sometime between the ninth and the fifteenth century. The Mappila offspring of these mixed marriages were introduced to Islam and simultaneously to maritime trading by their Arab fathers. Doubtless these steps had improved their economic conditions and uplifted them socially; but only marginally.[10] Social status and wealth were too intimately linked to caste in Malabar to have allowed any drastic change in the position of the erstwhile fisherfolk. On the whole, the lack of social respectability and resources prevented the Mappilas from becoming independent maritime merchants in significant numbers. Consequently, when the Portuguese came to Malabar in 1498, the community, with notable exceptions like the Ali Rajas, mainly comprised of brokers, transporters and 'petty' traders.[11] This scenario did not alter drastically in the following centuries.

The Ali Rajas were a cut above the ordinary Mappilas. They were the leading maritime merchants and suppliers of assorted goods from Malabar and the adjacent regions before the 1780s. The Mappila merchants of Calicut, with their ostentatious lifestyle could never really outclass them; at least not on a sustained basis.[12] They were handicapped by their failure to own vast landholdings and to exercise the same measure of control over strategic markets and trade routes like the Arakkal chieftains. The Ali Rajas had painstakingly created an exclusive sphere of influence out of an intricate web of shared interests with the Nambudiri landowners and Nair rulers on one hand, and with a host of maritime and inland merchants on the other. These connections had been painstakingly nurtured for centuries. It was impossible for new aspirants, especially those with low-caste credentials, to carve out an area of predominance as extensive or as well-entrenched as theirs.

The Arakkal clansmen also perpetuated the social divide by not marrying the 'low-caste' Mappilas. Yet the unthinkable happened at the turn of the eighteenth century. Despite his 'petty trader' past, Choucara Moosa, a Mappila merchant of Tellicherry succeeded in arranging a match betweeen his nephew and a grand niece of Kunhi Amsi at the end of the eighteenth century. It was a sign of the changing times that his successor Ali Bibi Junnuma Bi Valiya Tangul accepted this proposal despite her misgivings.[13] She really did not have much of a choice. The Choucara family, headed by Moosa had forged ahead of the Arakkal clan both as far as maritime trade and control of the hinterland were concerned. There had even been times when Moosa had bailed a beleaguered Bibi out of trouble. She dared not to reject this proposal and antagonize Moosa for life.[14] The phenomenal prosperity of the Choucaras reflected the far-reaching changes that had followed the breakdown of the traditional heirarchies of power and the ascendance of the English East India Company in Malabar at the close of the eighteenth century.

The complex sphere of influence

In the period preceding these momentous changes, the Ali Rajas did not have to make the kind of compromises that the Ali Bibi was forced to make. They could rely on their own sphere of influence to recover their losses. It is impossible however to define the boundaries of this area of predominance. But despite its complexities, certain features stand out in clear relief. Firstly, it was extremely unstable. It shrank and expanded to adjust to the minutest fluctuation in their fortunes. There were times, such as in 1746,[15] when it did not extend beyond the walls of their mud fort in Cannanore, and also others such as in 1771, when it stretched from the coast to the foot-hills of the western ghats.[16]

Secondly, the sphere of influence of the Arakkal chiefs could be further sub-divided into two interdependent sectors—one the maritime circuit and the other, their area of predominance in the hinterland.

Thirdly, it was not one but two spheres of formal and informal influence. The sphere of formal influence could be demarcated in terms of the actual landholdings and area of political predominance of the Ali Rajas. It was superimposed on a more intangible sphere of undefined 'space' which these chieftains controlled because of their aristocratic background and by virtue of their kinship, community and business ties. Since there were too many overlaps, no clear separation of these two spheres is feasible. It is evident though that even in the worst of times when the formal sphere of influence had all but disappeared, the informal one endured and provided sustenance.

Finally, we would do well to remember that in spite of their upper caste elitism, the Ali Rajas fraternized with the ordinary Mappilas. They could ill-afford to alienate the humbler members of their community, especially since it was on their support that the Arakkal sphere of influence flourished. The Ali Rajas took enormous pains to foster their loyalty through social interaction and through business dealings.

The maritime circuit

Sea-trade was the main source of wealth for the Ali Rajas and the sector that provided livelihood to hundreds of Mappilas. The major break for the Ali Rajas came sometime in the twelfth century when the Kolattiri Raja allowed them to colonize the Lakshadweep in return for an annual tribute of 18,000 fanams. This enabled the Arakkal chiefs to export coconuts, coconut products and fine quality coir manufactured under their close supervision on the islands. Sea-trade received a further boost during the tenure of Ali Moosa who took charge of the clan in 1183–4. Under him the Arakkal family conquered the Maldives and assumed control over the islands' vast store of cowries, fish, coconuts and coconut products. The Ali Rajas also profited from the transhipment of goods from India, Red Sea and the Far Eastern ports. In time the Mappila chieftains became carriers of indigenous and transhipped goods from the islands to ports in the Red Sea, Persian Gulf, China, Bengal, Coromandel, Gujarat and Konkan.[17]

Concurrently with their acquisition of the Lakshadweep and Maldives in the late twelfth century, the Ali Rajas also consolidated their hold over the Malabar coast and exported goods from the mainland. Cannanore port was the focal point of all their maritime activities in the eighteenth century. Smaller ports such as Kavai, Pudiyangadi and Dharmapatnam in northern Malabar operated as satellites of Cannanore. Their leverage also extended in varying degrees to the south as far as Calicut and to the north as far as Mangalore. The Ali Rajas exported Malabari pepper and coconuts, Peria and Koorgi cardamom, Mysorean sandalwood, Kanarese rice, Lakshadweep coir and Maldivan cowries in their ships to distant markets in the Indian Ocean. Besides these direct exports, the Arakkal chiefs also sold some consignments to ships coming to Cannanore from Gujarat, Bengal and Macau. Finally, they accepted orders for Malabari and Mysorean goods from other reputed suppliers in Mangalore, Calicut and Cochin. These different channels of export provided opportunities of employment to Mappilas belonging to different economic strata.[18]

The Ali Rajas engaged a huge force consisting mainly of Mappilas for the collection of goods from the islands, from Malabar and from Kanara and for their redistribution to other centres like Calicut and for export abroad. The number of Mappilas engaged in these operations swelled sharply after the sixteenth century since cargoes had to be split into smaller parcels and sent through circuitous routes to various points to preempt their confiscation by the European East India Companies. Starting with the Portuguese who arrived in Malabar in 1498, the Dutch, the English and the French did not allow a market-driven pricing mechanism to prevail. Instead they all tried to forcibly buy large quantities of pepper at uneconomical rates from the Malayali rulers and the Mappila merchants.[19] The European companies closely monitored sea-trade in Malabar in order to enforce a complete monopoly over the sale of spices and subsequently over the sale of aromatic and hard woods. Any vessel which did not get prior clearance to navigate and to transport goods risked attacks by their vigilant, patrol boats. But regardless of the intimidation, the 'smuggling' of Malabari spices and other goods continued unabatedly, although at a much higher transportation cost. Despite the larger overheads, the Malabari exporters found it more viable to resort to clandestine shipments rather than accept the customers and the circuits of trade thrust upon them by the European East India companies.[20]

Enlargement of the conflict

By their persistent defiance of the restrictions on indigenous trade, the Ali Rajas got embroiled in very expensive and protracted conflicts with the European companies of trade in Malabar. The recurring friction with the English factory in Tellicherry in the early eighteenth century could in one sense be viewed as a part of an ongoing war. But a closer scrutiny would reveal that a subtle change had taken place. While the struggle to uphold the freedom of the seas continued, the contest itself was no longer restricted to the seas or to intense lobbying for trading rights in the Nair courts. In a major departure from the past, it had spilled over deep into the hinterland where the contestants tried to directly access centres of cultivation, inland markets and arterial routes to gain a better control over the inventories, warehoused for export at different sites.

The expansion of the conflict in the Kolattiri realm had been triggered off by a new breed of English officials and their Topas or 'half-caste' Christian interpreters. These men took advantage of the local warfare between the Ali Rajas and the Chirakkal Nairs who constituted the most powerful faction among the Kolattiri aristocrats to penetrate into the interior in 1722. The Tellicherry officials pretended to act sanctimoniously when they helped the Chirakkal Raja to avenge the insult that he had suffered at the hands of the Ali Raja. The Mappila chieftain had supposedly ambushed a retinue of a close relative of the Nair king and publicly flogged the aristocrat in 1722. But the French disputed this allegation and claimed that no disrespect had been shown to the prince. Though we have no means of ascertaining the truth, the fact remains that the Tellicherry officials had set a dangerous precedent.[21] Thereafter they took it upon themselves to regularly intervene, on one pretext or the other, and by direct or indirect means in the hinterland to appropriate goods on easier terms. This essay examines the enlargement of the conflict and the sharp fissures that appeared in the Malabari society and polity as a result of this intervention.

Ironically, the hardened approach adopted by the English towards the Ali Rajas coincided with the softening of the Dutch towards them. The Dutch had decided to scale down their establishment in northern Malabar and to use the Ali Rajas as their suppliers in Cannanore. Even the French seemed well disposed towards them. In fact, had it not been for their support in 1746 and 1747, the Ali Rajas might have got annihilated by the English Company quite early in the century.[22] The two decades were the darkest period in the history of the Arakkal house. It affected the maritime activities of the family which virtually came to a standstill during this phase.

The murder of Ali Raja Kunhi Mammali in 1727, possibly at the instigation of the Tellicherry officials inaugurated a period of acute strife for the Arakkal chieftains. Thereafter, for almost three decades they fought a series of wars with the Nair rulers, especially with the Chirakkal Raja, the Tellicherry factory and the Ikkeri forces from Bednur. The two *Ilaya* Rajas or the husbands of the Ali Bibis, the female successors of Kunhi Mammali, faced a two-pronged attack from their enemies on land as well as on the high seas. As the cost of military campaigns escalatd, the Ali Bibis were compelled to borrow large sums of money from every available source including the Tellicherry factory.[23] Since most of these resources were utilized to fight wars, practically nothing remained for overseas trade. Matters were further compounded by the English officials confiscating the ships of the clan to recover their loans.[24] In 1736 they even refused to issue passes to ships belonging to the Arakkal family on the grounds that the clansmen 'smuggled' pepper to Calicut.[25] The crisis deepened in 1747. The Tellicherry factory stepped up their vigil to such an extent that it was impossible for any boat to enter or leave Cannanore unaccosted by their patrol boats.[26] But they were not able to sustain this blockade after a couple of years.

Fortunately for the Arakkal clansmen, a strong Ali Raja assumed charge in 1744–5. Within a decade, this man was able to stem the rot and even restore some of the lost glory of the Arakkal house. He first liquidated the family debt to the English factory with generous financial assistance from the Mappila merchant, Poquoe Moosa Marakkar of Travancore in 1747.[27] The Ali Raja next concentrated on neutralizing the English embargoes on the Cannanore trade by appealing for help to the Dutch officials in Cannanore and to the French in Mahe. While these allies interceded forcefully on his behalf, the Ali Raja parleyed with the Angrias of Konkan and drew up plans for joint naval action against the English. With pressure mounting from all sides, the Tellicherry officials capitulated. They started re-issuing passes to the ocean-going ships belonging to the Ali Rajas in 1756.[28] This is where the case rested when Kunhi Amsi took charge of the clan sometime in the late '50s or in the early '60s.

Apart from Poquoe Moosa, there were many other prosperous Mappila merchants who intermittently collaborated with the Ali Rajas in coastal trade. These men were united in their common struggle against European interference in indigenous trade, particularly against the surveillance and seizure of their crafts by the European patrol boats. They responded to this menace by distributing their inventories along the seaboard and then by moving the cargo in stages to the main export centres like Calicut. The merchants of Vadakara and Kotta closely cooperated with the Ali Rajas in this phased transportation of goods.[29] There was a historical bond between them. In the mid-sixteenth century, Balia Hassan, a member of the Arakkal clan had fought along with the Kunjali Marakkars of Kotta against the Portuguese authority in Cannanore. These men died in the course of their campaign for indigenous autonomy in trade and were venerated as martyrs by the Mappilas.[30] In the eighteenth century the Kotta Marakkars and the Arakkal chiefs once again united to face a common enemy. It was now not so much the Portuguese as much as the English patrol boats which targeted their crafts for systematic harassment.

To the south of Kotta, there was another group of influential Mappilas in Koilandi allied to the Ali Rajas Their leaders, the Siddi Syeds were ship-owning merchants who traded with the Red Sea ports. They also enjoyed the additional distinction of being religious leaders. The Ali Rajas often made good use of their exalted position to mobilize the Mappilas in their own favour. In 1746, the Siddi Syeds helped to disuse a flash-point in which the reigning Ali Raja came perilously close to being deposed by the Mappilas of Valarapatnam.[31] Finally, the Arakkal chiefs counted on the goodwill of the Calicut merchants. Apart from the commercial ties, the relationship between the two parties was further strengthened through matrimonial alliances. At least two of the Bibis in the eighteenth century were married to businessmen of this port.[32]

The hinterland base

The Arakkal sphere of influence was not limited to the coast but extended deep into the interior. The Ali Rajas and their friends like Camall Mopla were major landholders. Before the last quarter of the eighteenth century no mercantile syndicate had as much say in the procurement and in the transportation of pepper as the group headed by the Ali Rajas. There were doubtlessly many Mappila merchants outside this coterie who owned pepper plantations and coconut groves too. But their individual holdings were scattered and insignificant as compared to those belongng to the Arakkal clansmen, in terms of size, contiguity and the powers accompanying them.

The Ali Rajas occupied extensive agricultural land, covering several districts in which the best quality pepper, rice and coconuts were cultivated under various land tenures. Certain portions came to them as *anubhogam* or rent-free land which the Nair princes gave them in exchange for military service at various points in time.[33] The Ali Rajas had also taken large tracts under the *kanum* tenure or lease from the Nair princes and the *devasthanams* (temple estates). Finally the Ali Rajas had reclaimed barren stretches of land and transformed them into rice fields, pepper plantations and coconut groves under the *kuzhikanum* tenure.[34]

These various categories of landholding belonging to the Ali Rajas were clustered around the rivers Valarapatnam, Taliparambu, Kodoli and Dharmapatnam in northern Kolattiri. They contained important markets and trade routes that gave the Ali Rajas an automatic advantage over their rivals. Some of the markets were not mere collection points for pepper and coconuts but also transhipment centres for the Mysorean sandalwood and cardamom from Koorg and Wynad. These commodities were grown in the districts bordering Malabar or across the ghats. They were transported to the coast through the rivers and path-ways that the Ali Rajas and their associates had helped to forge for centuries. The efforts to build a network of inland routes, connecting Malabar to the adjoining regions of Mysore, Kanara, Bednur and the Carnatic had intensified after the advent of the Europeans and as a consequence of their intrusion into coastal trade. They were meant to increase road traffic and to provide a safer alternative to movement of goods by sea.

The Ali Rajas controlled strategic points along some of the trade routes that traversed the Periapatam pass. During his campaign in Malabar, Haider Ali of Mysore took this factor into account when he asked Kunhi Amsi to supervise the military operations in Malabar in 1766. Through his actions Haider Ali acknowledged the privileged position of the Ali Rajas within the hierarchy of power in the region. Many of the title deeds of the Arakkal landholdings also bore testimony to this reality. They incorporated special features that gave the Ali Rajas more than physical control over the land and its produce. *Deshadhipatyam* was for instance one such element that conferred on the Ali Rajas the right to 'govern' people living in selected areas within their holdings. Deshadhipatyam or 'royalty' as the English referred to it was appended separately to special categories of land and gave the title-holder the right to regulate the movement of goods and to monitor the sale of the produce.[35] The island of Dharmapatnam which formed a part of the exclusive domain of the Ali Rajas was covered by this special clause. The *janmakar* or the original landlord which included the Chirakkal Raja and several devasthanam authorities seldom interfered in the management of the island though they legally had the right to do so. Moreover, by virtue of being a *separate* privilege accompanying certain landholdings, deshadhipatyam was liable to cancellation and re-leasing to another aspirant, without the physical eviction of the earlier tenant. The janmakar however had not exercised this prerogative with the Ali Rajas before the 1730s.[36]

The Ali Rajas had nurtured their landed interests by staying on the right side of the Kolattiri aristocracy. They had also consolidated their position by subletting their holdings to Mappila cultivators. The districts of Cherakunnu, Kunjimangalam, Rhandaterra and Dharmapatnam island had considerable Mappila population. It was no coincidence that large portions of these areas were owned, leased or reclaimed either by the Ali Rajas or by their Mappila friends like Camall Mopla of Madayi.[37]

Division of the Mappila 'constituency'

The Ali Rajas nurtured a huge 'constituency' of Mappila merchants through a close interplay of personal empathy and economic ties. Their overlapping spheres of landed and business interests on one hand and social and political influence on the other stretched across a vast hinterland which sustained the ports between Kavai and Calicut in the early eighteenth century.[38] Given the enormous richness of this field, it was only natural that the other syndicates of trade should have wanted a share of the more lucrative sectors within it. The Ali Rajas encountered fierce competition from the Tellicherry factory and from their interpreters, the Rodriguez, along two interregional circuits of trade. One was the Valarapatnam–Taliparambu waterway that connected the coast to the upstream Mappila markets like Mattambi, Madakkara, Valarapatnam, Taliparambu, Irkur and Srikandapuram which in turn were linked through broken pathways to Koorg and Mysore. The other interregional route was the Anjarkandi, Dharmapatnam and Kodoli riverine system that converged on Dharmapatnam island. This network of streams encompassed Mappila agricultural strongholds such as Dharmapatnam Rhandaterra,

Anjarkandi and markets like Benghat, Agar, Cadrur, Choudar and Kotiath. It also had linkages with overland routes connecting Malabar to Wynad, Koorg and Mysore. Quantities of the best quality Malabari pepper, coconut and timber, Peria and Koorgi cardamom and Mysorean sandalwood transited through the Valarapatnam and Dharmapatnam waterways to the coast.[39]

There were cracks in the Mappila 'constituency' after an infamous incident in which a Chirakkal prince was allegedly denigrated by the Ali Raja in 1722. The ramifications were however not felt until the mid '30s.[40] The eighteenth century had started on an optimistic note for the Ali Rajas and the euphoria lasted for at least the first three decades.[41] As business flourished and the cash-flow increased, the Ali Rajas drew up ambitious plans for exercising tighter political control over the markets along the Valarapatnam and Taliparambu waterway. The idea was to acquire deshadhipatyam rights over them. Initially, the Mappila inhabitants of Srikandapuram, Valarapatnam and Taliparambu markets responded enthusiastically. They already shared common ties of culture and trade with the Ali Rajas. The prospects of getting more closely integrated into the Cannanore syndicate seemed like a step in the right direction to them at the opening of the eighteenth century.[42]

Things however did not work out the way envisaged by the Ali Rajas. Their plans for enlarging their landholding and political predominance through a military alliance with the Udaimangalam faction of the Kolattiri Nairs did not materialize. The Udaimangalam princes, who ruled the areas around the Valarapatnam and Taliparambu rivers, were locked in a fratricidal war with the Chirakkal Nairs to prevent the usurpation of the same territories by the latter.[43] They consequently welcomed the help proffered by the Arakkal chieftains and received their proposals of expansion favourably. The incident in which the Chirakkal prince was humiliated by the Ali Raja in 1722 was in fact a part of this larger conflict in which the Arakkal clansmen were allied to the Udaimangalam faction. The Tellicherry factory however gave it a totally different slant. They accused the Mappila chieftain of vaulting ambition and reckless behaviour towards their Hindu overlord.

From their side the Ali Rajas had miscalculated the cost of exploiting the internal dissensions within the Kolattiri family. In the long run they gained little and in the process got alienated, firstly from the Mappilas in the Valarapatnam complex, and then from those in the Dharmapatnam complex as well. Unfortunately, their loss proved to be a major gain for the Tellicherry factory and the Rodriguez. The

Arakkal chiefs had never bargained for external intervention. But once fighting had erupted, the Chirakkal Raja took the disastrous course of appealing first to the Tellicherry factory in 1722 and then to the Ikkeri Raja of Bednur in 1729–30 for assistance.[44]

In the initial stages of the conflict with Chirakkal, the Mappila 'bazaarmen' from Valarapatnam and Cherakunnu took a joint stand in favour of the Ali Raja and the Udaimangalam Nairs. But the fighting in terms of human suffering and devastation of property proved to be too expensive. In 1728, Valarapatnam was completely ransacked by the Chirakkal forces and around 600 Mappila women and children lost their lives.[45] The Mappila combatants were also demoralized by the murder of the Ali Raja Kunhi Mammali by a close family member in 1727. That the man should have been poisoned during his *haj* pilgrimage revealed the sharp division within the Arakkal clan. It also demonstrated the ominous capabilities of Domingo Rodriguez (senior) to divide the clansmen and their Mappila supporters. The death of Ali Raja Kunhi Mammali was followed by the lacklustre regimes of the two Ali Bibis.[46]

There were no immediate defections from the Ali Raja's camp in the aftermath of Kunhi Mammali's death and the debacle of the Ilaya Raja in Valarapatnam in 1728. This was partly so because the Siddis of Koilandi provided armed reinforcements to the Mappila coalition in 1730. And the supporters were also encouraged to remain loyal because the fighting had ended. But truce was always too short-lived and was inevitably followed by more bloodshed. For more than two decades after the massacre of Valarapatnam in 1728, the two successive Ilaya Rajas 'brought' brief interludes of peace by paying huge indemnities. They often raised the money by selling gold ornaments and other precious belongings of their Mappila supporters.[47] The instability and the financial demands of the war aroused the resentment of the Valarapatnam 'bazaarmen'. The victims also noticed that each time they returned to pick up the pieces of their shattered lives, the English officials and the Rodriguez stirred up fresh trouble between the Chirakkal Raja and the Arakkal chieftains. The continuous violence gave the Tellicherry syndicate long-term control over the Nair Raja and enfeebled the Ali Rajas. This recurring trend convinced the Mappila of Valarapatnam that they would enjoy greater stability under English protection.[48]

The inhabitants of Valarapatnam bazaar decided to break free of the Ali Rajas and to work for Pallicutta Mapla, the *mudaliar* or the market leader of Valarapatnam. Since Pallicutta had been specially chosen by Domingo Rodriguez of the Tellicherry factory to represent his own and the interests of the Tellicherry factory in Valarapatnam, the Mappilas had in effect transferred their allegiance to the English Company in 1746.[49] The large-scale defection from the Ali Raja camp enabled the Tellicherry syndicate to vastly improve its standing in the main Valarapatnam market and in the adjoining areas. At this point the Rodriguez seemed like the prinicpal victors of the local wars, waged since 1722 between the Udaimangalam–Ali Raja combine and the Chirakkal forces and between the Ali Rajas and the English factory. But in the long run it was not they but the Mappila 'petty traders' within the Tellicherry syndicate who were the principal beneficiaries of the internal dissensions among the Kolattiri aristocrats. The Mappila traders penetrated into the Valarapatnam complex and expanded their business operations under the protection of the English Company.[50] This coterie was headed by Combem Allupy who was the maternal uncle of Moosa and the architect of the Choucara fortunes.

The repercussions of what transpired along the Valarapatnam river adversely affected the relationship between the Ali Rajas and the Mappilas who lived along the Dharmapatnam–Anjarakandi–Kodoli waterway. The financial burden of the internecine warfare as well as the Bednur invasion (1729–34) had impoverished the Kolattiri princes. The Nair rulers sustained the fighting by borrowing heavily from the English Company. The Nairs later repaid the loans by 'alienating' political control over strategic markets, arterial routes and pepper-rich tracts in the hinterland to the Tellicherry factory. In many instances this was done by divesting the Ali Rajas of the territories and privileges, conferred earlier. At the instigation of the English officials and the Rodriguez, the Rajas of Chirakkal and Kotiath of the Kolattiri realm revoked the deshadhipatyam of Dharmapatnam island and of Rhandaterra district of the Ali Rajas in 1728–29. The 'alienation' of political power and its transference to the English Company took place in gradual stages and was completed in the case of Dharmapatnam in 1749 and for Rhandaterra in 1760. This was a grievous blow for the Ali Rajas.[51]

Though the sub-tenants of the Arakkal chieftains were never evicted from Dharmapatnam and Rhandaterra, the revocation of deshadhipatyam partly in 1726 and then fully in 1736 impaired their capacity to transport and consequently also to procure goods in both these areas. Up to 1736 the Ali Rajas had enjoyed the exclusive right of carrying goods in small boats up and down the Dharmapatnam river.[52] But once deshadhipatyam over the island was lost, the British stepped in and started manipulating inland and interregional trade to their own advantage. They also scrutinized the credentials of itinerant merchants and blocked the entry of persons suspected of proximity to the Ali Rajas. After 1736 it was the Tellicherry officials who decided as to who would be allowed to set up shop or be granted land on sublease in both Rhandaterra and Dharmapatnam. As expected, they exercised these prerogatives in favour of 'friendly' Mappila merchants.[53]

The English factory had dealt a double blow to the Ali Rajas. Firstly, it systematically and successfully eroded their economic base in the hinterland. Secondly, it patronized the Mappilas who defected from their camp, in the wake of their declining influence in Dharmapatnam, as a deliberate strategy to undermine community support for the Arakkal house. For the Mappilas, like Paraporem Cunhiseu of Kotiath who changed sides after 1736, it was more a matter of necessity rather than political opportunism.[54] Significantly, like Cunhiseu the Mappila contractors of the Tellicherry factory which included the Choucaras originally hailed from the landlocked principality of Kotiath that lay just behind Dharmapatnam island. All of them came to be officially registered as the suppliers of the Tellicherry factory during the 1730s. It may be therefore presumed that soon after the Arakkal chiefs had lost political control over Dharmapatnam river and island, these merchants had no option but to start working for the English factory and the Rodriguez. This arrangement allowed them free access to the coast and the opportunity to ply their crafts under English passes.

The Kotiath merchants, subsequently known as the 'bazaar' merchants of Tellicherry entered into a long and fruitful partnership with the English officials and the Topas interpreters. These business transactions occurred at the official as well private levels and proved to be mutually beneficial, more so for the Mappila merchants. They had after all been nothing more than 'petty traders' before the middle of the eighteenth century. Yet, with the patronage of the factory officials, the Choucaras created an expanding sphere of influence that steadily swallowed up large chunks of the Arakkal domain. By the 1770s they had become the richest and the most powerful lessees of Rhandaterra district. What is noteworthy is that the Chirakkal and Kotiath Raja who were both landlord and temple adhikaris of these areas overlooked their low-caste credentials and allowed them to become major landholders.[55] Since none of this would have been possible without the patronage of the English officials, it could be said that the Company had socially elevated the Choucaras and reduced the gap between the Mappila upstarts and the Ali Rajas. The 'half caste' Rodriguez likewise benefitted considerably from their long association with the English factory. Despite their low-caste origin, they became janmakar or 'absolute' owners of Kallai which lay contiguous to Rhandaterra and close to the Valarapatnam–Taliparambu route.[56]

The Mappila coalition

The Arakkal sphere of influence went through a cycle of peaks and troughs. In 1727 it acquired greater homogeneity when Kunhi Mammali removed the 'barrier' to the extensive, pepper-rich territories around Kodoli fort.[57] But after three decades of internecine wars under the captaincy of two weak Ilaya Rajas, it resembled a patchwork of scattered pockets of influence in 1746. The large-scale defections by the Valarapatnam merchants however coincided with the ascension of a new Ali Raja and the predecessor of Kunhi Amsi. He was able to restore the balance of power in favour of the Ali Rajas through hard work and personal charisma. He exploited his friendship with the French factory officials in Mahe and with the Siddis of Koilandi to explore new areas in the hinterland. As a result of his efforts, the Arakkal house forged close ties with the 'bazaarmen' of Peringatur market in the distant Kanagamala hills in the Irvenad principality in 1747.[58] This expansion into areas south of the Dharmapatnam river prepared the ground for the formation of the Mappila coalition under Kunhi Amsi in 1766.

The exact year in which Kunhi Amsi assumed charge of the Cannanore government is not known. What is definite though is that he was at the helm of the affairs when Haider Ali conquered Kanara in 1761. Kunhi Amsi was an ambitious man and he wasted no time in convincing the Mysorean ruler of the merits of conquering a rich province like Malabar. His aim was not so much to promote Haider Ali's interests as to use the invasion to impede his rivals and to improve his own standing in the province. By 1763 Kunhi Amsi had entered into a military alliance with the Mysorean ruler and drawn up a blueprint for the invasion.[59] The Ali Raja proved to be an extremely useful ally. He acted as a bridge between Haider Ali and the principal Mappila merchants of the Kolattiri kingdom. The finalization of the military pact between the two allies in 1763 was followed by talks between the Mysorean ruler and important Mappila merchants of Mahe like Condutti Babchy in 1764–5.[60] Some understanding was also reached with Coota Moosa of Irkur, Anna Babachy of Irvenad, Alam Sially of Muttungal and Vadakara, the Siddis of Koilandi and finally Mamaley Craw of Bednur. These businessmen participated in the invasion under the leadership of Kunhi Amsi. With the birth of the Mappila coalition in 1766, the Arakkal sphere of influence had expanded beyond the borders of the Kolattiri kingdom.[61]

Levelling with the Nair Rajas

In 1766, as Haider Ali's army swept through Malabar, Kunhi Amsi realized his long-cherished dream of becoming a Raja, on par with the autonomous Nair Rajas of Kolattiri. Haider Ali formally ratified this by proclaiming him ruler of Mappilas living between Karwar and Kanyakumari and by making him a tributary in Kolattiri.[62] Kunhi Amsi's achievements constituted a major victory for the entire Arakkal clan. It was a negation of the permanent state of demotion in which the Arakkal chieftains had been placed as a consequence of Kulangara's conversion to Islam and as a result of his becoming a maritime trader.

Kunhi Amsi's sudden elevation within the political hierarchy and his unprecedented prosperity as an overseas merchant evoked sharp reactions in Malabar. The European Companies of trade, in particular, responded negatively to these developments. None of these agencies, not even the French Company which was friendly with the Ali Rajas, was happy to see the Nair defence crumble almost without any resistance. They were dismayed by the fact that in spite of prior knowledge of the invasion, the rulers had made no coordinated efforts to preempt it. Instead, faced with the complete rout of their small and ill-equipped forces, the aristocrats fled from their realms.[63] Some like the Chirakkal Raja took refuge in Tellicherry, others like the Kotiath Raja sought asylum in Travancore and many more like the Palazhi Raja and the Nambiars withdrew to the nearby hills. However, after the initial trauma, the Nair kings and noblemen returned repeatedly to reclaim their territories. For the next twenty-six years Haider Ali and his son Tipu Sultan got embroiled in three major wars and innumberable local conflicts to save their conquered territories from being taken back again and again by the vanquished Nairs and the English Company in Malabar. Our study tries to gauge the impact of this political stalemate on the hinterland and maritime trade of the Ali Rajas first between 1766 and 1774 and then betweeen 1774 and 1780.[64]

The sudden rise (1766–74)

After the Nair debacle of 1766 and the establishment of the Mysorean regime, the European and Indian syndicates of trade in Malabar faced the grim reality of redefining their position with reference to the new regime and the Mappila coalition under Kunhi Amsi. The European companies were the hardest hit because they automatically lost their privileged status with the collapse of the old order. They discovered to their utter dismay that their factories in northern Malabar could no longer bank on the commercial and political concessions that they had acquired through a series of treaties with the Nair Rajas since the sixteenth century. These agreements either became inoperative or had to be re-validated by the Mysorean *sarkar* on the payment of large sums of money or supply of arms. What proved to be particularly galling is that they had to often negotiate the terms and conditions of renewal with Kunhi Amsi who became Haider Ali's principal administrator and tax-collector in the Kolattiri domains.

The sudden enlargement of the Ali Raja's role in the hinterland created a daunting set of problems for the mercantile groups outside the Mappila coalition. The French trading company in Mahe had, for example, to prod the coalition members to get its routine shipments of pepper guaranteed by treaties with the Raja of Kadattanad. The merchandise refused to move unless the Ali Raja sent specific instructions to the Mappila *muppans* (leaders) in charge of inland markets and roadways.[65] The Tellicherry factory was placed in a similar predicament. The English officials had to seek special authorization from Kunhi Amsi for transporting the pepper from the Rhandaterra district into the English settlement. That the Company should have been forced to observe this procedure in spite of exercising deshadhipatyam over Rhandaterra rankled in the minds of the English officials and strengthened their resolve to bring back the Rajas.[66]

In the post-invasion period, the Ali Raja made a mockery of the concessions that the English factory had extracted from the Chirakkal Raja, especially those granting it special status in the markets around the Valarapatnam and Taliparambu rivers. In 1766 Mammali Craw, a close relative of the Ali Rajas, swept into this area with the Mysorean army and drove out the representatives of the factory from the complex. He thereby nullified the benefits accruing to the English company and their contractors from the acquisition of deshadhipatyam or 'royalty' over Valarapatnam market and river in the previous year. In one fell swoop in 1766, Mammali Craw had undone all this and avenged the insults that his ancestors had suffered in the same market in 1746.[67] The discomfiture of the English Company, following its loss of influence in Valarapatnam also placed merchant Domingo Rodriguez (junior) in an unenviable position. He incurred huge losses when Kunhi Amsi ransacked and later occupied his warehouses in Irkur in 1771. There was a ruthless edge to the Ali Raja's attacks on the property of the Topas merchant.[68] It was unlikely that the Mappila chieftain had forgotten the relentless campaign of his grandfather, Domingo Rodriguez (senior) to isolate and undermine the Arakkal family.

After more than half century of persistent efforts, the Arakkal clansmen managed to extend their formal sphere of influence over the markets and trade routes around the Valarapatnam and Taliparambu rivers in 1766. Kunhi Amsi immediately followed up the political gains with important infrastructural changes to enhance the volume of maritime and riverine traffic in Cannanore and in the Valarapatnam complex. He integrated them into one interdependent circuit by constructing the ten mile-long Sultan's canal to connect the backwaters of the coast near Cannanore with the Valarapatnam–Taliparambu waterway in 1766. The canal released an uninterrupted supply of water into the grid and prevented the silting of the intermeshed branches of rivers in the hinterland. With the opening of many sections earlier clogged by the silt, the boatmen were no longer obliged to make circuitous detours in this marshy area.[69]

The Sultan's canal also solved the problem of overcrowding in the Cannanore harbour. It facilitated the movement of medium-sized boats, directly from the port to the different riverine markets like Valarapatnam and Irkur. With the steady rise in maritime traffic in Cannanore, Kunhi Amsi also decided to upgrade the harbour facilities. He purchased the St. Angelo fort, adjoining his own jetty in Cannanore from the Dutch East India Company for a sum of Rs 160,000 in March 1771. Along with these infrastructural developments, Kunhi Amsi simultaneously expanded his fleet to include three extra ocean-going ships, six gallivats and nine grabs.[70]

The wedding feast

The wedding feast of 1771 was the high point in the history of the Ali Rajas in the eighteenth century. After several false starts, Kunhi Amsi had finally realized the goals towards which his ancestor Rajas had striven since the early eighteenth century. Things could not have been better. The maritime trade of the Arakkal house had flourished like never before. Its dominance over the hinterland likewise had spread far beyond the Kolattiri domains. It was only in the fitness of things that Kunhi Amsi decided to host a very lavish, eight-day long feast to celebrate the marriage of his niece in Cannanore. The response from the Mappila coalition was overwhelming. According to an eye-witness account, Mappilas from all walks of life and from every part of Malabar came to wish the couple with rich gifts. From his side, Kunhi Amsi played a good host and served abundant quantities of rice and fish. He also fired 120 canons to commemorate the marriage and to also ensure that the event registered with the European officials in neighbouring Telicherry and Mahe. These officials had studiously maintained an outward facade of indifference. But they were actually deeply troubled by the close camaraderie between the Mappila guests and Kunhi Amsi who all ate and slept under the open skies for one whole week.

This idyllic picture of community solidarity was however flawed. The Ali Raja struck a jarring note when at the end of the week-long rejoicing he demanded a substantial sum of money as 'tribute' from the richer merchants. Each of their individual contribution was calculated according to the merchant's financial standing and the amounts were pegged somewhere between Rs 6,000 and Rs 10,000. To make things worse, he even detained the merchants in Cannanore and released them only after they had made arrangements for payment. Many of the guests were justly outraged and believed that Kunhi Amsi had stepped out of line by forcing them to pay 'tribute'.[71]

The decline (1774–80)

Pockets of simmering discontent began to fester within the Mappila coalition after 1774. The absence of rapport betweeen Kunhi Amsi and his new adherents stood out in sharp relief to the cohesiveness characterizing the earlier group led by his predecessors. The Arakkal chiefs had always blended emotive appeals to community loyalties with hard-nosed economic policies to rally their supporters. Their task was made easier by the fact that many of their adherents were tenants of close business associates who had depended on the Ali Rajas for their livelihood for generations together. In marked contrast to this well-knit group, the coalition led by Kunhi Amsi was cobbled together by political opportunism and unrealistic hopes of prosperity. It was comprised of market leaders belonging to the scattered bazaars, many of which lay beyond the pale of traditional influence of the Ali Rajas. These new followers remained united just as long as it helped them to flourish and broke away at the first signs of trouble.

After 1774 the coalition partners felt disillusioned with Haider Ali's indifference and with the failure of Ali Raja Kunhi Amsi to ensure a more meaningful role for them in the hinterland trade of Malabar. Once the euphoria of the early military success had passed, they realized that Haider Ali was fighting on too many fronts to be of any use to them in Malabar. The ruler had to deal on one hand with disaffection in Mysore and with the hostility of the English Company and of the Marathas, on the other. After two years of continuous fighting, barely after the First Anglo-Mysore War had ended in 1769, his territories were attacked by the Marathas. The war with Peshwa Madhav Rao lasted till 1772.[72] Encircled on all sides by his enemies, Haider Ali found it progressively hard to redeploy his forces to quell the Nair insurrections in Malabar. With no logistic support from the

Mysorean army, the Ali Raja could not function properly. He was further handicapped by the fact that his own troops were requisitioned by Haider Ali from time to time. Consequently, Kunhi Amsi could neither supervize the movement of goods nor collect taxes due to the prevalent lawlessness in northern Malabar.[73] The displaced Kolattiri aristocrats came back from time to time to attack him and the coalition partners for usurping their rights and for dishonouring the original covenant of Arayan Kulangara. In their eyes, Kunhi Amsi had overstepped his authority by entering the 'hallowed' precincts of the elite and especially by levying taxes—something that even the Nair Rajas had never dared to do before.[74]

The Ali Raja collected taxes on behalf of the Mysorean sarkar. Haider Ali had introduced taxation in the form of *ad hoc* contribution after 1766 and then on the basis of a proper computation of the produce after 1774. In a sense he had theoretically authorized the Mappila merchants to by-pass the multilayered chain of command of the Nairs and to procure the taxable commodities directly from the fields in Malabar. Initially the scheme proved to be tremendously advantageous for the merchants who sold prodigious quantities of pepper to foreign ships and then handed over a fixed amount to the sarkar as tribute through the Ali Raja. But soon the 'bazaarmen' encountered very stiff resistance from the dispossessed landlords and rulers who had earlier sold the harvest in wholesale at places and prices of their convenience.[75]

The rulers of Malabar had prior to 1766 been overseers of enormous landholdings and devasthanam property belonging to the Nair and Nambudiri oligarchies. Due to their immense ceremonial powers and armed following, these quasi-autonomous landowners had ensured that the Rajas had the right to levy duties of various kinds but not collect agricultural taxes. The idea of rulers claiming a definite share of the income from land was unacceptable and became absolutely odious when the tax collectors also happened to be Mappila merchants. Outraged by the prospects of handing over a part of their produce to the coalition, the Malayali elite plotted with the English officials to drive out the Ali Raja's men from their territories. It is noteworthy that in spite of their general hostility towards the Mappilas, the aristocrats and the gentry readily sold their pepper to the Mappila contractors of Tellicherry, particularly to the Choucaras. With the diversion or the 'smuggling' of the commodities that were either grown or transported through Malabar to Tellicherry, the Choucaras rose in the esteem of the Mappila commodity brokers. The coalition partners realized that it was more profitable to sell the merchandise to the Choucaras who enjoyed the patronage of the English company and the Nair aristocrats than to Kunhi Amsi who was at loggerheads with both.[76]

The European fears of being deprived of their share of the Malabari commodities by the Mappila coalition proved in the long run to be totally unfounded. Kunhi Amsi's effectiveness as a revenue collector and consequently as a wholesaler of Malabari spices was impaired by the unreliability of Mysorean support, by the hostility of the exiled Nairs and by his own inability to control his coalition partners. In the mid-'70s the Mappila collector and merchant of Irvenad, Anna Babachery decided unilaterally to extort spices and money from the Kotiath Nairs much in excess of the assessment. Though this operation was ratified neither by Haider Ali nor by Kunhi Amsi, Anna Babachery came to symbolize the ugly face of the coalition.[77] He had also set a bad precedent. Soon there were other coalition partners who broke free of Kunhi Amsi and sold pepper and other commodities to the highest bidder which in most cases happened to be the Choucaras.

Kunhi Amsi fell from Haider Ali's grace in 1774. Owing to the huge arrears in tribute, mainly due to defaults by the coalition partners, Haider dismissed him from the office of revenue collector in the Kolattiri realm. Instead he reinstated the Nair kings in their respective principalities on the assurance that they would pay a fixed *peshkash* or annual tribute.[78] The Ali Raja felt humiliated; more so because Haider Ali had acted on the advice of his arch enemy Domingo Rodriguez (junior). The Topas merchant had resigned from his job as interpreter in the Tellicherry factory and joined the service of the Mysorean ruler in 1774. He was rewarded for changing sides and replaced the Ali Raja as tax collector in the Chirakkal domain in 1774–5.[79] At this point in time it seemed as if the wheels of fortune had once again turned in favour of Rodriguez. But in reality it proved to be a temporary reprieve. Four years later when the Second Anglo-Mysore War broke out in Malabar, Domingo Rodriguez incurred huge losses and ultimately died in disgrace.[80]

Unlike Domingo Rodriguez, Ali Raja Kunhi Amsi was spared the trauma of suffering monetary losses and prestige during the Second Anglo-Mysore War which broke out in 1780. He died a year earlier and bequeathed a troubled legacy to his niece and successor Junnuma Bi, Valiya Tangul.[81] His ally, Haider Ali also passed away in 1782, leaving behind his son, Tipu Sultan to prosecute the war vigorously. Tipu Sultan more than lived up to his expectations and concluded the war by imposing a humiliating peace on the English East India Company in 1784. But neither the defeat of its bitter foe, the English

Company nor the return of its ally Tipu Sultan as the ruler of Malabar could restore the balance of power in favour of the Arakkal house. Too much had been lost during the war. Mappila shipping, especially the Arakkal merchant navy had been reduced to absolute shambles by the English at sea. In 1783, the English army had also rampaged through Cannanore, looted its treasure and taken the important members of the family as hostages. A war-weary and a bankrupt Bibi had been forced to sue for peace and raise money for their ransom through her 'banker' Choucara Moosa. She had mortgaged the coir of her Lakshadweep islands to this Mappila merchant from Tellicherry.[82] This was a major blow in a series of setbacks on the road to decline. Although Tipu Sultan had won the war in 1784, the Arakkal family had lost all hopes of recovering their former preeminence. Consequently, Ali Bibi gradually got reconciled to playing a more subordinate role to Moosa who had emerged as the undisputed market leader among the Mappila business fraternity in Malabar. This progressively conditioned her and many of the richer merchants to the notion of living under the English Company's political and commerical hegemony which became a reality in Malabar in 1792.[83]

Conclusion

The great expectations that were aroused by the fanfare with which the Ali Raja Kunhi Amsi had launched himself at the wedding feast of 1771 were belied by later events. He could not rise to the demands of his role as market leader of the entire Kolattiri realm. Yet it was not entirely his failure. A large share of the blame rested with his ally, Haider Ali who could neither bring political stability nor implement the ambitious economic programmes that he wished to jointly execute with Kunhi Amsi. As a result, after a brief taste of prosperity in the period between 1766 and 1774, the Ali Raja's associates began to incur heavy losses in trade. Some of this was due to the antipathy of the Nairs and the rest because of the serious economic recession that hit Malabar between 1778 and 1779. The list of bankrupt maritime merchants included Condutti Babachey, Siddi Chekaderaman of Koilandi and Alam Sially of Vadakkara.[84]

It was against this backdrop of political chaos and economic decline that the Second Anglo-Mysore War broke out in Malabar in 1780. The Mappila coalition was once again revived by the Ilaya Raja or Junnuma Bi's husband. But the partners were too disillusioned with Haider Ali and no longer viewed him as their saviour. If despite everything they still decided to support him in the Second Anglo-Mysore War which lasted from 1780 to 1784, it was because their own relationship with the Nairs had deteriorated beyond redemption and not out of any sense of loyalty for the Mysorean ruler.[85] Many on being approached by Choucara Combem Allupy, the uncle of Moosa, even toyed with the idea of joining the English side in the war. Some even defected in the course of the conflict and fought side by side with the Choucaras.[86] As the war progressed, Moosa emerged as the accepted leader of the Mappilas. The ascendance of this man in Mappila business circles symbolized the victory of the English Company over the Ali Rajas of Cannanore.

There was a fatal flaw in the conflict between the Ali Rajas and the English Company for supremacy in maritime trade in the eighteenth century. The scope had widened beyond the seas and spilled over into the hinterland where it had got internalized. Instead of concentrating all their energies on checking the growing influence of the English in the region, the Arakkal chieftains dissipated them through their confrontation with the Nair aristocracy. The intrusion of the Mappilas into Nair preserves was initially preemptive. It was meant to neutralize the English military and diplomatic manoeuvres aimed at denying the supporters of the Ali Rajas free access to the strategic routes and inland markets. Later, especially after Haider Ali's invasion in 1766, the focus of the struggle changed. It was no longer envisaged as a damage control measure but as a means to aggrandize at the cost of the Malayali elite in the hinterland. This resulted in endless and bitter disputes on the question of 'authority' vested in the successive Mappila chieftains of Cannanore.

The internecine warfare between the Malayali mercantile and ruling groups and between them and the English and other European companies ushered in a period of political upheaval such as had never been witnessed in Malabar before the eighteenth century. The problem was further compounded by the invasions from Bednur in 1727 and Mysore in 1766. With increasing number of belligerents wanting to manipulate the system of procurement, the Nair ruling clans and Mappila mercantile groups split internally and regrouped as loose federations of vested interest with no permanent loyalties. This was the most pernicious side of this conflict. It transformed by stages the local skirmish beween the Ali Raja and the Chirakkal Raja in 1722 into a major regional war in 1780 which embroiled the warring groups of Nairs, competing factions of Malayali merchants, rival European companies of trade and their Indian partners, and finally invaders from Bednur in 1729 and from Mysore in 1766.

The financial burden and the effects of constant political turmoil had a negative impact on the Mappila support base of the Ali Rajas.

From the mid-eighteenth century, the number of defections from the Arakkal to the rival camp of the Choucaras of Tellicherry rose appreciably. They reflected an attitudinal shift among a section of Mappila merchants, headed by the Ali Bibi. The ground was laid for drastic changes. The Arakkal group, so zealously committed to checking the intrusion of the English Company in indigenous trade, was influenced by the Choucaras to soften, firstly towards the Company, and then get reconciled to the entire question of British rule in the province in 1792. Under the British government, the descendants of the mighty Ada Raja, the Lord of the Seas, took their place among the ordinary suppliers of pepper of the East India Company.

NOTES

1. Refer to W. Logan's *Malabar* (3 volumes, henceforth simply Logan), vol.I, Madras, 1951, foot note on p.358 for a chronological list of the Ali Rajas in the eighteenth century.

2. *See Nouvelles Acquisitions Francaises* in the Bibliotheque Nationale de France, Paris (henceforth simply NAF) 9368 Notes, extraites des lettres d'un officier de cavalarie qui a voyage aux Indes Orientales, Mahe, 1771, pp.165–7.

3. For a general history of Haider Ali's activities in Malabar *see* B. Sheikh Ali, *English Relations with Haider Ali*, Mysore, 1963.

4. For background information *see* G. Bouchon, *Mamale de Cannanor. Un adversaire de l'Inde Portuguaise [1504–28]* (Henceforth simply Bouchon/ *Mamale*), Paris, 1976; Logan, vol.1, pp.313–17.

5. A. Martineau, *Les Origines De Mahe de Malabar* (henceforth Martineau/ *Origines*), Paris, 1917, pp.6–11.

6. Logan, vol.1, pp.313–17.

7. E. Thurston, *Castes and Tribes of Southern India* (henceforth simply Thurston), vol.2, Madras, 1909, pp.92, 95; J.C. Visscher, *Letters from Malabar* (henceforth simply Visscher), Madras, 1862, p.130.

8. Thurston, vol.5, pp.297, 306.

9. Logan, vol.1, pp.313–17.

10. *British Parliamentary Papers,* vol.6, Ireland, 1969, p.298; G. Bouchon, 'Les Mussulman du Kerala al'Epoque du Decouverte Portuguaise,' *Mare Luso-Indicum,* vol.2, Geneva, 1972, pp.3–59.

11. Bouchon/*Mamale,* pp.119–20.

12. Visscher, p.118.

13. A.P. Umarkutti, *History of the Keyis of Malabar,* Cannanore, 1916, p.35. I am grateful to Shri M. Narayan Kutti for translating the Malayalam account into English for me.

14. Diary of the Malabar Commission in the Tamilnadu Archives, Madras (henceforth simply DMC.), 1667–B, Cannanore, 30 March 1793, p.208.

15. *Tellicherry Consultations* (a series of 21 volumes and henceforth *Tel. Con.*) vol.16, Madras, 1933–36, p.146.

16. TDG. 1485, 16 March 1773, pp.69–71.

17. DMC. 1667–B, Cannanore 30th March 1793, pp.113–18; Logan, vol.1, footnote on p.358; Bouchon/*Mamale,* pp.119–28.

18. *See* Colonies. Series C2 in the Archives Nationales de France, Paris (henceforth simply Col. C2) 78, 3 Jun 1740; A. Hamilton's *A New Account of the East Indies* (henceforth Hamilton), Edinburgh, 1727, pp.291–5; Martineau/ *Origines,* pp.6, 7.

19. For a general background of the confrontation between the Malabari traders and the Europeans refer to Sheikh Zain-ud-din, *Tohfut-ul-Mujahideen* (tr. by M. Rowlandson), London, 1883 and also K.M. Panikkar's *A History of Malabar,* Annamalainagar, 1960.

20. Tellicherry Diaries (General) in the Tamilnadu Archives (henceforth simply TDG) 25–A, Cannanore, 31 March 1757, pp.182–3.

21. For the details *see* Visscher, pp.119–20 and *also Letters to Tellicherry (1736–38),* vol.2 (henceforth simply *Let. Tel.*), Madras, 1934, p.34.

22. *Correspondence,* vol.4, pp.60–1; *Tel. Con.* 16, p.203 and *Tel. Con.* 17–A, p.243.

23. *Tel. Con.* 11, p.83 and *Tel. Con.* 13, p.143.

24. *Tel. Con.* 17–A, p.243.

25. *Tel. Con.* 10, p.49.

26. *Tel. Con.* 16, p.28–9.

27. *Tel. Con.* 17–A, p.243.

28. TDG. 24–A, 7 February 1756, p.146.

29. *Tel. Con.* 17–b, pp.26, 60.

30. Bouchon/*Mamale,* pp.172–3.

31. NAF. 9063, 11 December 1767, p.27; *Tel. Con.* 17–A, p.42.

32. DMC. 1667–B, Cannanore, 30 March 1793, pp.113–9.

33. Logan, vol.2, p.cxcviii for the definition of *anubhogam* and *also* Logan, vol.1, footnote on p.358.

34. DMC. 1667–B, Cannanore, 30 March 1793, 113–9; *Tel. Con.* 12, p.178 and *also* Logan, vol.3 treaties of 7 September 1749, pp.50–3.

35. Logan, vol.2, appendix III for the definition of *deshadhipatyam.*

36. *Let. Tel.* 2, p.34.

37. DMC. 1667–A, Valarapatnam, 20 April 1793, pp.481–3; *Tel. Con.* 16, p.146.

38. RMC. 1679, Palghat, 3 October 1793, p.59.

39. Ruchira Banerjee, 'The Mercantile Network of Malabar c. 1760–1780' (unpublished thesis and henceforth simply 'Network'), Bombay, 1993, chapter III.

40. Col. C2 75, Mahe, 15 January 1735, p.263.

41. *Correspondance,* vol.4, pp.60–61.

42. *See* principal Mappila towns in Logan, vol.2, Appendix XXI.

43. *Tel. Con.* 16, pp.144–5.

44. *Reports of a Joint Commission from Bengal and Bombay, Appointed to*

Inspect into the State and Condition of the Province of Malabar in the Years 1792 and 1793 (henceforth simply *Reports of a Joint Commission*), Madras, 1862, pp.16, 18; Martineau/*Origines,* pp.238–61.

45. *Tel. Con.* 3, p.63.

46. *Correspondance,* vol.1, p.361, Logan, vol.1, p.359.

47. *Tel. Con.* 3, p.11 and *Tel. Con.* 16, p.74.

48. Ibid., pp.70–5, 80–81, 123, 145; *Tel. Con.* 8, p.82.

49. *Tel. Con.* 16, p.90.

50. *Tel. Con.* 15, p.61.

51. *Reports of a Joint Commission,* pp.17, 18; *Tel. Con.* 12, p.178.

52. Ibid. AN, Col. C2 75, Mahe 15 January 1735, p.263; Logan, vol.1, p.11.

53. Public Department Diary in the Maharashtra State Archives, Bombay (henceforth PDD), 37(I) 28 August 1761; *Tel. Con.* 2, pp.22–5 and *Tel. Con.* 10, pp.6, 9, 14, 99.

54. *Tel. Con.* 7, p.56 and *Tel. Con.* 10, p.50 mark the change from friendliness to hostility.

55. TDG. 1511, 25 December 1792, pp.109–11; *Tel. Con.* 11, pp.146–7, 88–9; *Tel. Con.* 12, p.178.

56. Refer to sale deed in Logan, vol.3, p.60.

57. *Tel. Con.* 2, p.112.

58. Martineau/*Origines,* pp.272–3; *Tel. Con.* 17–A, 192.

59. PDD. 40(I), Bombay, 26 March 1763, p.171.

60. NAF. 9063, 10 June 1765, p.1.

61. DMC. 1668–B, Memorial of the Late and Present State of Levenaddu, pp.974–6; TDG. 1480, 7 May 1770, p.122; NAF. 9072, 9 May 1769, pp.6–7; NAF. 9064, 9 February 1767, p.59.

62 NAF. 9368, Notes, extraites des lettres d'un officier du cavalrie qui a voyage aux Indes Orientales, Mahe, 1777, pp.165–8.

63. NAF. 9031, 30 September 1766, pp.218–20.

64. Banerjee, 'Network', chapter 2.

65 NAF. 9064, 31 January 1768, p.89.

66. TDG. 1480, 9 April 1770, p.99.

67. NAF. 9072, 6 May 1769, pp.6–7; NAF. 9068, 18 September 1767 pp.24–5; Secretariat Inward Letter Book in the Maharashtra state Archives (henceforth simply SILB.) 23, 11 April 1770, pp.390–1.

68 TDG. 1485, 16 March 1773, pp.69–71.

69. DMC. 1667–B, Cannanore, 30 March 1793, pp.113–18; Logan. vol.1, p.9.

70. NAF. 9368, Notes, extraites des lettres d'un officier du cavalrie qui a voyage aux Indes Orientales, p.165; NAF. 9032, 18 March 1771, p.710.

71. NAF. 9368, Notes extraites des lettres d'un officier du cavalrie qui a voyage aux Indes Orientales, pp.165–9.

72. NAF. 9032, 13 September 1769; M. Hasan, *History of Tipu Sultan,* Calcutta, 1971, pp.10–11.

73. NAF. 9032, pp.394, 398–9, 403, 407, 427, 450–1.

74. Ibid., DMC. 1668–B, Memorial of the Late and Present State of

Levenaddu, pp.974–6; Banerjee, 'Network', chapter 2.

75. SILB. 23, 20 November 1770; TA., DMC. 1667–B, Cannanore, 30 March 1793.

76. NAF. 9032, 11 May 1769, p.589; Banerjee, 'Network', chapter 2.

77. NAF. 9025, 4 May 1775, p.60.

78. *Reports of a Joint Commission,* pp.12–17.

79. SILB. 28, 28 February 1775, p.104.

80. TDG. 1494, 30 September 1782, p.287.

81. TDG. 1490, 23 January 1779, p.14.

82 DMC. 1667–B, Cannanore 30 March 1793, p.218.

83. Ibid., pp.113–18.

84. NAF. 9063, 23 January and 24 April 1773, pp.82–9.

85. TDG. 1490, 23 September 1779, p.14.

86. Ibid., 10 December 1779, p.298.

6

Exploring the Hinterland: Trade and Politics in the Arcot Niẓāmat (1700–1732)

MUZAFFAR ALAM
SANJAY SUBRAHMANYAM

'Finally, the problem had political rather than economic dimensions. If there was a crisis in the Ottoman empire, it does not in fact concern a true economic crisis—at least internally—but instead a political crisis whose origins should be sought in part in the appetites of the Great Powers; and as for the reproach that one can address to the Ottomans, would it not be of having been unable to build barriers before these appetites...?'

—Robert Mantran, 'The Transformation of Trade in the Ottoman Empire in the Eighteenth Century'[1]

Introduction

As elsewhere in the Indian subcontinent, the early eighteenth century in the northern Tamil country saw the rise to prominence of a new type of state, the autonomous *niẓāmat*, or what the British were apt to call the 'Nawabi' state, operating under the carapace of Mughal sovereignty. For some other parts of India, notably Bengal under Murshid Quli Khan (1700–27), Shuja-ud-din (1727–39), and their successors, the story has been told often enough for us to be familiar both with its broad outlines, and its myriad unresolved contradictions.[2] The northern Tamil country or Karnatak Payanghat in the Mughal terminology of the epoch, is another story. For here the attention of historians has traditionally perked up only with the Anglo-French wars of the 1740s, a period on which H.H. Dodwell laid his imprimatur, for better or for worse, for the generations to follow.[3] Commenting on this in his classic and oft-cited essay 'Trade and Politics in eighteenth century India' (1970), Ashin Das Gupta remarked that it seemed impossible to compare the pattern of development on the Coromandel coast in the eighteenth century with that in Gujarat and Bengal 'because of the paucity of our knowledge about it'.[4] Where he did consider himself on safe enough ground was for the period after 1730, and more particularly once into the 1740s and 1750s, the years when he could make use of Ananda Ranga Pillai's celebrated and voluminous diary (or at least its incomplete translation into English).[5]

Writing seventeen years later in a chapter on 'India and the Indian Ocean in the eighteenth Century' in the well-known volume on Indian Ocean history he jointly edited, Das Gupta was able to advance somewhat further, mainly on the basis of the monograph published by Sinnappah Arasaratnam shortly earlier (in 1986, to be precise).[6] He pointed now to the continuity of the trade of Tamil Maraikkayar merchants (calling them 'Chulias', in deference to Arasaratnam) in ports such as Kadalur, Naguru and Mahmud Bandar (Porto Novo).[7] Elsewhere, in the central part of the Coromandel coast, he underlined the relative success of Mylapore or São Tomé (known by then in English records as San Thome). 'This port', wrote Das Gupta, 'formerly a Portuguese enclave under its Mughal administrators successfully challenged the English establishment and drew to itself much of the trade still going towards the west mainly in the vessels of the Pathan merchants and even the trade of English private merchants coming from the east'. Yet, once more, searching for details of the sort Das Gupta is able to provide for Bengal and Gujarat, we are left frustrated. The problem is partly one of identifying the participants in commercial networks and placing them in some form of recognizable sociological framework; but it also lies in supplying the missing ties between 'trade' and 'politics'. What, after all, was the political context of these shifting mercantile fortunes, beyond the familiar cliches of greedy revenue-farmers, and unstable local despots? As Das Gupta himself remarks, 'The hinterland is just as important if we wish to understand the history of the Coromandel coast'.[8]

The present essay attempts to sketch, albeit in a preliminary fashion, the main lines of development in the hinterland, or the Arcot niẓāmat under first, Da'ud Khan Panni, and then the founder of the Nawayat 'dynasty', Muhammad Sa'id, or Sa'adatullah Khan. It does so using some materials of a sort familiar to readers of Das Gupta's work, namely the very extensive account of the Venetian adventurer Nicolò Manuzzi (1639–1717), and the Dutch East India Company records; but it is also concerned to explore other materials, both in Persian and, to a more limited extent, in Tamil. We argue that the Arcot state attempted to keep a relatively tight hold on the conduct of external commerce, and that Sa'adatullah Khan in this respect followed the trend set by the formidable Da'ud Khan Panni, his predecessor in the niẓāmat. However, we also point to the evolution between the earlier and the later decades of our period, especially in relation to the role played by newcomers from North India in this context, notably the redoubtable network of Khatris (and to an extent, Kayasthas and Gujaratis) that developed in this period. And finally, we argue that the 1730s mark a turning point in this respect, for it is now that the balance between the niẓāmat and European (English and French) political power turns unfavourable to the former, eventually leading to the widespread fiscal crisis that gripped states in Tamilnadu in the latter half of the eighteenth century.[9] We would thus caution against working backwards from the period after 1730, to generalize the relationship of trade and politics in the Karnatak Payanghat in the early years of the niẓāmat.

Political geography and political economy

A somewhat longer-term reflection may not be wholly out of place to set the stage. Between the mid-sixteenth century and the 1640s, the area between the rivers Krishna and Kollidam in south-eastern India was a heavily contested region. In the years before 1550, the area had been under Vijayanagara domination, and towns such as Kondavidu, Venkatagiri, Udayagiri, Siddhavatam, Velur, Padaividu and Arni had palyed an important role in regional geo-politics during the reigns of Krishnadevaraya (1509–29) and Achyutadevaraya (1529–42). These centres all came to be fortified in the course of the fifteenth and sixteenth centuries, and were the places of residence of a variety of Velama and Reddi lineages from Andhra, and occasionally of migrant Kannadiga warrior families.[10] Then, in the second half of the sixteenth century, a realignment took place in the region, during the rule of the fourth (or Aravidu) dynasty of Vijayanagara. Faced with pressure from the Golkonda Sultanate to the north, some of the towns and fortresses on the southern fringes of the Krishna, like Kondavidu, changed hands several times. The Aravidu rulers for their part installed themselves after 1590 in Chandragiri, in the Tirupati region further to the south, giving that centre a particular political and even economic importance. Still further into the Tamil country, Senji emerged as the major political and commercial centre, outstripping such towns as Arni and Padaividu. While Arni continued to have a certain importance, Padaividu had fallen into decline by 1590. Senji was now the seat of a Nayaka dynasty, which ruled from the mid-sixteenth to the mid-seventeenth centuries, in the very area which was later to form the core of the niẓāmat of Arcot.

The political geography of the region is well-described by European observers in the 1610s and 1620s. The three main seats of political power, as they saw it, were Chandragiri, Senji and Velur—the last of these a centre which was used by the Aravidus from 1602 as an alternate capital. From these fortified centres, the Aravidu Rayas and the Senji Nayakas collected agrarian and other revenues, using a system of revenue-farming, with the farmers very largely being Balijas, Beri Chettis and Komatis.[11] The area, while agriculturally poorer than the Krishna delta to the north or the Kaveri delta to the south, nevertheless afforded a quite reasonable revenue from its production of commercial crops like rice, cotton, indigo and sugar, and from taxes on textile production—which was carried out mostly in the villages along the coast. The whole area between Kunjimedu and Armagon (the so-called central Coromandel region) produced textiles which were much in demand in the Southeast Asian market. Ports like Parangippettai (Porto Novo), Tirupapuliyur, Puducheri, Devanampattinam, Mylapore and Pulicat exported these products and channelized the imports of precious metals, copper, porcelain, pepper, spices, horses and elephants to the inland courts, and to other smaller consuming centres.[12] From 1640, Madras gradually emerged as the major centre of external trade, while further south, the relatively obscure port of Sadras (Sadrangapatnam) also grew in importance after 1660.

The revenue-potential of the region and those lying still further south eventually attracted the attention of the Sultanates of Bijapur and Golkonda, with whom the Vijayanagara rulers had maintained an uneasy political equilibrium since the 1570s. In the late 1630s and 1640s, Bijapur and Golkonda launched a series of major campaigns directed at the Aravidus and Senji Nayakas. By the 1650s, Golkonda conquests engineered under the generalship of Mir Muhammad Sayyid Ardistani extended almost as far as Mylapore along the coast, and included most of erstwhile domains of the Chandragiri Raja.[13] Bijapur's ascendancy, on the other hand, extended via Mysore to encompass much of the Senji Nayakas' former territories, and eventually posed a threat to the Nayakas of Tanjavur. The last ruler of the Aravidu dynasty, Sriranga Raya, resisted by both military and diplomatic means, unlike the Senji dynasty which capitulated and allied itself with Golkonda's Mir Jumla, Mir Muhammad Sayyid. Sriranga attempted in the 1650s to negotiate with Prince Aurangzeb, at the time *ṣūbadār* of the Deccan, to retain a position for himself as a tributary chieftain under Mughal suzerainty.[14] In this, he largely failed, and his territories passed under Golkonda control, to remain there until 1687.

The precise nature of the fiscal arrangements put in place in their

Karnatak conquests by Bijapur and Golkonda is unknown to us. It appears, however, that revenue-farming persisted at least in the coastal districts. In formal terms, the Golkonda authorities followed their normal practice of administering the region through a number of *ṭarafdārs* and *ḥawaldārs,* and the area as a whole was given to the charge of first Mir Muhammad Sayyid, then to Raza Quli Beg (Neknam Khan), and in the 1670s and early 1680s to Akkanna Pandit.[15] Muhammad Sayyid, who manipulated the region virtually as a semi-independent state, chose as his centre of operations the hitherto obscure fort of Gandikota, transforming it in the space of a decade into a major fortress-town. The centre of Gurramkonda, which had in the early decades of the seventeenth century played a role of importance as the residence of the family of Gobburi Obaraja, as well as Chandragiri itself, were eclipsed by Gandikota. The *ṭaraf* Karnatak, with its 16 *sarkārs* and 162 *parganas* is believed to have had as its *jama'* in 1685–6 a sum of eight million rupees (2.67 million *huns*). When Golkonda fell to Aurangzeb in 1687, these revenues came to be attached to the Mughal state.[16]

In 1688, soon after the conquest, Aurangzeb detached twelve sarkârs south of the Gundalakamma river, and placed them under a separate *faujdār*, with his seat at Kanchipuram. The former Golkonda noble, 'Ali 'Askar Khan, was the first appointee to this post, and he was followed by 'Ali Mardan Khan in 1690, then Zu'lfiqar Khan, and eventually Da'ud Khan Panni. The faujdār attempted to administer the erstwhile Golkonda territories, while further to the south, Mughal armies engaged in combat with the Marathas, who laid claim to the areas conquered by Bijapur in the 1640s. The struggle centred largely around Senji, where Rajaram of the Bhonsle clan had installed himself; Senji fell in 1698 to Zu'lfiqar Khan after a protracted siege. It is significant that for purposes of revenue classification, though, the areas of Senji (Nusratgadh), Velur, Dharmavaram, and so on, were included, still in 1705–7, under the separate head *mulk-i maftūḥa* ('the conquered territories'). The twelve sarkārs which were included under the 'regular' territories were further divided into two groups. Five were included in *ṣūba* Karnatak, and seven in ṣūba Karnatak Payanghat. In the former category were the sarkārs of Siddhavatam, Gandikota, Gutti, Gurramkonda and Kumbum; in the latter were the coastal sarkārs of Addanki, Tadimari, Narasipur, Sarvepalli, Chandragiri, Chengalapattu, and Kanchipuram.

In 1706, the total jama' of these twelve sarkārs and the mulk-i maftūḥa added up to some fifteen million rupees, obviously somewhat more than what had been extracted by Golkonda in 1685–86. This was not done by a thorough-going revenue re-survey, which none of the faujdârs and *dīwāns* before 1710 seem to have been able to manage, but rather by continued recourse to revenue-farmers (*mustājirs* and *ijāradārs*), and also by extending control over regions in the interior where Golkonda control had been limited, or contested by Bijapur. The two decades after Mughal conquest see changes, but they are not always the predictable ones. Large amounts of the jama' were alienated, for example, in jāgīr rs given to specific Velama notables of the area, to persuade them to support the Mughals. In the second half of the 1690s, Kumara Yachama Naidu of the Recherla clan was given a jāgīr extending over Venkatagiri, Nellore and Tirupati, and worth over 2.5 million rupees in jama', besides a *manṣab* of 6000/6000.[17] To compensate these large alienations, additional tributes were occasionally levied on the Maratha Rajas of Tanjavur, on the Wodeyars at Srirangapatnam, and the Madurai Nayakas.[18] The whole revenue system bore the stamp of hasty improvisation, and this is understandable when we see that as late as 1706, 5.2 million rupees from the jama' was set aside for *sīh-bandī*, the maintenance of troops. Such a high degree of militarization in relation to available resources brings home the fact that even in the early eighteenth century, the Karnatak was still a frontier area, not only on account of the Marathas, but because the Velama, Reddi and other warrior clans of the region remained unsubdued. The conflict that eventually led Zu'lfiqar Khan to behead the powerful Kumara Yachama Naidu is one sign of the tension that simmered beneath the surface of the accomodation that the Mughals sought to make in these years.[19] It was from this apparently unpromising raw material that Sa'adatullah Khan carved the Arcot 'kingdom' in the second and third decade of the eighteenth century.

The emergence of Arcot from about 1700 was part of a somewhat larger process. Da'ud Khan Panni, whom we have already noticed as faujdār of the Karnatak in the early eighteenth century also harboured ambitions of creating a territorial base for his family, which was of Afghan origin, descended from a certain Khizr Khan Panni. When Da'ud Khan was appointed ṣūbadār of the Deccan in around 1710, he thus brought his brother Ibrahim Khan to Hyderabad, as *nā'ib ṣūbadār*; earlier members of his family had played roles of significance in the Payanghat. In 1715, Da'ud Khan was eventually killed in battle while opposing Sayyid Husain 'Ali Khan Barha, but by that time Ibrahim Khan had established himself as first *kotwāl* and then faujdār of the interior town of Karnul. His descendants Alf Khan and Himmat Bahadur Khan, succeeded to the positions of Nawabs of Qamarnagar (Karnul); eventually, in 1751, Himmat Bahadur

Khan was killed by the forces of the Hyderabad ruler, Salabat Jang, after having played a major role in the succession struggle that followed Nizam-ul-mulk Asaf Jah's death in 1748 by having a hand in the death of two of the major contenders, Nasir Jang and Muzaffar Jang. Karnul was plundered in 1751, and Himmat Bahadur Khan's family and children were taken prisoner, though his descendants were later partly reinstated. Elsewhere, in Kadappa, another Mughal noble, 'Abd-un-Nabi Khan Miyana emerged as faujdār by the 1720s, while 'Abd-ul Majid Khan, grandson of a former Bijapur noble 'Abd-ul-Karim Khan, held a similar position at Bankapur. Further west, in Chittur, Sira and Dodballapur, other faujdārs sought a similar position: Amin Khan and his successor 'Abd-ul-Rasul Khan at Sira, and Tahir Muhammad Khan at Chittur. It is thus worth bearing in mind that several of the major nobles who accompanied Aurangzeb or Zu'lfiqar Khan Nusrat Jang to the Karnatak sought to put down local roots in the years between 1700 and 1725; this has certain parallels with Mir Jumla's own attempts to create a sub-state centred around Gandikota in the 1640s and 1650s, but at the same time has something original about it. The attempt in the early eighteenth century to transform faujdārīs into compact regional 'kingdoms' under the umbrella of Mughal suzerainty required the partial displacement of autochthonous lineages (of Telugu or Kannada origin), the creation or expansion of a court-centre (Kadappa, Karnul, Savanur, Sira, Dodballapur, or Bankapur) with a regional idiom, and also negotiation with the great power-broker, Nizam-ul-Mulk Asaf Jah, who ultimately held the balance in the region after the mid-1720s.

The table below summarizes the broad fiscal situation in the Karnatak a decade after the fall of Senji to Zu'lfiqar Khan's forces. The materials have been collated from the researches of J.F. Richards and M.A. Nayeem into the Persian records of the still-expanding Mughal state, and offer us a glimpse of the raw materials from which the Arcot state could be constructed in the decades that followed.[20]

Table: The Fiscal Situation in the Karnatak (c. 1706)

(in rupees)

A. Disbursements		B. Revenue–Resources	
		I. *Ṣūba* Karnatak:	
Kh̲ālis̱a	990,679	I. 1 *Sarkār* Kumbum	1,077,098
Major *Jāgīrs*	908,486	I. 2 *Sarkār* Gutti	896,869
Minor *Jāgīrs*	3,171,861	I. 3 *Sarkār* Gandikota	1,168,865
Sinhbandî	5,249,305	I. 4 *Sarkār* Siddhavatam	757,171
Outside *Jāgīrs*	2,013,875	I. *Sarkār* Gurramkonda	765,453
Poligars etc	2,629,217	Total	4,665,456
Pā'ibâqî	662,649		
TOTAL	15,626,072		

contd...

(in rupees)

B. *Revenue-Resources*

II.	*Ṣūba* Karnatak Payanghat	
II. 1	*Sarkār* Addanki	427,236
II. 2	*Sarkār* Sarvepalli	675,637
II. 3	*Sarkār* Narasipur	582,943
II. 4	*Sarkār* Tadimari	484,760
II. 5	*Sarkār* Chandragiri	507,616
II. 6	*Sarkār* Chengalapattu	501,415
II. 7	*Sarkār* Kanchi	1,015,523
	Total	4,195,130
III.	Mulk-i maftūḥa	6,765,484
	TOTAL	15,57444

We may make what we will of this miraculously 'balanced' budget, which obviously involved a certain fiscal sleight-of-hand. Of particular significance is the relative importance of the southern 'newly conquered' territories in the whole, since the northern and relatively arid part of the Karnatak Payanghat represented a less likely fiscal source than the areas further south.

The foundation of Arcot

The standard source through which historians have hitherto reconstructed the early history of the Arcot niẕāmat is a chronicle in Persian, the *Tūzak-i Wālājāhī*, composed by Munshi Burhan Khan ibn Sayyid Hasan, born in Tiruchirappalli, but descended from ancestors who had long resided in Bijapur. The text was written in the years 1781–6, thus in the reign of Nawwab Muhammad 'Ali Walajah at Arcot. This fact ideologically charges the text somewhat, and provides it with a particular slant concerning the early rulers of Arcot; the author is divided between a desire to justify the creation of the sub-state and a certain desire to downplay the role of, in particular, Sa'adatullah Khan. Further, and interestingly, Burhan Khan writes from an explicitly Shi'a perspective, which also lends a special flavour to his version of the past. The *Tūzak-i Wālājāhī* extends and elaborates on an earlier text by the *malik-ush-shu'rā* of the Arcot court, Mir Isma'il Khan Abjadi, who had written a *maṣnawī* on the exploits of the first of the Walajah rulers, Anwar-ud-Din Khan, entitled *Anwar Nāma,* in 1760–61.[21]

Burhan Khan begins his account with a mention of how the *mulk-i Karnātak* was made up of two parts, the Balaghat and the Payanghat; it was in the latter that the ṣūba of Arcot lay, having formerly been ruled over by Hindu (*hunūd*) Rajas from their capital at Senji. Aurangzeb had however sent Zu'lfiqar Khan to settle the area and the latter had done so, taking over the Payanghat area, but also forcing the *zamīndārs* of Tiruchi, Tanjavur, Ramnad and other regions to submit. The account continues:

'When Zu'lfiqar Khan Bahadur was busy subduing the Payanghat, he chose the bank of a river and the skirt of a forest as the camping ground for the army of Islam, and for raising the standards of the victorious forces. Twelve long years of continuous habitation replaced the tents by thatched houses which, in the course of time, changed into tiled ones; when it became the capital (*qarārgāh-i ḥakim*), it gradually developed into a big town (*shahr-i 'aẓīm*) and became famous on the lips of one and all'.[22]

Burhan even provides us the etymology of the name, from *ār* (Tamil for river), and *kātu* (for forest); the combination of river and forest are thus said to have lain at the root of the town. He goes on to note the other names of Arcot, Dār al-Nūr and Muhammadpur, as it came to be called in the second half of the eighteenth century. This is a prelude to his description of the *nāẓims* of the area, beginning with Zu'lfiqar Khan, 'of imposing stature, noble-minded, good-natured, and of universal generosity', and an *iṣnā'asharī* Shi'a to boot. He is supposed to have administered the affairs of the Karnatak for twelve years, then giving way to his deputy (*nā'ib*), the Afghan Da'ud Khan Panni, and returning to Delhi.

Burhan's sources, dependent though he no doubt was on collective local memory, were largely reliable in the instance, though Arcot had already existed before 1700, and does find some mention in the accounts of the campaigns of the period when Zu'lfiqar Khan still dominated the region.[23] The fact remains that in the 1690s, Arcot was a minor fortress and a way-station; later, it became a major political centre. In the Dutch letters before about 1705, the tendency is to refer to the Nawab as resident in a camp (*leger*); only thereafter does Arcot ('Arkadoe') receive the epithet of 'the place of His Excellency's usual residence' (*de plaetse van Syn Excellenties ordinaire residentie*). Zu'lfiqar Khan and then Da'ud Khan may be thought, therefore, to have considerably consolidated the centre of Arcot, while at the same time maintaining a rather close eye on what transpired on the coast. Senji, which as noted above, had been captured from the Marathas in February 1698 after a protracted siege, had been given over to a *qil'adār* of Bundela extraction; the other major centre in the region with accumulated political prestige, namely Velur, was after its capture from the Marathas in the latter half of 1702 handed over to the charge of Ghulam 'Ali Khan, brother of the dīwān Muhammad Sa'id. In sum, rather than making use of one of the existing prestigious centres of the area, the niẕāmat chose, even after it had captured Senji and Velur, to opt for a new centre, no doubt in order to distinguish the new dispensation from those that had preceded it.

The *Tūzak-i Wālājāhī* does not enter into these details, but instead contents itself with recounting minor anecdotes concerning Da'ud Khan's rule, taking particular note of his fondness for ferocious dogs that he bred. The account of his niẕāmat concludes with some enigmatic details:

He was very fond of sea voyage (*sair-i daryā*). On the coast of the roaring sea adjoining the port of Mylapore (*bandar Mailāpūr*), he erected a building whose beauty was beyond description. During these days of dilapidation and ruin (the 1770s), the construction of a building of equal beauty is beyond human power (*g̱ẖair imkān*)'.[24]

An interesting variant to the *Tūzak's* perspective is provided by the early nineteenth-century regional chronicle in Tamil of Senji Narayana Pillai, entitled the *Karnāṭaka rājākkaḷ cavistāra carittiram*.[25] Here is how the early settlement of Arcot was summed up from oral tradition by Senji Narayana a century after the event, with the emphasis shifted somewhat from Zu'lfiqar Khan to Da'ud Khan Panni.

Navab Dvud Khan settled himself with his troops on the southern bank of the Palar river, in the province of Arcot. This place became the town (*paṭṭaṇam*) of Arcot. It was here that he resided in order to exercise the *faujdāri* (Tamil: *pauvucutāri*) of the Karnatak. Thus, from the Killedars of the Karnatak, and from the Killedars, Jagirdars, Mansabdars, Rajas, Palaiyakkarars et cetera (*vakaiyṟā*) settled by the Navab Amir ul-Umara (Zulfiqar Khan), he collected the appropriate *nazr* and tribute-instalments (*nacarum pēshkistiyum*). He sent *āmils* to the remaining *k̲h̲āliṣa* (Tamil: *kālacā*) ta'alluqas (*tālukas*) to collect the land-revenues (*amānī*) and port-duties, and together with the revenue-farms (*icārā*), every year had fifteen lakhs of rupees sent punctually to the *ḥuẕūr* (Tamil: *ucūrukku*) as had been decided. He constructed a fort and bungalows at Mylapur, and governed the lands of the Karnatak with justice (*nītiyāy*) until the Fasli Year 1114, all the while resident at Arcot.[26]

Da'ud Khan Panni is, of course, one of those important and enigmatic personages who occupy considerable space in the Mughal chronicles between the last years of Aurangzeb, and the early years of Farrukhsiyar. His father, Khizr Khan Panni, is known to have belonged to an Afghan family of Mahdawi leanings, and entered the service of the 'Adil Shahi rulers of Bijapur in the third quarter of the seventeenth century after an earlier career as a trader. Da'ud Khan for his part moved to

Mughal service by 1682, in which year he, his brother Sulaiman Khan, and his uncle Ranmast Khan are to be found receiving robes of honour (*khil'ats*) from Aurangzeb in the Deccan.[27] By 1700, he was firmly associated with Zu'lfiqar Khan in his Deccan campaigns; the following year, 1701, he was appointed Zu'lfiqar Khan's deputy (nā'ib) in the Karnatak Haidarabadi, and began to reside at Arcot. This association with the 'Irani' faction brought him the condemnation of Mughal chroniclers such as Khafi Khan, who makes it a point in his *Muntakhab ul-Lubāb* to paint Da'ud Khan in dark hues, as one who secretly negotiated with the Marathas, who had excessive truck with Hindus in general (his close associate being a certain Hiraman Baksariya), whose character was unreasonable, and who was even probably impotent! Contrasted with him is the flower of the Turani notables, especially Chin Qilich Khan (later to be celebrated as Nizam-ul-mulk Asaf Jah).[28]

By early 1704, Da'ud Khan had been promoted to the high mansab of 6000/6000, and given a position as nā'ib of Prince Kam Bakhsh in ṣūba Bijapur; however, it is clear that he continued to operate out of the Senji–Arcot region for the most part. Indeed, he remained associated with that region until 1713, when he was transferred to Gujarat; he was eventually killed on 6 September 1715 near Burhanpur, in a battle that came to be celebrated in both the Persian chronicles and semi-literary texts in Marathi.[29]

Now, Da'ud Khan is also the subject of considerable discussion in Nicolò Manuzzi's *Storia del Mogol,* since Manuzzi had fairly extensive dealings with him through the first decade of the eighteenth century, while resident at Madras. Manuzzi's portrayal of him, based on a mixture of rumour and direct observation, is startling: here is a veritable monster, who dashes his own female infants to the ground and kills them (*pace* Kamsa and his nieces and nephews), sets his vicious dogs on unsuspecting victims, is constantly drunk on imported European wine, and so on. The picaresque aspects of Manuzzi's account aside, what emerges from his detailed description of dealings between Arcot and Madras is the underlying tone of hostility that characterized the relationship between the English Company and the emerging autonomous niẓāmat. Indeed, glimpses of hostile relations can be seen as early as 1696, when Sulaiman Khan Panni, the brother of Da'ud Khan held charge of the region around Porto Novo. In February 1698, the English Company, fearing an attack on their Fort St David at Devanampattinam, repulsed a Mughal party that was at the gates of the fortress, killing Da'ud Khan's own brother-in-law in the process. After several months of hostilities, the English governor at Madras was obliged to pay an indemnity to Zu'lfiqar Khan to settle the matter.

We may imagine the situation as viewed from a Mughal perspective. Arriving on the Coromandel coast, they found themselves confronted in the late 1680s by a whole series of European fortified settlements, of a sort that they did not easily permit elsewhere in their domains. Of these, the most significant were the Dutch Casteel Geldria at Pulicat, the English Fort St George at Madras (both in former Golkonda territories), and Fort St David at Devanampattinam (Kadalur) in the Karnatak Bijapuri; while other fortresses such as Tranquebar and Nagapattinam fell under the rule of the Maratha dynasty at Tanjavur. While the Mughals did have some experience in dealing with such Portuguese fortresses as Daman and Diu, they were also embroiled in a rather violent quarrel in the 1680s with the English, which augured ill for their future relationship; relations with the Dutch in Surat and elsewhere at this time were, as Ashin Das Gupta has shown, rather vitiated by issues of convoying vessels to the Red Sea in the face of the threat posed by European piracy in the western Indian Ocean.[30] One possible strategy was thus for the Dutch or English to develop a relationship with the regional Mughal elite, insulated from the possible repercussions of what might transpire in Gujarat or Bengal.

The search for likely sympathizers was thus a pressing priority for the Europeans. In these years, the letters of the Dutch East India Company, like those of the English, point to the gradual rise of Da'ud Khan Panni, as Zu'lfiqar Khan's preoccupations took him away from the Karnatak region without his abandoning that area entirely however. The main power-broker through whom the Dutch dealt with Da'ud Khan was a Maharashtrian Brahmin, Krishnaji Pandit, referred to on more than one occasion as the factotum (*albeschik*) of the former. It was Krishnaji who broke the news to the Dutch in April–May 1702, that orders had arrived from the 'emperor's court' (*keijsers hof*) that all the European nations on the Coromandel coast were to be dealt with as enemies and eventually expelled, adding somewhat ironically that 'since this was not really possible to put such a thing into effect, a beginning had been made with the English', with the others to follow in due course![31] This was the thin edge of the wedge for negotiations concerning the weaver and washer villages around Pulicat that the VOC controlled, and on account of which they had a fiscal dispute with the Mughal *dīwān*.

It is thus clear that these European-controlled ports accounted for a good deal of the trade of the region (even if we cannot attempt a precise quantification), while retaining a distasteful status from the

Mughal point of view of *peshkash*-paying autonomous centres. The situation is brought home to us clearly when we consider Manuzzi's account of his own mission in January 1701 to the Mughal camp in Arcot, on behalf of Governor Thomas Pitt at Fort St George. He carried letters for Da'ud Khan, with whom he had a previous acquaintance, as also for the dīwān of the Karnatak Payanghat, Muhammad Sa'id; accompanied by the Brahmin and Company factotum Ramappa, Manuzzi took along a gift of about Rs 3000 to 4000, two cannons, some scarlet and some gold-cloth, mirrors, pistols, and a variety of odds and ends to be distributed to notables. On arriving at Arcot, Manuzzi was allowed to see Da'ud Khan, who apparently complained to him of the lack of courtesy on the part of the English (in contrast with their Portuguese neighbours, who had been reinstated after a gap of several decades in São Tomé). Manuzzi claims that he was let down in his mission by Ramappa, who behaved in a duplicitous and devious fashion, trying to hold back the present in cash for Da'ud Khan. An aspect worth remarking of Manuzzi's account is his meeting with the 'chief minister' or dīwān, Muhammad Sa'id, described by him as 'one of the most polished men to be found among the Mahomedans', who 'invited me to his table and entertained me magnificently'.

At the same time, the resentment felt by the Mughals against the English as a consequence of the dealings at Devanampattinam in 1698 resurfaced rapidly. Manuzzi reports how he protested his own transparent sincerity as intermediary, but also reports Da'ud Khan's response.

> His reply was that, as for me, he would do anything I wanted but that the English, settled within the country of the king, his master, possessed a strong place most useful and highly suitable for all sorts of merchandise and traffic. They had always been left undisturbed, and yet, without regard to the past, they now treated him in the most cavalier spirit, and gave him next to nothing. They failed to reflect that they had enriched themselves in his country to a most extraordinary degree. He believed that they must have forgotten that he was general over the province of the Karnatak, and that since the fall of the Golkonda kingdom they had rendered no account of their administration, good or bad, commencing with 1686. Nor had they accounted for the revenues from tobacco, betel, wine etcetera, which reached a considerable sum every year.[32]

Manuzzi's own reply, whether real or invented *ex post facto,* is not devoid of interest. He stressed, first, the fact that Madras had been created by the English from a 'vast plain full of sand, uninhabited', and transformed by them into a port that was 'highly populous, full of active merchants and other residents'. The good government of the English, and their sense of justice was responsible for this; this was why so many merchants, weavers and printers of cloth had decided to reside there. If Da'ud Khan took harsh measures against them, the English would simply leave the place, and the other European nations would follow them from Coromandel. The losers would be the local merchants and weavers who earned lakhs of pagodas each year in the process of trade. At the same time (and there is a contradiction in the argument here), the English would very likely resort to violence if expelled, and 'seize every ship they came across, and thereby spread ruin and desolation throughout the Moghul empire'.There is nothing particularly novel about these arguments, indeed their interest lies precisely in their very familiar character. The English provide safety, security and justice; they bring in gold and silver coins, and provide a livelihood for local merchants and weavers. On the one hand, they are really indifferent to whether they are allowed to trade or not ('they set little store by the place'), and on the other, they were to be feared at sea, where their capacity to generate violence was considerable. In any event, Manuzzi's mission cannot be judged a success, since (despite his own typically self-congratulatory version), it turns out that Governor Pitt and his Council were rather unhappy with Da'ud Khan's treatment of their letters.[33]

Several months later, while *en route* from Arcot to Tanjavur to collect an annual peshkash from the Maratha rulers, Da'ud Khan once more made direct contact with the English. In May 1701, he is known to have been given a gift by the chief of Fort St. David, who met him near Kadalur; on his return, he is also reported to have visited the French at Pondicherry, the Dutch at Sadrasapatnam, and finally the English at Madras. The last of these visits occurred in July 1701, and both in this year, and in 1702, on the occasion of another visit, the procedure followed by Da'ud Khan is significant. He appears consistently to have set down his camp in Mylapore (São Tomé), dealing from there with the English. This port was to be given a privileged role in his conception of things, and this is doubtless the reason why in August 1702, the dīwān Muhammad Sa'id is reported by Manuzzi in Mylapore, having given orders to build an 'earthen wall to be made all around San Thome, including not only the quarter of the Mahomedans, but that in which the Portuguese dwell'.[34] Again, in November 1706, when Da'ud Khan paid a visit to the Madras region, he is reported to have stayed first at St Thomas Mount, and then in São Tomé, 'in a large tent erected on the sea-shore and fitted with carpets'.[35] Manuzzi notes that a particular complicity existed between him and the Portuguese Bishop of Mylapore, Padre Gaspar Afonso Álvares S.J., until the latter died in office in November 1708.

It is clear enough that the attempt to re-develop São Tomé was part of a larger strategy on the part of Da'ud Khan. From these years date the presence in Mylapore of a number of important 'Pathan' merchants, to whom reference has already been made above; these men were obviously Indo–Afghans from Bijapur, and encouraged to settle there by Da'ud Khan. Basing himself on English records, for example, S. Arasaratnam argues that Da'ud Khan's subordinates deliberately kept taxes low in the port (at 2 1/2 per cent on imports and exports), gave traders full exemption from inland duties for a time, and even established a mint there in 1707. He traces the trade of these 'Pathans' (the term being found in the English records) to such places as Pegu, Tenasserim, Bengal, Surat, Mokha and the Persian Gulf, in brief over a series of regions both east and west. Further, he insists that these traders 'had close links with Mughal administrators', and that at times their trade was directly financed by sleeping partners who were themselves 'wealthy officials' (and who kept two-thirds of the profits).[36] In the 1710s, in S. Arasaratnam's view, the trade of São Tomé would have been at least half that of Madras, and even if it declined in the 1720s, it continued to worry the English Company as late as the 1730s and 1740s, so that they seized control of the port as soon as they could, in the late 1740s.[37]

It was somewhat paradoxical that the settlement where their activity was focused was São Tomé, which had had an altogether checkered history from the 1510s, when the first private Portuguese traders settled there. Created as a bishopric and city (*Cidade*) in 1606, São Tomé suffered in the first half of the seventeenth century from the vicinity of the Dutch at Pulicat, who kept up a sustained attack on private Portuguese shipping from the town.[38] In 1662, São Tomé was captured by Golkonda forces, and thereafter it came briefly under French control. However, in the late 1680s, the Portuguese made a further attempt to resettle the town with a Mughal *farmān,* with the intention of attracting those Portuguese traders who had settled in Madras (under English protection) and in Porto Novo, to resume trade in the port. This attempt seems to have met with only rather limited success. Besides the Bishop, Padre Gaspar Afonso Álvares, the governor of the *Estado da Índia,* D. Rodrigo da Costa had pinned his hopes on the Madras merchant Lucas Luís de Oliveira and the Porto Novo-based entrepreneur, Manuel Teixeira Pinto, who also find uncomplimentary mention in Manuzzi's account.[39]

The coexistence between Afghans and Indo-Portuguese appears to have been distinctly uncomfortable, but the Portuguese had little other choice in the matter. Violent incidents flared up from time to time, for instance in the first year of the captaincy of Nuno Sodré Frade, who replaced Mateus Carvalho da Silva in 1704. The presence of a Mughal faujdār in the vicinity (in 1704, a certain Mir 'Usman, or Sayyid 'Usman) did not help calm matters either. Manuzzi provides us a detailed account, confirmed by English Company records, of a public disturbance in São Tomé on 4 October 1704, on the occasion of the procession of the Feast of the Rosary. Several of the faujdār's men are said to have been killed or injured, as were some Portuguese. The captain Nuno Sodré Frade himself was wounded, and abandoned by his compatriots; chagrined by this, he asked that he be relieved of his post in Goa, shortly thereafter.[40]

At the same time, it is clear that Da'ud Khan's plans in respect of São Tomé could not be fully carried through. He had built a fine residence there, as noted by both the Indo-Persian and Tamil chronicling traditions cited above; but his real purpose of fortifying the port remained unfulfilled. Manuzzi makes mention of it, in relation to his account of events in the year 1706, as follows:

> I have already mentioned that the officials governing the Karnatik requested leave from the Mogul to build a new fortress at the port of San Thome. His Majesty refused his permission upon the excuse that the Europeans would take possession of it, since it was so close to the sea. Nay, he would be highly pleased if they could be deprived of those towns where they already resided.[41]

Of the European nations, the Portuguese were obviously the most vulnerable by the early eighteenth century. The English for their part sheltered more or less behind the walls of Fort St George, secured their position through a combination of threats, tributes and diplomacy. The French at Pondicherry were in an intermediate position, and hence made a far more concerted effort to woo Da'ud Khan (whom they descirbe in their letters as an *'amy de la Nation'*), while at the same time making it a point to maintain good relations with the powerful Bundela qil' adār of Senji, Sarup Singh. Again, this was in contrast with the English at Fort St David, whose relations with Sarup Singh were at best strained, and at worst downright violent. As early as 1704, they claimed that the Senji governor was planning to 'break down the Banks of the River (Ponnaiyar) and turne the Course of the water from coming into the Right Honourable Companies Bounds', and hence sent out troops to Tirupapuliyur to 'deter him from that Villainous designe'.[42] But things only went from bad to worse. In 1710, for example, in the course of a dispute over some defaulting revenue-farmers who had taken refuge with the English, Sarup Singh (or, as the English letters term him, 'that stupid inhuman Creature Suroop Sing') took it upon himself to capture and hold prisoner two English Company servants, Captain Hugonin and Ensign Reay, in his stronghold of Senji; the English Company then attacked and burnt some fifty villages in the region, destroying thousands of pagodas worth of rice that awaited harvest.[43] The hostilities, in which the English Company servant Gabriel Roberts had a major (and, as it later turned out, somewhat unsavoury) role to play, continued intermittently for nearly two years, with the articles of peace being signed only in May 1712.[44] English attitudes on the affair veer uncertainly between shrill self-righteousness and a certain remorse. In one letter dated 25 October 1711, the factors at Fort St David admit to their superiors in Madras: 'Wee must Indeed owne there is no [...] express order for Commencing a Warr or Plundering the Country & Destroying that vast quantity of Grain but the Gentlemen concerned desire youll be pleas'd to Consider that as they were Oblig'd in Duty they acquainted their superiors at Fort St. George of every pace they tooke'. They then go on rather shamefacedly to declare: 'But the Destruction of 50, or 60,000 Pagodas worth of Graine, about 52 villages & Townes among which was his (Sarup Singh's) favourite Towne Yembollam and Killing the Pandarum there are things which really makes his demands carry too much justice with them'.[45] We may note, as an aside, that in the course of negotiations in January 1712, we come across the figure of 'Senhor Nichola Manuch, formerly inhabitant of Madras now at Pondicherry', who had interceded in the affair with the Mughal administration at Arcot, describing 'our (the English) quarrell with Surop Singh with advantage on our side'.[46]

Finally, the Dutch East India Company occupied an interesting place in the Karnatak scheme of things, less bellicose than the English, less marginal than the French or the Portuguese. By the early years of the eighteenth century, the Dutch headquarters on the Coromandel coast had been established firmly at their fortress in Nagapattinam (from where they had expelled the Portuguese in 1658), which gave the Dutch a rather different perspective on matters than when they had operated out of a centre further north, in their Casteel Geldria at Pulicat. The main Dutch centres that lay under the control of Arcot were, from north to south, Pulicat, Sadras, and Porto Novo, but they also had a less significant interest in ports such as Kunjimedu and Kovalam (Covelong).

In order to protect their interests in these ports, the Dutch had, as we have seen, an ally in the Mughal camp in the early years of the eighteenth century: this was Krishnaji Pandit, with whom they kept up a close correspondence. Besides, they also made an effort to keep up a flow of minor gifts (*schenkagie*) to the major Mughal notables, the 'heer Nabab' (that is, Da'ud Khan), the dīwān, the *bak̲h̲shī,* as well as the faujdārs and ḥawaldārs who controlled the vicinity of the three ports in which they operated. On occasion, they also supplied Persian and Arabian horses as part of the package, and less frequently elephants from Sri Lanka (which the Maratha Rajas of Tanjavur, for their part, received regularly from them in gift). The main interlocutors of the Dutch were the ḥawaldārs in or around the three ports we have mentioned, as also the faujdārs at Ponneri (near Pulicat), and his counterparts at Chengalapattu, Chidambaram and Tirukasugudam. But there was another factor to be taken into consideration too, particularly in the areas around Porto Novo and Sadras. The Mughals, like the Bijapur rulers before them, did not wholly succeed in displacing the autochthonous lineages of Tamil and Telugu *kāvalkārars* who collected transit-dues and a number of other cesses. These 'visiadoors' (as the Dutch termed them), continued in the early years of the eighteenth century to find mention in Dutch records, as did their conflicts with both the Mughal authorities and the Dutch themselves, on those occasions when they took on the transit-tolls (*cuṅkam*) in revenue-farm. In the years 1717–19, for example, severe conflicts broke out in the Sadrasapatnam area with the 'groote visiadoor', a certain Chinna Tambi Nayaka.[47]

In general, one is left with the impression that during the years when Da'ud Khan was at the helm of affairs in the Payanghat, Dutch affairs were in better favour with him than those of the English. Whether this was mainly due to the intervention of Krishnaji Pandit or not, we have no means of knowing for sure. Already in 1702, much before their quarrel with Sarup Singh, the English at Fort St. David seem to have been on bad terms once more with the Mughals, which the Dutch records go so far as to call a 'war between the English and the Moors'; in contrast, in September that year, the Dutch were invited by Da'ud Khan to settle at Kunjimedu, a port where the English Company had formerly had a factory, since abandoned. The situation was described thus in a Dutch letter from Nagapattinam to Batavia of Septmber 1702.

The region of Conimede lying in the kingdom of Singi has on account of a long drawn-out war been sufficiently depopulated, that the English, who had had the said place in their possession before this, seeing nothing more come out of it than excessive expenses, without it ever being brought around to a tranquil state of commerce and to some sales of goods or purchases of cloth, were obliged—the more so in order to be free of the vexations of the lords of the land (*lendregenten*) by which the said place was and still continually is plagued—to leave the said Conimede altogether and to bring their trade over to Tegenepatnam, where they were also followed by all the craftsmen (*arbeijtsluyden*) who were still over there.[48]

The place had thus lain practically 'deserted' for some years, until in 1701, Da'ud Khan had decided to 'present' it to the Dutch. But complications followed, that are not devoid of significance. For it soon transpired that Da'ud Khan's word was not enough. Instead, a document of 'confirmation' was needed from the dīwān Muhammad Sa'id, who declared himself ready to give it, but for the sum of Rs 8000 for himself, soon raised somewhat deviously to Rs 13,000, for himself, his secretary, and others. The Dutch fumed and fretted, but noted that the dīwān's star was distinctly on the rise already. The new faujdār of Chengalapattu, Buland Khan, was reputedly his man: other agents like his 'secretary' (on whom more below), also appear to have had a significant role to play in fiscal and financial matters in the region. We are still in a phase when Zu'lfiqar Khan ('de heer Julfacharchan' to the Dutch) held the key to affairs in the Payanghat, but it would appear that the balance of power between his subordinates Da'ud Khan and Muhammad Sa'id was still uncertain. The latter insisted, as we have noted above, that Da'ud Khan's grants (*qaul*) were of 'no worth so long as they were not given a *parwāna* of confirmation by the dīwān'; eventually the VOC was obliged, in August 1702, to send him the equivalent of Rs 13000 (3782 pagodas) to Arcot. But matters were then further delayed, since Muhammad Sa'id had gone to look to the affairs to Velur, recently taken from the Marathas (on account of the capture of which he had just received a manṣab of 3000/2000); all of this confirmed to the Dutch that the dīwān was not merely greedy and unreasonable in his claims, but also unreliable when it came to delivering his own *parwānas* and arranging *ḥasb-ul-ḥukms*.

In the years that followed, Muhammad Sa'id (or Sa'id Khan as he was now titled) appears to have fallen briefly into disgrace, perhaps on account of his disputes with Da'ud Khan concerning a number of matters.[49] In his place as dîwân, we find a certain Zia-ud-Din Khan ('Sawidichan'), who in turn put his own men into place, while at the same time maintaining a considerable role for Maharashtrian Brahmins (such as a certain Sankarji Malharji Pandit, an erstwhile opponent of the Mughals) in the fiscal administration, in deference to the continuing political weight of Krishnaji Pandit. It is with Zia-ud-Din Khan that the VOC had to deal concerning the problematic affair of the widow and daughter of a certain Pieter Josephszoon, taken into the household of a Persian merchant of Pulicat, Aqa Raza; the ḥawaldār of Pulicat, Sundardas, appears to have been somewhat less than sympathetic to the Dutch in this matter, as well as on the question of money-changing between silver rupees and gold pagodas.[50]

However, by early 1707, when news of the death of Aurangzeb and the prospects for the succession had begun to trickle into the Payanghat, Sa'id Khan had already been reinstated as dīwān. Da'ud Khan, absent at this time in the vicinity of Kadappa, appears to have been facing troubles within his own ranks in 1705–6, notably in the form of the faujdār of Palaiyamkottai, a fortress lying due west of Porto Novo in the hinterland. Instead of being supported in this by the court, Da'ud Khan had reputedly found Aurangzeb unsympathetic to his cause; one of the effects of bringing Sa'id Khan back into power was that he was able to intercede in the region, bringing in a certain 'Abd-un-Nabi Khan Miyana (already responsible for Porto Novo in about 1698, and later to achieve prominence in Kadappa), as faujdâr over Chidambaram in the place of the somewhat incompetent incumbent 'Inayat Khan.[51]

The rise of Sa'adatullah Khan

Detailed news of Aurangzeb's death first reached the Dutch in Nagapattinam on 7 April 1707, in the form of an *olai* (palm-leaf letter) from the VOC *wakīl,* the Brahmin Ramayya, who resided in Arcot, written on the first of that month. Ramayya, in turn, reported news that had arrived via Kadappa that Aurangzeb had died on 3 March at 2 o'clock in the afternoon, as well as the subsequent activities of Prince Muhammad A'zam and the *wazīr* Asad Khan. Da'ud Khan and Zu'lfiqar Khan were naturally supporters of this faction in the struggle (the wazîr being the latter's father), with difficulties being expected from Kam Bakhsh (who laid claim to the erstwhile Golkonda and Bijapur territories), and especially from Shah 'Alam, who was in north India and counted on a very substantial military backing. Ramayya sagely expected the struggle to last another two or three years at least, and was keeping himself informed through the Tirukasugudam faujdār, Shaikh Islam, as well as Da'ud Khan's factotum (albeschik) Krishnaji Pandit.[52]

Things did not quite turn out though as expected. A letter dated 15 February 1710 from Monsieur Hebert of the French Company in Pondicherry, explains the situation in the Karnatak to his superiors in the metropolis (with some minor inaccuracies) as follows:

The Great Mogol Aurengzeb being dead and having left three sons, who declared war in order to possess the kingdoms of their father, Azemtara who was the oldest (*sic*) having been defeated in the month of October 1708 (*sic*) by Chaalem his brother, he killed himself at the end of the combat; Cambax his other brother who had retired to Golconda was abandoned by his soldiers and wounded by Davud Kan governor of the Carnatic who made him prisoner; this prince died three days after, and Chaalem who is aged 70 years is left master of all the estates of his father. This prince has dispersed the Rajepoutes who during his absence had besieged Agra his capital.[53]

The letter-writer argues, moreover, that this succession struggle, which had the effect of diverting Da'ud Khan's energies towards the north, hence involuntarily interrupted a process of Mughal consolidation in the far south. In this region, kingdoms such as Madurai (under its Nayaka dynasty), Tanjavur (under a branch of the Bhonsles) and other territories still managed to preserve a limited degree of autonomy, paying peshkash to the Mughals only on the show of force. However, in Hebert's view, further campaigns were unlikely in view of the fact that Shah 'Alam 'likes war not at all, and has always led a soft and effeminate life'.

As is well-known, despite their having supported Prince Muhammad A'zam, the careers of neither Zu'lfiqar Khan nor Da'ud Khan suffered in the short-run after the defeat of their master. The former continued to be a power in Mughal politics until the ascension of Farrukhsiyar to the throne (when he was killed in ignominous circumstances, in 1713); the latter survived till 1715, as noted above, having played a stellar role in the defeat and capture of Kam Bakhsh together with his Afghan associates (*afg̱hānān hamrāh ī-ye Dā'ūd Ḵẖān*).[54] However, from about 1710, Da'ud Khan's influence in the Payanghat is decidedly of a lower order than before, as affairs of a different nature and scale occupy his time. Instead, it is increasingly the dīwān (always something of an *éminence grise*) who openly controls affairs, though as late as 1711, the clients of Da'ud Khan were not entirely devoid of influence in the zone.

Muhammad Sa'id, who from about 1710 was definitively titled Sa'adatullah Khan (a title that he had originally had from Aurangzeb, who had then later named him Kifayat Khan, 'Economical' Khan—a title that its recepient naturally disliked!), now strove with some vigour to carve out a viable domain in the Karnatak Payanghat, a domain that would offer him sufficient autonomy, while nevertheless stopping considerably short of a direct repudiation of Mughal rule.[55] He can be observed at work both from the Persian materials produced at his own behest, and from the letters and papers of the European factories perched on the very edge of his zone of operations. It is inevitable that the latter, while not uniformly hostile in character, are nevertheless rather less complimentary to him than his own panegyrists.[56]

A major source for an understanding of Sa'adatullah Khan's functioning in the 1710s is a Persian text patronized by him, the *Sa'īd Nāma* of Jaswant Rai Munshi.[57] This elaborate work, in ornate rhymed Persian prose (*nasr-i musajja'*) was authored by a poet and writer in Sa'adatullah Khan's circle, himself a Jalput Saraswat Brahmin with origins in northern India. It is made up of three *daftars,* with a fourth having been planned but never written by its author, and carries the account of the activities of its hero (the Sa'id of the title) as far as 1723, beginning with his birth at Bijapur on Wednesday 17 Jumada I 1061 (28 April 1651). It stresses the high birth of Muhammad Sa'id, whose father it is noted was Muhammad 'Ali bin Ahmad bin Sa'id-ud-Din bin Muhammad Sa'id of the Banu Hashim, whose family had migrated from Medina to Ahmadabad in about 810 AH, during the rule of Sultan Ahmad Shah Gujarati. Subsequently, after Akbar's conquest of Gujarat, they had moved to Nizam Shahi service in Ahmadnagar (receiving a large part of the Konkan in *tuyūl*), and then eventually—after Mahabat Khan's campaigns in the area in the seventeenth century—to the service of the 'Adil Shahis of Bijapur, coming to be a part of the community called the Nawayats (newcomers) in the Deccan.[58] At the time the clan moved to Bijapur, it is noted that its head was a certain Qazi Sa'id, who was normally a part of the vanguard of the Bijapuri army. On his death in battle, his nephew Mulla Ahmad Nawayat continued to play a role of great significance; he was thus named governor (*ḥāris*) of Bidar, before joining Mughal service through the intercession of Shayista Khan, with the high rank of 6000/6000.[59] Muhammad Sa'id's father, it is noted, was related through marriage as *hamzulf,* or 'co-brother-in-law' in common north Indian usage, to Mulla Ahmad. Returning thus to our hero, he had been born at dawn, and in view of the very auspicious hour of his birth, the leading astrologers of Bijapur such as Mulla Murtaza Mashhadi and Mulla Abu'l Hasan were called in; they all concurred on reading his horoscope (*zāicha* or *tāli'nāma*) that he had a great future, and suggested he be named Muhammad Sa'id (meaning 'auspicious').

The text goes on to note a few details of Muhammad Sa'id's early career, such as that he had been faujdār at Ramgir in Bidar before coming to the Payanghat; he was married for the first time in 1671 to the daughter of Mukhlis Khan, but apparently had no male children.[60] Burhan Khan, in the *Tūzak-i Wālājāhī*, provides us some further rather curious details on the manner in which Muhammad Sa'id was recruited into Mughal service, together with what another text insists was his older brother (*birādar-i buzurg*) Ghulam 'Ali.[61] It is claimed that the two brothers, who were 'in miserable circumstances in the Konkan', attempted to ingratiate themselves to Aurangzeb through his ba<u>kh</u>shī. However, while the other brother Ghulam 'Ali passed muster, Muhammad Sa'id, 'with his emaciated body and short stature' (*az naḥāfat-i jism wa qaṣr-i qāmat*) was rejected for Mughal service. He is then reported to have had recourse to a maker of magic amulets (*ṣāḥib-i da'wat*), who gave him one such *ta'wīẕ* to conceal in his turban, in order to influence the emperor. Muhammad Sa'id was then assigned a place in the last row of an audience by the ba<u>kh</u>shī. However, since Aurangzeb recognized an unnatural influence at work on himself in respect of this man whom he had already rejected, he guessed at once that the amulet-maker was behind the affair. The amulet was seized and sent back, with a stern message to the sāhib-i da'wat not to interfere in the affairs of kings, but Muhammad Sa'id was let into Mughal service at a lowly level with an admonition. Burhan concludes his story:

> Now, it is in the power of God to raise an ant (*mūr*) to the rank of Solomon (*manṣab-i sulaimānī*) and defeat human rationality (*'aql-i insānī*). The raising up from beggary (*gadā'ī*) to the position of a Sultan (*daulat-i sulṭānī*), which seems not to stand to reason is worked out in the unseen *darbār* of the Almighty. Muhammad Sa'id from the position of a servant (*naukarī*) found his entry, as days rolled on, into the group of *manṣabdārs* (*ba murūr-i aiyām dar zumra-i manṣabdārān dā<u>kh</u>il yāft*).[62]

Uncomplimentary reflections and mildly scandalous stories of this type were permitted to the chronicler of the Walajahs, but would surely have been out of place coming from Jaswant Rai's pen. Burhan Khan does have a number of positive things to say about Muhammad Sa'id though, mixed with somewhat sly remarks. Thus, the major passage in the *Tūzak* on his administration runs as follows:

> In the *sūba* of Arcot, he was for twenty years *nā'ib* to the *nāẓim* and for five years, *nāẓim*. The fame of his administration was sung for twenty-five years on the whole. He devoted his high purpose to the welfare of the creation and to the organization of his army. He was an *iṣnā'sharī*, and had faith in the sect of Ja'far. He had in his heart the interests of his relatives and the members of his family, and he invited them from the Konkan and bestowed

upon them forts and jāgirs (*ham-quam wa'ashīrat-i kẖwud rā az Kūkan talbīd wa qilā 'wa jāgīrāt bakẖshīd*). His younger brother Ghulam 'Ali who was at the court of the Padshah, was granted the *jāgīr* of Velur, and given the title of Khan. He tried to comfort and console the poor, the orphan and the needy. The people regarded his days as the best of the past (*zamān-i ū rā bihtarīn az min sābiq mī guftand*), and were of one accord in praising the justice of his *niẓāmat*.[63]

Thus, combined with an implicit criticism for his 'nepotism' is the fulsome if formulaic praise for his concern for the poor and needy in this very brief summing up of a career that lasted, by Burhan's own admission, some twenty-five years in the Payanghat. In contrast, the other text with which we are concerned, the *Sa'īd Nāma,* sets out to do far more justice to its subject. But before entering into this text, we may turn briefly to the career of its author, details of which he himself provides us both here and elsewhere. Jaswant Rai, as noted above, was a Saraswat Brahmin, the son of a certain Bhagwant Rai, in turn the son of Sundardas. At four generations removed in the ancestry was a certain Malik Debani, who had like his ancestors resided in Ghazni. Expelled in the last part of the fourteenth century from there (at the time of Timur), Malik Debani had apparently moved to Lahore, and then to Kakriwal (west of Patiala), where he became a *zamīndār*. However, Jaswant Rai reports, his son Malik Hardas had a taste for letters, and hence left home to become a *munshī,* so that the family became attached to the household of a certain Jalal Khan Kakar (and his descendants, Kakar Khan and Purdil Khan). In the time of Aurangzeb, he reports, Jaswant Rai had first made the acquaintance of Muhammad Sa'id (in 1118 AH). by writing a *qaṣīda* in his praise. Pleased, the latter had appointed him his official biographer, in which matter the intercession of a certain Lala Dakhni Rai (on whom more below) had been of aid as well.

The *Sa'id Nāma* begins with characteristic praise for the Almighty (who had caused the tender buds of the poet's heart to blossom forth into the full bloom of floral poesy); particular praise (*manqabat*) then follows for Imam 'Ali bin Abi Talib and the five members of the Prophet's family, in keeping with the *isnā'asharī* proclivities of Sa'adatullah Khan that have been already noted above. The main body of the work then details Sa'adatullah Khan's attempts to 'settle' the area of the Payanghat and his relations with the refractory zamīndārs in annual campaigns to collect peshkash; these include the Madurai Nayaka dynasty by then resident at Tiruchirappalli, and the Maratha rajas of Tanjavur. Year after year, even as an aged warior of seventy, Sa'adatullah Khan seems to have set out personally to demand their dues from these rulers in an unending series of confrontations and minor skirmishes. As it happens, this is confirmed both by the Dutch Company's records, and by the peshkash documents of the region.[64] Interspersed with these details of unending campaigns are Jaswant Rai's own poetic efforts, for the work is written in a Persian that is extremely (and surely deliberately) ornate, challenging the reader to keep up with the author.

The *Sa'īd Nāma,* like the *Tūzak-i Wālājāhī,* mentions the presence of a large number of Nawayats who had either accompanied Muhammad Sa'id, or had been invited by him to follow once he had attained a position of power. His brother, Ghulam 'Ali Khan, *qil'adār* of Velur, is the best known of these, but a number of others are also worthy of mention, such as his brother-in-law Muhammad Shafi', and his nephew Muhammad Sadiq, both of whom held positions of importance in the administration. Others, notably Afghans and men from Badakhshan, were not absent either in the campaigns of the 1710s: men such as Ghalib Muhammad Khan, Daulat Khan Khizrza'i, or Roshan Beg Khan. Amongst the Mughal functionaries who came south with the Mughal advance, and settled down in the Karnatak Payanghat in these years, were also men of other ethnicities; Iranians who had once been associated with Zu'lfiqar Khan, Bundelas and Shekhawats amongst the Rajputs, and so on. Perhaps most significantly from our point of view, there was also a very large number of Khatris, who even find mention in the Tamil chronicle we have mentioned earlier, the *Karnāṭaka rājākkaḷ cavistāra carittiram.* Indeed, according to this text, when orders came from the Mughal court to name Da'ud Khan faujdâr of the Karnatak with Muhammad Sa'id as his dīwān, the posts of both *dīwān peshkar,* and *sarrishtadār* were given over to Khatris.

Indeed, the reader of the *Sa'īd Nāma* soon perceives that the text is about two heroes rather than one. Omnipresent in the text, and constantly active as an agent and advisor to Sa'adatullah Khan is the figure, already noted briefly above, of Lala Dakhni Rai.[65] This character is introduced into the text fairly early on; it turns out that his father, Khushhal Rai, had already been associated with Muhammad Sa'id early in his career. This man, in turn the son of a certain Sadanand Qutb-ud-din Khani, hailed from the celebrated town of Badayun in Hindustan. Other members of the family may also be found in the entourage of Muhammad Sa'id: notably Dakhni Rai's uncle Anandi Das, and his son Khub Chand, the latter (in Jaswant Rai's words), having 'been brought up from his childhood in the court of the Nawab'. Other figures that we shall have occasion to encounter include the coastal ḥawaldārs Dayaram and Sundardas, and Lala Todar Mal, who often acted as Sa'adatullah Khan's representative in diplomatic and revenue affairs.[66]

The close relationship between Jaswant Rai, a Saraswat Brahmin, and these Khatris, is not entirely surprising. Commenting on the situation in the Bengal niẓāmat in the early eighteenth century, where too the Khatris played a role of some importance, John McLane notes their close ties with their *purohits,* the Saraswats, with whom they even practised commensality with a relative degree of facility.[67] Elsewhere in the Mughal domains, a similar place to that of the Khatris was held by the Kayasthas, notably in Hyderabad once it came to be dominaed by the Turani faction of Nizam-ul-mulk Asaf Jah.[68]

Mentions of Dakhni Rai can be found in the Dutch records as early as 1702 (*'sijnen secretaris ... Deckenerauw'*), but mention of the former as the 'factotum' of Sa'adatullah Khan (the preferred Dutch usage of the epoch, albeschik) must await the 1701s. In point of fact, the domination of the Khatris appears to have been contested in a lively fashion in the transition from Da'ud Khan to Sa'adatullah Khan. In 1711, for example, the Dutch letters report the temporary absence of Sa'adatullah Khan in Mysore, where he had gone on a tribute-gathering mission from the Wodeyars (*sijn optogt tegen den Maijsoerder*); in place in Arcot were his brother's son, Muhammad Sadiq (to whom the Dutch addressed the dues from their revenue-farm over Sadrasapatnam, where incidentally they had begun fortifications), and a certain Ja'far Khan, who was apparently a sort of privileged agent.[69] Earlier in the same year, it is reported that Dayaram and Sundardas, both of whom had positions in the fiscal hierarchy near Pulicat, had been displaced, and Maharashtrian Brahmins—namely a certain Narasimha Rao, and Raghuji Pandit—put in their place.[70] The letters attribute these local rivalries in turn to the larger rivalry between Da'ud Khan (who still cast a residual shadow over the area), and Sa'adatullah Khan. The former continued to act, in part through Krishnaji Pandit, but more especially through Shaikh Islam, the faujdār of Pulicat.

In 1712, however, Sa'adatullah Khan found his hand strengthened, as the Dutch letters make clear. In late November that year, the Nagapattinam Council takes note of his departure from Tanjavur, where he had been to collect his peshkash, and settle residual matters stemming from the death on 28 September 1711 of Shahaji, and the succession of his brother Sarabhoji. However, rather than return to Arcot, 'the usual place of his residence', Sa'adatullah Khan had decided to go to Velur, in view of some important news.

He had received good news from the royal camp (*hof leger*), that the new emperor (Jahandar Shah) had given him, the duan (*dīwān*) the title of Nabab, and a mancep (*manṣab*) of a thousand riders, and for the payment of the said riders had assigned him some land in Jagier or rent.[71]

Sa'adatullah Khan had then returned to Arcot, but then gone on to Velur *en route* to his annual tribute-gathering mission to Mysore. The VOC officials realized that he had now become thoroughly entrenched, and began to wonder what to offer him in gift. These reflections continued into the next year, by which time the Company was aware of great changes in the Mughal domains, with the accession of Farrukhsiyar to the throne. Taking advantage of these rumours and confusions, the Dutch managed to put off their gift to Sa'adatullah Khan, despite the fact that the English in Madras and the French in Pondicherry stole a march on them thereby. In August 1713, in a letter, the VOC Council declared itself content with Sa'adatullah, and even with their dealings with his albeschik Dakhni Rai for the most part. They admitted that so far, the factories in southern Coromandel had been relatively peaceful and tranquil during his time, but also expressed scepticism concerning how long this could last, given the fact that the 'Moorish government' was always plagued by a greed for money.[72] In the case of Sa'adatullah Khan too, they were afraid that the desire for money ate away at his bosom (*'de geld sugt in sijnen boesem zo wel als bij andere regenten'*), and that at some time or the other, this would have its effect.

These prejudices were subsequently confirmed in the VOC's eyes by the troublesome affair of Periya Chinna Tambi Maraikkayar, an important Muslim merchant of Porto Novo, who died in 1712, leaving a sum of money that was disputed between his nephews Khoja Maraikkayar, Chinna Chinna Tambi Maraikkayar and Ibrahim Maraikkayar, with the last two having complained to Arcot about the role of the first in the division of the estate (*boedel*). The affair has that baroque quality to it that the VOC's dealings with Indian rulers often did, with small issues being blown out of all proportion. It turned out that the Company was itself directly concerned, to the extent that the former governor Joannes van Steeland had for some reason taken into his charge a chest containing *olais* and accounts of the Maraikkayars, which his heirs claimed had a bearing on their dispute. It was further claimed that the Maraikkayar had personally given the sum of 2600 pagodas (or 15,600 *florins*) to Steeland, a fact that his successors in the Company administration were unwilling to admit.

A considerable correspondence hence developed over the years

1714 and 1715 on the question, with the ḥawaldār of Porto Novo, Venkatarayalu, playing a role therein, to mediate with the new na'ib dīwān at Arcot, Muhammad Sadiq. The comings and goings of emissaries, the exchange of letters with the Company wakīl at Arcot Tiruvengada Ayyan, and the receipt of parwānas is noted in the Dutch factory records, both from the 'Nabab', and from Dakhni Rai's relative, Lala Todar Mal ('den heer Todderamaloe'), who was on his way to collect the peshkash from Tanjavur and Tiruchi in July 1714.[73] We also get a rare glimpse here into the role of other minor Kayastha or Khatri administrators (Madho Das, Beni Das) in the affair. By early September, the VOC Council had decided it was not worthwhile to put their factories in Porto Novo, Sadras and Pulicat at risk over this affair, and it was hence decided to send the sealed chest (which had languished thus far in the Company's warehouse at Nagapattinam) by a special sloop to Porto Novo. However, the money that Van Steeland had reputedly taken proved a more difficult question to resolve, since one suspects that this had to do with his private affairs rather than Company business. The Company's partial capitulation was the result of considerable pressure, for, in August 1714, a party of twelve horsemen and some foot-soldiers had arrived in Porto Novo with a peremptory demand in the name of Sa'adatullah Khan, that Khoja Maraikkayar be handed over to them, and with letters containing further threats.[74] Khoja Maraikkayar is known to have been detained for more than a year thereafter in Arcot, until the matter was settled to the satisfaction of the rival heirs; he eventually returned to Porto Novo from Arcot and Velur only in February 1716, with matters settled more or less to his liking too; his rivals, Chinna Chinna Tambi and Ibrahim Maraikkayar are reported meanwhile to have settled down in Madras or Mylapore.[75]

Finally, in 1715, the Company had to undergo still further humiliation, being obliged at last to hand over the sum of 2600 pagodas that was claimed from Steeland by Sa'adatullah Khan's *chūbdār* ('staff-bearer'), Muhammad Husain, sent expressly for this purpose. The Nagapattinam Council's resolution of 5 February 1715, summed up in a later letter to Batavia, sets out the pros and cons in the affair.[76] On the one hand, the VOC was convinced that the niẓāmat had too much at stake in Dutch trade at Porto Novo and Sadras, which brought in considerable revenues (*redelijk schat*) to Arcot, to actually implement its threats. But, it was argued, even if an interruption of two to three weeks was imposed (by means of an inland blockade) on these factories, two to three months' worth of trade could be lost, in view of the time taken to get back to a state of normalcy, and because of the advances already given out for textile procurement. This loss would hence easily mount to far more than the 15,600 florins that were demanded, indeed so much so that a loss of face could be countenanced to maintain the trade channels. The Dutch were also aware that all was not well in the Khoja Maraikkayar affair from certain other points of view; it turned out that the chest that they had had in their custody (allegedly sealed on Periya Chinna Tambi's death in 1712), had been tampered with, a fact that could thus cause problems if investigated too closely.

Consolidating a kingdom

There was, of course, one remotely possible solution, for the VOC's officials had now begun to hope that sooner or later Sa'adatullah Khan would be recalled by the court to the Deccan, or even to Delhi. The departure of Chin Qilich Khan ('Siglischan') as ṣūbadār of the Deccan, and the arrival of Sayyid Husain 'Ali Khan gave them some more hope, but it was soon dashed; whatever the changes further north, Sa'adatullah Khan was there to stay.[77] The fact that in the early part of Farrukhsiyar's reign he had taken care to send large remittances to Delhi, 14.4 lakhs of rupees and five elephants in one version, 25 lakh rupees and an unspecified number of elephants (*chand fīl*) in another, as well as gifts of semi-precious stones, could only have helped strengthen his case for staying on .[78] In this process of looking to its own rather narrow interests, the Dutch also (rather curiously) forgot to take note of a rather significant set of events that took place in the immediate hinterland of Porto Novo and Sadras in the latter half of 1714, and which marks a significant point of inflection in the consolidation of Sa'adatullah Khan's position.

We refer here to the question of Senji, which has been discussed by us elsewhere at considerable length, not only in its literal aspects (the crushing of a recalcitrant qil'adār), but for its symbolism in terms of redefining the relationship between Sa'adatullah Khan and the very mixed stratum of zamīndārs, some of them members of relatively ancient lineages (like the Velugoti Rajas of Venkatagiri, who were Velamas), others more recent arrivals from the north, most notably Afghans and Rajputs.[79] Let us recall too the particular prestige of Senji, which together with Velur was on older political centre of gravity, besides having the reputation of being an unassailable fortress. It was from Senji that the Telugu Nayakas had ruled over Tondaimandalam, the core of the region that formed the Arcot niẓāmat; and it was here too that the governors of Bijapur had been located after their conquest of the region in 1649, building a number of imposing monuments there. Again, Senji had formed the major locus of Maratha resistance to Mughal designs in the 1690s, frustrating a Mughal siege force for long years until its capitulation in 1698, the year when it came to be renamed Nusratgadh after its conqueror, Zu'lfiqar Khan Nusrat Jang. The Dutch factors who had a long if selective memory, still called the hinterland of Porto Novo and Sadras 'the kingdom of Senji' (*Singijse rijck*) in the eighteenth century. Thus, we insist, the importance, both real and symbolic, of Senji was not a purely partisan invention of Senji Narayanan Pillai, writing his chronicle of the *Karnāṭaka rājākkaḷ* in the early nineteenth century.

The much-reviled qil'adār resident there in the early eighteenth century, Sarup Singh, belonged to a minor Bundela lineage from Jetpur, and was like a number of his clansmen associated with Zu'lfiqar Khan in his campaigns. We have already noted his difficulties with the English Company in Fort St. David in the early 1700s; in contrast, his relations with the Dutch and the French seem to have been relatively free of problems. However, his death in December 1713 precipitated a crisis of some dimensions, for a number of reasons. In a letter of February 1714, the French governor Du Livier at Fort St. Louis in Pondicherry, described the situation in the following terms to his principals in France:

> I have received news of the death of a Gentile Prince called Soubrousingue [Sarup Singh], governing the Gingy country fifteen leagues from here, that he had handed over his Government to his brother while awaiting the return of his son who was at the Court to solicit the continuation [of the qil'adārī], and that the Divan of Chief Intendant named Mathmet Sal [Muhammad Sa'id] had sent 200 horsemen and 500 pions, to extract a considerable sum from the successor of this governor, and the restitution of several villages, that he claims that the late Prince had usurped from the estates of the Mogol, and which he had given to this Company and that of England, as also to the Paliagares [*pāḷaiyakkārars*] or Chiefs of the Forests. It is said that he has so far extracted the sum of 400,000 Rupees which make up 600,000 *livres* in French money, and we assured that he is about to send 100 horsemen and 200 men on foot to seize not only the said villages, but also those which we were given in gift by Daoud Khan, former viceroy of this province, a friend of our nation, and who is at present in Guzerat....[80]

In short, while the Dutch in Porto Novo were preoccupied with Periya Chinna Tambi Maraikkayar's affairs, trouble was brewing in the not-so-distant hinterland. These troubles find echoes in the English records of Fort St. David, and also merited a long series of dispatches from Pondicherry that have been analysed by us elsewhere. Rather than rehearse the perspective of the European records, we shall approach the problem here from another viewpoint, that of Jaswant

Rai's Persian chronicle, which equally devotes considerable attention to the 'conquest' of Senji after the Bundela rebellion there.

To this chronicler, the Senji campaign was a mark of Divine Grace, for it showed that Sa'adatullah Khan was no ordinary mortal, but a man cut out for great things. Thus, his chapter on the revolt of the Bundelas and their alliance with the Marathas (to be found in the second *daftar* of his chronicle) begins by noting the following.

When God, the Eternal and Omnipotent, bestows on anybody age and status from the beginning of (his) existence, and makes him as strong as the foundations of the sky, if someone else, out of short-sightedness, jealousy and malice tries to pull him down, and spares no effort in his vile designs, his efforts will soon come to naught, and in a few days the edifice of his dreams will be washed away, and be uprooted from its foundation. This maxim is best illustrated in the case of Rup Singh, otherwise known as Tej Singh, son of Sarup Singh, son of Mitr Sen, son of Chandrabhan, son of Nar Singh Dev Bundela, who in the peaceful days of Jalal-ud-Din Muhammad Akbar, at the instance of Nur-ud-Din Muhammad Jahangir had killed that savant, that unparalleled mole on the face of the word and poetry, the fragrance of amber on the brow of meanings new and old, the sugar-crunching parrot of the Garden of Revelation (*ilhām*), the singing nightingale of the garden of wisdom (*ifhām*)—may God bless him—Shaikh Abu'l Fazl ibn Mubarak, while he was on his return from the spacious country of the Deccan at a place near Gwalior, which is like the flower-garden of everlasting spring, and had earned for himself, on that account, the contempt and condemnation of both the worlds.[81]

Jaswant Rai thus makes sure that the reader realizes what sort of antecedents these Bundelas had, and, in case the point should have escaped, reiterates, 'And since it is futile to expect good fruit from a bad tree, or try to cultivate in a barren field, his grandson too trod the path of his forbear, as the (Qur'anic) saying has it: Everything ultimately returns to its source'.

The outline of past events is then sketched out. Sarup Singh had 'ruled well for seventeen years' (since the fall of Senji to the Mughals in 1698), and had brought in a large number of Bundelas to aid him; besides Sa'adatullah Khan considered him to be a close associate. However, on his death, his son Tej Singh decided to rebel, by refusing to hand over the prebend (*tuyūl*) to the official (*mutaṣaddī-i pā'ibāqī*) who had been sent to recover it for the royal treasury. Instead, he is reported to have set about repairing the fortress and getting munitions ready; he is equally reported to have had relations with Narada and Mahada, the sons of the Maratha war-leader Baharji Ghorpade, whose raids in the region are mentioned by the Dutch as early as 1707.[82]

Besides offerings to hand over Senji to the Marathas, he is said to have mounted a joint attack with them on the fortress of Satgadh, lying in the interior, in the region controlled by Tahir Muhammad Khan, faujdâr of Sira. The latter complained to Sa'adatullah Khan, who thus left from Velur on his campaign; after a halt at Gudiyattam, he and Tahir Khan defeated their opponents, and went on to Dodballapur. Thereafter, he returned to Velur, deputing Lala Dakhni Rai to take care of the affairs of Senji.

The chronicle now turns its attention to Dakhni Rai's proceedings. He is reported to have first gone to Arni, brought together some forces there, and also sent out spies to enquire on Tej Singh's activities. Gathering that the latter was in no mood for peace, he suggested Sa'adatullah Khan might want to join him from Velur. On the 9 Ramazan 1125 AH, despite the fact that he was fasting, Sa'adatullah Khan set out for the rendezvous at Arni, accompanied by the chronicler Jaswant Rai. At this stage, Sarup Singh's brother, Sultan Singh, who was rather more prudent than his nephew, sent envoys pleading for peace. But Tej Singh himself was unmoved, forcing the Arcot forces to move, first to Chettapattu, and then to Devanur. Still, Sa'adatullah Khan, it is noted, chose peace over war, sending out Lala Todar Mal and three others to parley with Tej Singh, while at the same time awaiting the 'Id, an excellent occasion as it turns out for Jaswant Rai to demonstrate his poetic talents.

Rather than a long drawn-out siege, the affair finished rather quickly. It was early October 1714, the returning north-east monsoon was on the Tamil country, and the Arcot army made its way with some difficulty on that account. Sa'adatullah Khan had, besides his generals such as Daulat Khan Khizrza'i and Imam-ud-Din Khan, the aid of some Maratha auxiliaries under Subhanji, and the Velugoti forces commanded by Bangaru Yachama Nayaka. Further, Jaswant Singh Shekhawat and the versatile Lala Dakhni Rai were also present to lead a part of the expeditionary force. Crossing difficult and marshy ground, the Arcot forces were camped on the banks of the Varahanadi river, when they were suddenly attacked, first by an advance force under a certain Bapu Rai, and then by Tej Singh himself, with a force of a mere one hundred and seventy horsemen. His lightning attack on Sa'adatullah Khan's vanguard very nearly carried the day, and Jaswant Rai himself admits that 'the fate of the battle on that day hung in balance'. He goes on to state, giving this opponent his due, after all that Tej Singh left no stone unturned of prowess, courage and dexterity in the art of war. But since Fate had decreed otherwise, and the Grace of God was with the Nawab, the helper of the poor and the oppressed, Tej Singh fell from his horse wounded and dying, and as many as one hundred and seventy heroes also fell around him.[83]

These bodies were eventually sent back to Senji fort, where the wives of the Rajputs became *satīs*, in a collective conflagration witnessed by Jaswant Rai. Despite some residual resistance on the part of the other Bundelas, the fortress was occupied by the end of 1714, and a new qil'adār appointed. However, Sa'adatullah Khan did not remain long there. Having ordered the construction of a mosque at the foot of the Rajagiri fort, and improvements to the Chettikulam tank, he is reported to have departed on 12 Zi'l Hijja 1125 (early 1715), for Tiruvannamalai. His brother-in-law, Muhammad Shafi' was left there as administrator. Senji would never serve Sa'adatullah Khan as his political capital, for the choice of Arcot had already been made. On the other hand, a particular effort would be made to affirm the symbolic nature of the 're-conquest' in 1714. Besides a victory inscription on the east (Pondicherry) gate, declaring that 'Islam has expelled Infidelity' (*kard islām kufr rā bīrūn*), a mosque was built (as noted above), as also an 'Idgah and a fountain. All of these carry inscriptions of Sa'adatullah Khan within three years of his quelling the Bundela rebellion.[84]

Senji also came to serve another purpose, as a place of incarceration. Thus, in late 1717, the Dutch Council at Nagapattinam reports a rather curious incident, also noted in some of the Persian chronicles. A man allegedly called 'Aqibat Mahmud, but claiming to be the Mughal prince Muhammad Akbar (referred to by the Dutch as 'the legitimate Mogol prince Sulthan Mahometh'), had decided in 1713–14 to make a bid for the Mughal throne, and hence set out for the Deccan (perhaps from Bengal).[85] First wrecked and brought ashore at Srikakulam, he had not found the welcome there to his taste, and decided to head further south. However, after an armed conflict, Sa'adatullah Khan had decided to seize him, and hold him prisoner in Senji, rather than let him continue in his ambitions. This he managed to do, despite the fact that 'Aqibat Mahmud was supported in his endeavours by a number of local pāḷaiyakkārars. One of his representatives, a Telugu Brahmin, had however managed to escape, and wrote letters from Devanampattinam to the Dutch, asking them for help to set his master free, offering them the total control of the ports of Masulipatnam, Karedu, Ramayyapatnam, Pulicat, Sadrasapatnam, and Porto Novo, in exchange.[86] The Company prudently declined, but it is noteworthy that Sa'adatullah Khan too would give no room for such adventurism. His role was to watch developments at the Mughal centre, and play his cards with prudence to consolidate his regional position; adventurism on a grand pan-Indian scale was simply not his style.

Nevertheless, with the capture of Senji,and the defeat of a powerful combination of zamīndārī and Maratha interests, there is a perceptible change in Sa'adatullah Khan's level of confidence and the nature and extent of his projects. To be sure, he remained in the latter half of the 1710s (and even later) vulnerable to Maratha attacks, buying off threats from the Ghorpades and others on more than one occasion. However, it is clear that a concerted attempt was now made to go beyond the idea of a mere conquest-state. True, the idea of frontier state-building remains: Sa'adatullah Khan continues his own (or his representatives') annual peshkash-gathering expeditions to Tiruchi and Tanjavur on the one hand, and, albeit less regularly, to Mysore on the other. But a new wave of market-building and a renewed and vigorous presence in the ports of the sea-coast is visible, with the idea of placing Arcot at the centre of not merely a fiscal but a commercial network.

However, we should not leave the reader with the impression that consolidating the 'kingdom' of Arcot was a matter of trade alone. Sa'adatullah Khan, on replacing Schafi' Khan as dīwān of both the Karnataks, had made a particular effort at fiscal management, if we are to believe Jaswant Rai. He had had fiscal details prepared for each village, with the aid of *deshmukhs*, *deshpandes* and *kulkarnis*. Equally, the *chaukīs* were systematically strengthened, while markets, bazaars, and such centres were put under the overall charge of a nā'ib dīwān with a mutaṣaddi in charge of each one. A *dastūr* (or regulation) was defined for the traders (*bepārīs*), and at the same time, details of all the prebends of all manṣabdārs in the region were also made ready. The man who was initially placed in charge of many of these operations was a certain 'Alam Chand Khatri from the Punjab.[87] But Sa'adatullah Khan also made every effort to make Arcot appear to be a courtly centre, as well as taking upon himself the image of a ruler. The chronicle that he commissioned is unsparing in its details, telling us about his daily schedule as if he were no less than a minor monarch. This was already during Aurangzeb's lifetime, and was clearly still another of the sources of conflict between Sa'adatullah Khan and Da'ud Khan Panni.

From about 1710, Sa'adatullah Khan and those allied with him had spared no effort to transform and improve Arcot even further. Tanks had been dug, and trees planted; new and exotic fruits and vegetables had been brought in and planted in places such as the special gardens called Humayun Bagh and Nau Jahan Bagh. In Jaswant Rai's vision, the city had become full of gardens, while a number of new *ḥavelīs* too had been made inside the qil'a. Indeed, it is noted that Da'ud Khan's old ḥavelī had now proven inadequate, so that Muhammad Sharif, the *mīr-i 'imārat,* was asked to supervise a new ḥavelī on the edge of a tank, outside the fort. While not on campaign, here is how the chronicler describes, in an idealized form, the life led by Sa'adatullah Khan in this prosperous new centre. Rising in the morning, he is said to begin the day by reading Qur'an and theology. Then he went on to the *dīwānī,* to take care of fiscal affairs, and to conduct discussions with the *'ulamā'*. At mid-day, after prayers, he is portrayed first meditating alone, and then meeting persons concerned with the administration. Interestingly, these included *faqīrs* and dervishes, poor widows and other needy persons, in a series of activities that culminated with the late afternoon prayer. Now, at last, there was a bit of physical exercise in the polo (*chaugān*) field, and Sa'adatullah Khan and his friends also engage in martial activities. As the lamps would come on, he would listen to poetry, stories and history, with men such as the celebrated Shaikh Muhammad Amin ibn Bani Isra'il of Meerut.[88] After the last prayer, he usually returned home, but at times there was music by men such as La'l Khan Dholakiya Zu'lfiqarkhani and his sons; in the court was also resident a certain Jan Sen, who claimed to be descended from no less a personage than Miyan Tansen, as well as another musician, Hasan Khan Kalawant Mukhliskhani from Aurangabad. At times, the works of great poets were heard, and these included Mirza 'Abdul Qadir Bedil, Nasir 'Ali Sarhindi, and some Deccani poets such as Nusrati. A particular annual feature was the celebration of Muharram in Arcot. *Marṣīyas* were read in the Deccani tongue, and in this month the Nawab asserted his identity as a Shi'a.[89]

We are aware that one of Sa'adatullah Khan's pet projects after the fall of Senji was the idea of building a fortified port-town, in imitation of, and as a riposte to, the European efforts in that direction (and perhaps not unlike Da'ud Khan's earlier plans for Mylapore). As it turns out, the European menace finds repeated mention in Jaswant Rai's chronicle. Already, while discussing the fall of Velur into Mughal hands in 1702, he notes that the expedition against the fort were in part due to the fact that the emperor's orders concerning the coming and going of ships (*jahāzāt*) were not properly executed. The man who held charge of Velur on behalf of Rajaram, a certain Sankarji Malharji (mentioned briefly above), was suspected of relations with the Europeans in the ports of the Karnatak (*kulāh-poshān-i banādir-i darya kanār-i Karnātak dayār*) who for their part were notorious for creating all sorts of problems with their invidious dealings.[90] A decade later, just before the capture of Senji, mention is similarly made of the link between hinterland politics and the Europeans (notably the English) perched on the coast in their enclaves. In particular, there are references to Sa'adatullah Khan's military expeditions against the powerful pāḷaiyakkārar Chellappa Nayaka (called '*Chīl Ẕalīl*', or 'Chil, the mean' in the chronicle), who from his base near Tiruvannamalai had build links with the 'hat-wearers' (*kulāh-poshān*), creating considerable trouble in the towns and villages around Senji, by attacking old hereditary zamīndârs as well as traders and travellers from Tiruchi, Tanjavur and Rameswaram.[91] Da'ud Khan had proved incapable of controlling the depredations of this man, and finally it had as usual fallen to Lala Dakhni Rai and his relatives to take care of the matter.

All of this provides us with useful background material, showing that maritime affairs were a lasting concern of Sa'adatullah Khan, who came moreover from stock that had always laid stress of both *tijārat* (trade) and *zara'at* (agriculture).[92] His choice in terms of a port from which to make a statement fell on Kovalam (Covelong), a port a few miles to the north of Sadrasapatnam, where the VOC had one of its important factories. In 1717, the process of building Sa'adat Pattan (or Bandar) began, a port to which the Arcot régime made every effort to attract both local and distant merchants, much to the unhappiness of both the English and Dutch. The *Sa'id Nāma* has a fairly elaborate discussion, both of the circumstances leading to the foundation, and the act of foundation itself. Jaswant Rai approaches the issue indirectly, by noting the existence of conflicts between the faujdār Dayaram and the English in Madras, which he attibutes to the fact that the *firangīs* of the town (which he terms Chinnapattan) had begun to construct buildings between their place of residence and Mylapore. The unruly elements (*aubāshān*) of the town of Madras had encouraged the English in this design, and once the conflict became open, the Europeans had managed to defeat Dayaram, and in the process his son Basant Rai had been killed. The Persian chronicler goes on to note that Dayaram had been supported throughout in this struggle by Sayyid 'Usman (or Qadir 'Ali Khan), who was resident at Mylapore. As for Sa'adatullah Khan himself, we are left with the impression that he had always had reservations concerning Dayaram's actions in this regard, as well as those of Qadir 'Ali Khan.[93]

Nevertheless, Jaswant Rai would have us believe that as a consequence of conflicts such as that described above, Sa'adatullah

Khan was rather concerned with finding means of dealing with the Europeans. Once certain pressing affairs in the Balaghat had been settled, the chronicle's attention turns first to the process of building *peths* in the interior, an activity that was apparently supported in the period by a powerful (and, thus far, rather obscure) magnate-figure, a certain Baisaji Bhakariya.[94] Lala Dakhni Rai too is known to have taken a lively interest in the matter through the construction of the important new interior market-town of Sa'adat Nagar (founded on 10 Zu'l-qada 1126 AH, and completed the following year), at three *kos* distance from Arcot. In it, there were not merely shops for Hindus and Muslims, and resthouses for travellers, but reservoirs, bunds and gardens.[95]

All of this serves as a preamble for the main action that concerns us, namely the actual decision to build up Sa'adat Pattan or Sa'adat Bandar which Jaswant Rai suggests was taken in 1130 AH. It was not that there was a particular shortage of ports in Payanghat, he notes, but the problem with the European 'hat-wearers' of Chinnapattan and elsewhere was great in a number of them. Given that their fortress was protected by the sea, they had become arrogant over time; even large traders resident in Bandar Mylapore had problems with them. Hence, Sa'adatullah Khan in the goodness of his heart had thought that building a port with his own name (the name of a man who had, in his time, broken the *kulāh-poshān*) near Mylapore, with a goodly fort, and lovely buildings, with Hindu and Muslim quarters, would help settle the matter. In fact, this question had, in Jaswant Rai's view, been dear to his master's heart for a long time, but it was only now that he had brought it before Dakhni Rai. The ever-active Dakhni Rai hence chose a site and invited him there to inspect it; the Nawab made his visit duly, praised God at the sea's shore, and gave Jaswant Rai an occasion to compose further poetry.[96] The Christian churches in the vicinity were inspected, and specific mention is made of the Armenian churches, which were rather different from those of the Europeans. The chronicler's curiosity extends towards the nearby Europeans too, and he notes having seen the beautiful European women, and observed their evening parties.[97] The Nawab's party thus fell to exchanging and reciting poetry, profiting from the presence of various other notables on the occasion; the main subject around which their poetic imaginations revolved was that, inevitably, of the topos of *firang,* the land of the Franks. Soon after this visit, the chronicler notes, work began in earnest; gardens were constructed, buildings were put up, and eminent traders were brought in to settle there. As for Sa'adatullah Khan, having left his subordinates in charge of the affair, he apparently returned to Arcot via Kanchi, reflecting all the while on the need to build way-stations, and houses, in order to facilitate trade and merchant activity. Besides Dakhni Rai, it is noted that a certain Qadir Husain Khan Yazna played a major role in the affair, which took on a greater urgency after the formal inauguration of Sa'adat Pattan, at a suitably auspicious time on Thursday, 12 Rajab 1131. On this day, the fort and the palace had their foundations laid, and the new name given officially to the town; it is noted that merchants, whether Indians, Southeast Asians, Armenians and European, were encouraged to settle there, and bring big ships to trade.[98] Once the construction had been completed, the Nawab himself visited the spot in order to reassure the traders on Saturday, 29 Shawwal 1131. There, however, he learnt of rebellions among the local pāḷaiyakkārars, and had to leave post-haste to attend to them, after having remained a mere two days in Sa'adat Pattan; on his departure, it is noted that he was accompanied by the commander of the Tiruchi forces, Ramanna.

The delights of the high-flown literary description of Jaswant Rai aside, it is clear that this was not a project that eventually enjoyed a great success though. Of the Europeans, the only ones who participated in it were the Ostenders, who had arrived off the Coromandel coast in May 1719 in their ship *Keyser Carolus VI*. The Dutch were little enthused by the presence of this new set of European traders, who were likely to bid up the prices of procurement in their view. The comportment of the commander of the Ostenders, the St Malo-based Frenchman Godefroy de la Merveille, failed to work marvels on them, and they were distressed by the very large sum of Rs 80,000 the Ostenders reportedly paid Sa'adatullah Khan to be allowed to settle in Kovalam (Sa'adat Pattan) and Porto Novo.[99] Matters were worsened from the VOC viewpoint by the fact that it was a famine year in the area north of the Kollidam as far as Pulicat, so that despite imports of rice from the Kaveri delta, it was proving difficult to have weavers meet orders. More rivalry was the last thing the Dutch Company, never noted for its competitive spirit at the best of times, wanted at this time. The very rapid failure of Sa'adat Pattan can be explained by a series of factors. By the late 1710s, the situation was even less propitious for a new port, operating outside of European networks in southern Coromandel, than a decade earlier. On the one hand, there was Madras, on the other Pondicherry and Nagapattinam, which straddled the space in which other ports such as Kovalam tried to breathe. The surviving ports from which Indian shipowners operated were enclaves of communities such as the

Maraikkayars, namely Porto Novo and Naguru, and their relative weight in the external trade remains a matter of debate.

The remaining years of Sa'adatullah Khan's career that are recounted in the *Sa'īd Nāma* (which finishes abruptly in 1723) continue to harbour instances of conflicts with Europeans, and especially the English at Madras (Chinnapattan). Jaswant Rai reports how in 1723, the Nawab, who at that time was visiting Sa'adat Pattan, had decided to pay an impromptu visit to Mylapore, staying en route at a place that the chronicler terms Firangi Kot. Reaching Mylapore in the morning, Sa'adatullah Khan sojourned in the house and garden of Aqa Muqim, *mutaṣaddī* of the port (who also bore the title of Ahsan Khan). Traders from the ports used the occasion to come and visit the Nawab and offer presents; a stern message was equally sent out to the Madras governor to pay up arrears of tribute that were due to Arcot. Mention is equally made of Rama Chetty and Loachma Rao Sahu (two resident merchants of Madras) who possessed great buildings in many of the ports of the coast, and were apparently leading traders in the Karnatak. However, since they had become exceedingly arrogant as a result of English protection, the Nawab was obliged to send them a message to bring them down to earth too, from the 'wine of arrogance' they had drunk.[100] While the English and those under their protection were viewed with particular discontent, troubles with the Dutch too came to the surface in this period. In Aprill 1722, a letter from Sa'adatullah Khan to the Dutch Governor in Nagapattinam, Gerrit Westrenen noted for example that the former had sent his chûbdâr, a certain Shitab Khan, and several other subordinates to Jaffna and Colombo for the purchase of elephants and other goods; these men had been ill-treated by the Dutch there, and even imprisoned. The nāẓim thus voiced his unhappiness in no uncertain terms, for this was still another instance of European recalcitrance.[101]

From Sa'adat Pattan to Sidi Jauhar Bandar

As Jaswant Rai's chronicle draws to a close in the years 1134/1723, we learn of the return of Sa'adatullah Khan from his visit to the coast and to gather peshkash, and his entry into Arcot on Friday 21 Sha'aban. But appropriately, the last references in the text are to the Nawab's *alter ego,* Lala Dakhni Rai (who has now been exalted in status to Rai Dakhni Ram), and who after a visit to Vishnu Kanchi and Siva Kanchi returned to the capital a day after his master. We learn moreover that his wife had died on Friday, 11 Rajab 1134; and that he was being persuaded by his friends to marry the daughter of Madari Lal from Hyderabad, an event that eventually occurred on 5 Ramazan 1134.

Interestingly, the re-marriage of Dakhni Rai also finds mention in the Dutch records, in the context of the rapidly declining fortunes of Sa'adat Pattan (or 'Kouwelang', as the Dutch factors continued to call it). The Dutch factors at Sadrasapatnam, Van Outvelt and Turnhout, reported the imminent visit of 'de heer Nabab' and 'zinn duan Deckenaraijen' to the 'town and fortress of Kowalam' in late March 1723, noting besides that they were very likely to pay a visit to the Dutch factory on their return. As usual, wrangles began on the giving of gifts, which the messengers from Arcot hinted strongly should be given; the Dutch factors for their part could offer only some scarlet, rosewater and sandalwood. Then, on 5 April, news arrived that the Nawab had left Lalapettai (perhaps a market-town named for Lala Dakhni Rai), for Kaveripak, and that Dakhni Rai (who had been held up for a day or two 'due to a heathen festival') would soon join him. The Dutch factors took the occasion to ruminate on the fate of Sa'adat Pattan.

> From Kowelang, the last reports state that the palce and the little fort (*kasteeltje*) put up there, are in great dilapidation, and the bulwarks have all caved in; some 80 houses have been abandoned by their owners, 70 still stand covered with their tiles, and 115 with straw; of 80 boutiques only 30 are still used, and all the buildings are in very bad shape, but now with the rumoured arrival of the Nabab there, the inhabitants are being forced by the son of the regent with violence to repair their houses. The Ostenders are still there, three persons strong besides a priest (*paap*); their chief now once again obtains 100 ropias per month for his expenses from the above-mentioned regent [or] his son. He knows how to keep the natives continually fed with the hope of the imminent arrival of their ships. So, he says he has received letters from there, and spreads it about that in such and such a place a certain number of ships are ready, and in this way manages to carry on. How long this can last, one cannot say with certainty...[102]

The Dutch governor at Nagapattinam, Westrenen, in a slightly later missive (of September the same year), notes not only the visit in question but the particular need to give a substantial present (*een sinal geschenkji*) to Dakhni Rai 'to felicitate him for his marriage'.

Thus, despite this obstinate show of interest, by 1723, the Sa'adat Pattan project was no longer viable, even if it has been noted that 'Pathan' merchants from the coast continued to use the port to a limited extent as late as the 1730s.[103] True, Kovalam continued to play an administrative role into the end of the 1720s, and we note the role played by the faujdâr resident there, a certain Bada Sahib, in the years around 1728.[104] Meanwhile, we may note that Sa'adatullah Khan's interests obliged him to turn elsewhere. The year 1724 witnessed a substantial crisis in Deccan politics, with the defeat of the sūbadār Mubariz Khan by Nizam-ul-mulk Asaf Jah, who managed as a consequence to impose himself on Arcot as a superior authority. Since we are aware that Arcot chose to support Mubariz Khan in this struggle (despatching Diler Khan, Ghalib Khan and 'Abd-un-Nabi Khan Miyana to fight at Shakar Kheda), Sa'adatullah Khan obviously found himself awkwardly placed in the affair.[105] The next year, troubles in the Mysore area reared their head, and the nāẓim was obliged himself to lead an expedition there against the Wodeyars.[106]

Finally, the second half of the 1720s we see a rearrangement in Arcot politics of which we can only dimly glimpse the outlines. The fortunes of the Khatri magnates who had so clearly dominated the previous fifteen years are somewhat on the wane now (with the possible exceptions of first, Khub Chand, and second 'Alam Chand Khatri), and new figures may be found jockeying for power. Amongst these was Ghulam Imam Husain Khan (or 'Imam Sahib'), who would play a major rōle in the Arcot area with a direct interest in trade at the French port of Pondicherry through the 1730s, eventually leaving to be named faujdār of Masulipatnam under Nizam-ul-mulk in about 1740.[107] In 1728, it was Ghulam Imam Husain Khan who was named qil'adār of a new fortress to be built at the coast in Alambaram, just south of Sadrasapatnam. The project is redolent of the earlier attempt at Sa'adat Pattan, save that on this occasion the nāẓim did not sink his own prestige into it directly. Rather he left matters on the one hand to Qadir Husain Khan, and on the other to a notable whose name suggests his Abyssinian origins, namely Sidi Jauhar Khan. The latter is reported by the Dutch in September 1728, who were as before distressed by the affair, to have decided to build a 'stronghold or fortress' there, on a flat space created by the dunes, 'made up with five bulwarks, with its front extending to the north'. The front of this fortress would be very close to the area where the Dutch Company was asked to build a factory, indeed it would lie right by the place where the nāẓim's flag would fly. Furthermore, it is noted that a number of leading merchants from Arcot had been asked to participate in building up the port, to be called Sidi Jauhar Bandar. They included Shankar Parikh, Venkatapati Chetti, Sunku Narayanappa Chetti, Sunnampettai Rama Chetti, as also men such as the leading *ṣarrāf* Sangana, as well as a certain 'Samarauw', described as Sidi Jauhar Khan's factotum (albeschik). As many as forty-two new houses were under construction, half for various unnamed Arcot merchants, others for men like 'Samarauw' and his brother Baba Rao, the ḥawaldār Dhondhu Pandit, as well as the leading merchants mentioned above.[108]

We are aware that although Sa'adatullah Khan asked the French

Company, among others, to participate in making the new port a success, Sidi Jauhar Bandar too had a rather limited success. Sinnappah Arasaratnam notes that Sidi Jauhar Khan went very far in his effort to establish the port, 'abolished all customs on imports and exports for five years, and all inland import duties from there to Arcot'.[109] Further north along the coast, members of Sa'adatullah Khan's own family, such as Baqir 'Ali Khan continued to evince a considerable interest in these very years in providing a countervailing force to that of the Europeans so far as maritime trade was concerned.[110] These efforts continued beyond the death of the old warrior Sa'adatullah Khan himself on 8 October 1732, and in 1734 (when the departing Dutch governor Adriaan Pla left a memoir for his successor), the men to reckon with were still Sidi Jauhar Khan and his trusted subordinate ('desselfs vertrouwde') Imam Sahib.[111] Indeed, the former had just received confirmation from the Mughal court (or so the Dutch stated) of his extensive control of the coastal region stretching from Pulicat to Alambaram. Less than a decade later, by the early 1740s, however, the political climate in the region would be completely transformed. Men like Ghulam Imam Husain Khan would now be obliged to find a niche for themselves further north, in the territories directly controlled by Nizam-ul-mulk, and even this could not last into the 1750s. A new political dispensation would be put into place in Arcot (with the ascension of the Walajah dynasty under English patronage), and control over the activites of the kulāh-poshān would now be a distant thought for participants in the political system.

Conclusion

Between the 1960s and the early 1980s, the years during which Ashin Das Gupta published both *Malabar in Asian Trade, 1740–1800,* and *Indian Merchants and the Decline of Surat, c. 1700–1750,* a rather clear division of labour existed in the field of 'medieval Indian history' between maritime historians and land-lubbers.[112] The former worked largely with European records, the latter with indigenous ones (including those in Persian). The former concerned himself or herself with the fate of port-cities, and of the manufacturing centres around them, the latter with agrarian production, peasants, prebend-holders and inland cities. True, William Foster's *The English Factories in India* was there for all to pillage at will, but for the rest, the worlds and sources of the twain did not meet. This arrangement, which seems for a quarter-century to have appeared largely satisfactory to all concerned, was challenged in the course of the 1980s by a number of authors. For this challenge to fructify, some conceptual changes were necessary, and in the first place the assumption that the world of inland politics existed as a separate and autarchic domain, which could be invoked as a *deus ex machina* to 'explain' the rise and fall of trading systems was called into question. We are, as it happens, still at the questioning stage, but gradually accumulating studies have helped break down the disciplinary Berlin Wall erected in the 1960s. It is now possible to pose even the history of inland regions in relation to the problem of trade routes and the control over them, rather than simply assume that the agrarian overlords who controlled such regions regarded trade with disdain for reasons of caste ideology, steppe mentality, or whatever else.[113] Our essay has thus tried, in spite of its many limitations, to further this methodological *entente*, by deliberately juxtaposing the 'internal' and 'external' perspectives.

Readers of the above pages would naturally have been struck by possible parallels with the rather better-known case of the Bengal niẕāmat (evoked at the outset), where too a process of 'regional centralization' with implications for the control of external trade was begun by Murshid Quli Khan.[114] Some similar *dramatis personae* can be found in the two cases, from the Khatris (who founded some powerful zamîndârîs in Bengal), to the Armenians, as well as other groups operating within the overarchinng Mughal system as it still functioned in the early eighteenth century. We shall not pursue this comparison further here, and content ourselves merely with noting that as the Mughal centre was weakening under Farrukhsiyar and Muhammad Shah, the strategies and institutions associated with Mughal rule were often gaining hold in the peripheries. As two maritime provinces, Bengal and the Karnatak Payanghat often presented similar opportunities to ambitious notables, be they Afghans, Nawayats or Shaikhzadas.

Yet, in the case of the Karnatak Payanghat, the picture has often been clouded by the persistent view that the years after the 1680s represent a phase of more-or-less unremitting gloom. In even the relatively nuanced picture presented by S. Arasaratham for the years up to 1740, we are left with a view of 'the breakdown of hinterland administration, the consequent disruption of communication between port and hinterland, the impoverishment of merchant groups, [and] the declining profitability of trade'; elsewhere, we hear from him of 'the messy process of the establishment of Mughal administration over the Karnatak [which] seems to have ... [caused] an increase in the number of inland customs posts along major land routes and in and out of major market towns'.[115] Arasaratnam does qualify this view, particularly in relation to what he depicts as the conspicuous success of 'Pathan' merchants trading out of São Tomé in these very years, but the overall image of Mughal expansion in the region leading to a collapse in the commercial potential of the hinterland lingers. Contrasted to this is the view presented in a recent work by the historian of French trade in the Indian Ocean, Catherine Manning: for here, S'adatullah Khan is portrayed as a ruler who 'efficiently centralised and organized his administration', controlled all the key strategic nodes in his domain, and campaigned energetically to raise resources so that he could 'maintain his army and bureaucracy and pay the necessary tribute to Hyderabad'. Indeed, writes Manning, Sa'adatullah Khan's 'policies were in many ways textbook examples of the building of a successor state under the shelter of Mughal rule'.[116]

On the face of it, our position may appear rather closer to that of Manning than of Arasaratnam, even if we are not perfectly sure of what the 'textbook' in question really was. Of course, we should caution against being seduced by the rhetoric and the triumphalist rhymed prose of Jaswant Rai; but it is nevertheless the prose, we must stress, of a chronicler associated with an expanding rather than a declining state. The Arcot niẕāmat was not created by the energy of its Nawayat ruler or the literary alchemy of his chronicler, but by a combination of circumstances, and the intervention of a number of groups, including some that were relatively new to the Tamil landscape. As a centralizing regional dispensation, with the potential of a substantial coastline before it, the drive to the control of the ports was a natural outgrowth of the niẕāmat's consolidation. But its European opponents were already rather too well-entrenched by 1710 for them to be dislodged summarily from their coastal settlements, or even brought around to substantially less recalcitrant behaviour. To compete with them was possible either for communities with a well-defined trading niche (thus, the Maraikkayars of Porto Novo or Naguru), or exceptionally for groups such as the mysterious 'Pathans' of São Tomé, whose internal articulation as a community is one of a number of questions that surely deserve closer investigation.[117] The eventual consequences of this slowly shifting balance of commercial and political power would surface suddenly, in the middle years of the century. The nāẕims of the 1710s and 1720s would thus be transformed, within a generation of their deaths, into the representatives of a rather distant Ancien Régime. And chroniclers in Persian and Tamil as diverse as Burhan Khan Handi and Senji Narayanan Pillai would be left to ruefully recall the 'good old days', of Da'ud Khan Panni and Sa'adatulah Khan.

NOTES

*: *Acknowledgements:* We are grateful to Jaivir Singh and Jatinder Gurbax Singh for having brought the interest of the *Sa'īd Nāma* to our notice, and having provided us with a microfilm of the text. This essay forms part of an ongoing project on the history of the fortress of Nusratgadh Senji and the Arcot region, and the problem of 'régimes of historicity' in eighteenth-century South India.

1. Robert Mantran, 'Transformation du commerce dans 1 'Empire ottoman dans le dix-huitième siècle', in Thomas Naff and Roger Owen, (eds), *Studies in Eighteenth Century Islamic History,* Carbondale, 1977, p. 235 (original citation in French).

2. See, for example, the recent account in John R. McLane, *Land and local Kingship in Eighteenth-century Bengal,* Cambridge, 1993.

3. Cf. H.H. Dodwell, *Dupleix and Clive: The Beginnings of Empire,* London, 1926.

4. Ashin Das Gupta, 'Trade and politics in 18th-century India', in D.S. Richards, (ed.), *Islam and the Trade of Asia,* Philadelphia, 1970, p.202, reprinted in Das Gupta, *Merchants of Maritime India, 1500–1800,* Aldershot, 1994.

5. J. Frederick Price and K. Rangachari, (eds), *The Private Diary of Ananda Ranga Pillai, Dubash to Joseph Francois Dupleix, Governor of Pondicherry,* 12 vols, Madras, 1904–28; for one of the copies of the rather more extensive Tamil manuscript, Bibliotheque Nationale de France, Paris, Mss. Tamoul 144–53, *Ānandaraṅgappiḷḷaiti ṉasaridai,* 12 vols More recently, for the years 1778 to 1792, we have another published diary (albeit of lesser interest), Ma. Kopalakichnan, (ed.), *Iraṇṭām Vīrānāyakkar Nāṭkuṟippu (1778–92),* Chennai/Madras, 1992.

6. S. Arasaratnam, *Merchants, Companies and Commerce on the Coromandel Coast, 1650–1740,* Delhi, 1986. For the debate around this work, see Sanjay Subrahmanyam, 'Asian Trade and European Affluence? : Coromandel, 1650 to 1740', *Modern Asian Studies,* vol. XXII, No. 1, 1988, pp.179–88, and the reply by Arasaratnam, 'Coromandel revisited: Problems and issues on Indian maritime history', *The Indian Economic and Social History Review,* vol. XXVI, No. 1, 1989. The narrative is continued more recently, within roughly the same paradigm, in S. Arasaratnam, *Maritime Commerce and English Power: Southeast India, 1750–1800,* New Delhi, 1996.

7. This idea was further explored in Bhaswati Bhattacharya, 'The Dutch East India Company and the Trade of the Chulias in the Bay of Bengal in the Late Eighteenth Century', in K.S. Mathew, (ed.), *Mariners, Merchants and Oceans: Studies in Maritime History,* New Delhi, 1995, pp.347–61.

8. Ashin Das Gupta, 'India and the Indian Ocean in the 18th century', in A. Das Gupta and M.N. Pearson, (eds), *India and the Indian Ocean, 1500–1800,* Calcutta, 1987, pp.131–61, citations on pp.146–7.

9. For this transition, see the remarks in Catherine Manning, *Fortunes à Faire: The French in Asian Trade, 1719–48,* Aldershot, 1996, pp.206–8. For a related case-study from an area slightly further south, see Sanjay

Subrahmanyam, 'The Politics of Fiscal Decline: A Reconsideration of Maratha Ṭanjavur, 1676–1799', *The Indian Economic and Social History Review,* vol. XXXII, No. 2, 1995, pp.177–217.

10. Cf. the important analysis in Noboru Karashima, *Towards a New Formation: South India under Vijayanagar Rule,* Delhi, 1992, pp.15–63; also David Shulman and Sanjay Subrahmanyam, 'The men who would be king?—The politics of expansion in early 17th century northern Tamilnadu', *Modern Asian Studies,* vol. XXIV, No. 2, 1990, pp.225–48.

11. For details, see V. Narayana Rao, David Shulman and Sanjay Subrahmanyam, *Symbols of Substance: Court and State in Nayaka-period Tamil Nadu,* Delhi, 1992, pp.82–112.

12. Cf. the extensive discussion of these questions in Sanjay Subrahmanyam, *The Political Economy of Commerce: Southern India, 1500–1650,* Cambridge, 1990.

13. For details, see Jagadish Narayan Sarkar, *The Life of Mir Jumla, the General of Aurangzeb,* 2nd edition, New Delhi, 1979.

14. For details, see the correspondence in Shaikh Abu'l Fath Qabil Khan, *Ādāb-i'Alamgīrī,* (ed.) 'Abdul Ghafur Chaudhuri, 2 vols, Lahore, 1971, vol. I, pp.168–73, 269–71, 305–8, 346–7. For an earlier discussion, also see Sanjay Subrahmanyam, 'an Eastern *El-Dorado:* The Tirumala–Tirupati Temple-complex in Early European Views and Ambitions, 1540–1660', in David Shulman, (ed.), *Syllables of Sky: Studies in South Indian Civilization in Honour of Velcheru Narayana Rao,* Delhi, 1995, pp.338–90.

15. Political details may be found in H.K. Sherwani, *History of the Quṭb Shāhi Dynasty,* New Delhi, 1974, pp.448–62, 626–34.

16. Sherwani, *Quṭb Shāhi Dynasty,* pp.655–6, citing Girdharilal Ahqar, *Tārīkh-i Ẓafarah,* Gorakhpur, 1927 (compiled in 1771–72, on the basis of late seventeenth-century data).

17. For an excellent discussion, see J.F. Richards, 'The Hyderabad Karnatik, 1687–1707', *Modern Asian Studies,* vol. IX, 1975, pp.241–60; also, more generally, the discussion in J.F. Richards, *Mughal Administration in Golconda,* Oxford, 1875.

18. Some details may be found in M.A. Nayeem, 'Mughal documents relating to the *Peshkash* of the Zamindars of South India, 1694–1752', *The Indian Economic and Social History Review,* vol. XII, No. 4, 1975, pp.425–32.

19. Yachama Nayaka (or Naidu) was a member of the well-known Velugoti family of Telugu warriors, of the Velama caste and the Recherla *gotra;* for details of this family, later better known as the Rajas of Venkatagiri, see N. Venkataramanayya, (ed.), *Velugōṭivāri vaṃsāvali,* Madras, 1939, and the discussion in Shulman and Subrahmanyam, 'The men who would be king?', cited above.

20. Cf. M.A. Nayeem, *Mughal Administration of Deccan under Nizamul Mulk Asaf Jah (1720–48 AD),* Bombay, 1985, pp.104–26.

21. Mir Isma'il Khan Abjadi, *Kullīyāt-i-Abjadī,* 3 vols, (eds) S. Muhammad Husayn Nainar and Muhammad Husayn Mahvi, Madras, 1944–51, vol.I (for the *Anwar Nāma*).

22. Munshi Burhan Khan Handi, *Tūzak-i Wālājāhī,* (ed.) T. Chandrasekharan and Syed Hamza Hosain Omari, Madras, 1957, p.68; *Tūzak-i Wālābjābī of Burhān ibn Hasan,* tr. S. Muhammad Husayn Nainar, vol. I, Madras, 1934, pp.59–60.

23. See the contemporary account by Bhimsen, *Nuskha-i Dilkusha,* tr. Jadunath Sarkar, in V.G. Khobrekar, (ed.), *Sir Jadunath Sarkar Birth Centenary Commemoration Volume: English Translation of Tārīkh-i-Dilkasha (Memoirs of Bhimsen Relating to Aurangzib's Deccan Campaigns),* Bombay, 1972, pp.200–1, 206.

24. Burhan, *Tūzak* (text), p.72; *Tūzak* (translation), p.64.

25. *Karnāṭaka rājākkaḷ cavistāra carittiram,* (ed.) V.R. Ramachandra Dikshitar, Madras, 1952.

26. *Karnāṭaka rājākkaḷ cavistāra carittiram,* pp.42–3.

27. Saqui Must'ad Khan, *Ma'āsir-i 'Alamgīrī: A History of the Emperor Aurangzib-'Alamgīr (Reign 1658–1707 AD),* tr. Jadunath Sarkar, reprint, Calcutta, 1986, pp.137–8. For later details of Da'ud Khan's career, see pp.260 (1700), 298–9 (1705), *passim.*

28. Muhammad Hashim Khafi Khan, *Muntakhab ul-Lubāb,* 2 vols, eds. K.D. Ahmad and T. Wolseley Haig, Calcutta, 1869, vol. II, pp.750–4.

29. Muhammad Hadi Kamwar Khan, *Tazkirat-us-Salāṭīn Chaghtā,* (ed.) Muzaffar Alam, Bombay, 1980, p. 212–3; 'Dāvud Khān Pannīci bakhar', in *Sanshodhan,* vol. XVIII, Nos. 3–4, 1949, pp.113–17.

30. Ashin Das Gupta, *Indian Merchants and the Decline of Surat, c. 1700–1750,* Wiesbaden, 1979, reprint, New Delhi, 1994, ch. 2.

31. Algemeen Rijksarchief, The Hague (henceforth ARA), Overgekomen Brieven en Papieren (henceforth OBP), VOC, 1664, 'Translaet brief door de heer Kistnosie Pandiet uijt het moors leger voor Mandras ... den 3en Meij 1702 ontfangen', pp.197–9.

32. Niccolao Manucci [Nicolò Manuzzi], *Mogul India, or Storia do Mogor,* tr. William Irvine, 4 vols, London, 1907–8, reprint, Delhi, 1990, vol. III, pp.369–70. Unfortunately, the full original text of Manucci has never been published, only the earlier sections thereof. For these sections (which do not include vols III and IV of the translation), see Piero Falchetta. (ed.), *Storia del Mogol di Nicolò Manuzzi veneziano,* 2 vols, Milan, 1986.

33. For details from the English documents of the period, see Henry Davison Love, *Vestiges of Old Madras, 1640–1800: Traced from the East India Company's Records preserved at Fort St. George and the India Office, and from Other sources,* 3 vols, London, 1913, especially vols I and II.

34. Manucci, *Storia,* vol. III, p.274.

35. Ibid., vol. IV, p.123.

36. Arasaratnam, *Merchants, Companies and Commerce,* pp.171–2. Note that the Persian chronicles too develop this association (practically a cliché in Tamilnadu today), between Afghans and money-lending (*istiqrāẓ);* cf. the chronicle of Jaswant Rai cited below (especially fl. 133b).

37. Of obvious interest in this connection is the document in the Biblioteca da Ajuda, Lisbon, Codex 49–I–57, containing a Portuguese complaint against the English seizure; also see Biblioteca Publica e Arquivo Distrital, Evora,

Map Section, P/1–8, for a map of São Tome as it was when handed to the English in 1749.

38. Sanjay Subrahmanyam, *Improvising Empire: Portuguese Trade and Settlement in the Bay of Bengal, 1500–1700,* Delhi, 1990, pp.47–67, 188–215.

39. Manucci, *Storia,* vol. III, pp.120–2; also see the discussion in Sanjay Subrahmanyam, *The Portuguese Empire in Asia, 1500–1700: A Political and Economic History,* London, 1993, pp.202–7.

40. Ibid., pp.204–5, citing letters in the *Boletim da Filmoteca Ultramarina Portuguesa,* nos. 38–40, pp.231, 260–2.

41. Manucci, *Storia,* vol. IV, p.254.

42. Records of Fort St. George (henceforth RFSG), *Letters to Fort St. George 1703–1704,* vol. IX, Madras, 1931, Gabriel Roberts and Council at Fort St. David to Thomas Pitt at Fort St. George, 27 April 1704, pp.20–1 (and for the sequel, the letter of 6 May 1704, p.38).

43. For details of these hostilites, see RFSG, *Letters to Fort St. George 1711,* vol. XII, Madras, 1931, pp.11–12, 15–16, 51–52, 81–2, 113–14, 121–2, *passim.*

44. RFSG, *Diary and Consultation book of 1713,* Madras, 1920, pp.75–6, 88, 183, passim.

45. RFSG, *Letters to Fort St. George 1711,* p.114, Robert Raworth and Council at Fort St. David, 25 October 1711, to Edward Harrison etc at Fort St. George. We may note that the tendency by now was to blame all ills on the villainy of Gabriel Roberts.

46. RFSG, *Diary and Consultation Book of 1712,* Madras, 1929, pp.5–6.

47. ARA, OBP, VOC. 1912, *Letter from Adriaan de Visser etc at Nagapattinam to Batavia,* 21 August 1718, pp.16–17.

48. ARA, OBP. VOC. 1664, pp. 534–5, *Governor Dirck Comans and Council at Nagapattinam to Batavia,* 30 September 1702.

49. These may have included disputes over the administration of Da'ud Khan's jâgir in Wakinkheda, which Sa'id Khan had given out in *ta'ahhud* ('lease contract').

50. ARA, OBP, VOC. 1745, *Governor Joannes van Steeland and Council at Nagapattinam to Batavia,* 31 March 1707, pp. 37–8, 64, *passim.* Manucci, *Storia,* vol. IV, pp.254–5, has a confused account of the incident.

51. ARA, OBP, VOL. 1745, *Nagapattinam to Batavia,* 31 March 1707, pp.58–9.

52. ARA, OBP, VOC. 1745, 'Translaet Mallabaarse ole door s'Comps courantier den bramine Rama-aijen uijt Arkadoe (...)', pp.149–52.

53. Archives Nationales, Paris (henceforth AN), *Archives du Ministère des Colonies,* Correspondance Générale, C^2 69, fls 1–24, lettre de Mr Hebert a Pondichéry le 15 février 1710.

54. Kamwar Khan, *Tazkirat-us-Salātīn Chaghtā,* p.36.

55. See the brief discussion in Susan Bayly, *Saints, Goddesses and Kings: Muslims and Christians in South Indian Society, 1700–1900,* Cambridge, 1989, pp.151–4; also N.S. Ramaswami, *Political History of Carnatic under the Nawabs,* New Delhi, 1984.

56. Muhammad Sa'id also appears as Sa'adatullah Khan in the standard Mughal biographical dictionary, Shahnawaz Khan Samsam-ud-Daulah,

Ma'āṣir-ul-Umarā, ed. Maulavi 'Abd ur-Rahim and Ashraf 'Ali, 3 vols, Calcutta, 1888–95, vol. II. pp.513–14.

57. Oriental and India Office Collections, London (henceforth OIOC), Persian Mss. I.O. 3177 (Ethé 2843), fls 1–184 (copy dated 1849); in the same Mss, fls 1–37 is the *Waqā'i'-i Sa'ādat* taking the history of Arcot to Ghulam Murtaza Khan. Incidentally, we may note the existence of another text incorrectly attributed to Jaswant Rai; this appears in Muhammad Yusuf Kokan and Syed Hamza Hussain, eds, 'Musawaddat-e-Jaswant Rai,' *Bulletin of the Government Oriental Manuscripts Library*, Madras, vol II, No. 2, 1949, pp.129–47.

58. Cf. S.A.R. Bokhari, 'Carnatic under the Nawabs as Revealed through "Sayeed Nama" of Juswant Rai', M. Litt. thesis, Department of Indian History, University of Madras, 1965, pp.37–41.

59. Jaswant Rai, *Sa'īd Nāma*, fls 16a–19a.

60. The first wife of Sa'adatullah Khan is reported by Jaswant Rai (*Sa'īd Nāma*, fls 40a–40b), to have died at Arcot on 14 Muharram 1114 AH, despite the ministrations of doctors of four schools (*firangīya, tilangīya, hindīya* and *yūnānīya*). He is then reported to have remarried the next year in Velur, on 27 Rajab 1115, but only under some persuasion; his bride was the daughter of Qazi Shaikh urf Shaikh Husain, and 3 lakh rupees (*'ālamgīrī*) was given as bride-price.

61. OIOC, I.O. 3177, *Waqā'ī- Sa'ādat*, fl. 2b.

62. Burhan, *Tūzak*, (text), pp.74–5; translation, pp.67–8 (modified slightly here).

63. Burhan, *Tūzak*, (text), p.75; translation, p.68.

64. For one of a number of examples, ARA, OBP. VOC, 1863, fls 295v–296r, *Letter from Daniel Bernard and Council at Nagapattinam to Batavia*, 10 August 1715, where Sa'adatullah Khan is mentioned as being at Chidambaram, while on his return from Tiruchirapalli to Arcot.

65. On the ambiguous image of the Khatris, between merchants and warriors (and their consequent self-image in the eighteenth century), see Muzaffar Alam and Sanjay Subrahmanyam, 'Discovering the Familiar: Notes on the Travel-Account of Anand Ram Mukhlis', *South Asia Research*, vol. XVI, No. 2, 1996, pp.131-54.

66. For a list of Dakhni Rai's main relations in the Karnatak, see Jaswant Rai, *Sa'īd Nāma*, fls 59b–60a. Those listed include Lala Danishmand, Lala Khub Chand, Mukund Rai, Debi Chand, Budh Chand, Todar Mal, Ganj Mal, Nawal Chand, Tika Ram Munshi, Rup Narayan and Diyanat Rai.

67. McLane, *Land and Local Kingship*, pp.131–4.

68. Cf. Karen Leonard, 'The Hyderabad Political System and its Participants' *Journal of Asian Studies*, vol. XXX, No. 2, 1971, pp.569–82.

69. ARA, OBP, VOC. 1811, *Daniel Bernard and Council at Nagapattinam to Batavia*, 28 November 1711, p.58.

70. ARA, OBP. VOC. 1811, *Daniel Bernard and Council at Nagapattinam* to Batavia, 10 July 1711, pp.108–10.

71. ARA, OBP, VOC. 1842, *Daniel Bernard and Council at Nagapattinam to Batavia*, 28 November 1712, pp.53–4.

72. ARA, OBP, VOC. 1842, *Daniel Bernard and Council at Nagapattinam to Batavia,* 30 August 1713, pp.367–9.

73. ARA, OBP. VOC. 1849, *Daniel Bernard and Council at Nagapattinam to Batavia,* 6 September 1714, fls. 366–8.

74. ARA, OBP. VOC. 1855, *Letters from Daniel Bernard and Council at Nagapattinam to Batavia,* dated 21 April, 7 August and 6 September 1714, pp.7–10, 115–16, and 213–14.

75. ARA, OBP, 1884, *Letters from Daniel Bernard and Council, and Adriaan de Visser and Council at Nagapattinam to Batavia,* dated 12 February 1716 and 30 April 1716, pp. 84–6, 247–9.

76. ARA, OBP, VOC. 1869, *Daniel Bernard and Council at Nagapattinam to Batavia,* 23 April 1715, pp. 121–30.

77. ARA, OBP, VOC. 1869, *Daniel Bernard and Council at Nagapattinam to Batavia,* 10 August 1715, pp.267–9.

78. Kamwar Khan, *Tazkirat-us-Salātīn Chag̲htā,* pp.187 and 193 (for different accounts of the remittance): p. 199 (for a description of a piece of pale amber, *ambar-i ashhab,* worth some one lakh rupees).

79. Cf. Sanjay Subrahmanyam, 'Friday's Child: Or how Tej Singh became Desingurâja', in J.F. Richards et al., (eds), *The Making of Indo–Muslim Identity in Pre-colonial India,* Durham: University of Carolina Press, 1998 (forthcoming).

80. AN, *Archives du Ministère des Colonies,* Correspondance Générale, C[2] 69 (1710–76), letter from M. Du Livier, 14 fevrier 1714, fos. 76v–77r.

81. Jaswant Rai, *Sa'īd Nāma,* fl. 101a. Bokhari, 'Carnatic under the Nawabs', p.191, translation revised and corrected.

82. ARA, OBP, VOC. 1745, Joannes van Steeland and Council to Batavia, 31 March 1707, pp. 58–9: 'Op de tijdinge dat de marattys sterck 25,000 ruiters onder hare hoofden Damasie en Baijrosie Gorpadda weder naar dese Carnaticase Landen quamen afsacken, is den heeer Julfacarchan in aantogt geweest ...'.

83. Bokhari, 'Carnatic under the Nawabs', p.198.

84. Muhammad Yousuf Kokan, *Arabic and Persian in Carnatic, 1710–1960,* Madras, 1974, pp.16–17, 36; also Ziyaud-Din A. Desai, *A Topographical List of Arabic, Persian ad Urdu Inscriptions of South India,* New Delhi, 1989, Nos. 453 and 454.

85. Kamwar Khan, *Tazkirat-us-Salātīn Chag̲htā,* p. 196, giving details obtained *az waqā' i'-i Dakan;* for further details, see Jaswant Rai, *Sa'īd Nāma,* fls 95a–95b.

86. ARA, OBP, VOC. 1896, *Adriaan de Visser and Council at Nagapattinam to Batavia,* 30 November 1717, pp.17–18. The fact that the so-called Mughal Prince Muhammad Akbar was confined at Senji is confirmed by a Marathi document, OIOC, Mackenzie Collection, General, vol. IX, 13 (e), pp.140–61.

87. Jaswant Rai, *Sa'īd Nāma,* fls 31a–31b. For a more general reflection on the role of Punjabi Khatris in early eighteenth-century Mughal politics, see Muzaffar Alam, *The Crisis of Empire in Mughal North India: Awadh and the Punjab, 1707–48,* Delhi, 1986, pp.169–74, 183–4, 203, *passim.*

88. Muhammad Amin was not merely a poet (cf. Kokan, *Arabic and Persian in Carnatic*), but a well-known *munshī*; cf. OIOC, I.O. 2894 (Ethé 2122), for the *Majma' ul-inshā'*, collected by him in 1733–4, and which includes some letters from the Karnatak Payanghat. Several copies of the text exist, including one in the Bibliothèque Nationale de France, Paris (Blochet, vol. I, No. 708).

89. Jaswant Rai, *Sa'īd Nāma*, fls 34b–37a.

90. Ibid., fls 27b–28a.

91. Cf. RFSG, *Letters to Fort St. George 1711*, p. 16, where he appears as 'Chela Nargue a great Pulligar near Chingee [who] has desir'd our protection for some of his people at Trepopolore'. It is further noted that he is 'a profest Enemy to Suroop Sing'. Also see ibid, pp.51, 68, and 122, for details of his opportunistic alliance with the English.

92. OIOC, I.O. 3177, *Waqā' i'-i Sa'ādat*, fl. 2b.

93. Jaswant Rai, *Sa'īd Nāma*, fl. 138b.

94. Baisaji Bhakariya has already found mention in the chronicle (fls 58a–59a) as a man who had helped set up a number of *peths* in both the Balaghat and the Payanghat; he was hence awarded the *qānūngo'ī* of the whole Deccan.

95. Jaswant Rai, *Sa'īd Nāma*, fl. 146a, *passim*. Similarly, for the foundation of the market-town of Fath Nagar, near Senji, by Basant Rai (probably the brother of Jaswant Rai) in 1128 AH, see fl. 128b.

96. For a collection of his poems, see OIOC, I.O. 1454 (Ethé 1695), *Dīwān-i Munshī* (collected around 1712 AD). Other copies are listed in the Asiatic Society of Bengal, Calcutta, and the Government Oriental Manuscripts Library, Madras (Islamic Manuscripts Catalogue, vol. I, No. 93, *Kulliyāt-i Munshī*).

97. Compare the accounts in John O'Kane, (trans), *The Ship of Sulaiman*, London, 1972, and Sayyid Muhammad 'Ali al-Husaini, *Tārikh-i rāḥat-afzā*, (ed.) S. Khurshid 'Ali, Hyderabad, 1947, cited in Simon Digby, 'Indo-Persian Narratives of Travel of the Close of the 18th and beginning of the 19th century', unpublished paper presented at a conference on 'Traditions: Transmission or Invention? The Resources of History', EFEO-IFP, Pondicherry, 15–17 January, 1997.

98. Jaswant Rai, *Sa'īd Nāma*, fls 148a–150b; also see Arasaratnam, *Merchants, Cmpanies and Commerce*, pp.22–3, 173.

99. ARA, OBP, VOC. 1927 *Adriaan de Visser and Council at Nagapattinam to Batavia*, 18 August 1719, pp.37–40. The Ostenders' local broker in this affair was a certain Mara Chetti, well-known to the VOC. For brief discussions, also see Manning, *Fortunes à faire*, pp.111–2, and Jan Parmentier, *De holle compagnie: Smokkel en legale handel onder Zuidnederlandse vlag in Bengalen, ca. 1720–44*, Hilversum, 1992, pp.9–14.

100. Jaswant Rai, *Sa'īd Nāma*, fls 181a–82a.

101. ARA, OBP, VOC. 1981, Book II, 'Translaet Persiaanse missive geschreven door den Nabab Sadoulachan ... ontfangen den 8e April Anno 1722', p.240.

102. ARA, OBP, VOC. 1997, letters from Van Outvelt and Turnhout at Sadrasapatnam to Westrenen at Nagapattinam, dated 21 March and 9 April 1723, pp.281–9 (citation from pp. 287–8).

103. Arasaratnam, *Merchants, Companies and Commerce,* p.173.

104. ARA, OBP, VOC. 2102, pp.69–70, *passim,* for the correspondence between the faujdār at Kovalam, the faujdār at Ponneri Mirza Baha-ud-Din, the Dutch chief at Pulicat, and the *dīwān* at Arcot, Mulla Shaikh Hasan, especially on the subject of minting rights.

105. OIOC, I.O. 3177, *Waqā'i'-i Sa'ādat,* fl. 11b.

106. For details, see Sanjay Subrahmanyam, 'Warfare and state finance in Wodeyar Mysore, 17245: A missionary perspective', *The Indian Economic and Social History Review,* vol. XXVI, No. 2, 1989, pp.203–33.

107. For a brief summing up of his career, see Manning, *Fortunes à faire,* pp.208–9.

108. ARA, OBP, VOC. 2102, letter from Sadrasapatnam factors to Nagapattinam, 18 September 1728, fls 163–93, especially fls 174–7.

109. Arasaratnam, *Merchants, Companies and Commerce,* pp.172–3.

110. ARA, OBP, VOC. 2243, translations of diverse Persian letters by Sa'adatullah Khan, Imam Sahib, Bada Sahib and Sa'id Mustafa, dated 1731, pp.2023–51.

111. ARA, Hoge Regering van Batavia, No. 340, *Memorie* left by Governor Adriaan Pla for successor Elias Guillot, Nagapattinam, 28 February 1734, fls. 30–1.

112. Cf. the eloquent statement in Das Gupta, 'The maritime merchant [of medieval India], c. 1500–1800', Presidential Address to the Medieval Section, Indian History Congress, 35th Session, Jadavpur University, 1974, reproduced in Das Gupta, *Merchants of Maritime India, 1500–1800,* Essay III.

113. Cf. Muzaffar Alam, 'Trade, State Policy and Regional Change: Aspects of Mughal-Uzbek Commercial Relations, c. 1550–1750', *Journal of the Economic and Social History of the Orient,* vol. XXXVII, No. 3, 1994, pp.202–27, for a case-study; also Sanjay Subrahmanyam, 'Of *Imārat* and *Tijārat*: Asian Merchants and State Power in the Western Indian Ocean, 1400–1750', *Comparative Studies in Society and History, vol. XXXVII,* No. 4, 1995, pp.750–80, for an overview of positions, and a broad attempt at reinterpretation.

114. See the relevant sections in Muzaffar Alam and Sanjay Subrahmanyam, 'Introduction', in Alam and Subrahmanyam, (eds), *The Mughal State, 1526–50,* Delhi, 1998.

115. Arasaratnam, *Merchants, Companies and Commerce,* pp.168, 354–5.

116. Manning, *Fortunes à faire,* p.207.

117. Notably, it is clearly important to work through the surviving administrative papers of the Arcot niẓāmat, in the National Archives of India, New Delhi (Inayat Jang Collection), and the Andhra Pradesh State Archives, Hyderabad (both of which have already been used to an extent by Richards, *Mughal Administration in Golconda,* and Nayeem, *Mughal Administration of Deccan*). We hope to return to these in a later essay.

7

European Corporate Enterprises and the Politics of Trade in India, 1600–1800

OM PRAKASH

Throughout the early modern period, India was at the centre of the trading activites of the European corporate enterprises as well as of the private European traders operating in Asia. While the corporate groups by and large took care of the inter-continental trade, the trade within Asia was carried on mainly by the private traders, many of whom were simultaneously employed by one or the other of the corporate groups. The only major exception to this pattern was the Dutch East India Company (VOC) which, in addition to being a major participant in Euro-Asian trade, also engaged in a substantial amount of trade within Asia as an integral part of its overall trading strategy. This essay first establishes the centrality of India in both the Euro-Asian as well as the intra-Asian trading networks of the Europeans. It then goes into the question of the political and economic environment in which Europeans functioned in different parts of Asia. The cases of the Indonesian archipelago, Japan and India are then analysed to bring out the marked differences in this respect. Finally, the essay comments on the radically altered situation within India, following the wresting of political authority in Bengal by the English East India Company, during the second half of the eighteenth century.

I

In keeping with the traditional composition of the Asian imports into Europe, the principal item procured by the Portuguese *Estado da India*—the first of the European corporate groups to come to Asia—was spices, overwhelmingly pepper, though some other goods were also procured. One ordinarily associates the spice trade with primarily the Indonesian archipelago (Sumatran pepper and Moluccan cloves, nutmeg and mace) and only marginally with Sri Lanka (cinnamon) and the south-west coast of India (pepper). This characterization, however, is totally inapplicable to the Portuguese case. Their early occupation of Malacca (1511) notwithstanding, the bulk of their pepper procurement was from the Malabar region (and later Kanara as well) on the south-west coast of India. This made India their principal theatre of operation throughout the century and a half of their trading history between Europe and Asia.[1] It was only in the context of their intra-Asian trade that the Portuguese connection with other parts of Asia, including China and Japan, became quantitatively significant.

This pattern of the domination of the Euro-Asian seaborne trade by India, however, changed when the Dutch and the English East India companies appeared on the Asian scene in the beginning of the seventeenth century. The shift of the Asian *loci* of the Euro-Asian trade from India to the Indonesian archipelago around this time was dictated by the fact that both the Dutch and the English procured their spices from Indonesia. But about three-quarters of a century later, the Asian *loci* again began to shift back to India. This happened because, over this period, the composition of the Asian imports into Europe changed dramatically in favour of goods procured predominantly from India. In the case of the Dutch East India Company, for example, spices, including pepper, came down from an imposing 74 per cent of the total imports in 1619–21 to 68 per cent during 1648–50 and to a mere 23 per cent during 1698–1700. On the other hand, textiles and raw silk went up from 16 per cent in 1619–21 to an incredible 55 per cent at the end of the seventeenth century. There was a decline thereafter, but in 1778–80 textiles and raw silk accounted for half of the total imports.[2] Because of the smaller geographical range of the Asian operations of the English East India Company, goods procured in India accounted for an even greater proportion of the total Asian imports into England. At the end of the seventeenth century, this figure stood at as much as 95 per cent and at 84 per cent in 1738–40.

If India was at the centre of the European trading companies' Euro-Asian trade, it was equally central to the extensive amount of trade the Europeans, both the corporate enterprises as well as private traders, carried on within Asia using the Indian Ocean–South China Sea trading network. The critical role played by India was as much a function of her capacity to provide cost–competitive manufactured goods—predominantly cotton and other textiles—in the case of the Europeans engaged in intra-Asian trade, as it had been traditionally in the case of the Indian and other Asian merchants similarly engaged in this trade. The principal European corporate enterprise engaged in intra-Asian trade in a substantial manner and as an integral part of its total trading strategy, namely the Dutch East India Company, got involved in this trade in the first place in order to procure Indian coarse cotton textiles at source. These textiles were the principal medium of exchange throughout the Malay Indonesian archipelago and it was nearly impossible for the Company to obtain supplies of pepper and other spices except in exchange for these textiles. While these textiles could have been procured within the region at places such as Acheh, the acute business instinct of the Company took it, within a few years of its arrival in Asia, to their source, the Coromandel coast and Gujarat. The large and assured availability of highly cost-competitive textiles in India with a large demand both in Southeast Asia and West Asia was thus the starting point of the Dutch East India Company's involvement in intra-Asia trade, which eventually grew to a point where this branch of trade became of as much concern to the Company as its Euro-Asian trade. As early as 1612, Hendrik Brouwer, a future governor-general of the East Indies, had described the Coromandel coast as the left arm of the Moluccas and the surrounding islands because without textiles that come from there, the trade in the Moluccas will be dead.[3]

The three principal elements in the Dutch strategy of participation in intra-Asian trade were Indian textiles and raw silk, Indonesian spices, and Japanese silver. The initial supply of investment funds brought in from Holland was invested first in Indian textiles, a large part of which was then sold against spices. While a part of the spices was sent home, the remainder constituted, together with the remaining Indian textiles, the basis of entry into a number of branches of trade within Asia. Among the most prized of these was the trade with Japan, where nearly half of the value of the goods sent consisted of Indian textiles and raw silk. As of 1639, when the 'closed country' era began in Japan, the Dutch East India Company was the only European entity permitted to operate in the country, giving the Company a significant differential advantage over its rivals. This advantage lay in the large amount of silver, a critical input for the Indian and several other trading areas, that the Japan trade provided. Given the large and persistent differential in the gold-silver bi-metallic ratio between the two countries, it was highly advantageous for the Company to convert a large part of the Japanese silver it procured into gold at Taiwan. The Chinese gold could then be invested profitably in the procurement of textiles on the Coromandel coast, where the basic currency unit in use was the gold *pagoda*. The point to emphasize is that, by about the middle of the 17th century, the

Dutch East India Company had become a major participant in intra-Asian trade, with trading links all along the great arc of Asian trade. Indian textiles, raw silk, and later opium, which turned out to be a highly profitable item, sold in large quantities all over the Indonesian archipelago, were among the key commodities in the Dutch Company's framework of intra-Asian trade. Given the importance the Company attached to this trade, its employees were not allowed to engage in it on their individual account. That, however, did not prevent them from doing so on a fairly large scale on a clandestine basis. Indeed, in a high-value, low-bulk item such as opium which was ideal for contraband trade, the volume of the clandestine trade was often as large as that on the Company's own account.[4]

Turning next to the English East India Company and the private English traders, one finds that while the involvement of the Company in intra-Asian trade was negligible and confined essentially to the first half of the 17th century, private English traders based in India constituted by far the largest and the most enduring group of Europeans engaged in the trade of the Indian Ocean and the South China Sea. These traders operated from ports on both the east and the west coasts of India. Over the 17th and the early years of the 18th century, the Coromandel ports witnessed English trading activity on a much larger scale than did ports in Bengal. Masulipatnam was the principal port used on the Coromandel coast, but around the turn of the century more and more private English shipping moved on to Madras. In Bengal, the principal port was Hugli until it was replaced by Calcutta in the early years of the 18th century. In course of time, Calcutta emerged as the most important port of English private trade in India. On the west coast, English private trade began at Surat in the early years of the 17th century, but moved on to Bombay in the 18th century.

II

What was the nature of the political and economic environment in which the European corporate groups and the private traders were obliged to function while carrying on their trading activities in the Indian subcontinent? In other words, if the range of alternative scenarios under which the Europeans functioned in different parts of Asia in the early modern period is conceptualized as a broad spectrum, where precisely would South Asia figure in that spectrum? One might begin by drawing attention to the fact that in the pre-European phase of the history of commercial exchange in the Indian Ocean–South China Sea complex, there was a well-established tradition of foreign merchants being welcome at the Asian ports, since they were perceived as providers of additional business to the local merchants and of additional income by way of customs duties etc. to the ruling authorities. The visiting as well as the resident foreign merchants were, by and large, left to manage their affairs themselves, including the arrangements they might make with their local counterparts, their business dealings in the market, and so on, without the administration unduly interfering in their decision-making processes. The Asian port at which such autonomy was allowed in the most unconstrained fashion was probably that of Malacca, which in the course of the 15th century had become a major centre of international exchange, and a meeting point of traders from the East and the West. Foreign merchants resident in, and operating from, the port could broadly be divided into four groups: (a) the Gujaratis, (b) other Indian merchant groups and merchants from Burma, (c) the merchants from Southeast Asia up to and including the Phillippines, and (d) the merchants from East Asia, including the Chinese, the Japanese and the Okinawans. Each of these four groups was even allowed to have a *shahbandar* of its own, who managed the affairs of that particular community autonomously of the local authorities.

To what extent was this scenario modified by the arrival of the Europeans in the Indian Ocean at the beginning of the 16th century? By far the most crucial element in the new situation was the armed superiority of European ships over their Asian counterparts. A glaring example of this disparity was provided in April 1612 when six English ships congregated off the Arabian coast and hijacked, in succession, fifteen passing Mughal ships from India, culminating in the capture of the great 1000-ton vessel *Rahimi,* which belonged to the mother of the Mughal emperor. The prizes were taken to a nearby anchorage and plundered at will. It is true that the *Rahimi* was armed with some fifteen pieces of artillery and that the soldiers aboard her carried muskets, but these were merely anti-personnel weapons. Indian vessels, which often relied on rope and treenails to hold their planks in place, lacked the strength both to withstand heavy artillery bombardment from without, and to absorb the recoil of large ordinance firing from within.[5] The fact that the English could do this with impunity reflected not only the vulnerability of the Indian mercantile vessels but also the absence of a Mughal navy capable of retaliating against such high-handed action. The flotilla at Dacca and the fleet maintained by the Sidis at Janjira near Bombay were clearly inadequate to support an offensive against European ships. It was indeed not without reason that in 1662, on being approached on behalf of the king of the Maldive islands to use his good offices to persuade Emperor Aurangzeb to impose a ban on English and Dutch shipping to the islands, the *faujdar* of Balasore pointed out that even if the emperor could be persuaded to oblige the king, he was in no position to do so since he was 'master only of land and not of the sea'.[6]

An early institutionalized consequence of European naval superiority was the requirement that the Portuguese, almost immediately on their arrival in the western Indian Ocean, imposed on Asian shipping to obtain from them, before each voyage, a license in the form of a *cartaz*. The document obliged the Asian ship to call at a Portuguese-controlled port and to pay customs duties before it proceeded on its voyage to ports enumerated in the document. While it is ture that the distorting effects of this innovation in reorienting the direction of Indian merchants' trade were relatively limited, it was nevertheless instrumental in bringing about a quiet revolution in the organizational structure of Asian trade. For the first time in the history of this trade, the unfettered and absolute freedom of navigation on the high seas stood compromised.

In the 17th century, the Dutch, the English, and the French companies also took over the cartaz system from the Portuguese, though in a modified format and under the nomenclature of the 'pass' or the 'passport' system. It was, however, only the Dutch East India Company which, given its high stakes in intra-Asian trade, took the system with a certain amount of seriousness. The Vernigele Oostindische Compagnie (VOC) also followed the Portuguese precedent in attempting to monopolize both the Euro-Asian and the intra-Asian trade in spices. By the early 1620s, on the basis of agreements wrested from the authorities in many of the islands in the Moluccas, the Dutch had acquired effective monopsony rights in nutmeg and mace. The case of cloves was somewhat more complex. There was large-scale smuggling between the producing areas and Makassar, enabling the English, among others, to obtain large quantities of this spice. Though from 1643 onwards the VOC had managed to reduce such smuggling, it was only after the conquest of Makassar in 1669 that the Dutch fully controlled the trade in cloves. Finally, as far as pepper—which was a substantially more important item of investment in the Indies than all the other spices put together—was concerned, inspite of the conclusion of exclusive agreements with a number of states in the region, the Company never acquired effective monopsony rights in the spice.

The totality of the control achieved by the VOC in the case of spices other than pepper in the Euro-Asian trade is exemplified by the almost incredible fact that for the entire period between 1677 and 1744, the Company managed to sell cloves in Amsterdam at the fixed price of 75 stivers per Dutch pound.[7] A similar stranglehold was enjoyed by the Company in the intra-Asian trade in these spices. The fact that the Moluccas enjoyed world monopoly in the production of these spices, grown in particular islands covering a limited geographical space, which could be effectively policed, was the key to the success of the VOC in controlling the production and the trade in these items. By the same token, pepper, which was grown on the island of Sumatra over extensive tracts, could never be brought under the monopoly net, the formal monopsony agreements with several regional powers notwithstanding. For precisely the same reason, the Portuguese had an essentially similar experience with this spice on the south-west coast of India in the sixteenth century.

What did the Dutch spice monopoly entail for the Company on the one hand, and for the producers and the Asian traders dealing in them on the other? I have argued elsewhere that by increasing the rate of gross profit on these spices to incredibly high levels, often running to a thousand or more per cent, the spice monopoly became a major element in the unquestioned domination of Euro-Asian trade by the Dutch through the 17th century. A similar domination was achieved in the intra-Asian trade by using the spice monopoly as a major entry device into many branches of the network. The unusually high profit was, of course, at the expense of the producers of these spices, as well as the Indonesian and other Asian traders who used to carry on a large-scale intra-Asian trade in them. This can be seen as institutionalized coercion by one group over another that had not been a feature of Asian trade in the pre-European phase. In terms of the placement in the spectrum discussed earlier, the situation in the Indonesian archipelago would indeed represent one end of the spectrum with a clear-cut and substantive differential advantage available to the VOC.

Together with the spice monopoly, exclusive access to the bullion-providing Japan trade was the other principal circumstance behind the VOC's unprecedented success in penetrating the Indian Ocean–South China Sea trading network. But ironically, the conditions under which the Company was obliged to operate in Japan were diametrically opposite to those in the Indonesian archipelago, placing the Company, as it were, at the other end of the spectrum of conditions under which the European corporate enterprises functioned in Asia. In a coercion-based regime, if it was the VOC that resorted to coercion over the producing and the trading groups in the Indonesian archipelago, it was itself the victim of coercion at the hands of the political and the commercial establishment in Japan.

The beginnings of the rise of a non-market governed commercial regime in Japan can be traced to 1604 when, under a new arrangement termed the *pancado,* the Portuguese were obliged to sell their principal import into Japan, namely Chinese raw silk, at a price determined arbitrarily by a guild monopsony consisting of a group of merchants from the five imperial cities of Edo (Tokyo), Osaka, Kyoto, Sakai and Nagasaki. In 1631, when they protested against the arrangement, the Portuguese were told that they were free to leave the country. In 1633, they actually had to sell at prices lower than even the pancado price.[8] The same year the pancado arrangement was extended to cover a part of the Chinese raw silk brought in by the Dutch East India Company as well. Following the promulgation, in June 1636, of the *sakoku* or the 'closed country' edict and the expulsion of the Portuguese in 1639 consequent on the suspected involvement of their Catholic missionaries in the Shimbara rebellion in 1637, the Dutch became the only European merchant-group to be allowed to operate in Japan. In May 1641, they were ordered to move to the islet of Deshima, off the Nagasaki harbour, to which they were henceforth confined, besides being subjected to a range of commercial restrictions. These included a ban on the export of gold; the prescription of days on which the Company could offer its goods for sale, until which time they had to be kept in sealed warehouses; and the extension of the pancado system to the entire lot of Chinese raw silk the Company imported into Japan. The 1672 introduction of the system of *shih shobai,* which the Dutch translated as *taxatie-handel* (appraised trade), effectively extended the pancado system to all imports. On the basis of the samples collected from the Dutch factors, the defferent commodities imported were evaluated unilaterally by selected members of the Nagasaki Chamber of Commerce. This arrangement had an immediate and substantial adverse effect on the profitability of the trade, and in 1675 the Batavia Council wrote to the governor of Nagasaki that although the Company traded with 'all corners of the globe', it had 'never yet found a single other place where the purchaser fixed the price'.[9] The appeal that the 'appraised trade' system be rescined, however, fell on deaf ears and the Dutch chief at Nagasaki, Martinus Ceaser, could do little but express his frustration as follows, 'But it seems that the Japanese have finally laid aside all sense of honour and decency whilst we perforce must dance to their piping in everything'.[10] The fact that the

Japan trade was nevertheless of enormous value for the Company through the 17th century only serves to underscore the critical role that bullion played in the early–modern Asian trade.

What was the situation in India which, as we have seen, was at the centre of the Europeans' trading activities? In the 16th century, the Portuguese managed to obtain monopsonistic privileges in the procurement of pepper on the Malabar coast. On the strength of the assistance provided to the raja of Cochin in throwing the Portuguese out, the Dutch East India Company inherited, in 1663, similar monopsonistic privileges. But given identical problems of policing and enforcement, the situation was indeed comparable to that in Sumatra rather than that in the Molluccas.

Outside of the Malabar coast, however, the situation in India was very much in the mould of the Malacca model, characterized by the absence of coercion on either side. In terms of the spectrum of alternative scenarios, the placement of the Europeans operating in India would be right in the middle of the spectrum. In the subcontinent, the relationship between the ruling authorities and the different European groups was by and large an amicable one, based essentially on perceived mutual advantage. The authorities basically looked upon the European companies' trade in their area as a net addition with the attendant benefits that such growth of trade entailed for the economy. More immediately, the resultant increase in the customs revenue, which in the case of the Mughal empire accrued directly to the central treasury, and probably constituted a head of revenue in importance next only to land revenue, was an important consideration. An equally important consideration would seem to have been the 'bullion for goods' character of the Europeans' trade. The fact that the companies paid for the goods obtained in the subcontinent overwhelmingly in terms of precious metals made them probably the single-most important conduit for the import of these metals into the country. The domestic output of these metals being practically nil, their import, in reasonably large quantities, was critical, among other things, for the successful conduct of the subcontinent's monetary system. As a result European requests for permission to trade and the establishment of factories were routinely granted by Mughal imperial authorities and by regional authorities in the Coromandel coast. The rate of customs duty that European companies were obliged to pay was ordinarily the same as that payable by the Indian and other Asian merchants operating from the region. Indeed, imperial administration often went a step further and exempted these companies from the payment of transit (*rahdari*) duties, giving them a differential advantage *vis-à-vis* their own nationals. It is another matter that local and the provincial authorities, whose income streams would have been adversely affected by such exemption, usually managed to ignore imperial orders and continued charging rahdari duties. Under this dispensation, the companies operated in the market basically as yet another group of merchants availing no special privileges in their dealings with the Indian merchants or artisans. By the same token, they were at liberty to function in the system like any other merchant group, without restriction on the use of systematic infrastructure. Their factors and representatives were allowed to travel throughout the empire, buy and sell where they found it most profitable to do so, and deal with their Indian counterparts on terms strictly determined by the market.

The absence of coercion, however, did not preclude occasional conflict between Indian political authorties, on the one hand, and European trading companies, on the other. In such an event, both sides were concerned that the conflict did not escalate beyond a point. At work was, indeed, a rather finely tuned balance between unquestioned European maritime superiority as against their almost total vulnerability on land for a long time. Scholars such as Frederick C. Lane and, more recently, Niels Steensgaard have gone to the extent of arguing that 'the principal export of pre-industrial Europe to the rest of the world was violence'. While there is an element of truth in this formulation, it is imperative that it is not torn out of context. Violence on the sea was a weapon of the last resort to be used as sparingly as possible, for the simple reason that it was by no means a costless process. Ordinarily, both sides would first seek to resolve conflict and only in the event of a deadlock would either side resort to actual violence.

An example of a potential area of conflict between the authorities and the Dutch East India Company, given its large-scale participation in intra-Asian trade, was the violation of the Company's pass policy by the Indian merchants engaged in the Indian Ocean trade. The trouble the Company faced at Surat in 1648–9 is a case in point. Following the conquest of Malacca in 1641, and the subsequent conclusion of monopsony agreements with the principal tin producing regions in the Malay peninsula, the Company sought to restrict direct access for Indian vessels to the 'tin ports' north of Malacca, and get them to carry out all their trade at Malacca itself. This strategy, however, proved largely ineffective as long as these vessels had continuing free access to the Bay of Bengal port of Acheh on the northern tip of Sumatra. The extensive trade carried on by Acheh merchants with

Sumatran and Malayan ports made Acheh a large market for Indian textiles, as well as a major procurement point for items such as pepper and tin. Indeed, on the basis of the passes issued by the queen of Acheh, it was even posssible for the Indian merchants to sail to the east Sumatran and west Malayan ports and carry on trade there. Particularly useful in this regard was the link to Perak, then a vassal state of Acheh and abundantly provided with tin. The implications of this for the VOC were quite severe. In 1646, no tin could be bought in the Malay peninsula and no pepper could be sold at Malacca. A full-scale response was evidently called for and on 3 July 1647, Batavia resolved that 'the Moors of Surat, Coromandel, Bengal, Pegu, etc. be prohibited from the trade both in Achin [Acheh] and in the tin quarters [of peninsular Malaya] on pain of seizure [of their vessels] as legitimate prize if they come there in the future'. Patrolling of the approaches to Acheh, as well as to ports such as Kedah, Perak and Johor was intensified. The factors in India were instructed not to issue passes for Acheh or any of the other ports declared out of bounds.[11]

The reaction to this severely restrictionist policy was sharp, at least at Surat. When passes for Acheh were refused, Mughal authorities banned the loading of Dutch ships at the port. That was not all: in April 1648, the local Dutch factory was stormed by a force of 150 men. One Dutchman was killed, two others wounded and goods worth f.27,000 plundered. The attackers were never identified, but it was a clear message signalling the displeasure of both the Mughal authorities as well as the local merchants. Johan Tack, the Company's man at Agra, sought the Court's intervention in the restitution of the plundered goods. With the help of one of the *umara* at the Court, Haqiqat Khan, who was generally favourably inclined to the Company, an audience with Shahjahan was obtained. The emperor promised to grant a *farman* directing the *mutasaddi* of Surat to compensate the Company for the plundered goods. But before the farman could be issued, a delegation of Surat merchants arrived at the Court. They could not prevent the grant of the farman, but ensured that it was a very different kind of document. All that the farman did was to say that the local authorities at Surat would do their best to trace the plundered goods. The factors saw no point in even bringing the document to the attention of the mutasaddi. The Company then decided to retaliate at sea. A fleet sent from Batavia for the purpose arrived too late in 1648 to attack the Indian ships returning from Mocha. But the following year, two Gujarati ships on their way back from Mocha and carrying a cargo worth more than one and a half million guilders were seized just outside Surat. Following negotiations between the Company, the local authorities, and some of the leading merchants of the city, the Company's two-fold demand for compensation for the plundered goods and a promise to stop the Surat ships' attempted voyages to Acheh, Perak, Kedah and Phuket, etc. was accepted. In return, the Company released the seized ships and the cargo to the lawful owners.[12]

The implications of the Company's pass policy during these years were somewhat less severe on the Coromandel coast. The problems there revolved mainly around the issue of the refusal of passses for the ships of the all-powerful noble, Mir Jumla. Following the seizure in 1647 of tin worth 2000 rials off Perak, from a ship of the Mir because it did not carry a Dutch pass, the governor of Masulipatnam, a subordinate of Mir Jumla, asked for restitution. Peace was bought temporarily by a promise to do the needful and by agreeing to sell the entire stock of cloves in the Company's warehouses in Coromandel together with a certain amount of copper to the Mir. But the tin had not been returned by 1651 leading to obstruction of the Company's textile trade in the region. It was only after Commissioner Dirck Steur went to see Mir Jumla that an agreement emerged. The Company reiterated its promise to return the tin, besides undertaking to buy its textiles, at specified places only, from the representatives of the Mir. But problems surfaced again following the seizure of one of Mir Jumla's ships, the *Nazareth,* off Malacca, for flying the Portuguese flag after the Dutch–Portuguese truce had ended. Matters came to a head in 1653 when Mir Jumla threatened to attack Fort Geldria unless the *Nazareth* and its cargo were released immediately and passes granted for the Portuguese controlled ports in Sri Lanka. It was then decided to meet a part of the Mir's claims in respect of the goods carried by the *Nazareth*. Besides, passes were to be issued to all subjects of Golconda for ports under the jurisdiction of the king of Kandi and for Acheh. The only stipulation made regarding the latter was that in the event of the blockade of the port by the Dutch, ships sailing for Acheh would agree to proceed to another destination approved by the Company. It was, however, only at the end of 1655 that compensation in respect of the *Nazareth* was paid. The Company also conceded the Mir's right to trade with Makassar, Bantam and Kedah, as well as to send goods to Malacca aboard the Company's ships. In return, Mir Jumla agreed not to send ships to Jaffanapatnam in view of the ongoing Dutch–Portuguese struggle there.[13]

III

The conditions and circumstances under which the European corporate enterprises functioned in India, however, underwent a sea change in the second half of the 18th century, with the position of the English East India Company in parts of the subcontinent fast approaching that of the VOC in the Indonesian archipelago. The political control now exercised by the English East India Company gave it substantial differential advantage *vis-à-vis* both the rival European companies as well as the intermediary merchants and artisans. The terms and conditions the Company imposed on those doing business with it were no longer determined by the market: indeed, these people were no longer always free even to determine whether to do business with the Company at all. In Gujarat, this situation developed after the English take-over of the Surat castle in 1759. On the Coromandel coast, the 1750s and the 1760s witnessed the acquisition, by the Company, of extensive land revenue collection rights in key textile producing districts in the northern Circars and central Coromandel, giving it unprecedented control over textile merchants and weavers in the area. S. Arasaratnam has described in some detail the Company's coercive textile procurement practices in the region, including the demarcation of looms on which textiles would henceforth be produced exclusively for the Company.[14]

It was, however, in Bengal, where the Company first obtained formal *diwani* rights in 1765, that the full impact of the Company's new status was in evidence. At one level, there was a fundamental alteration for the worse in the nature of the relationship between the English Company on the one hand and the intermediary merchant and artisanal groups on the other. Gross abuse of the newly found political power available to the English factors turned this relationship into one of widespread coercion and oppression. This is perhaps best illustrated by the manner of procurement of textiles at Kharpai. Soon after the assumption of diwani rights in 1765, the Commercial Resident of the area arranged for information to be collected regarding the number of weavers, looms, pieces of textiles of different kinds manufactured in each *aurung* in his area annually, the number ordinarily procured by rival European trading companies as well as private merchants each year, and so on.[15] Since the Company's textile requirements took precedence over everyone else's, individual *paikars* of the Company were allotted weavers who were banned from working for anyone else till such time as they had met their contractual obligations towards the Company. The terms offered by the Company to the paikars and, in turn, by the latter to the weavers were extraordinarily poor. The perennial complaint of the weavers was that the price allowed them by the Company hardly covered the cost of the raw material. In 1767, the weavers went so far as to send a delegation to Calcutta with a petition (*arzi*) requesting that the prices offered to them be increased to at least afford them a subsistence wage. They did manage to obtain an order directing the Commercial Resident, identified in a Dutch report as one Bathoe, to do the needful. But this evidently was no more than an eyewash because Bathoe not only openly disregarded the order but even threatened to have the weavers arrested in case they continued with their efforts.[16]

The textiles received from the paikars were classified by the Company's evaluators from quality one to five. Pieces not found good enough to make even quality five were rejected as 'firty' (ferreted). A rough idea of what the Company subjected the weavers to can be formed by the fact that pieces classified as third quality would gladly have been accepted by the Dutch Company as first quality at a considerably higher price.[17] It is remarkable that even the pieces rejected by the Company as 'firty' had a profitable market. The margin between the price that these pieces fetched in the open market, and the rate at which they had been evaluated by the Company before being rejected, conveys some idea of the extent of exploitation of the weavers. This margin was shared clandestinely between the Commercial Resident, the chief *gumashta* and the paikars. To take an example from 1767, Resident Bathoe rejected 896 pieces of textiles as 'firty' that year. Many of these pieces were eventually sold by paikars in the open market at between 6.5 to 7 rupees higher per piece than the price at which they had been evaluated by the Company's factors before being rejected. Bathoe had returned the pieces to the paikars after keeping a margin of Rs 3 per piece for himself and Re 0.5 per piece for the chief gumashta, Radhamohan Basak. But even after paying 3.5 rupees extra, the paikars managed to earn a net profit of 3 to 3.5 rupees per piece for themselves.[18] Besides, the Company also exploited the weaver by manipulating the raw material market to its advantage. It was reported in 1767, for example, that Resident Bathoe had bought silk yarn from the producers at 16 *tolas* to a rupee and had supplied it to weavers at 7 to 9 tolas per rupee. The profits were shown in the Bardwan accounts of the Company.[19]

In 1771, the Board of Trade reverted to the contract system and formally invited local merchants to supply to the Company. But in its actual working, the new arrangement represented no more than a change in form and left the content by and large unchanged. Often, the Commercial Residents themselves undertook the responsibility of supplying to the Company on a contractual basis. After 1774, their names were listed as direct suppliers to the Company and an official agency commission payable to them was agreed upon.[20]

A by-product of the political ascendancy of the English Company in Bengal was the growing range of problems created for its European rivals, the Dutch and the French East India companies. The growing English stranglehold on the weavers, obliging an increasing number of them to work exclusively for itself, made it difficult for the Dutch and the French to procure an adequate quantity of textiles. Within a few months of Plassey, the English factors were reported to be forcibly taking away pieces woven for the Dutch.[21] In October 1758, when the Dutch protested against English highhandedness in having pieces under production for their Company torn away from the looms, the English officials promised redress but nothing was actually done.[22] In the early 1760s, the Commercial Residents at Malda and Midnapur were instructed to ensure that the best weavers of Jagannathpur, Olmara and the neighbouring aurungs worked exclusively for the English.[23]

With a view to finding a lasting solution to the problem, the Dutch proposed to the English in 1767 that they should be assigned weavers in the various aurungs who would then be allowed to work for them without hindrance. Since formally the English took the position that the Dutch, as indeed all other Europeans, were perfectly free to carry on their trade in the region, this was agreed to in principle, but eventually nothing came of the proposal.[24] A Fort William public notification, dated 28 April 1775, even asserted

> that the weavers of the province of Bengal and Bihar should enjoy a perfect and entire liberty to deal with any persons whom they pleased and that no person should use force of any kind to oblige the weavers or other manufacturers to receive advances of money or to engage in contracts for the provision of clothes against their will, and that all persons offending against this order should suffer severe punishment.[25]

The charade continued in the English response, dated 8 September 1785, to a Dutch memorandum:

> Under your agents, they [the weavers] may work more freely perhaps than under our own, and you may rest assured that we shall not countenance the servants or gomastahs of our own Board of Trade in any attempts that they may make to oppress the natives who work for you and not us, or prevent your employment of their industry. The weaver who works for your Company contributes equally to pay the revenue, with the weaver who works for our own Board of Trade, and perhaps more so. And an extension to the sale of Bengal manufacture is more profitable to Great Britain than a monopoly in the purchase of such goods as would restrain the manufacture.[26]

The truth, however, was otherwise and the Dutch procurement continued to suffer heavily. The situation was exploited fully by the merchants. On an average, the Dutch factors were obliged to pay about 25 per cent higher than what the English Company paid for comparable varieties.[27] Also, the VOC often found it difficult to get an adequate number of merchants unless a continuous increase in the price was agreed to.[28]

The replacement of a market-determined relationship between the English East India Company and the Bengali artisanal and mercantile groups by a relationship marked by a clear-cut domination by the Company had important implications for the relative share of these groups in the total value of the ouput produced. On the basis of its political muscle, the Company enforced unilaterally determined below-market terms on the producers of and the dealers in commodities such as textiles and opium. The blatant manner in which this was done, robbing in the process the producers and the merchants of a good part of what was legitimately due to them would, in turn, have distorted the incentive structure in manufacturing and other production in the province. This, combined with the official Company and the unofficial private English traders' monopolies in commodities such as salt and opium, is likely to have brought about a certain amount of decline in the value of the total output produced in the province, though it is not possible to indicate even broadly the extent of this decline.

There were other negative implications as well. English Company exports to Europe were now financed in part by the diversion of a part of the Bengal revenues for the procurement of the export cargo. To that extent, these exports now became 'unrequited', involving a drain of resources from the country—a theme that has legitimately attracted a great deal of attention in the Indian nationalist historical writings of the nineteenth century. Another part of the exports was financed on the basis of the rupee funds obtained against bills of exchange issued to private European merchants and payable in London and other European capitals. These merchants bought these bills mainly as a device of remitting their Indian savings home. Between the Bengal surplus revenues and the rupee receipts obtained against bills of exchange, the Company found itself in a position to suspend altogether the import of treasure from home for nearly a quarter of a century, evidently causing the shortage of money in the province that several contemporaries noted and commented upon. It was only in 1784 that these imports were resumed, partly for investment in the procurement of export goods and partly to further strengthen the Company's military presence—a necessary prelude to the conquest of other parts of the subcontinent.

NOTES

1. V. Magelhaes–Godinho, *Os Descrobrimentos e a Economia Mundial* (Lisbon, 1963–71), vol. III, pp.10–11, 73–5; A.R. Disney, *Twilight of the Pepper Empire, Portuguese Trade in Southwest India in the Early Seventeenth Century* (Cambridge, Mass., 1978), Appendix 2.2, p.162.

2. J.R. Bruin, F.S. Gaastra, and I. Schoffer, *Dutch-Asiatic Shipping in the 17th and 18th Centuries* (The Hague, 1987), vol.1, Table 41, p.192.

3. J.E. Heeres (ed.), *Corpus-Diplomaticum Neerlando-Indicum* (The Hague, 1907), vol.I, p.154.

4. Om Prakash, *The Dutch East India Company and the Economy of Bengal 1630–1720* (Princeton, 1985), pp.15–23, 83–9.

5. Geoffrey Parker, *The Military Revolution, Military Innovation and the Rise of the West, 1500–1800* (Cambridge, 1988), pp.107–8.

6. *Algemeen Rijksarchief* (ARA), letter from the Dutch Director at Hugli to Batavia, 26 October 1662, VOC 1240, f.1380 vo.

7. Kristof Glamann, *Dutch–Asiatic Trade, 1620–1740* (Copenhagen/The Hague, 1958), p.33.

8. George Bryan Souza, *The Survival of Empire: Portuguese Trade and Society in China and the South China Sea, 1630–1754* (Cambridge, 1986), p.60.

9. Pieter van Dam, in F.W. Stapel et al (ed.) *Beschryvinge van de Oost-Indische Compagnie* (The Hague, 1927–54), Book II, Part I, p.454.

10. C.R. Boxer, 'Jan Compagnie in Japan 1672–74 or Anglo–Dutch Rivalry in Japan and Formosa', *Transactions of the Asiatic Society of Japan,* Second Series, 7 (1930), p.170.

11. S. Arasaratnam, 'Some notes on the Dutch in Malacca and the Indo-Malayan trade 1641–70', *Journal of South-East Asian History,* vol.X(3), 1969, pp.480–90.

12. H.W. van Santen, *De Verenidge Oost-Indische Compagnie in Gujarat en Hindustan, 1620–60* (Leiden, 1982), pp.21–4.

13. Tapan Raychaudhuri, *Jan Company in Coromandel, 1605–1690* (The Hague, 1962), pp.48–51.

14. S. Arasaratnam, 'Weavers, Merchants and Company: The Handloom Industry in Southeastern India 1750–1790', *The Indian Economic and Social History Review,* vol.XVII(3), 1980, pp.257–81.

15. ARA, J.M. Ross at Khirpai to Director at Hugli, 18 July 1767, Appendix D, *Hooge Regering Batavia* (hereafter HRB), 247.

16. ARA, J.M. Ross at Khirpai to Director at Hugli, 16 May 1767, Appendix C2, HRB 247.

17. ARA, J.M. Ross at Khirpai to Director at Hugli, Appendix A, HRB 247.

18. ARA, J.M. Ross at Khirpai to Director at Hugli, 18 July 1767, Appendix

D, HRB 247.

19. ARA, J.M. Ross at Khirpai to Director at Hugli, Appendix A, HRB 247; also Appendix D, HRB 247.

20. Hameeda Hossain, *The Company Weavers of Bengal, the East India Company and the Organization of Textile Production in Bengal, 1750–1813* (Delhi, 1988), pp.90–1.

21. G.C. Klerk de Reus, 'De expeditie naar Bangale in 1759', *De Indische Gids,* vol.11, 1889, p.2099.

22. ARA, Memoir prepared by Dutch Director, George Louis Vernet, and submitted to the English on 10 May 1768, HRB 247.

23. ARA, Memoir by Taillefert for his successor, George Louis Vernet, 7 November 1763, HRB 246.

24. ARA, Memoir prepared by Dutch Director, George Louis Vernet, and submitted to the English on 10 May 1768, HRB 247; J.M. Ross at Khirpai to Director at Hugli, 8 July 1767, Appendix D, HRB 247.

25. ARA, The notification signed by J.P. Auriol, Assistant Secretary, HRB 253.

26. ARA, The English Company reply dated 8 September 1785 to the second Dutch memorandum, Mcpherson and Council to Eilbracht and van Citters, HRB 211.

27. To take a specific example, in 1767, against Rs 10 per piece paid by the English for a particular variety, the Dutch had to pay Rs 12:7 annas, ARA, J.M. Ross to Director at Hugli, Appendix A, HRB 247; J.M. Ross to Director at Hugli dated 12 May 1767, Appendix C, HRB 247.

28. ARA, Memoir by George Vernet for his successor, Faure, 8 March 1770, HRB 249; Memoir by outgoing Director Johannes Bacheracht for his successor, J.M. Ross, dated 31 July 1776, HRB 252.

8

Trade and Traders in the Bay of Bengal: Fifteenth to Nineteenth Centuries

KENNETH MCPHERSON

Introduction

During the eighteenth century, the maritime trade of the Bay of Bengal underwent profound changes. These changes culminated in the nineteenth century when European intrusion, and the creation of European territorial empires along the littoral of the Bay, undermined the role of indigenous mercantile groups and seafarers. European economic and political activity also fundamentally altered major directions of cargo flows as well as the composition of these cargoes.

From the early centuries of the present era, the maritime trade of the Bay of Bengal had been based upon servicing market demand along the littoral, and the transhipment of goods between the Arabian Sea and Southeast and East Asia. Few of the cargoes included goods from outside the Indian Ocean region—apart from Chinese exports such as pottery, porcelain and silk—and generally comprised the raw and processed products of the region. Such cargoes varied enormously in content and volume over time, but the basic structure of a distinctive Bay of Bengal maritime trade system remained remarkably consistent until the eighteenth century.

This trade network involved people from many communities in South Asia, and also peoples from Southeast Asia. Indeed, the development of a Bay of Bengal trading system was based upon the existence of two older maritime systems: one, based on an axis within Southeast Asia linking Sri Lanka, eastern India, Bengal and the Arakan coast, the other on an axis within Southeast Asia linking the mainland—from the Irrawaddy to the Mekong—with the Indonesian archipelago.

The timing of the conjunction of these two systems remains vague. By the third and fourth centuries AD, cargoes from the eastern reaches of South Asia were despatched to points on the Malay peninsula and the Tenasserim coast. At markets on these coasts south Asian merchants collected return cargoes of commodities gathered from elsewhere in South-east Asia by indigenous peoples. At the same time, there is evidence of the earliest Chinese maritime contacts with Southeast Asia which increased sporadically in coming centuries.

The ebb and flow of this maritime trade varied greatly over time as did the composition of cargoes. It depended essentially on the prosperity of littoral markets as consumers of goods produced within the boundaries of the Bay of Bengal and beyond. In turn, the prosperity of these markets was dependent upon the fate of states which controlled the littoral lands. Cargoes across the Bay of Bengal were, in the pre-modern era, subject to a great range of risks. Nature presented its own challenges, but in an age of limited communication technology market fluctuations added another great risk factor.

The picture of maritime trade across the Bay of Bengal before the arrival of Europeans late in the fifteenth century is riddled with lacunae. Historians have explored parts of the region, but largely in the context of the political boundaries imposed by European colonizers. British India, the Netherlands East Indies, Singapore, the Malayan peninsula, Thailand and Sri Lanka have been treated as discrete historical entities. There have been exceptions and scholars such as Coedes, Snouck Hurgronje, Schrieke and Van Leur 'did not stop short at political boundaries in the Bay of Bengal'.[1] Largely due to their efforts the history of the Bay of Bengal as an arena of human activity was given credence, if only in the sense that they individually managed to throw light on some of the historical strands which bound it into a distinctive centre of human intercourse. But they painted a large canvas, and there remains much we do not know about the history of the Bay of Bengal as a discrete entity. In addition to lacunae in the maritime histories of important areas such as Sri Lanka, and the Arakan and Tenasserim coasts, our knowledge of the maritime history of other areas such as the Coromandel coast, the Malay peninsula and insular Southeast Asia is periodic rather than continuous, and delineated by modern political boundaries.

If our knowledge of the mechanics of the maritime trade of the Bay of Bengal is piecemeal, our knowledge of the people involved in the trade is even more limited. This is a critical gap for the historian of the area, for without some understanding of the actors it is difficult if not impossible to understand the well-springs of maritime trade and its vital linkage with land-based human history. It is this point that Ashin Das Gupta has underscored in his work on South Asia and the maritime history of the Arabian Sea. His histories of Surat and the Malabar coast, although set in a specific time frame and focussed on a small geographic area, illustrate for the historian the central need to evaluate changes in maritime trade in the context of human activity on land as well as on sea.

To understand the profound changes which began to re-shape the maritime world of the Bay of Bengal in the eighteenth century, we must focus on the people involved in that world. Merchants, sailors, shipbuilders and rulers did not create trade *per se,* rather they took advantage of economic opportunities. Conversely, these participants could have their lives and fortunes adversely changed by economic and political events over which they had no control.

Whilst our knowledge of the human face of the maritime world of the Bay of Bengal before the eighteenth century is very limited, it is possible to gain some insights into specific areas at specific times. Such snapshots cannot substitute for a thorougoing history, but they provide leads for further research and the basis for some general conclusions. In this context, South Asian traders at Melaka and Southeast Asia in the fifteenth and sixteenth centuries, Indo-Portuguese traders on the Coromandel coast in the seventeenth and eighteenth centuries, and the establishment of a British Indian outpost at Penang in the late eighteenth century, highlight some of the fundamental changes which occurred in the history of the maritime world of the Bay of Bengal between the fifteenth and eighteenth centuries. In addition, such studies illustrate the nexus between human fortunes and the arcane workings of economic and political history.

Continuities and change

One of the major problems in the historiography of the Bay of Bengal until recently has been the tendency of scholars to segregate historical time in Asia into pre-European and European periods. This has discouraged the study of historical continuities in Asia, and has obscured the reality that fundamental changes in the nature and composition of trade across the Indian Ocean were not sudden, or of necessity associated with the arrival of the Portuguese, but took centuries to unfold. From the fifteenth to the eighteenth centuries, maritime trade across the Bay of Bengal continued to involve vigorous indigenous groups as partners in the evolution of European economic interest in the area.

When Europeans first arrived they did not overwhelm a 'traditional' maritime system in the Bay of Bengal, but rather they altered some of the aspects of that system, and at the same time integrated into it. The alterations they affected were associated with the diversion of some local cargoes, such as spices and pepper, more directly to

European markets. Their integration reflected their need to finance trading ventures and access cargoes for Europe at a time when local demand for European imports, apart from specie, was very limited. To survive, European traders had to find a niche in maritime trade between markets within the Bay of Bengal: the so-called 'country trade'. Lacking the ability to control markets, production areas and sealanes across the entire Indian Ocean, Europeans were forced to an accommodation with local trading groups and rulers in many areas, most particularly in the Bay of Bengal. During the eighteenth century, however, economic changes in European taste and the creation of a British territorial empire in India ushered in sweeping changes in the nature of trade across the Bay of Bengal, which finally overwhelmed vestiges of the pre-European trading system.

Merchants and sailors: Chulias, Klings and the Melaka trade

When the Portuguese first entered the Bay of Bengal they came across a flourishing trading system which linked the ports along the littoral of the Bay with one another and with ports in south–western India, Gujarat and West Asia. Pre-eminent amongst the indigenous traders and seafarers involved in this trade were two South Asian trading communities, the Chulias and Klings.[2]

As early as the twelfth century AD, Kling merchants and shipowners dominated trade between southern China and the Bay of Bengal through Quanzhou, where they built a substantial temple modelled on the great Meenakshi temple at Madurai. However, during the next century they were displaced by their Chinese rivals and by Muslims from various parts of the Indian Ocean littoral.

By the fourteenth century AD, Muslim traders and seafarers were to be found in all the ports of the Indian Ocean, from the Mozambique coast to Southeast Asia. This spectacular expansion of Muslim enterprise has been paralleled in the historical mind with the eclipse of Hindu enterprise in maritime trade. It certainly appears that there was a relative decline in the number of Hindus travelling as seafarers and traders, but the decline was far from absolute. Gujaratis, for example, both Hindu and Muslim, continued to frequent the ports of east Africa, and remained particularly numerous on the very profitable run between western India and Southeast Asia where Indian cotton cloth was in great demand. Similarly, on the Coromandel coast where Kling traders may not have voyaged as frequently as in earlier centuries, they appear to have retained close financial links with both shipping and seaborne trade, often in partnership with Chulias. Indeed, although Gujarati Muslims dominated South Asian maritime enterprise in the western Indian Ocean along with their

Hindu compatriots, Indian trade across the Bay of Bengal was dominated by a combine of Muslim Chulias and Hindu Klings from the Coromandel coast.

Although the Klings lost out on the direct trade with China they retained an important position in the trade between the Coromandel ports and Burma and the Malay peninsula. In fifteenth-century Melaka they were one of the most powerful foreign communities, with a Bendara in the Sultan's council and their own quarter known as Kampong Keling. In the same century, an Italian traveller, Conti, commented on the wealth of Melaka's Chulia community noting that they were '...very rich, so much so that some will carry on their business in forty of their own ships each of which is valued at 50,000 gold pieces.'[3]

Whilst Melaka was the centre of Kling and Chulia settlement and trade in Southeast Asia in the fifteenth century, considerable numbers were active in Patani on the east coast of the Malay peninsula where they engaged in the lucrative trade with the Thai kingdom of Ayuthia. Others were scattered in small communities along the Tenasserim coast as far north as Pegu.

The main export cargoes carried eastwards by Klings and Chulias comprised cotton cloth, ranging from the luxurious to the common. Return cargoes were dominated by tin, rare timber, exotic tropical products such as gum and medicinal drugs, pepper and spices. Tin, timber and jungle raw materials were probably collected from a variety of small coastal market places, whereas pepper and spices were most likely collected at the great entrepot of Melaka where fleets from the Indonesian archipelago unloaded cargoes gathered from Sumatra, Java and the Molouccas. On their return voyages these fleets carried south Asian cotton cloth to the far reaches of insular Southeast Asia. Ports on the Tenasserim coast and on the east coast of the Malay peninsula were likewise the points from which South Asia cotton cloth was distributed to the market places of mainland Southeast Asia.

It is not clear what the respective roles of the Klings and Chulias were in this trade. Present evidence suggests that the Chulias were both merchants and shipowners, whilst the Klings were rarely referred to as shipowners. We do know that the collection and distribution of goods from the Tamil hinterland to the Coromandel ports was controlled by powerful Hindu merchant guilds. It may not, therefore, be too much to assume that there was a symbiotic relationship between Klings and Chulias centred upon the Coromandel ports, and that Klings may have investd in Chulia shipping.[4]

With the capture of Melaka by the Portuguese in 1511, the Chulias —as Muslims—fled the port and sought shelter in other ports outside Portuguese control on the eastern shores of the Bay of Bengal. In contrast, the Klings flourished under Portuguese (and from 1641, Dutch) control in Melaka where they benefitted from the exclusion of South Asian and WestAsian Muslims. In addition, it seems likely that from this period the Klings once more emerged as shipowners. Muslim-owned vessels were, initially at least, barred from Melaka, and there was insufficient Portuguese-owned shipping to carry cargoes between Melaka and the Portuguese settlements in South Asia let alone to ports outside Portuguese control. The Klings were ideally situated to take advantage of this situation. As Macgregor pointed out, in the early years of the Portuguese occupation of Melaka, Kling merchants 'assisted the Portuguese in business matters...loaned their slaves in times of war, and, sometimes money as well'[5]. Indeed, so dependent were the Portuguese on local trading partners that by the late sixteenth century they were busy wooing the Chulias back to Melaka.[6]

Some Chulias did return to Melaka, but for the most part they focussed on ports outside Portuguese control. One area in particular attracted both Chulias and Klings: the Tenasserim coast gateway to the profitable trans-isthmian route from Pegu to the Thai capital of Ayuthia. Along the coast Kling and Chulia merchants dealt in a wide variety of export goods such as cotton textiles and tobacco from Tamil Nadu in return for cargoes of tin. By the early-seventeenth century, when the English and Dutch attempted to break into the Ayuthia trade, they found Coromandel interests well entrenched and encountered and dealt with Coromandel merchants in Southeast Asian ports stretching from Aceh to Manila. But, the central area of Chulia activity was within a diaspora which stretched from the Coromandel ports of Porto Novo and Cuddalore to the tin-exporting ports of the Tenasserim coast, Perak and Johore. Their ships carried cargoes of tin from Southeast Asia to the Coromandel coast where the tin was then re-exported on European-owned vessels.

Chulias and Klings were eagerly sought as partners in enterprise by the various European companies operating out of ports on the Coromandel coast and in Southeast Asia. On the Coromandel coast the English Company, the East India Company (the EIC) and Dutch Company, Verenigde Oostindische Compagnie (the VOC) sought their cooperation as a means of accessing the trading networks of Southeast Asia. In Southeast Asia, the Portuguese came to value them at Melaka as did their successors, the Dutch.

The trading alliance between the Chulias and Dutch, however, collapsed in the early-eighteenth century when the Chulias fell foul of Dutch ambition in the Malay peninsula. The Chulias provided the tin-rich Malay sultanates with links to the Coromandel coast at a time when Dutch ambitions were to create an exclusive mercantile system in insular Southeast Asia which incorporated the Malay peninsula. Perhaps because of the prominent role they played in the tin trade of various Malay sultanates which resisted Dutch claims to hegemony, the Chulias were expelled from Melaka in the early-eighteenth century. In contrast, the Dutch continued to cultivate the Kling community in Melaka.

The Chulias removed themselves northwards away from the baleful attention of the Dutch. By the middle of the eighteenth century large numbers of them had settled along the Kedah coast and on Phuket island from where they controlled the tin trade with the Coromandel coast. This trade inevitably brought them into close contact with expanding British commercial interest on the Coromandel coast which were beginning to focus more sharply on Southeast Asia.

Until the eighteenth century, groups such as the Chulias and the Klings were vitally important to the operations of the EIC on the Coromandel coast. Not only did they provide vital cargoes of Southeast Asian commodities, but they distributed cotton textiles from southern India into markets on the eastern shore of the Bay and into Southeast Asia. In the absence of any Company base in Southeast Asia (apart from Benkulu on the western coast of Sumatra) the British were vitally dependent upon partnerships with groups such as the Chulias and Klings.

Outpost and outcastes: the Portuguese on the Coromandel Coast[7]

The Chulias and Klings were the first partners Europeans sought as they edged into the trade of the Bay of Bengal in the sixteenth and early seventeenth centuries. But, from the early seventeenth century, the English, Dutch, Danes and French were also keen to incorporate the skills and knowledge of Portuguese commodities in southern India in their drive to penetrate maritime trade networks into Southeast Asia.

During the sixteenth and seventeenth centuries, the Portuguese established a flourishing unofficial trading presence on the Coromandel coast. Neglected by historians, this presence is worth a study as it provides an excellent example of how early European traders had to cooperate with indigenous traders and seamen, and subsequently with one another, to gain a foothold in the maritime economy of the Bay of Bengal. In addition, the history of the community illustrates the changes wrought by European enterprise upon the traditional maritime world of the Bay of Bengal, as their interests expanded and became less reliant upon indigenous collaborators.

Whilst not addressing directly the question of indigenous and European cooperation in the Indian Ocean, Holden Furber wrote in 1951 that 'nationality stopped east of the Cape', and that business interests encouraged cooperation between the Portuguese, Dutch, English, Danes and French 'in their common desire for individual gain'.[8] Private traders of all nations were enmeshed with one another in the interlocking networks of Asian trade. Sometimes they were friends, sometimes enemies, but the pursuit of profit frequently cut across formal political loyalties. Furber provided a fascinating example of this intermingling of interests when he detailed the first Danish attempt to enter the Manila trade from their base at Tranquebar in 1745. The initiator was the commander of the French factory at Pondicherry, Dupleix. The Danes provided the ship, the former French vessel the *Restancier* (renamed the *Dansborg*), which was registered in the name of a Chulia merchant. A Kling provided the cargo, and the ship was crewed by a Danish captain, a Scots supercargo, and two Portuguese *mestiços* who were mate and helmsman.[9]

The Portuguese settlements on the Coromandel coast had a tenuous relationship with the *Estado da India* based at Goa. Throughout the sixteenth and seventeenth centuries, the *Estado* vainly sought to impose its authority on the prosperous communities of Portuguese private traders in Pulicat, Porto Novo (Parangi Pettai), São Tomé and Nagapattinam on the southern Coromandel coast.[10] The Portuguese on the coast lived on the frontiers of the *Estado,* and developed a very profitable and extensive commercial network within the fabric of Asian maritime trade across the Bay of Bengal between India, Southeast Asia and China. Unlike their compatriots in Melaka they worked closely with local Muslims—such as the Chulias of Nagapattinam[11]—as well as with the Klings.

The first Portuguese settlements on the southern Coromandel coast were established at Pulicat and São Tomé in 1521, followed in the 1530s by Nagapattinam and Porto Novo. Their prosperity was based on the export of locally woven textiles designed and painted for markets in Southeast Asia and, to a more limited extent, on the sale of rice to the Portuguese in Sri Lanka. By the middle of the sixteenth century, Nagapattinam on the Kaveri delta was the most important of all these ports and possessed what was probably the finest natural harbour on the coast. São Tomé had no natural harbour, and it depended on nearby Pulicat for an all-weather anchorage to protect its ships during the monsoons.

The Portuguese authorities at Goa attempted to exercise some control over the Portuguese inhabitants of these ports through the appointment of a 'Captain Major' for each port, although political authority resided with local Indian rulers. Goa hoped to control the spiritual life of the local Portuguese through a bishopric established at São Tomé in 1606, and attempted to order their trading activities by institutionalizing a system of concession voyages between the Coromandel coast and Southeast Asia. But this economic regulation was flouted, and private Portuguese traders developed their own links to ports around the Bay of Bengal.

In 1613, the Dutch took Pulicat from official Portuguese control. This event caused some panic in São Tomé and a temporary decline in its fortunes. But Nagapattinam continued to prosper, and its Portuguese inhabitants eagerly cooperated with the Danish factory at Tranquebar, which was settled in 1620.[12] Indeed, this pragmatism in commerce was fast becoming a hallmark of the Portuguese trader on the Coromandel coast. In Pulicat, for example, there was a community of Portuguese *overloopers* (interlopers) from São Tomé in the service of the VOC as early as 1615. By the 1640s these settlers 'were even acting as middlemen in the purchase of textiles' for the VOC.[13]

Whilst the loss of Pulicat was a blow to the prestige of the *Estado* and to the fortunes of São Tomé, it had minimal impact on the Portuguese at Nagapattinam. They quickly moved into the Makassar, Manila and Pegu trade, as well as increasing their trade with Portuguese settlements at Hughli and Chittagong in Bengal. The career of Francisco Vieira is typical of this adjustment. Born in Portugal, Vieira lived in Nagapattinam in the 1620s, then moved eventually to Makassar where he played a central role in the development of that kingdom's export trade in cooperation with merchants from all other nations, until finally brought to heel by the Dutch in the 1660s. As Boxer comments

> His career exemplifies an aspect of the Portuguese presence in Asia which is too often disregarded; for it is commonly believed that the Portuguese were essentially warriors and missionaries rather than traders and merchants, and that they were unable to compete effectively with their Dutch and English rivals.[14]

In 1632, Portuguese trade with Bengal received a near fatal blow when the Mughals drove them from Hughli. Nagapattinam balanced the loss of its Bengal markets by increasing its trade with Makassar. The port even recovered some share of its former trade with Bengal when the Portuguese established a new settlement at Balasore in the 1640s which 'continued to present a...serious problem' to their Dutch rivals in the area.[15] But Dutch rivalry on the Coromandel was becoming an increasing threat to Portuguese interests as they began to extend their activities south from Pulicat, in an attempt to capture the textile export trade of the Portuguese. Dutch attacks on Portuguese shipping increased and some Portuguese took to flying the English flag in an attempt to avoid Dutch harassment.[16] The Dutch were aware of what was going on, but they could do little to stop the practice.

Indeed, it was the English who were emerging as allies of the Portuguese on the Coromandel coast. Relations between the *Estado* and the English may have been shaky, but beyond the formal boundaries of the *Estado*, private Portuguese traders were learning to extract advantages from mounting Anglo-Dutch rivalry and enmity. Initially, Anglo-Portuguese relations on the Coromandel coast were poor. In contrast, the English and the Dutch appeared firm friends. But this halcyon period of Anglo-Dutch relations ended abruptly on the Coromandel coast when news was received of the 'Amboyna Massacre', and when the Dutch authorities at Pulicat sharply increased the rent they charged the English for warehouse space.

The breakdown in the Anglo-Dutch accord on the Coromandel coast led to the establishment of the English factory at Madras (Fort St George). Their new base was to the south of Pulicat and within walking distance of São Tomé.

The English at Fort St George were keen to encourage Portuguese settlement, and amongst the original party of settlers were a few Portuguese merchants.[17] To attract Portuguese they were offered freedom of religion, housing subsidies and the same commercial privileges as English private traders, provided they paid a 4 per cent customs duty. The Company encouraged Portuguese settlement because 'The residence of the Portugalls was reckoned a cause of increase of trade and the Companies customes'[18], and in 1680 the Council of Fort St George reported that 'our greatest income arises from the customs upon...Portuguese commerce.'[19] The Danes at Tranquebar and the French at Pondicherry, which was established in 1672, were also keen to attract Portuguese settlers to their ports.

The settlement of Portuguese in Madras was encouraged by increasing Dutch attacks on their shipping and posts along the coast, and by the Dutch capture of Melaka which threatened their access to the harbours of Southeast Asia. But the Portuguese traders of São Tomé, Porto Novo and Nagapattinam for the most part did not desert their ports, and intensified their sale of cloth at Makassar as well as at Manila where they had access to supplies of New World silver. Boyajian, indeed, has argued that by the 1630s resident Portuguese traders in India, the *casados,* had redirected their Asian trade away from Goa and the Cape of Good Hope to the Coromandel coast. In this process they pioneered a regular trade with Manila and the Indonesian archipelago, which was much more profitable than participation in the *carreira* and 'country trade' of the western Indian Ocean.[20]

It was this resurgent trade into Southeast Asia which piqued the English and illustrates the complex nature of Anglo-Portuguese 'friendship' on the Coromandel coast. Whilst the English welcomed Portuguese settlers to Madras, they considered the Portuguese from Nagapattinam in particular as their most serious rivals in Makassar, where their profits from the clove trade were rapidly falling in the face of massive cloth imports by the Portuguese from the Coromandel coast. Unable to confront the Portuguese directly, the English changed tack, and the authorities at the EIC's main factory at Surat attempted to break into the Manila market in the 1640s, but with no success, despite the fact that 'a Portugall Negro' was involved as intermediary.[21]

Whilst in overall terms at this period Nagapattinam was the most serious rival of the English at Madras, it was the presence of São Tomé, just a short walk to the south, which daily irked the factors at Fort St George. The situation was more than a little bizarre. Each morning large numbers of Portuguese from São Tomé walked along the beach to trade and work in Madras, each evening they returned home. The Captain Major of São Tomé fulminated and the bishop remonstrated, but the Portuguese of São Tomé were quite happy to work for and with the English. Official relations between the two settlements were strained. In 1642, Goa sent extra troops to São Tomé as a warning to the English, much to the annoyance of its Portuguese inhabitants who had to support them, and in 1646 the English assisted the sultan of Golconda when he unsuccessfully laid siege to the Portuguese settlement.[22] In general, however, official relations on the spot were reasonably good, if for no other reson than during the 1640s and 50s both the English and the Portuguese on the Coromandel coast were plagued by turbulent hinterlands, as the Hindu-ruled state of Vijayanagara collapsed under pressure from the Muslim-ruled state of Bijapur. In turn, Bijapur fell to its co-religionists from Golconda. Neither the local English, nor the local

Portuguese, were a match for the roving armies which at various times laid siege to São Tomé, Porto Novo and Fort St George.

In Burma, the VOC also faced problems with the Portuguese, and reacted more violently than the EIC by stepping up the intensity of its attacks on Nagapattinam. So fierce was its onslaught that in 1643 the Portuguese at Nagapattinam finally accepted the authority of Goa and a fortress was constructed.[23] The construction of the fort did not ultimately save Nagapattinam which fell to the Dutch in 1658. Some Portuguese accepted Dutch rule, but the majority dispersed to São Tomé, Porto Novo, Tranquebar and Madras.

After suffering a siege by the forces of the kingdom of Bijapur in 1661, São Tomé was captured in the following year by an army from the kingdom of Golconda which held the port until 1672. In that year it was taken and held by the French before reverting to a joint Muslim–VOC occupation in 1674. The VOC now regarded the port as of little significance as it was largely decayed. A few of its Portuguese inhabitants remained, their numbers augmented by some refugees from Nagapattinam, but the majority had fled to Madras where the most important Portuguese merchants were now located.

In 1687, some of these merchants, annoyed by the Company demanding extra taxes and customs payments in advance, began negotiating with the ruler of Golconda (and then with the Mughals who conquered Golconda) to resettle the largely ruined site of Sào Tomé. Despite the opposition of the EIC they were successful, and 'privately, basefully and ungratefully sneaked away.'[24] The flag of Portugal was raised once more over the town, but practical support was not forthcoming from Lisbon or Goa. Lisbon's interests was now focussed on Mozambique and Goa, and as far as the Bay of Bengal was concerned 'Lisbon suffered from amnesia'.[25]

The English were opposed to the reestablishment of São Tomé for several reasons. Generally speaking they were increasingly concerned by the growth of French influence on the Coromandel coast, particularly after the settlement of Pondicherry in 1672, and viewed with suspicion the many signs of Franco-Portuguese friendship. More immediately they feared a revival of independent Portuguese commerce in the area and the defection of Portuguese soldiers and civilians from Madras, where they outnumbered the English by more than six to one.[26]

Despite the antipathy of Madras and the indifference of Lisbon, São Tomé survived as a moderately successful port until the mid 1700s, with links stretching across the Bay of Bengal to Bengal, Burma and Manila. Its prosperity was enhanced by the support of the local Muslim ruler (the Nawab of Arcot, successor to the Mughal rulers) who patronized the port in an attempt to undermine the commercial pretensions of the English at Madras. Indeed, by the early 1700s the value of São Tomé's trade was nealy one third that of Madras.[27] The English tried a variety of means to undermine this trade, but it was not curbed until they took advantage of Portuguese–French collaboration at the height of Anglo-French conflict in southern India in 1749, to occupy the port.

Whilst São Tomé's fortunes fluctuated, Porto Novo fell to the Dutch in 1690. In the 1660s the Portuguese of Porto Novo had taken over Nagapattinam's Manila trade, and merchants such as Manual Teixeira Pinto were courted by the EIC 'with a view to promoting their own trade'.[28] Such merchants built up considerable fortunes although they 'carefully maintained a distance from the imperial structure of the *Estado'*.[29] By the 1680s, Porto Novo was the most prominent port south of Madras and dominated by Portuguese and Chulia traders whose ships sailed to Pegu, Aceh, Melaka, Goa and Manila. But, Madras was an irresistible magnet for many local Portuguese, and the focus of Portuguese commercial activity on the Coromandel coast was firmly centred on the city by the beginning of the eighteenth century.

By the end of the seventeenth century, the Dutch were a spent force on the Coromandel coast and, ironically, were survived by still-thriving Portuguese commercial groups. The reasons for the decline of the VOC in the area are complex. In part they relate to its inflexible commercial policies and need for a high level of profits, compared with Portuguese private traders who dealt in a wider variety of commodities and were content with smaller profit margins.[30]

By 1700, all the Portuguese settlements on the Coromandel coast, with the exception of São Tomé, had vanished. The most thriving Portuguese community was located in Madras, which was until the early decades of the eighteenth century, a predominantly Portuguese rather than an English city in terms of European population and language.[31] The Portuguese moved into the commercial world of Madras with little or no trouble. Their knowledge of the markets of the Bay of Bengal and Southeast Asia was invaluable both to the EIC and to English private traders who were not slow to make use of their expertise. This was particularly true when the English renewed their attempts to break into the Manila trade which the Spanish jealously guarded.

The EIC was determined to access the flow of silver from Mexico and Peru to Manila to finance its growing trade with China. In both

Bengal (where an English factory had been established at Calcutta in 1690) and at Madras, the EIC needed Manila silver to pay for its purchases in India and to obtain export cargoes in China. As mentioned above, as early as 1644 the EIC factory at Surat had attempted to break into the Manila trade using a Portuguese intermediary, but with little success. By the 1670s fresh attempts were underway at Madras, encouraged by growing Spanish interest in trade between Manila, Bengal, São Tomé, the Malabar coast and Surat. This paralleled a similar attempt by the EIC factors at Bantam in the Indonesian islands, before they were expelled by the Dutch in 1682.[32] The Spanish were primarily interested in purchasing textiles, and in both Calcutta and Madras there is evidence of local Portuguese acting as agents for the Spanish as well as for the EIC. On the Coromandel coast the EIC was 'surreptitiously...utilizing the services of the Indo-Portuguese merchants of St. Thomas and Madras' to trade privately with Manila.[33]

Not only were Portuguese merchants used as intermediaries but there was extensive use of Portuguese pilots, interpreters and ships registered as Portuguese-owned and carrying Portuguese names. In 1684, William Dampier commented that 'Sometimes the English merchants of Fort St. George send their ships [to the Philippines] as it were by Stealth, under the charge of Portuguese Pilots', and by the 1690s it was regular practice at Madras to issue passes to English 'Manilha Shipps' to 'goe under Portigues coulers'.[34]

This practice continued into the eighteenth century. Of 114 voyages on the Madras–Manila–Madras run between 1707 and 1752, 25 per cent of the ships involved were registered as owned by Madras Portuguese. By the 1740s, however, the frequency of Portuguese ownership was declining, and in the 1750s, the English at Madras were legislating to prevent cargoes on the Manila run being laden on vessels flying the Portuguese and French flags before English ships had obtained full cargoes.[35]

This change in tack on the part of the authorities at Madras was due to an increase in available British tonnage. This led to competition on the coast for cargoes, and to an increasing self-confidence amongst local British merchants which was leading them away from a reliance upon Portuguese expertise. But the decline of Portuguese-owned shipping on the coast was also probably due to the relative paucity of Portuguese venture capital needed for investment in modern shipping. The Portuguese were still players in the seaborne commerce of the coast, but they were being reduced by a shortage of capital to minor partners of the British. As late as 1749 there were still a few very wealthy Portuguese in Madras, such as Antonia de Madeiros (widow of 'Lewis Madeira', shipowner) who loaned the Company a fortune in 1749 when it was fighting the French, but relatively the number and wealth of the Portuguese had declined in relation to the English community and to Hindu mercantile groups such as the Chettiars.[36]

It would seem that English antipathy was not directed at local Portuguese, but rather against Portuguese from Macao who began to make inroads into the Malabar sugar and Bengal silk trade by the 1720s. What the legislation in Madras does suggest, in the context of the occupation of São Tomé in 1749, was that the EIC was not prepared to tolerate Portuguese operating outside the British commercial system, although they were quite happy to take advantage of their expertise within the system.

By the middle of the eighteenth century, Portuguese maritime activity out of eastern India was in sharp decline. Portuguese merchants were still prominent in cities such as Calcutta and Madras, but they were for the most part land-bound merchants. There are no indications that the previously prominent role played by local Portuguese in shipping across the Bay of Bengal had been maintained. Vessels flying the Portuguese flag were still sailed from Madras and Calcutta, but the flag was now one of convenience, and ownership of most of these vessels had in most instances passed to British and Indian interests.

The mid-eighteenth century also marked a turning point in relations between British and Portuguese at the local level on the Coromandel coast. The Anglo-French war of the mid century cast a slur on the loyalty of many Portuguese in Madras. Local Roman Catholic clergy were penalized for collaboration with the French who occupied Fort St George in 1749, with the result that the two Catholic churches in the Fort were demolished by the British in 1752 although compensation was later paid. In addition, the fortunes of several Portuguese were confiscated and the attempts of the Portuguese at Goa to recover São Tomé were brusquely rejected.[37] Not all wealthy Portuguese in Madras suffered during this period, but as a community they were in decline literally and in the eyes of the authorities who had found new partners in the rapidly changing economic world of South Asia. In the late eighteenth century, however, there was to be one last revival of Anglo-Portuguese commercial collaboration in the Bay of Bengal. This resulted from the final attempt of the British to break into the Manila market.[38]

In the 1780s, the Spanish government had barred all European shipping, except that of the Portuguese, from the trade of Manila. But pressure built up in Spain from merchants to permit direct trade to Asia and to abandon the one permitted annual voyage between Acapulco and Manila. In 1785, the annual galleon was abandoned and the Royal Spanish Philippine Company was founded to promote direct trade between Spain and Manila.

The major problem facing the Company was access to adequate supplies of Asian goods (particularly Indian textiles) at Manila.[39] To overcome the shortage of supplies of Asian goods, the Company began to develop a clandestine trade with Madras and Calcutta. The Company's first agent in India was the Portuguese business house of J. & L. da Costa with offices in Madras and Calcutta.[40] Between 1787 and 1790, 5 to 7 ships were involved in this Bengal–Manila trade, all of which sailed the Portuguese flag and had British and Portuguese commanders. But in 1790, the Spanish opened Manila to all European shipping and this event, in effect, marked the end of the era of Anglo-Portuguese mercantile cooperation in the Bay of Bengal and Southeast Asia.

By the beginning of the nineteenth century the British were all but masters of the European commerce in the Indian Ocean and politically had finally trounced both the French and the Dutch in the region. In addition, the EIC was in the process of being reduced to the governing agency of British India and lost its trade monopoly. This opened the trade of Asia to the full impact of emerging European and north-American capitalism. At one level, one could argue that having penetrated the major Asian markets, now that they had no need of the Portuguese, the British cast them aside. To a certain extent it may be that this view informed British attitudes. But, it could also be argued that changing economic and commercial circumstances overtook the Portuguese merchants of Asia and made them irrelevant.

Fundamental changes in shipping were underway which reduced the importance of locally-owned shipping in Asia. Local shipowners had no access to new shipping technologies relating to speed, cargo capacity and safety. Europeans, particularly the British, developed and controlled this new technology and undermined the commercial viability of local merchants and shipowners in Asia, reducing them at best to the role of agents dependant upon their ability to service European business houses.

The Indo-Portuguese merchants and shipowners of South Asia shared the fate of many local entrepreneurs who had been intimately involved with the establishment of British commerce in South and South–east Asia. Hindu, Muslim and 'Portuguese' merchants had collaborated successfully with British merchants throughout the seventeenth and eighteenth centuries, but in the course of the early nineteenth century they fell victims to major economic changes in Europe which changed the rules of Indian Ocean commerce. Until the eighteenth century, the major profits from Indian Ocean trade were made from trade within the Indian Ocean. From the mid-eighteenth century this was reversed, with profits from the direct trade between the region and Europe far exceeding those made from intra-regional trading voyages. In this redirection of maritime trade, indigenous merchants (and by the eighteenth century, the Portuguese of South Asia could be considered indigenous) were at a disadvantage compared to the British in terms of capital and market access. The result was that they moved from economic relationships based upon relative equality to one of subordination.[41]

Penang: the Indian emporium

As the old commercial alliance between the Portuguese and the British in the Bay of Bengal waned, there was a rapid increase in British maritime activity in the area. This was in part stimulated by the acquisition of Indian territories which produced export commodities such as textiles, opium and indigo. A further stimulation came from Europe where the changing market demand led to the eclipse of 'traditional' European cargoes of spices, pepper and textiles by new cargoes of Chinese tea and a variety of tropical raw materials.

Put most simply, the interest of Europeans in the maritime trading world of the Bay of Bengal shifted during the late eighteenth century. No longer were they seeking cargoes for Europe from the area, but rather they began trading the exports of the area into Southeast and East Asia in return for new commodities in demand in Europe.

In August 1786, Captain Francis Light, a former opium trader on the Kedah coast, took possession of the island of Penang on behalf of the EIC under lease from the Sultan of Kedah.

The decision to establish a new commercial base in Southeast Asia was taken in the context of the EIC's traditional commercial and strategic interests. But its foundation coincided with the beginning of a new trade era in Southeast Asia, which came of age in 1819 when Stamford Raffles established the free port of Singapore. The history of Penang can only be understood in the context of a rapidly changing era of commerce and strategy, as the major European powers underwent profound economic transformations and competed for ascendancy on the world stage.

Singapore was a spectacular commercial success and marked the triumph of the doctrine of free trade over monopolistic forms of mercantilism, which had dominated European commerce with Asia from the sixteenth century. But the idea of a free port did not originate with Raffles, for in 1787 Sir John Macpherson, then Governor-General of India, wrote that:

> If the situation is favourable, the merchants will find their advantages in resorting with their goods to it, and as an inducement to them, we desire [to] refrain from levying any kind of duties or tax on goods landed or vessels importing at Prince of Wales Island [Penang], and it is our wish to make the port free to all nations.[42]

From its foundation, Penang was envisaged as a free port which held promise of opening the door to the China trade. Its establishment was both a precursor to a new age and the last gasp of the old. Its early years mark the break between traditional European commerce in Asian waters and the emergence of free-wheeling capitalistic enterprise which was given such vibrant from in Singapore after 1819.

The acquistion of Penang was undertaken without any detailed planning and in the desperate hope that a free port in Southeast Asia would link the India trade with China. The EIC was ill-prepared for such a venture, and it was simply concerned that the base should pay for itself as well as providing ready access to the highly profitable China tea trade. There was no model for the establishment of such a port, and ultimately the promise of Penang was to fall victim to changing imperial commercial and strategic concerns.

Penang was founded in the years of transition for British trade in Asia. It flourished very briefly as an entrepot for the China trade in the last years of the Company's monopoly of British trade in the East, and then metamorphosed into an entrepot for a much more geographically restricted area of Southeast Asia and the Bay of Bengal. Its enduring trade with China was based on the export of Southeast Asian commodities, rather than on any substantial linkages with the export trade of India for which it was initially conceived.

The reasons for the establishment of a British settlement at Penang relate to the financial and political state of the East India Company. By the middle of the eighteenth century, the EIC had been transformed from a monopolistic trading concern to the ruler of vast tracts of territory in the Indian sub-continent. This acquisition of territory made many individual fortunes, but it was a resource problem which stretched the finances of the EIC to breaking point. The EIC's profits were further undermined by declining demand in Europe for Indian cargoes, and the antipathy of the French, Dutch and Spanish on the waters of the Indian Ocean and in many Asian markets.

The great hope of the EIC was that it would break into new markets, the most profitable of which was the burgeoning China tea trade. But the China trade was problematical, given that the main EIC exports from India—cotton goods and opium—were not in great demand in China or were illegal imports. To obtain Chinese tea, the EIC had to trade Indian goods elsewhere in return for specie and commodities, such as pepper and tin, that could be traded in China for cargoes of tea. The potential market which attracted the EIC was insular Southeast Asia where there was a growing demand for Indian cloth and opium, and plentiful supplies of pepper, Spanish dollars and exotic tropical commodities which fetched good prices in China.

Insular Southeast Asia, however, was largely barred to EIC trade by the Dutch who jealously guarded their expanding empire. In the Philippines too the Spanish were generally hostile to the EIC.

On the Malay peninsula, however, Dutch influence had not stretched northwards beyond their great fortress at Melaka, and local rulers were keen to involve the EIC as a counterweight to Dutch pretensions and the growing power of the Burmese and Thai kingdoms. In addition, EIC agents and individual British merchants—such as Light—reported that local trading groups and rulers in insular Southeast Asia, from the Riau islands to Sulawesi, were keen to escape the Dutch trading monopoly by dealing directly with the EIC to purchase Indian cargoes in return for commodities (and Spanish silver dollars) which could be traded profitably with China.

From the 1760s, the Company was courted by the rulers of Riau and Kedah who were under pressure from the Dutch. In 1768, an anonymous Company agent was approached by the Sultan of Riau to have:

> an English resident to reside on Pulo Byang, for the convenience of carrying on Trade with the English, and would be very glad to contract a nearer acquaintance and friendship with that nation for several reasons, first for the advantage of Trade and Manufactures on the island of Byntang [Bintan] where he resides, secondly he is an independent King, as yet unmolested by any European Nation, and of late years his Port is become a place of considerable Trade particularly frequented by the English, which occasions the Dutch to look on this Port as their rival; they have already insulted several Pires [*prahus*] belonging to that Port, this gives the King a great deal of uneasiness and makes him apprehensive that they will soon go further [and] he asked me seriously what method he should take to prevent his being molested by that Barbarous Nation as he calls the Dutch.[43]

The writer went on to note that Bintan was frequented by a great number of vessels from Borneo, Bali, Java, Thailand, Cambodia and Cochin-China. It would therefore be a fine port to link into the China trade, given local demand for Indian goods and the possibility of purchasing cargoes for sale in China.

But the EIC did nothing until the early 1780s. In September 1780, Captain James Scott, a 'Country Trader' (an independent British merchant who traded in cooperation with the East India Company in Asia) and partner of Francis Light, reported to the Company that the island of Penang should be equipped as a naval base, given the growing hostility of the Dutch at Melaka astride 'the thoroughfare of our Europe, Madras, Bengal, Bombay and China ships'.[44]

The strategic alarm was calculated to provoke the Company to action. By the early 1780s, the EIC was increasingly concerned that both the Dutch and the French were expanding their interests to the detriment of British commerce in Southeast Asia. Fears were voiced that the French were determined to secure the tin trade of the Tenasserim coast, and that the Dutch were expanding into the Malay peninsula to 'entirely prevent any other Nation from having any share in the Trade of these countries.'[45] In addition, the Company was growing more desperate to 'secure a market for the disposal of the Opium produced in Bengal'.[46]

By early 1786, the EIC has decided to establish a base at Penang which it regarded as ideally suited for the China trade and as a penal settlement for Indian criminals. It was also believed that possession of Penang would gurard against Dutch antipathy. In resolving to accept the offer of the Sultan of Kedah, the Board of the East India Company noted that:

> an Establishment properly secured at this place will connect the Bengal trade with that of China and is much wanted as well as for the promotion of that valuable Commerce as to afford a windward port of refreshment and repair to the King's, the Company's and the Country Ships. The Harbour of Pinang will be particularly convenient to the Company's ships which proceed from Madras, Bombay and [the] Ganges for China and it will afford a station from which His Majesty's Squadron may at any season proceed to the support of the Company's settlements upon either Coast and as the Dutch have taken possession of Rhio, in fact of all the Malacca ports, Pinang will afford a mart for the praus of the Eastern Seas and the sale of our opium.[47]

No mention was made of the French. However, in his letter to the Secret Committee of the Company's Board of Directors in January 1786 concerning the acquisition of Penang, the Governor-General, Sir John Macpherson, noted that 'I have long had my eye to the movements of the French at Pegu and Cochin China' where they had recently obtained permission to establish factories.[48]

In the treaty signed between the Sultan of Kedah and the EIC on 2 March 1786, the Company agreed to keep armed vessels permanently in the area to guard the island and coast and to promote 'free trade for all nations'[49].

During the first thirty years of its existence, Penang developed into a substantial port whose population grew from 986 in 1786 to *c.* 30,000 in 1805, comprising Chinese, Chulias, Malays, Arabs, Europeans and various other communities from across Southeast Asia.[50]

Although Penang was sparsely inhabited when the Company took possession, the Kedah coast has long been frequented by indigenous vessels from eastern India, Burma and the Indonesian archipelago. Kedah merchants were active in the tin trade throughout the peninsula and insular Southeast Asia, Bugis brought spices from the Moluccas, Chinese junks came annually and the ruler of Kedah 'was by the 1750s equipping his own vessels to send to India, to the annoyance of the Dutch'[51].

Within days of its proclamation as a Company settlement, Penang attracted a polyglot collection of inhabitants: Malays, local Christians and Chinese, Eurasians, and Chulia merchants who established the first bazaar.[52] Light immediately tackled the question of financing the Company's China trade, particularly as the Company was still not certain that they would retain the Penang base if it did not quickly return a profit.[53] He noted that many of the Company's China-bound vessels arrived at Penang in ballast, and suggested that local goods should be stockpiled at the port for carriage to China in place of ballast. To obtain local goods, Light requestd regular supplies of the Company's opium.[54]

Initially, Penang flourished. There was a steady influx of settlers ranging from Bengali convicts to Chinese artisans. From the first days of its existence, the most prosperous, if not the most numerous, section of the population were Chinese, whose activities as artisans and shopkeepers were highly praised by the British. The Chulias were less well regarded, and Light found them not 'worthy of much confidence or fear as subjects'.[55] Unlike the Chinese, many of the Chulias were seasonal visitors, and 'the vessels from the coast [of India] bring over annually 1,500 or 2,000 men'.[56]

Despite Dutch antipathy, Penang rapidly developed into a flourishing commercial base, and the Company held high hopes that it would soon evolve into the major entrepot for the China trade. Records relating to trade are patchy, but it certainly seems that the port soon attracted a large number of substantial indigenous and

European-owned sailing crafts, plus literally thousands of *prahus* annually. In 1786–7, for example, out of 42 ships that called at Penang, 17 came from Pegu, Mergui, Ache, Melaka or eastward; 6 from Nagore, Nagapattinam, Porto Novo, Tranquebar and Pondicherry; 11 from Bengal, 7 from Canton and Macao; and 1 from America.[57] In addition to these listed vessels, fleets of Bugi prahus arrived annually (1836 in 1799 and 3328 in 1802[58]) bringing millions of Spanish silver dollars to be exchanged for Bengal opium and south Indian piece-goods.[59]

Throughout the 1790s, the number of country craft and prahus visiting Penang increased rapidly, as did the total volume of trade. Imports increased nearly eightfold between 1789 and 1792, and exports rose from Spanish dollars 2.71 million to 31.74 million. In this period, Light was able to sell large consignments of Company opium, and remitted several hundred thousand Spanish silver dollars to China for the purchase of tea.[60]

By the first decade of the nineteenth century, Penang was flourishing: but not quite in the manner the EIC had envisaged. Penang had certainly become a trade centre, although it was visited more frequently by country ships and prahus than by the Company's ships. The Company was certainly accruing silver dollars and exotic cargoes for sale in China, but the true prosperity of Penang was based on trade which operated independently of the Company's needs. Penang had become a major entrepot for local rather than international trade. The greater volume of its commerce was with adjacent indigenously-controlled ports, ranging from Sumatra to Burma and southern India, rather than directly with the Company's ports in India and with China. Few Company ships picked up substantial cargoes at Penang, and the Company was increasingly concerned that its official establishment on the island was still in debt to the Bengal treasury.

The reality was that British trade with China was changing. An increasing number of Company ships sailed with full cargoes from India and no longer called at Penang to pick up goods for sale in China.[61] By the early nineteenth century, Penang's links with China were greatly weakened in terms of the Company's trade with that country.

In addition to Penang's increasing irrelevance to the Company's China trade, serious concerns were being voiced that Penang was located too far from the major maritime trade routes in Southeast Asia to continue as the major British commercial base in the area. Stamford Raffles, then a young Assistant Secretary at Penang, was, for example, by 1808 advocating that Penang be abandoned in favour of Melaka which he claimed was a much better anchorage.[62] Penang was indeed too far from the major centres of commercial activity. Another argument for the relocation of Britain's major base in Southeast Asia was that there was little demand for Penang's produce, or its re-exports, beyond an arc of ports stretching around the Bay of Bengal from northern Sumatra to southern India.

But dreams were slow to die. The Company lost its trade monopoly in 1813 and lingered on as little more than the managing agency of India for the British government, but it was loathe to radically alter its establishment in Southeast Asia once peace was agreed with the Dutch, and Melaka and Java were returned to them. The harsh reality was, however, that Penang was still losing money, and in 1819, Stamford Raffles had established an alternative commercial base on the island of Singapore which immediately attracted Chinese settlers from Penang, the annual fleets of Bugi prahus which had formerly patronized the port, private British merchants and Chulia and Arab traders. Penang's fortunes were further depleted by 1819 as the Chinese demand for opium increased and for Penang's re-exports declined.[63] The India–China trade was no longer posited upon the entrepot functions of Penang, whose inhabitants prospered on a much more geographically-restricted range of commercial transactions.

Conclusion

Between the fifteenth and nineteenth centuries, maritime trade in the Bay of Bengal changed considerably. In the fifteenth century, there existed a 'traditional' maritime trading system within the Bay of Bengal with direct links into other parts of the Indian Ocean region and East Asia, and indirectly into the Mediterranean. In the sixteenth century, European intruders entered the Bay of Bengal where, until the late eighteenth century, their fortunes were largely dependent upon indigenous partners and finding means to work the 'traditional' maritime system to their own benefit. Europeans introduced direct economic linkages with Europe, but dealt mainly in traditional export cargoes from the Bay of Bengal and other parts of the Indian Ocean region.

By the late eighteenth century, fundamental changes in European demand and European political power in the Indian Ocean region led to new types of commercial practice in the region. Europeans were now extracting new cargoes and exerting new pressures, and their reliance upon indigenous partners declined. Until this period we have seen how first the Portuguese and then the Dutch interacted with traditional mercantile groups, particularly those from southern India. The British, too, were vitally dependent upon such groups, and also upon the skills and expertise of local Portuguese. By the late eighteenth century, the British had passed beyond collaboration with the Portuguese as their interests in trade grew more varied and complex. New economic and political demands and interests focussed the British away from old partnerships and geographic areas of interests.

The result was that by the end of the eighteenth century the 'traditional' maritime trading system of the Bay of Bengal no longer served European interests. Indigenous partners were dispensed with, and if they survived at all it was in a dependent position within a Western hegemonic economic system. British maritime interest had moved eastward across the Bay of Bengal, from India to Southeast Asia. Indian cargoes were still vital to their trading interests, but not Indian partners.

NOTES

1. Patricia Rueb, 'Trade and Civilization in Early Modern Times', *IIAS Newsletter,* 8, 1996, 20–1.

2. Chulia was a common term used in the Malay peninsula to refer to Tamil-speaking Muslims from the Coromandel coast. Kling was a collective term, interchangeable with Chetty, used to refer to Hindu merchants from the Coromandel coast drawn from three linguistic groups: Tamil, Telugu and Kannada.

3. S. Digby, 'The Maritime Trade of India' in T. Raychaudhuri, and I. Habib, (eds) *The Cambridge History of India,* vol. 1 (Delhi, 1984), 156.

4. For a more detailed treatment of the Chulia and Klings in Southeast Asia during this period see: K. McPherson, 'Chulias and Klings: Indigenous Trade Diasporas and European Penetration of the Indian Ocean Littoral' in Giorgio Borsa, (ed.) *Trade and Politics in the Indian Ocean* (Delhi, 1990), 33–46.

5. A. Macgregor, 'Notes on the Portuguese in Malaya' in the *Journal of the Malay Branch of the Royal Asiatic Society,* vol. XXVIII, part II (May 1955), 26. See also S. Arasaratnam, *Merchants, Companies and Commerce on the Coromandel Coast 1650–1740* (Delhi, 1986), 114–15.

6. S. Arasratnam, *Merchants, Companies and Commerce.*

7. For a more detailed treatment of the Portuguese on the Coromandel coast see: K. McPherson, 'Enemies or Friends? The Portuguese, the British and the Survival of Portuguese Commerce in the Bay of Bengal and Southeast Asia from the Late Seventeenth to the Late Nineteenth Century', in F.A. Dutra, and J.C. dos Santos, (eds) *The Portuguese in the Pacific* (Santa Barbara, 1995), 211–37.

8. H. Furber, *John Company at Work. A Study of European Expansion in India in the Late Eighteenth Century* (Harvard, 1951), 19.

9. H. Furber, *Rival Empires of Trade in the Orient 1600–1800* (Minneapolis, 1978), 287–8.

10. S. Subrahmanyam, *The Portuguese Empire in Asia 1500–1700* (London, 1993), 70–2.

11. S. Subrahmanyam, *The Political Economy of Commerce: Southern India, 1500–1650* (Cambridge, 1990), 195.

12. Ibid., 206.

13. Ibid., 205 and *Improvising Empire; Portuguese Trade and Settlement in the Bay Bengal 1500–1700* (Delhi, 1990), 75.

14. C. Boxer, *Francisco Vieira de Figuiredo: A Portuguese Merchant Adventurer in South East Asia 1624–1667* (The Hague, 1967), 50.

15. T. Raychaudhuri, *Jan Company in Coromandel 1605–1690. A Study in the Interrelations of European Commerce and Traditional Economies* ('S-Gravenhage, 1962), 76–7; N. Manucci, *Memoirs of the Mogul Court* (Folio Society, London, nd) 64.

16. T. Raychaudhuri, *Jan Company in Coromandel,* 106.

17. J. Talboys Wheeler, *Madras in the Olden Times* (Madras, 1882), 674: quoted from the 'Official Investigation Into The Administration of Madras 1675–76'; H.D. Love, *Vestiges of Old Madras* (London, 1913), vol.1, 25–6.

18. H.D. Love, *Vestiges of Old Madras,* 183.

19. S.D. Quiason, *English 'Country Trade' With the Philippines 1644–1765* (Quezon City, 1966), 38.

20. J.C. Boyajian, *Portuguese Trade in Asia under the Habsburgs 1580–1640* (Baltimore, 1993).

21. S.D. Quiason, *English 'Country Trade',* 5–6.

22. H.D. Love, *Vestiges of Old Madras,* 43, 76.

23. S. Subrahmanyam, *The Political Economy,* 211–12.

24. J. Talboys Wheeler, *Madras in Older Times,* quoted on 94.

25. S. Subrahmanyam, *The Political Economy,* 200–1.

26. Ibid., 94.

27. S. Subrahmanyam, *The Political Economy,* 205–6; S. Arasaratnam, *Merchants, Companies and Commerce,* 161, 169.

28. S. Subrahmanyam, *Improvising Empire,* 81, 234.

29. Ibid..

30. Ibid., 95.

31. H.D. Love, *Vestiges of Old Madras,* 181.

32. H. Furber, *John Company at Work,* 271–2.

33. S.D. Quiason, *English 'Country Trade',* 36–7.

34. Ibid., 39.

35. Ibid., 68–70, 89.

36. H.D. Love, *Vestiges of Old Madras,* 395, vol.3, 39.

37. Ibid., vol. 2, 400–1, 465.

38. Ibid., 251.

39. W.E. Cheong, 'An Anglo–Spanish–Portuguese Clandestine Trade

Between the Ports of British India and Manila, 1785–1790', *Philippine Historical Review,* vol.1 (1), 1965, 82.

40. H.D. Love, *Vestiges of Old Madras,* vol.3, 488.

41. K. McPherson, *The Indian Ocean. A History of People and the Sea* (Delhi, 1993), 270–1.

42. Sir Frank Swettenham, *British Malaya: An Account of the Origin and Progress of British Influence in Malaya* (London, 1906), 54.

43. India Office Records, G/34/1, Straits Settlements 1760–95 (hereafter referred to as SS), Miscellaneous Papers, unsigned report, Fort St George (Madras), 1 February 1769 'Of the trade of Rhio and the Establishment of a Factory on Pulo Byang'.

44. India Office Records, G/34/1, SS, Miscellaneous Papers, extract of letters from Captain James Scott, September 1780.

45. Ibid., letter from Light, copy dated 18 March 1784, Fort St George (Madras); Ibid.,'Information from Captain Light in respect to the late attack of the Dutch on Rhio, the attempts of the Malays against Malacca and the establishment of a factory at Poolipinan [Penang]', 10 April 1784, Fort St George.

46. Ibid., extract of a General Letter from Bengal, 23 August 1784.

47. Ibid., 2 March 1786.

48. Ibid., letter from Macpherson, 26 January 1786 and letter received from Light, 25 January 1786.

49. Ibid..

50. India Office Records, G/34/3, BC, Bengal Council Minute, 13 December 1786; Ibid., Miscellaneous Documents and Reports, 'Report of Lieutenant Governor R.T. Farquhar on his term of office', 18 September 1805: Farquhar estimated the population at *c.* 30,000 but Tregonning estimated it at *c.* 20,000 in 1811, K.C. Tregonning *The British in Malaya: The First Forty Years 1786–1836* (Tucson, 1965), 57.

51. Dianne Lewis, 'Kedah—the Development of a Malay State' in A. Reid, and L. Castles, (eds), *Pre-Colonnial State Systems in Southeast Asia* (JMBRAS Monograph No.6, Kuala Lumpur, 1975), 40.

52. K.C. Tregonning, *The British in Malaya,* 43–5.

53. John Bastin, and Robin H. Winks, (compilers), *Malaysia. Selected Historical Readings* (Nendeln, KTO Press, 1979), 125–6.

54. India Office Records, G/34/2, BC, Bengal Council Meeting 13 December 1786, letter from Light, 15 September 1786.

55. India Office Records G/34/6, BC, Bengal Council Minute 1 August 1794 enclosing a letter from Light dated 25 January 1794.

56. Ibid..

57. K.C. Tregonning, *The British in Malaya,* 110.

58. Ibid., 119.

59. India Office Records, G/34/3, BC, Bengal Council Minute 13 February 1788, letter from Light dated 10 January 1788.

60. India Office Records, G/34/5, BC, Bengal Council Minute, 5 April 1793; Ibid., 15 October 1788 as an example of sums remitted.

61. K.C. Tregonning, *The British in Malaya,* 124.

62. India Office Records, G/34/9, Miscellaneous Documents and Reports, letter from Raffles dated 7 November 1808.

63. K.C. Tregonning, *The British in Malaya,* 124.

9

The Eastward Trade of India in the Eighteenth Century

S. ARASARATNAM

Through most of the 17th century, India's Asian trade flowed eastwards and westwards in roughly equal proportions. Generally speaking, ports of the west coast of India conducted most of their trade across the Arabian Sea into West Asia and east Africa, and ports of the east coast predominantly traded eastwards across the Bay of Bengal into Southeast Asia. There were periods when west coast ships sailed eastwards across the Bay of Bengal and east coast ships westwards across the Arabian Sea. But these formed a small proportion of the total seaborne trade conducted from the respective regions. The obvious geographic proximity and the shorter sailing times created a close nexus between different ports of these two coasts and the nearest destinations across the ocean. Thus the great bulk of Gujarati trade and shipping from its major port of Surat in the second half of the 17th century was with the Red Sea, southern Arabia and the Persian Gulf. The same could be said about the long-distance sailings from Malabar ports. Likewise, and perhaps to an even greater degree, the bulk of the sailings from Coromandel were towards Southeast Asian destinations. The position is not clear with regard to Bengal, where voyages to Sri Lanka, Malabar, Surat and the Maldives were long-distance voyages, but shorter voyages to the western shores of the Bay of Bengal must have constituted a large part of the seaborne trade of that region.

Some major developments were taking place in the eastward trade of India in the 18th century. These developments were triggered both by internal changes taking place within the subcontinent as well as by external changes about realignments in its role in world trade in this period. It is the purpose of this paper to chart the phases of this easterly trade in the 18th century.

At the beginning of the 18th century, the evidence indicates that the direct trade between west coast ports of India and ports of Southeast Asia was tapering off. This was largely a continuation of developments that had taken place in the last quarter of the 17th century when the trade to West Asia had undergone a great expansion. While there is record of important Gujarati ships belonging to the Surat shipping magnates calling at ports such as Acheh and Melaka till the end of the 17th century, there is no evidence of their doing so in the 18th. The sailings to Bengal continued but not the sailing across the Bay of Bengal. Part of the reason for this may be that the Dutch had successfully dominated the market in western India for the profitable Southeast Asia Asian commodities. It could also be a function of a general decline in Gujarati trade and shipping which had begun in the last decades of the 18th century. There is even less evidence of sailings from Malabar ports into Southeast Asia. The bulk of their long-distance shipping appears to be directed to West Asia. In so far as they sailed eastwards, it was in shorter voyages to Coromandel ports. Thus at the beginning of our period, the decline of direct trade between western India and Southeast Asia is clearly established.[1]

At the same time there was a decline in the trade from east coast ports westwards across the Arabian Sea. This had always been a small proportion of the trade of the east coast and now it became even smaller. The bulk of the trade from this region flowed across the Bay of Bengal into various ports of Southeast Asia and beyond. Through the first four decades of the 18th century, this trade continued but with signs of diminution as the years advanced. In the first three decades all the evidence points to a steady trade from a number of outlets. Masulipatnam, the major Indian port of this coast, continued to be a centre of this trade but was certainly on a course of decline as far as long-distance voyages were concerned.[2] There are a number of factors that account for this. The annexation of Golconda by the Mughals had upset the power structure that had existed in the Krishna–Godavari delta and had dominated the administration of the port and its hinterland. Persian merchant magnates who had featured strongly in the trade of Masulipatnam had dispersed as a result of the fall of the sultanate of Golconda. These Persians, besides their strong trading connection with Surat, the Persian Gulf and the Red Sea, had also been strong in the Southeast Asian trade, to Acheh, Pegu and Tenasserim, among other Places.

Another factor which affected Masulipatnam's eastward trade was the constriction of the link between the port and the capital Hyderabad, and the frequent severing of communications between these regions.[3] The Golconda hinterland and the capital had been good markets for imports from Southeast Asia. The import of elephants from Pegu,

Tenasserim and Acheh had been most profitable to Masulipatnam merchants and the purchasers had been the rulers and generals of the Golconda state. Likewise, minerals such as tin and copper had been imported from Southeast Asia through this port and had sold well in the interior. In the 18th century, many of these internal markets appear to have been lost to these importers. Another factor was the fall from influence and from powerful positions of Persians and Indo-Muslims in the kingdom of Ayuthya towards the end of King Narai's reign. This also may have affected the trade between Masulipatnam and the southern provinces of Ayuthya bordering the Bay of Bengal. Several of these Persians were removed from administrative positions and had to leave the court.[4] It appears that in the 18th century Ayuthya's trade was oriented eastwards towards the South China Seas and Japan, though some sailings continued from east coast ports of India to Tenasserim. So through the first two decades of the century a few sailings took place from Masulipatnam to Tenasserim, Ujang Selang, Pegu and Acheh, probably from remaining elements of the old ship-owning merchants of that port. There is no evidence revealing the identity of these merchants.

More substantial evidence of eastwards sailing comes from ports futher to the south, from Madras, Sao Thome, Cuddalore, Pondicherry, Porto Novo and Nagore. In the first three decades there was considerable movement from Madras and Sao Thome. Madras, in particular, was attracting the shipping interests of the Coromandel coast. There are a number of reasons for this development. Madras was emerging as a major market for imports from Southeast Asia, while export commodities were readily available from any number of smaller ports to the north and east. It appears that Hindu-dominated shipping of the north Coromandel ports and of Paleacat was shifting to Madras and making it a base of its operations. Records of ship movements from Madras show the strength of this trade to Southeast Asia. The most popular destination was Pegu or Syriam, with about five to six Indian-owned vessels making return journeys to this destination. The Pegu connection was very strong with several Madras merchants having agents or members of their family network in that place. Also during this period, English records refer to ships of the 'King of Pegu' sailing to Madras, consigning goods for Chetty merchants and freighting goods for many of them. The names of the ships and the record of their owners wherever available show that they were equally distributed between Hindu and Muslim merchants. Many of the Hindus were of the Chetty caste, Tamil and Telugu, and many of the Muslims were Chulias domiciled in south Coromandel.[5]

There are signs of English participation from Madras in these early decades but as yet in modest proportions and often in partnership with Indians, jointlly owning ships and/or cargoes. The English secured settlement rights in Syriam and set up ship-building docks for their own use as well as for sale to purchasers.

It appears that in Syriam and Pegu Indians were having ships built for their use and may have turned to these parts for their shipping needs with the decline of the ship-building facilities in the Godavari delta.[6] Apart from sailing their own ships, it may be assumed that Indian merchants of Madras freighted goods in English vessels that were increasingly sailing from Madras to the Burmese coast from the 1730s. This trade to Pegu appears to be declining from the late 1730s and is probably linked to the political problems in lower Burma and the challenges faced by the Kingdom of Ava in its control of the coastal lowlands. Even the English appear to have abandoned their Syriam ship-building facilities since they were too costly and troublesome to maintain.[7]

There was also a continuity into the 18th century of the trade to Arakan which had been carried out from several Coromandel ports throughout the preceding century. It was a modest trade, usually two to three ships a year, and the sailings were from Madras. It was generally carried on by Indians but there is one instance in 1734 of an Armenian-owned ship sailing to Arakan and back.[8] It could well be that this was a joint venture between Armenians and Indians of Madras. The Armenians continued as a major force in the eastwards trade in the first half of the 18th century. This trade had a remarkable persistence and is recorded as continuing into the 1740s. The trade must have been the concern of particular commercial interests of Madras as there occurs the one ship that made several return journeys over several trading seasons.

Another popular destination of the eastwards trade was Tenasserim, the southern province of the kingdom of Ayuthya. This was a frequently sailed route with five or six vessels annually doing the return voyage from Madras. This had also been a popular route in the 17th century when the King of Ayuthya had established links with Bay of Bengal trade through this port. Now it appears that the nearly autonomous governors of these provinces fostered this trade and, as in Pegu, there were settlements of Indian merchants in this port and further to the south in Takuapa and the off-shore island of Ujang Selang. This entire region was rich in tin which was the major import into southern India. Ujang Selang was considered important enough for up to four ships to make the journey to that island. It is not known whether these were direct return sailings to that island or whether the ships touched on other ports on the mainland. The trade to these southern Siamese ports was carried on by Hindu and Muslim shipowners based in Madras but with domiciled agents in those ports who would transact business for them. As in the case of Pegu, these merchants had connections with local ruling groups. The European records speak of a 'King of Tenasserim' whose ships sailed[9] to Madras which probably refer to provincial rulers of the Siamese provinces.

Kedah was another place to which the eastward trade continued into the 18th century. Sailings from Madras to Kedah are recorded in the first three decades, but only one or two ships a year were involved. It is possible that there were more sailings from ports to the south of Madras. For the first few decades there is not as much evidence of the deep involvement of south Indian merchants in the Kedah trade as there is for the later part of the century, but this may be because this is not the concern of our major sources, the English and the Dutch Companies. Trade to Kedah was also conducted from the Nawab's port of San Thome, four miles south of Madras. Ships made San Thome their home port because of the incentives given by the Nawab in the first two decades of the century and the eastward trade embraced all places referred to above—Pegu, Tenasserim, Ujang Selang and Kedah. The participants were drawn from the same groups as constituted the shipowners of Madras with the addition of a Muslim trading community of Pathans who were probably from Masulipatnam and were attracted to settle in San Thome by the Nawab. The eastward trade of San Thome declined in the 1720s but picked up strongly in the 1730s along the customary routes.[10]

Trade to Melaka was also an element of the continuous functioning of the eastward trade of India in the 18th century. After a brief interruption, it had picked up towards the end of the 17th century and continued in the 18th. The Dutch were more liberal in their granting of passes to Indian ships of Coromandel, especially from Nagapatnam, with the intention of attracting trade to both these ports held by them. This relative freedom given to the trade to Meleka increased as the 18th century progressed and at least one or two ships owned by Indians called regularly at this port from Madras. There would have been more ships from the southern ports of Nagapatnam and Nagore calling at Melaka. It appears that often Melaka was not the port of destination for these ships but was a port of call on a round trip either to Acheh, Johore and southwards of Melaka or to Tenasserim, Ujang Selang to the north of it. Duties on textiles were still levied there, though not as high as in the preceding century, and a number of goods such as tin, pepper and spices were declared contraband. More than Melaka, Johore was the growth area for the eastward trade in the last decade of the 17th century and early decades of the 18th. Porto Novo and Nagore were the main ports of the trade to Johore and the Chulia Muslim shippers settled here were well entrenched in the trade with Johore and the Riau archipelago. The Chulias had factories in the up-river port of Pankor and extended their activities across the straits to Riau, Siak and other ports on the opposite east Sumatran coast.[11] This trade seems to have come to an end in the 1720s with civil war breaking out in the kingdom and external intervention from the Bugis and the Dutch.

Another important destination of the eastward trade was Acheh which had attracted trade from all the major trading regions of India on both its east and its west coasts. As noted above, the direct trade from Gujarat to Acheh had virtually come to an end in the early decades of the 18th century. Sailings from Bengal also appear to have dwindled to a trickle but the trade from southern Coromandel ports continued. In the first three decades there were sailings to Acheh from Madras, San Thome, Cuddalore, Porto Novo and Nagore. South Indian trading interests continued their linkages with the Sultans of Acheh and ships recorded as belonging to the Sultan sailed into Coromandel ports till the 1740s.[12] As in the case of Johore, civil unrest in Acheh appears to have caused a decline in this trade after this period. One feature that continued in the early decades of the 18th century was the freighting of Indian goods in Danish vessels starting from Tanquebar to Acheh and Johore. This had been very strong in the last quarter of the 17th century but subsequently declined in intensity and continued on a smaller scale. In 1731 for example, two Danish ships were freighted by Indian merchants to Acheh.[13]

The traditional pattern of Coromandel's eastward trade shows a continuity on a somewhat smaller scale. With the decline of Masulipatnam, the trade seems to have shifted southwards with Madras emerging as a focal point of this trade. The attractions offered by Madras were the expanding port and handling facilities, the security of merchant property, the arrangements for the marketing of imported commodities, the possibilities for accumulating capital for overseas venture, and the increasing involvement of English capital and English entrepreneurs in this trade. There is overwhelming evidence to show that Indian merchants all over the coast were floating loans in Madras to finance their voyages.[14] Often these were in small sums, subscribed by lenders drawn from a wide social spectrum and diverse ethnic groups. The respondentia loans system was widely used to finance voyages. The interest on such loans to the ports mentioned above ranged from 18 per cent to 25 per cent for a return voyage. There seemed no shortage of funds for prospective ventures. The people involved had been doing so for generations: Hindu Chetties of Telugu and Tamil castes, Chulia Muslims, remnants of the Masulipatnam Muslim shippers. Of the other groups that were entering this trade, the strongest were the Armenians, followed by Portuguese and English—both Company servants and free merchants. These groups will be discussed separately. While there were difficulties in this trade arising from political uncertainties in the destination of the trade, it seemed to affect the southern routes more than those to the north. Consequently there is a shift from ports such as Acheh, Johore and the east Sumatran coast to the Malay peninsula, southern Thailand and Burma.

The eastward trade from Bengal underwent considerable shifts in the early decades of the 18th century. The trade carried out by Indian merchants, which had embraced Pegu, Tenasserim, Kedah and Acheh in the second half of the 17th century, seems to have declined substantially in the first decades of the 18th. Balasore and Hughli had been the major ports for this trade, but sailings from both these ports dwindled to a trickle in these years. Up to 1720 there were a number of years when there was only one ship a year to Melaka or Kedah and none to Acheh. It was clear that the once flourishing Bengal trade to Acheh had come to an end.[15] With the establishment of Calcutta, Bengal shipping was attracted to that port over a period of time. Up till about 1730 Hughli held its own against Calcutta but started losing out to the English port after that date. Calcutta shipping increased substantially after 1721 and took over as the major port of Bengal. Up till the first four decades most of Calcutta's shipping was directed towards the west, to Malabar, Surat and West Asia. It may be assumed that this was also the case with Indian shipping from the Mughal port of Hughli. In the early decades four to five ships a year went eastwards. Their destinations were Pegu, Kedah, Ujang Selang and Melaka. It is clear that the main attention of both the Indian and English commercial interests of Bengal were in the westward rather than the eastward trade for the first three decades of the 18th century.[16] During this period the bulk of the eastward trade of India was conducted from the Coromandel coast and was largely in Indian hands but with major contributions coming from a range of new interests.

Important changes took place in the middle decades of the 18th century. Some of these changes were an acceleration of trends that were already visible. Certain lines of trade were opened up further. Many of the changes had to do with developments taking place in the three English settlements of Calcutta, Madras and Bombay. The Dutch had already been instrumental in altering some features of the eastward trade of India. They had taken over some of the carrying trade in this direction both in the exports and imports of India. One of the factors in the decline of Surat's eastward trade, for example, was the dominance the Dutch secured in some of the key commodities of this trade. This dominance continued into the 18th century. In the east coast, in Bengal and the Coromandel, the Dutch were carrying a good share of this eastward trade. The export of cotton and silk textiles from Bengal to Batavia for sale in the archipelago markets continued strongly into the first few decades. Subsequently, the export of opium increased markedly. Dutch exports of textiles from Coromandel to Batavia continued steadily. With the capture of Bantam in 1682, the Dutch had secured a captive market for the Coromandel textiles in Java, Sulawesi and the Moluccas. These places were all fed from Batavia where the Dutch held a textile monopoly. Coromandel textiles outstripped those from Gujarat and Bengal in the Dutch Company's orders from their Indian factories. By the mid-18th century, Coromandel textiles formed a large proportion of Dutch textile exports from India and provided the largest profit ratios as compared with other regions.[17] When the Dutch were short of funds for their purchases in India, they gave instructions to give priority to the needs of the Indies market over that of the European market. This success was achieved at the expense of Indian merchants of the Coromandel who had previously supplied these markets at considerable profit. The Dutch share of this market, however, was declining in the second half of the 18th century because of shortage of funds, shipping, and problems in the procurement of sufficient goods for the eastern markets.

From the early decades of the 18th century, significant moves from the English ports of Calcutta, Madras and Bombay to participate in the Asian eastward trade were visible. This came mainly from private entrepreneurs drawn from the servants of the East India Company and from free merchants settled in and around these ports. The Company itself did not carry on a systematic trade to the east in these decades, except to China. After the expulsion of the Company's factory in Bantam in 1682, it founded a settlement in Benkulen on the mid-west coast of Sumatra but it took many decades before the Company carried out a regular trade to that region. The first substantial participation of English private enterprise in the eastward trade was from Madras and Masulipatnam and gathered momentum in the 18th century. This was understandable as the ingredients for this trade were present there and could be readily utilized. The staple of the trade, textile exports to Southeast Asia, could be easily procured by shippers through the commercial relationships already in place for the Company's export trade to Europe. Company servants were beginning to accumulate capital and were expanding their seaborne trade from short coastal ventures to long-distance trading. Market expertise, both for imports and exports, was also readily available with Indian merchants settled in large numbers in Madras with whom senior Company servants were in commercial contact with mutual benefit. With the Company's custom at their command and various instruments of power at their disposal, these Company servants were ideally placed to penetrate the eastern trade. It is not, therefore, surprising that Madras emerged as the chief seat of English private trade eastwards.

In this same period, Calcutta's commercial expansion was directed more to the west than to the east. The sailings out of Calcutta in the first three decades show the preponderance of the westward trade. It is only after 1730 that the eastward trade picks up as part of a general expansion of English private trade in Asia.[18] Another cause may be that Bengal cottons and silks did not have such an extensive market in Southeast Asia as did those of Coromandel. Further, it was noted above that Indian merchants of Bengal were not prominent in the eastward trade which meant that English entrepreneurs did not have the advantage of collaboration with the local shipping interests as did those in Madras. The first beginnings of eastward trade from Calcutta took the form of round trips to Surat or Mokha, touching at Melaka or Kedah on the way. Also in the early decades some voyages skirted around the Bay of Bengal touching at Pegu, Tenasserim, Melaka and the east coast of India.

The growth of shipping and trade in Bombay was rather slow and dependent on the prospects of Surat. When the trade did grow, it followed the older patterns set in Surat and was dominated by coastal voyages on the west coast from Sind to Malabar and across the Arabian Sea to Gombroon, Basra, Muskat, Mokha and Jeddah.[19] When voyages to the east began, they were long-distance voyages to China, or Calcutta, via Melaka or any other port to the east of the Bay of Bengal. Bombay's main contact with Melaka in Southeast Asia was not surprising as English private trading interests of Bombay and Surat were closely involved with the Dutch officials of Surat and it appears that they helped carry on a contraband trade for these Dutch officials between Surat and Melaka.[20] One of the reasons for the absence of an extensive direct trade between Bombay and Southeast Asia was the fact that Gujarati textiles had ceased to be very profitable in Southeast Asian markets.

An important growth sector in the eastward trade of India was the trade with Manila which had its beginnings under the Portuguese and developed steadily from Madras with the migration of Portuguese merchants to Madras after the conquest of San Thome by Golconda in 1664. At first the participants were Company servants in partnership with Portuguese and Indian merchants of Madras. From the beginning of the 18th century this direct trade from Madras to Manila expanded with English free merchants, Portuguese and Indians as the principals. Ships of each of these groups in individual or shared ownership made regular voyages through most of the 18th century. Textiles from Madras had an excellent market in Manila. Large quantities of coarse calicoes, particularly the staple cotton white longcloth and the dyed and painted chintz and muslins, were the main cargo. These were readily available in Coromandel, being varieties traded in by the English Company, and could be procured through existing middleman channels at competitive prices. Some of these textiles were trans-shipped in the Manila galleons to Mexico. On the return these ships brought silver to Madras. In the lists of ships departing from Madras to Manila in the period 1707 to 1762, 24 ships have a clearly identified English ownership or interest, 17 are identifiable as Portuguese, 12 as Armenian and 6 as Indian. After 1740, no Indian-owned ship appears in the departure lists.[21]

Calcutta also entered the growing Manila trade. English free merchants' ships based in Calcutta began voyages to Manila from the 1720s. In the 1720s, ten ships were recorded as having left Calcutta for Manila, in the following decade there were six or seven, in the 1740s seven, and the trade appears to have come to an end in 1748.[22] Bengal silk and cotton textiles had a good market in Manila. Perhaps the absence of a Portuguese connection in Calcutta may have been an inhibiting factor in the capacity to organize ventures from Calcutta to Manila.

Another channel for Indian trade to Manila and other ports of Southeast Asia was the French after the reorganization of their Company in 1723. They employed their unused shipping in Pondicherry for these voyages to Manila, Tenasserim, Melaka and Acheh. Often these were in partnership with Indian merchants of the coast. The French were often short of capital and Indian merchants provided the bulk of the cargo that was carried in French ships. So great was the share of participation of these Indian merchants that these ships sometimes carried the names of these merchants. The French were newcomers to the eastward trade and were happy to accept the Indians into partnership, both in Company as well as in private ventures. Thus an expanding private French trade grew in Pondicherry similar to that of the English in Madras.[23]

From around the 1740s we enter a new phase in the eastward trade of India with the impetus provided by the English Company and, more intensively, by English private interests. Company ships were making regular voyages to China from the English Indian settlements of Calcutta, Madras and Bombay. By the late 1740s, about four Eastindiamen were sailing annually from Madras or Calcutta to China, calling at Melaka or Batavia on the way. They were freighting goods for the private trade from the three English settlements, besides loading Indian goods for China on the Company's behalf. The spectacular growth was in private shipping owned by English free merchants directed at Southeast Asian ports. This trade had a great deal in common with the traditional Asian trade that had been going on from the 17th century. It was aimed at the same places familiar to the old trade: Pegu, Syriam, Tenasserim, Ujang Selang, Kedah, Perak, Melaka and Acheh. The entry of these new participants gave a boost to the trade just when the old participants were beginning to be worn down.

Ingredients of this trade were broadly similar to what had been customary. Cotton and silk piece-goods of India were basic to the exports from India. These were drawn from all the regions of production—Gujarat, Bengal and Bihar, the Coromandel—depending on where the shippers were proceeding from. Different kinds of aromatic woods were carried. The export of opium increased, it became a major commodity, while earlier it had been a minor item. Apart from the produce of India, the ships carried a variety of goods of European origin which could be traded in Southeast Asia. Imports into India again consisted of goods which had traditionally been imported from that region—timber and wooden planks from Burma and Siam, ivory, tin, gums and resin, camphor, rattan, betel nuts and gold from several regions. Then there were Chinese and Japanese goods which these merchants procured at first from intermediary ports in Southeast Asia—porcelain, copper and sugar.

The trade had to be carried out over an extensive sea coast, buying and selling goods in small lots rather like the old peddling trade. The two major marts in this region were Batavia and Melaka, both controlled by the Dutch. Asian ports and the states that backed them had undergone a decline in the first half of the 18th century. It was only in Batavia and Melaka that goods could be unloaded on a large scale. There were a heap of restrictive regulations hampering trade but deals could be made with Dutch Company servants in these ports, through the intermediacy of their colleagues in Indian factories such as Surat, Chinsura (Bengal), Cochin and Nagapatnam. The Dutch had declared the Java seas east of the Straits of Melaka to the Moluccas a preserve of their exclusive trade. This claim was increasingly being challenged from the mid-18th century and English merchants were sailing to a number of places within this Dutch sphere of influence as well as to those on the outer fringes of the zones of control. The English Company was backing those interests which, in any case, were closely tied to senior Company servants of Calcutta, Madras and Bombay. It appears that, in their wake, Indian merchants who were surviving in the eastward trade saw opportunities that they seized. All in all, the eastward trade received a boost from the 1740s due to these developments.

One such area which was the subject of this expansion was the west coast of Sumatra where the English Company had settled in Benkulen after it was expelled from Bantam. For many decades after its foundation the settlement was a drain on the Company's resources, but from the 1730s a turn-around occured in its fortunes, largely through the perseverance and efforts of some Company servants in charge of the settlement. Pepper deliveries picked up at low prices and the Company decided to encourage this by providing incentives to its servants there and to private traders of the Indian mainland. From the 1740s this brought about an increasingly closer nexus between English settlements of India and Benkulen and surrounding ports of the west Sumatran coast. With the opening of new pepper supply centres along the coast, the demand for imports grew and the main source of these imports was India. English private traders in league with Company servants of Calcutta and Madras rapidly increased their trade from the 1750s. Textiles of the Coromandel and Bengal and opium from Bengal were the major exports from India. Madras officials and private traders had a special connection with the west Sumatran trade and enjoyed the larger share. The longcloth and the blue-dyed cloth of Madras were particularly desired here and the ships brought back tin, pepper and gold which was very profitable in Madras. The late 1750s saw a large increase in shipping from India, markets were over-stocked and the merchants branched out to other places along the coast to sell their goods. The trade had been dominated for long by interests from Madras and to a lesser extent Bengal, so that Bombay commercial interests complained about this domination and the trade had to be opened up for them as well in 1758.[24]

After the Seven Years War, when the French threat in the Indian Ocean had been effectively removed, there was a phenomenal growth in the eastward trade from India of both the Company and of English private trade. English shipping operations from the settlements increased year by year and the bulk of the sailings were to the east into Southeast Asia and the South China sea. The Company ships made direct voyages to China, calling usually at Melaka on the way, with a full cargo taken up at the port of departure in India. This cargo would be either on the Company's behalf or on freight for English free merchants. The exports of the company to Canton consisted of pepper, taken in at Malabar, opium becoming an important commodity from Bengal after the 1760s and raw cotton featuring prominently from Bombay after the 1780s. Thus the Company was not trading in any of the exports of India of its traditional Asian trade. Other goods for import into China such as tin, gambier, some spices were bought in Indian ports from private traders who had imported them from Southeast Asia. Apart from this, the Company's ships were taking bullion from India in large quantities up to the 1780s when opium and cotton sales in China increased and the drain of silver and gold from India caused probelms to commerce within India.[25]

It is with the expansion of English private trade to Southeast Asia that we reach a new phase in the eastward trade of India. These private traders were tapping many of the old markets for Indian exports and opening new markets and new routes into the islands. They were utilizing the Dutch-controlled ports of Melaka, Batavia, Surabaya and Macassar and getting the most out of a decaying Dutch trading system which had freed itself somewhat under the weight of inertia. The number of English vessels calling at Melaka doubled between 1770 and 1779.[26] But sailings to Melaka were no indication of the extent of this trade. Its real strength was in the outlying regions of Southeast Asia, along the west and east coast of the Malay Peninsula, in Johore and Riau, in Burma and Siam, Acheh and west Sumatra, Borneo and the Sulu Archipelago. Many of these places had featured continuously in the eastward trade of India for decades, others were new routes charted out by the omnipresent country vessels of these merchants.[27] Pegu and Tenasserim, which were important up to the mid-18th century, were not so in this phase of expansion, partly because of the contemporary political conflict between the Burmese and Thais. The trade to Acheh which had experienced a downturn in the mid-18th century now saw a revival and Acheh became an important port for the eastward trade driven both by the English and by Indian shippers. The great port of growing trade in these decades was Riau at the entrance to the Melaka Straits. It was a popular destination for the English country vessels and became a free port attracting trade from India, China and mainland and island Southeast Asia. On the Malay peninsula, Kedah underwent an expansion and Selangor and Perak experienced the spin-off effects of this trade. From these older centres, adventurous shippers sailed eastwards to Borneo, Bali and the Sulu archipelago impelled by the search for commodities for the China trade.

This English eastward trade of the last three decades was mainly carried out from Calcutta and Madras. There were two branches to this trade which sometimes converged. One, the most voluminous, was the direct trade between India and the various Southeast Asian destinations. It embraced the traditional items of the trade between India and Southeast Asia in its exports and imports and in this way was an extension of the customary trade exchanges. The imports into India were sold for internal consumption and for re-export for the China trade. The second branch of this trade had China as its destination but conducted a protracted trade in Southeast Asia for goods saleable in China and the ships proceeded to Canton. Both types of trade contributed to the increase of Indian exports, especially the textiles of the Coromandel and Bengal, leading to a spurt in production which had been stagnant during the Anglo-French wars and the Bengal revolutions. It led to a revival of commercial activity in the English ports and some of the Indian ports, as well as in the inland centres of production and marketing.

This revived trade did not lead to any marked influx of bullion as the traditional trade had provided. This was because of the peculiar characteristics of the trade and the way it was carried out. An important feature was that it was encouraged by the Company and grew as a means of providing specie to the Company in Canton to pay for its tea exports to Europe. The ships which had Canton as their destination deposited much of the proceeds of their trade in Southeast Asia and in China with the Company's treasury in Canton and drew Bills of Exchange on London.[28] A second feature was that the exports from India were themselves a means of remittance to London. The trade was a vehicle for the movement of wealth from India to Britain. A third feature was the nature of the imports to India consequent on the linkage with China. The ships which returned to India from China brought with them China goods in quantity of which silk and sugar-candy competed with Bengal produce and were able to outsell the latter. They deprived Bengal of its lucrative Surat market and contributed to a reduction in the trade between Bengal and western India.

Among the beneficiaries of this expansion of eastward trade were the old Indian merchant entrepreneurs who has been undergoing a difficult time in their trade to Southeast Asia. Now some of the former markets opened up further to Indian exports and these Indian shippers renewed their earlier contacts and networks in the Malay and Sumatran states. They more than held their own in places such as Acheh, Melaka and Kedah and were often utilized by the English merchants in forging links with indigenous trading interests of the region. Thus Chulia and Hindu Chetty ship-owning merchants were seen to be operating with renewed vigour from the 1770s, using Melaka and Kedah as bases where older settlements appear to be revived. Admittedly, the older ports of Porto Novo and Nagore which had been their centres of strength had declined after they had carved out a niche for themselves, had also passed under English control in 1783. They came to terms with the English, sailed out of English ports in south Coromandel and, when Penang was founded in 1786, were the first Indians to resort to that port and plant roots there from the very first years. They did likewise years later when Singapore was founded in 1819.

The eastward trade of India underwent major changes in the course of the 18th century. It has always been a major component of India's overseas trade but was subject to a variety of influences in this period. It continued to survive in the difficult first three decades when there were problems both with the Indian end and in the various Southeast Asian terminal points of the trade. In the middle decades, the traditional participants in the trade, both at the Indian and the Southeast Asian end, experienced major problems of instability and consequent decline. The wars on the subcontinent were a setback to the pursuit of this trade. But just at this time, there emerged a new force to pick up a declining trade. The great eastward drive of English Asian commerce with the massive expansion of English exports from China created ripples in the Asian maritime world. One of these was the trade between India and Southeast Asia. Because of the nature of this trade, it was double-edged in its impact, beneficial in some ways, harmful in others.

NOTES

1. Surat and Gujarat trade in the first decades of the 18th century have been studied in depth by A. Das Gupta in his *Indian Merchants and the Decline of Surat, c. 1700–1750* (Wiesbaden 1979).

2. Memoir of the arriving and departing private ships, sloops and vessels, 1 December 1709 to 31 August 1710 Archief VOC 1796, pp.28–38; Memoir of the arriving and departing ships at Masulipatnam from 1 September 1714 to 31 August 1715, Archief VOC 1869, pp.56–61; Ships arriving and departing at Masulipatnam, 26 December 1716 to 31 March 1717, Archief VOC 1896, pp.29–30; Arriving and departing ships at Masulipatnam from 1 September 1720 to 31 April 1721, Archief VOC 1962, ff.334–7; Memoir of all private vessels and other ships that arrived here (Masulipatnam) since 1 September (1727) to date (31 August 1728) Archief VOC 2101 ff.137–42.

3. For the political problems that beset this region, see J.F. Richards, *Mughal Administration in Golconda* (Oxford 1975), especially chapter IX and X.

4. A. Forbes, 'Tenasserim: The Thai Kingdom of Ayuthay's Link with the Indian Ocean', *Indian Ocean Newsletter* vol.3, no. 1. June, 1982, p.3.

5. Evidence of Madras shipping collected from diary entries in *Diary and Consultation Books Fort St George, 1700–1730* (Madras 1910–1950).

6. *Diary and Consultation Book,* Fort St George, 1725, 22 June 1725, *Despatches from England.* Records of Fort St George, 1728, p.6, *Despatches to England,* Fort St George 1727, p.135.

7. D.G.E. Hall, *A History of Southeast Asia* (london 1981, Fourth Edition), pp.406–7.

8. Mayor's Court Proceedings, Madras, 18 June 1734. India Office Library (IOL) 388/69.

9. *Public Consultations,* Fort St George, 1738, 1 May, 1738.

10. *Despatches from England,* Fort St George, 1732, pp.80,87. *Public Consultations,* Fort St George 1734, 26 November 1733, 7 January 1733–4.

11. *Diary and Consultations,* Fort St George, 1712, 4 October 1712.

12. H. Dodwell, *Calendar of the Madras Records 1740–44* (Madras 1917) pp.47, 58.

13. Governor and Council of Coromandel to Governor-General and Council, 27 October 1731, Archief VOC 2075 f.235.

14. The main source of evidence for this is the litigation in the Mayors Court between parties to respondentia loan transactions. Mayors Court Proceedings of 1700–1740.

15. The evidence has been assembled and discussed in Om Prakash, *The Dutch East India Company and the Economy of Bengal 1630–1720* (Princeton 1985), pp.225–9.

16. P.J. Marshall, *East Indian Fortunes. The British in Bengal in the Eighteenth Century* (Oxford 1976), pp.51–62.

17. Notice of cloth sold in Batavia. 1764–70. Archief VOC, Hooge Regeering 345.

18. Marshall, *East Indian Fortunes,* pp.75–91.

19. H. Furber, *Bombay Presidency in the Eighteenth Century* (Bombay 1962), pp.1–46.

20. Ibid., pp.54–61.

21. Shipping lists compiled and published in S.D. Quiason, *English 'Country Trade' in the Philippines, 1640–1765* (Quezon City 1966), chapter IV, especially pp.68–70.

22. Marshall, *East Indian Fortunes,* pp.88–90.

23. *Correspondance du Conseil Superieux de Pondichery et la Compagnie,* A Martineux (Pondicherry 1920), I, pp.14–17, 24.

24. R.J. Young, *The English East India Company and Trade on the West Coast of Sumatra 1730–1760,* Ph.D. thesis, University of Pennsylvania, 1970, pp.141–93.

25. H. Furber, *John Company at Work* (Cambridge, Mass. 1948), chapter V; E.H. Pritchard, *Anglo-Chinese Relations during the Seventeenth and Eighteenth Centuries* (Reprint, New York 1970), chapters VII and IX.

26. D. Lewis, 'The Growth of the County Trade to the Straits of Malacca 1760–1777', *Journal of the Malaysian Branch Royal Asiatic Society,* vol. XLIII, pt. II (1970), p.117.

27. D.K. Bassett, *British Trade and Policy in Indonesia and Malaysia in the late Eighteenth Century* (Zug 1971), chapters 1 and 2.

28. Pritchard, *Anglo-Chinese Relations,* pp.159, 166–8.

10

Indians in East Africa: the Early Modern Period

M.N. PEARSON

Ashin Das Gupta in his many publications told us a lot about trade and other contacts between the west coast of India and West Asia. My objective in this short tribute is to extend the picture to the south a little, and sketch in the broadest terms contacts between western India and the Swahili coast in that early modern period which he made his own.

To set the scene, I will first raise a matter of terminology. The area of water separating the two areas under discussion is conventionally referred to as the 'Arabian Sea'. To my mind this privileges 'Arabia' in a quite unjustified way. By 1500, Arab navigation to India was sparse in the extreme; the thrust was much more of Indians trading to the Arab world. Similarly, as regards the Swahili coast it has long been accepted that any notion of Arab colonization of the area, or indeed of deep Arab influence, is wide off the mark. The trend today is entirely to see Swahili culture as inextricably African, one variant within many of a very rich and complex African mosaic. True, being coastal the Swahili were more open to foreign influences than were their interior fellow-Bantu speakers, yet this cannot take away from their essentially African character.

If we discard 'Arabian', what then should we call this body of water? My suggestion is that we use a neologism, that is the 'Afrasian Sea'. The advantage of this term is that it nicely captures the essential fact that it joined two separate continents and that both are represented in the name.[1]

I

Studies of Indian diasporas are of course legion. Indeed, for a time we were told that India had a long and glorious history of overseas expansion, mostly cultural but some even military. No doubt these older studies were in part produced as part of the effort to emphasize, or create, a glorious past for India as it suffered under British rule.

Indian influence, not only cultural and religious but even political, was claimed to be dominant in Southeast Asia, at least at the time of the Cholas. Now, however, scholars of Southeast Asia are trying to reclaim the autonomy of their area. They modestly do not aspire to show the influence of their region elsewhere, but there has been a pronounced nativism, a stress on autonomy and lack of foreign influence. Indeed, I have even heard the term 'southeast Asia' itself being questioned, for it seems to imply that the area is in some way merely part of south, and east, Asia, in a way a residual category with little new coming from indigenous sources. Today's trend very strongly emphasizes the autonomy of the area, and in particular the way it has absorbed and transformed many influences from both south and east Asia and turned them into something distinctively 'southeast Asian.'[2]

The historiography of Greater India influenced the west rather less than it did the east. Nevertheless, some earlier studies still found vast Indian influence on the east African coast, and even inland. My aim is to investigate these claims in a little detail, and then try to sketch a more accurate depiction of the Indian presence in east Africa in the early modern period.

Referring to the period before the arrival of Europeans in 1498, Serjeant found a very substantial Indian presence on the coast. Indians were financiers, bankers, moneylenders and merchants, and indeed 'much of the ocean-going shipping was Indian-owned and Indian manned.'[3] The eminent Mozambiquean historian Rita-Ferreira made similar claims, and found both Hindus and Muslims from Gujarat playing a very large role from the late fourteenth century. Indeed, referring to a much longer period, he claimed that one could write a book called 'How India underdeveloped East Africa'.[4] Quite recently Teotonio de Souza veered in a similar direction. Describing the martyrdom of the early Jesuit Gonçalo de Silveira at the Mutapa court in March 1561, he wrote:

> The sudden change of attitude of the ruler of Monomotapa and the killing of the priest as a suspected agent of the Portuguese only confirms the close links that the Gujarati merchants of India maintained with the rulers of east Africa. It is not surprising therefore that the conversion and baptism of the ruler of Monomotapa at the hands of this Jesuit may have alarmed the bania merchants in the Rivers of Cuama [that is, the Zambezi valley].[5]

Unfortunately, the sources he cites to bolster this claim, one of them by me, do not support this statement, and indeed the copious documentation on this melancholy incident make it absolutely clear that it was Muslims, mostly African, whether from the coast or the interior, who instigated the murder.[6]

The thesis of a Greater India in east Africa found its fullest expression in an extraordinary American dissertation, two articles, and a book, all by Cyril A. Hromnik. The book, not surprisingly published in apartheid South Africa, was vigorously condemned as a racist tract at the time of its publication, and indeed Hromnik has not been heard from since.[7] To discuss all his lapses, exaggerations, unsubstantiated claims, and indeed his overt racism would be a tedious and unpleasant task. A few examples will suffice to give the flavour of his work.

The thesis, ostensibly a long, scholarly, well-documented study, in fact contains many problems. His focus is the role of Indian Christians, Canarins (that is, 'people from Kanara'), in the Zambezi valley and Zimbabwe plateau. This is an interesting and important topic; however he wildly exaggerates their role. For example, he claims that:

> It is a well documented fact that at the end of the fifteenth century Christians from Malabar were able to navigate their boats along the coast from Cochin and Cranganur as far as Malindi, Kilwa, Angoche, Moçambique, and most probably Sofala also.[8]

As an example of his argumentation, he notes, when describing the journey of the ill-fated Fr. Silveira to the interior that,

> He found Sena [on the lower Zambezi valley] to be a very large town where there are ten or fifteen Portuguese settlers, with some Christians from India. Since a very large town could not have been composed of the houses of fifteen Portuguese, there must have been many more Canarins than Portuguese.[9]

Soon after, he tells us that Indians had resided in Sena since the twelfth century, 'and in later centuries the town must have resembled a Goan village more than anything else as Canarins were its primary occupants.'[10]

The book is much worse. According to him, Great Zimbabwe is not African at all, while 'Africa owes its system of trade and currency, its metal technology and iron tools, and the terminology to express this entire complex of cultural development to India, Indonesia, China, with later contributions from the Muslim world and Europe.'[11] He claims that the famous carved doors of Lamu show Indian influence on the coast long before 1500, yet in fact none of the extant doors predate 1800. Indians began mining gold on the Zimbabwe plateau around the year 1000, and to cap it all, he proves that Indian trade was very extensive in earlier periods, else why was the Indian Ocean called 'Indian'?[12]

All of these accounts of Indian dominance of Africa, not just Hromnik's, are certainly stirring stuff, really hairy-chested claims of a vast Indian role far into the interior. Ashin Das Gupta from time to time chided me for my 'Indian-nativist' writings, for he considered them to be far too sympathetic to 'India' and far too derogatory of the Europeans, and especially the Portuguese. If this be true, then I should be thrilled to see, as de Souza claims, my favourite *bania* traders beating off an advance guard of European imperialism in the person of Fr. Silveira. Alas, the records cannot sustain these sorts of claims. It is time to turn to fact, not fancy, and attempt a broad-brush sketch of the role of Indians in east Africa in the early modern period.

II

One thing we certainly know is that Indian trade goods were overwhelmingly the main imports into east Africa over the whole of this period, regardless of who handled the actual exchange. In their early days the Portuguese built a fort at Sofala, and then tried to use trade goods from west Africa to buy gold, 'but the negroes of Sofala did not care for it, as they wanted articles which the Moors procured from India, especially from Cambay [a term used at this time for Gujarat in general].'[13] Among these goods, cotton cloths were overwhelmingly dominant, as indeed. Albuquerque found as early as 1514 when he described to his king the vast and intricate network of trade in this item.[14] When the Portuguese sacked Mombasa for the first time in 1505 they found

> in the city quantities of cotton cloth from Cambay because all this coast dresses in these cloths and has no others. In this way the captain-major gathered a great sum for the Sofala trade, finding a great number of very rich cloths, of silk and gold, carpets and saddle cloths, especially one carpet that cannot be bettered anywhere and which was sent to the king of Portugal with many other articles of great value.[15]

Other goods were also imported: wheat from Cambay, beads in enormous quantities, and also fine pieces of craft work, such as the 'bedstead of Cambay, wrought with gold and mother-of-pearl, a very beautiful thing...' which the ruler of Malindi gave to Vasco da Gama in 1502.[16]

The dominance of these goods is a rather strange phenomenon. It is unusual to find goods from one area so completely central in trade and exchange, regardless of who it was who brought them to the region. Whether it was Persians, Arabs, Indians or later Europeans, all of them depended on Indian goods, especially from Gujarat, for items which could find a market on the coast. We may note, however, that while Gujarati imports to the Swahili coast and parts of the interior were vital for the whole region, these goods did not make up a very substantial part of Gujarat's total exports. Edward Alpers has estimated the total at about 4 per cent only.[17] Tomé Pires' very well-known statement makes the same point, at least by omission: 'Cambay chiefly stretches out two arms, with her right arm she reaches out towards Aden and with the other towards Malacca, as the most important places to sail to, and the other places are held to be of less importance.'[18]

Indian, especially Gujarati, goods may have been central, but this is not to say that they came in only in Indian ships or were exchanged by Indian traders resident on the coast. We can now turn to a discussion of the role of Indian traders in east Africa.

It is very difficult to say anything very certain about the role of Indians before the arrival of the Portuguese, for the records are sparse. All we have are a few fragmentary mentions in Arabic sources, and some archaeological evidence. However, the accounts of the first Portuguese in the area, dating from 1498, can also be used to tell us what the situation was very late in the fifteenth century.

There are several problems with our sources before 1498. One is that trade between western India and the Swahili coast was often carried out with a stopover either in the Persian Gulf or Aden, or some other Hadramaut port. This raises the strong possibility that Indian goods may have been transhipped on the way, and thus taken to the Gulf or southern Arabia in Indian ships, and then transported onwards by west Asian traders, either Arabs or Persians. Further confusion comes from the fact that trade may have been handled by west Asian Muslims resident in western India, or alternatively by 'Indian Muslims', these being difficult to differentiate from Muslims from other areas. Perhaps this is the real point. The modern tendency to categorize people by nationality hardly applied in this early modern period; the distinction between say a Muslim who lived in India, one who visited India, one who traded in Indian goods, and one who was an agent for some other Muslim resident elsewhere is extremely nebulous. This was not, after all, a time when people had passports and citizenship of some particular country. Hindu merchants, if any, are of course much easier to identify, for they were certainly 'Indian'.

The dictatorship of the monsoons also complicates matters. Broadly speaking, the passage from India to the northern Swahili coast, that is down to Cape Delgado, can be done comfortably in one monsoon. However, south of there normally requires two. It seems that often the pattern was of trade goods being broken up on the north coast and taken further south in smaller, Swahili owned and operated, vessels.[19] Yet even this raises a problem. Foreign traders who arrived on one monsoon and left when the next started left themselves open to extortion, for the locals would simply raise their prices for the short time they were in port. In most other parts of monsoon Asia, traders solved this problem by staying over for a year, or more likely leaving an agent in place to buy when prices were low, and sell when they were high. This is to be seen in all the great port cities of the early modern Indian Ocean. It would be strange indeed if this was not done on the Swahili coast also.

So much for the difficulties. What we can say is that there is evidence of trade between India and east Africa from at least the beginning of the Common Era. It could well be that contact with the area north of Cape Delagodo was much earlier than with the region to the south of this commonly-used dividing line. Mudenge finds Indian contact with the former area from at least the first century, but with the latter only from around the eighth century.[20] The Periplus from the first century, and Masudi from the tenth, find extensive Indian trade in East Africa. Al Beruni early in the eleventh century claimed that 'The reason why in particular Somanath has become so famous is that it was a harbour for seafaring people, and a station for those who went to and fro between Sufala in the country of Zanj and China.' This of course refers to a time well before Kathiawar was conquered by Muslims, yet the quotation does not necessarily mean that Hindus from Somnath travelled to Africa. Al Idrisi in the twelfth century found Indians trading as far south as Sofala.[21]

III

The archaeological evidence confirms extensive Indian contact with the area. There is, for example, evidence of many Asian plants being grown in east Africa before the Portuguese arrived.[22] Indian influence has been found even from the period before the rise of Islam, that is the sixth and seventh centuries, in local pottery, for there have been finds of pots made with local clay but using Indian motifs.[23] The extant Cutchi doors of the coast, found especially in Zanzibar and Lamu today, date only from the very late eighteenth century, but archaeologists have found Indian motifs in architecture dating from much earlier times.[24] Perhaps again we should remember not to categorize things too strictly. A little while ago a bronze lion statuette was found at Shanga. It dates from around 1100. It seems clear it was used in Hindu *puja*, and this means it would hardly be sold or used by a non-Hindu. However, mosques in Shanga date from around

800. The object is a real puzzle, though it could be that it was used as regalia. The more general point is that at least by this time coastal communities all over the Indian Ocean were linked by travel and trade. Thus 'The Shanga lion must therefore not be so much "Indian" or "African" but "Indian Ocean" in attribution.'[25]

This does raise one other matter, which is whether the Indians who travelled and traded on the coast also settled. Horton and Blurton speculate that their lion was made to order by local Hindu crafts people in Shanga. We have just noted Indian influence on local pottery and architecture in the period before the arrival of the Portuguese. However, it could be, as Wilding suggests, that these Indian crafts people came in on one monsoon, did their work, and then left again.[26] So also, perhaps, with the traders, who also came in, traded, and left again. Yet this really seems to be very unlikely. As we noted, this sort of schedule would gravely disadvantage traders, and also crafts people, who surely would prefer to stay and profit from their superior expertise. Here however we presumably also need to differentiate between Indian Muslims and Hindus. Some years ago I produced a body of evidence which seemed to show that Hindus travelled by sea much more in this period than has been generally recognized (and I must record here that this article had an early outing at Santiniketan, under the auspices of Ashin Das Gupta).[27] Nevertheless, as a rule of thumb there can be little doubt that Muslims did travel more than Hindus.

If we turn now to the accounts of the very first Portuguese on the coast we can make more progress on this matter of whether or not Indians settled, always of course in the context of the undisputed dominance of Indian trade goods in the area.[28] The senior Indian historian, Tirmizi wrote that

> Unless more evidence is forthcoming, it is difficult to conjecture that there was a considerable Indian commercial community on the Swahili coast. The residence of Indian merchants on this coast was perhaps more seasonal than permanent before the nineteenth century.[29]

I will now accumulate the available evidence, which in sum seems to show that Indians, both Hindus and Muslims, certainly traded, and possibly settled, on the coast.

Most of our detailed information comes from Mombasa and Malindi, at that time the latter being much inferior to the former, let alone to Kilwa. We can briefly note what we know about three other Swahili port cities on the coast. In Mozambique, da Gama noted in 1498 'two captive Christian Indians', held by the local Muslims.[30] In Sofala, far to the south, we are merely told that there was a large trade in Gujarati products, carried there in small ships based at Kilwa, Mombasa and Melinde.[31] So also for Mogadishu in the far north, where Gujaratis themselves are described as having a direct large trade.[32]

Mombasa at 1500 was second only to Kilwa in its trade, or indeed, given the decline of the latter, may have been the premier port city of the coast at the time. Vasco da Gama was there in April 1498. One of the objectives of his voyage was to find the powerful Christian potentate Prester John. This meant he was keen to find Christians, and indeed he found some in Mombasa, or so he thought. Two fair-skinned Christians came on board the Portuguese ships, and later members of his expedition visited the houses of two Christian merchants, who 'showed them a paper, an object of their adoration, on which was a sketch of the Holy Ghost.' A footnote by none other than Richard Burton noted that this may have been a picture of an incarnation of Siva. Be that as it may, there is no doubt that these 'Christians' were in fact Hindus. As is well known, da Gama made the same mistake in Calicut next month, where he left still convinced that this port's Hindus were in fact somewhat schismatic Christians. However, these Hindu merchants, almost certainly Gujaratis, were mere sojourners, for the account of the voyage goes on to note that 'The Christian [sic. Hindu] merchants in the town are only temporary residents, and are held in much subjection, they not being allowed to do anything except by the order of the Moorish King.'[33]

The first viceroy, Francisco de Almeida, visited and sacked Mombasa in 1505. Several of the accounts of this early atrocity note the presence of three Gujarati ships in the port. They had already been unloaded, and run aground to be careened. They were well defended by their Muslim crew and the Portuguese withdrew. They did however acquire a vast booty in the town, and especially

> there were in the city quantities of cotton cloth from Cambay because all this coast dresses in these cloths and has no others. In this way the captain-major gathered a great sum for the Sofala trade, finding a great number of very rich cloths, of silk and gold, carpets and saddle cloths, especially one carpet that cannot be bettered anywhere and which was sent to the king of Portugal with many other articles of great value.[34]

The Portuguese spent longer in Malindi, and had better relations with the ruler, so information from this port city is relatively voluminous. Barbosa and Castanheda noted a large trade between the locals and the Muslims and Hindus of Cambay.[35] The fullest account of da Gama's first visit in 1498 comes from an anonymous description by an eye-witness. He described how

We found here four vessels belonging to Indian Christians. When they came for the first time on board Paulo da Gama's ship, the captain-major being there at the time, they were shown an altar-piece representing Our Lady at the foot of the cross, with Jesus Christ in her arms and the apostles around her. When the Indians saw this picture they prostrated themselves, and as long as we were there they came to say their prayers in front of it, bringing offerings of cloves, pepper and other thins. These Indian are tawny men; they wear little clothing and have long beards and long hair, which they braid. They told us they ate no beef. Their language differs from that of the Arabs, but some of them know a little of it, as they hold much intercourse with them.[36]

It seems clear that these Hindus came from Gujarat, for Gonçalves even calls them 'baneanes'.[37] Barros in his retrospective account, though one based on eye-witness testimony, noted both Muslims and Hindus from Cambay, and on the latter elaborated that these 'banians' were 'such devout followers of the teaching of Pythagoras that they will not even kill the insects by which they may be infested, and eat nothing which has life...' which may even lead one to identify them as Jains.[38] Castanheda has them variously coming from Cranganor and Cambay.[39] More to the point, he claims that they 'morão' in Malindi. This word means 'lived', and must be taken as quite strong evidence that these Hindus were resident; yet it could also mean they 'dwelt', not necessarily implying permanent residence. Castanheda also distinguishes between Arabian Muslims, whom he calls 'estrangeiros', or foreigners, and 'gente natural', or locals.

The next Portuguese visitor was Cabral in 1500. Accounts of his visit note the presence of three very rich Gujarati ships. Two different texts provide valuable descriptions of these ships. One put them at 200 tonnes each, and noted that

These naos have the superstructure built of cane and their hulls bound with ropes and caulked with pitch for the lack of nails; all the naos of these parts are fashioned so; they sail always with the wind astern for they cannot sail into the wind, and they have a quarter-deck.[40]

An anonymous account noted that 'Their hulls are well built of good wood, tied together with cord (for they have no nails), and they are covered with a mixture in which there is much incense. They have no castles except in the stern. These ships come to trade from parts of India.'[41] Finally, we have more evidence of Gujarati Hindus, possibly even Jains, in a description by a Spanish traveller from 1507. Figueroa told how

They went to Malindi, where the people live a frugal life. Called Gujarati, they are very withdrawn and sparing of conversation. Many of them will eat no living thing; by that I mean anything that must be killed and has blood. By another name they are known as Brahmans.[42]

There was at least one Hindu Gujarati still in Malindi in 1510, for in this year the Portuguese were selling the contents of a Gujarati ship which they had confiscated. Two items were sold to 'Gangua Guzurate'.[43]

It seems to be sound to use this early Portuguese documentation to also cast light on the situation for at least a little time before their arrival. What then can we say of the period around 1500? All the accounts note masssive trade by Gujaratis, as well as by Arabs and locals. Most of them say little about 'Indian' Muslims, presumably because they were indistinguishable from other visiting Muslims. The presence of Hindus, albeit often hopefully described as Christians, was much noted, and there is no doubt that these people were Hindus from Gujarat, though the extreme reverence for all forms of life may even point to Jains. What we do not know is whether or not these Gujaratis settled. The use of the word 'morão' may point to an affirmative answer, but on the other hand one account is definite that they were sojourners, and indeed were harshly treated.

IV

We have only scattered references to Indians trading on the coast in the sixteenth and seventeenth centuries. Portugal, of course, tried to impose its usual trade monopoly policies on the area. Their own records make it clear that there was much evasion, and indeed in the sixteenth century their power was limited to south of Cape Delgado. It was only with the acquisition of Mombasa in 1592, where they built Fort Jesus, that they had any sort of presence in the north. Consequently their records for the north are also scanty for the sixteenth century, and we must assume that Indians continued to trade there, along with Arabs and others. We do have one charming mention of their presence in the Lamu area in 1606. Fr. Gaspar de S. Bernadino arrived at Pate island, but none of the locals had had any experience with Christians or with Portuguese, and so had no idea how to treat this black-robed friar. Luckily, there were also present two Hindu merchants from Diu, who spoke good Portuguese. Diu of course had been under Portuguese rule for decades, so these two were able to act as intermediaries and tell the local ruler all about how priests behaved, such as their vows of poverty and chastity and their collection of alms.[44]

In the south the Portuguese established a strong base at Mozambique, and also the settlements of Sena and Tete, up the Zambezi river. Much evidence makes it clear that their trade control policies here also met with only limited success, for there was much evasion, especially by local and visiting Muslims. Gold from the Zimbabwe plateau was smuggled on a vast scale, as also were imports of Indian goods. And in any case the Portuguese, like everyone else, found the only trade items with any likelihood of finding a market were Indian products, especially cloths and beads. Thus to an extent Indian, Arab and other traders in the south were displaced by Portuguese, or ships licensed by the Portuguese, yet the products traded remained the same.

What is more interesting is to notice how Indians were able to operate within the entrails of the Portuguese quasi-empire in Mozambique. A sketch of how this operated will make up a contribution which has strong echoes in many other studies of indigenous assistance or cooperation in this somewhat ramshackle early modern empire.[45] When we look below the imperial Portuguese umbrella we find two distinct groups of Indians playing very different roles. By the eighteenth century, if not earlier, banias from Diu and elsewhere held a dominant position in the economy of the Portuguese area in the south, specializing especially in finance and money lending. The other Indian group were the Canarins, in other words Indian Christians, mostly from Goa, many of whom were *mestiços,* and who advanced far inland up the Zambezi valley and even to the Zimbabwe plateau. At first they operated in a subordinate position under the Portuguese, but by the later eighteenth century held dominant positions in those strange semi-feudal institutions, the *prazos* of the Zambezi valley. We will look at the Canarins first.

In broad terms the sequence is of Canarins coming in quite early in the sixteenth century and fulfilling subordinate roles in the Portuguese areas. However, through the seventeenth century they acquired a much larger role in trade, even on the plateau until they and the Portuguese were expelled by Changamire in 1693. In no way daunted, they then began to acquire prazos, and by the late eighteenth century it seems that most prazos were held by Goans, or people with some 'Indian' blood. The Portuguese complained from time to time about both their dominance of trade and then of the prazos, yet they also found that Canarins made much better and more willing settlers than did 'pure' Portuguese.

If we look first at the coast, in Sofala in the late 1580s there was a Christian settlement of some 600 souls, including Portuguese, mestiços, and 'gente da terra', which in this context means some

Indian Christians but mostly local African converts.[46] In the capital of Mozambique a Jesuit in 1568 found about 100 Portuguese householders, and about 200 Africans and mestiços.[47] This population seems to have grown rapidly, as late in the 1580s Fr. dos Santos found about 2000 Portuguese and other Christians.[48] We know little of the role of these Canarins, but the account of an English visitor from the mid-seventeenth century points to them being humble people who worked as lascars.[49] By the seventeenth century both Portuguese householders and also Canarins had occupied the mainland areas adjacent to Mozambique island, Mossuril and Cabeceiras. They married local Makua women, and created a distinctive hybrid littoral culture.[50]

As regards the interior, we again have some scattered evidence. Some of this comes as a consequence of what is perhaps the most famous event of the century for the Portuguese, the martyrdom of Fr. Silveira, and governor Barreto's subsequent punitive expedition. When the Father reached Sena, 260 km up the Zambezi in 1560, he found 10–15 Portuguese and also some Indian Christians.[51] He was accompanied on his journey by six Portuguese and a Canarin youth called Calisto.[52] Twelve years later the Portuguese sent off an ill-fated expedition to avenge Silveira's death. One of governor Barreto's five companies of troops consisted of 80 Canarins and locals, along with 60 Portuguese.[53] Further, the Portuguese also wanted to attack the ruler of Manica, in part at least because they claimed that he had on three separate occasions robbed Canarin traders.[54]

We have a few other indications of a sixteenth-century Canarin presence up the Zambezi. Fr. Santos in the late 1580s found 800 Christians in Sena, 50 of them Portuguese and the rest Indians and Africans. Further up river, at Tete, were 600 Christians, 40 Portuguese and the rest again Indian and African.[55] Early in the seventeenth century Fr. Avellar found 150 Portuguese in Sena, and 60–70 in Tete, in both cases along with 'many men of India'.[56] In 1633 we have news of the gardens of the Portuguese and natives of India at Sena, and indeed at this time, when the town was relatively prosperous, the population seems to have been very mixed indeed. At the school were sons of the Portuguese, but also children of Chinese, Javanese, Malabaris and Sinhalese, along with Africans and mulattoes.[57] At this same time António Bocarro noted both Portuguese and Indian Christians trading further inland.[58] Manuel de Costa, a Goan, was one of the wealthiest traders in the Zambezi valley in the mid-seventeenth century.[59] In the 1650s we even have a report of a Brahmin trading in ivory much further up river, though this could well be a misidentification.[60]

There is scattered evidence of Canarins trading in the interior in later times. Indeed, Newitt considers them to have been the dominant traders in the interior, as opposed to the Portuguese.[61] This role was facilitated by Portuguese policy, albeit inadvertently. In 1673 trade up the Zambezi was freed from the monopoly control of the governor of Mozambique, and became open to all. At the same time the Portuguese tried to restrict the opportunities this might open for the Canarins. All local ships leaving Mozambique for the Zambezi area were to be searched, and any Canarins found on board were to be thrown out, for they were considered to be very prejudicial to the commerce of the area. Similarly, the superintendent of the Portuguese factory at Sena was not to sell goods to them unless a Portuguese stood guarantor for them.[62] However, these racist and discriminatory policies met with little success. The Canarins moved in anyway. In 1690 the king complained bitterly about the effects of this opening. It was 'natives of this state', that is Canarins, who had moved in and quickly acquired a dominant role, very much to the detriment of the royal customs house. Their intense and expert competition had also led to a catastrophic fall in prices for cloth.[63] Finally, in 1690 the Portuguese decided to restrict trade again, this time to a state company.

Despite this, we have scattered evidence of Canarins continuing to trade in the interior. Fr. Conceição in 1696 noted some of them trading at what used to be a big fair. By 1696, however, Changamire had expelled all foreigners, including the Portuguese and the Canarins, from the interior. Even so some Canarins were able to make arrangements and stay. A place five-days journey inland from Tete had rich silver mines, in which Portuguese and Canarins stayed, among them one Domingos Carvalho. This enterprising trader made an agreement with the African now in charge of the area, to exchange cloth for silver, and for some time he did very well indeed.[64]

However, even from late in the sixteenth century some Portuguese had begun to acquire land on semi-feudal tenures in the Zambezi valley. The tendency for land control to replace trade (though of course the two were not totally mutually exclusive) accelerated through the next century, and perhaps reached its florescence once the Portuguese were expelled from the plateau in 1693. In the period before this the Portuguese in fact had actively promoted settlement, and increasingly looked to Goans to do this. Indeed, we have here an early version of planned settlement, a precursor of the famous Wakefield scheme which in the mid-nineteenth century resulted in colonies in several parts of New Zealand and Australia.

As early as 1679, the authorities in India were told that the ruler of Portugal had heard that there were Canarins and other natives in Portuguese India who could work in Mozambique and the Zambezi valley. They were told to look into this, for if it were true this would save the cost of populating the area with Portuguese from the metropolis.[65] Four years later the viceroy informed the king that 50 Canarins from Salcette and Ilhas, eight of them accompanied by their wives, were going off to the Zambezi area in a Portuguese ship.[66] A year later, in 1685, 18 Canarin couples, mostly farmers, arrived in Mozambique.[67] Fr. Conceição a decade later recommended bringing in more Goan families, as they were excellent traders. He also pointed out that the Portuguese women who arrived from time to time never had issue, except for one very young one. It would be best to bring in only very young Portuguese girls. The father also wanted to rebuild some of the ruined Portuguese forts in the area, for which task engineers, stone masons and carpenters were needed. However, it would be best if these workmen were Indians, for it was not suitable that Africans see Portuguese engaged in manual work.[68] In 1698 the king pointed out that it had always been difficult to get Portuguese to go to the Zambezi valley, and those who did usually died. It now became official policy that Canarins be encouraged, both men and women, merchants, craftsmen and farmers.[69]

These official schemes came to little, but informal settlement nevertheless proceeded. During the seventeenth and eighteenth centuries vast areas of land came to be controlled by Portuguese and Canarins. These were of course the famous prazos of the Zambezi valley. They have been much studied,[70] and in particular are now accepted as being essentially African institutions, rather than outposts of European imperialism. For our purposes, the point to note is that the prazos increasingly were controlled by Canarins, or by people with some Indian background. It is of course impossible, and undesirable, to be too specific about ethnicity at this time. Most of the *prazeiros* were probably mixtures of Indian, Portuguese and African ancestry.

Goan dominance seems to be a phenomenon of the later eighteenth century, and as this is really at the end of the early modern period with which I am concerned, I will only sketch this matter.[71] A census of Christians in the Zambezi valley from 1722[72] enumerated the following distribution: clearly Indians, that is Canarins, were far from dominant yet.

Table 1

Place	Portuguese and descendants Male	Female	Indians Male	Female	Natives
Sena	34	32	58	7	891
Gombe	8	7	4	1	101
Quelimane	10	9	10	6	16
Luabo	1	–	8	5	374
Manica	12	4	–	–	5
Sofala	13	13	9	1	279
Tete	24	36	16	8	768
Zumbo	67	27	23	–	300
Marave	3	–	11	11	180

But a half-century later this had changed. These new prazeiros dominated the province of Tete in Mozambique for most of the nineteenth century. They were heavily armed, and intermarried with locally powerful Africans. Indeed, the last of these independent feudatories was defeated and his territory incorporated into the Portuguese state of Mozambique only in 1888.[73]

It has been claimed that 'The Indian Ocean trade of 18th century Mozambique is essentially a story of the exploits of Banyan capitalism and Canarin backwoods traders.'[74] We can now turn to the activities of the other group of Indians who operated in Portuguese territory, the famous banias of Gujarat. They have of course been much studied in other regions.[75] Again I intend only a sketch to round off the story, for their dominance, like that of the Canarins in the prazos, lies later than my cut-off date of the end of the early modern period. We have scattered references to banias trading in the north, such as a petition from 'Amichande', the shahbandar of Massua, on the Ethiopian coast.[76] In 1671, the viceroy told the king he was not keen to stop the banias ['*gentios*'] of Diu from rebuilding their temples, and this favourable policy had been supported by D. Affonso Mendes, Patriarch of Ethiopia, as they had been helpful to him when he had been in Ethiopia.[77] Further south, in 1606 Fr. Gaspar de São Bernadino found two 'heathen merchants, natives of Diu' who knew Portuguese very well, at Siyu, on Pate Island.[78]

During most of the sixteenth and seventeenth centuries the Portuguese tried to regulate trade between their possessions in western India and Mozambique. There is evidence of extensive trade from Diu to Mozambique, done by banias from Diu and Surat. In 1639 a petition claimed that 1000 *bares* [240,000 kg] of cloth were going from Diu to Mozambique, while another petition from the next year found ivory worth 63,000 *pardaos* [Rs 113,400] coming in to Diu in the single month of October 1639.[79] It was around this time that there occurred a pronounced change in the priorities of the Portuguese state. By the end of the 1660s they had lost to the Dutch all of their possessions in Southeast Asia, and also Sri Lanka and the Malabar coast. East Africa thus became, at least by process of elimination, the most important trade area for the remaining Portuguese possessions in western India. In 1686 the Portuguese, having failed to make huge profits from their south-east African areas, decided to end the monopoly of the captain of Mozambique over the importation of Gujarati cloth into his port, and instead sell these rights to a merchant group from Diu. This was the famous, and ultimately unsuccessful, 'companhia de Mazanes de Dio', that is the Company of Banias. This entity has been much studied.[80]

A recent account claims that it in fact merely recognized an existing situation of bania dominance of Mozambique's trade.[81] It does, however, seem to have changed one aspect, which is that more and more banias now moved to this unhealthy island, and settled there and in its neighbourhood.[82] By at least early in the eighteenth century they held a stranglehold over the trade of the port and its neighbouring settlements on the mainland. There was in fact an influx of banias who controlled the wholesale and retail trade and also, so we are told, engaged in such manual occupations as barbers, watchmakers, and goldsmiths.[83] By the middle of the century banias owned 22 out of 37 retail shops in Mozambique, Mossuril and Cabeceiras (these two being on the mainland opposite the island). Banias dominated the whole economy of Mozambique and the coast. Some had huge incomes.[84] They had their own captain, who negotiated on their behalf with the Portuguese authorities.[85] Indeed, their commercial expertise and vast capital enabled them to out-compete the Portuguese themselves, while petty Swahili traders were also unable to match them. This of course led to considerable hostility from time to time, yet the Portuguese state needed them and their financial resources, so that official discrimination necessarily had usually to be moderated by this stark economic reality.[86] Mbwiliza in fact claims that at least in the first half of the eighteenth century Mozambique was 'in the orbit of Indian merchant capital. The only challenge to the grasp that the Banian merchants had, in alliance with Arab and Swahili middlemen, over trade in Mozambique came from French slave traders', who had entered the slave trade at Mozambique in the 1740s.[87] As a result, it has been claimed that 'National and religious ideologies gave way to a multiracial class ideology, symbolically expressed under a new identity of *homens do chapeu* [hat-weavers].'[88]

Nor did the banias restrict themselves to the coastal area around the port city of Mozambique. They spread inland also, or at least their influence did, for they usually used intermediaries for the interior trade. These African agents, called *patamares,* were hired by the banias. They led the caravans which carried Indian trade goods into the interior, to the Makua people in Makuani, where they were exchanged for ivory. The banias also took part in the trade in foodstuffs, and extended credit to Portuguese and Swahili elites.[89] The extent of their influence was shown, *inter alia,* in an episode in the 1740s. In 1744, Diu's banias resident in Mozambique Island had been forbidden to trade in or own slaves, for fear that they would convert their African slaves to Hinduism. This ridiculous Portuguese suspicion was vigorously rejected by the banias. They pointed out that for them the slave trade was vital, and they also needed to own slaves to work in their houses and ships. They threatened, in a familiar way, to move elsewhere if the ban was enforced. They also promised not to sell slaves to Muslims. Two years later the king backed them up. Indeed, they needed to be able to sell and own slaves, and in any case they had never converted slaves to Hinduism; rather they had allowed them to become Christians.[90] This positive Portuguese response, after a fatuous attempt at discrimination, was par for the course.

The remainder of the story can be very quickly sketched. It seems that the banias moved north later in the eighteenth century. In the first half of this century the northern Swahili coast had undergone a period of instability thanks to attacks by the Omanis. However, as Omani power was solidified the banias moved in under this new umbrella, and participated vigorously in the slave trade. They even ran the state's customs service and treasury.[91] Their descendants can be seen in Zanzibar today. Later again, at the end of the nineteenth century, many Indians moved into the new British colony of Kenya, and after World War I to Tanganyika as well. Again banias were prominent in merchant and money-lending.

V

The conclusion from all this seems to be that we must be careful not to exaggerate the role of Indians in east Africa in the early modern period. The enthusiastic claims of dominance, of a massive impact of Indians in the area, are wide of the mark. What we can say is that Indian goods certainly were the main imports to the region, and that Indians, mostly Muslim but also a number of Hindus, participated in trade on the coast long before the arrival of Europeans. Their role in the next century or so is comparatively poorly documented, but we find them continuing to trade either within or without the Portuguese monopoly system, both on the coast and, in the case of the Canarins, far inland also. Two groups of Indians secured a major role for themselves under the Portuguese imperial umbrella in the eighteenth century. Canarins played a large role in interior trade, and especially became one of the dominant groups, if not the main one, of those who held prazos. However, to distinguish Canarins, or to see them as quite distinct from other prazeiros would be incorrect. Intermarriage or at least interbreeding was wide spread, so that most 'Portuguese' had some African or Indian blood, just as did the Canarins. Few of them would be pure-blooded Indians who had converted to Catholicism. The other group was much more distinct, these being the banias who here as elsewhere played a large role in finance, trade and commerce. The Canarins continued their role in the Zambezi valley until near the end of the nineteenth century. The banias moved in under other imperial umbrellas in this century, first that of the Omanis and then at the end that of the British in the northern sector of the Swahili coast.

NOTES

1. For a fuller discussion of this matter see my *World History and the Indian Ocean: the Swahili Coast before Imperialism, 1450–1700,* Baltimore, Johns Hopkins University Press, in press, chapter 2.

2. See Lynda Norene Shaffer, *Maritime Southeast Asia to 1500,* Armonk, NY, 1996.

3. R.B. Serjeant, *The Portuguese off the South Arabian Coast,* Oxford, 1963, pp.3, 8–11.

4. A. Rita–Ferreira, 'Moçambique e os naturais da India Portuguesa', in Luis de Albuquerque and I. Guerreiro, eds, *II Seminário Internacional de história Indo-Portuguesa,* Lisbon, 1985, pp.617, 645. The late-fourteenth century date stems from the fact that Ibn Battuta in his account of 1331 did not mention Indians. The quotation of course is a parody on the title of Walter Rodney's well-known book *How Europe underdeveloped Africa,* Howard University Press, Washington D.C., revised edn. 1982. For similar wild claims of Indian presence, indeed dominance, see *inter alia,* R.R. Ramchandani, 'Indian Emigration to East African Countries from Ancient to Early Colonial Times, in *Mouvements de Populations dans l'Ocean Indian,* Paris, 1979, pp.309–29 and Prithvish Nag, 'The Indian Ocean, India and Africa: Historical and Geographical Perspectives,' in Satish Chandra, ed., *The*

Indian Ocean: Explorations in History, Commerce and Politics, New Delhi, 1987, pp.151–73.

5. T.R. de Souza, 'History of Mozambique: An Introduction to Bibliography', in *Purabhilekh–Puratatva,* VI, 1, 1988, p.66; T.R. de Souza, 'The Afro-Asian Church in the Portuguese Estado da India', in O.U. Kalu, ed., *African Church Historiography: An Ecumenical Perspective,* Bern, 1988, p.64.

6. Bertha Leite, *D. Gonçalo da Silveira,* Lisbon, 1946, pp.177–92; *Documenta Indica,* ed. J. Wicki et al., Rome, 1948, 20 vols to date, vol. V, *passim.*

7. Cyril Andrew Hromnik, 'Goa and Mozambique: the participation of Goans in Portuguese enterprise in the Rios de Cuama, 1501–1752', Ph.D. dissertation, Syracuse University, 1977; Cyril A. Hromnik, 'Background and content of the Historical Archives of Goa', *History in Africa,* V, 1978, pp.371–6; 'Canarins in the Rios de Cuama, 1501–76', *Journal of African Studies,* VI, 1, 1979, pp.27–37; Cyril A. Hromnik, *Indo-Africa: Toward a new understanding of the history of sub-Saharan Africa,* Cape Town, 1981. For reviews of the book see Martin Hall and C.H. Borland, 'The Indian Connection: An Assessment of Hromnik's "Indo–African",' *The South African Archaeological Bulletin,* vol. XXXVII, 1982, pp.75–80, and his response: Cyril A. Hromnik, 'African History and Africanist Orthodoxy: A Response to Hall and Borland', *The South African Archaeological Bulletin,* vol. XXXVIII, 1983, pp.36–9; see also reviews by C. Ehret, *International Journal of African Historical Studies,* XV, 3, 1982, pp.549–50, and C.P. Ownby, *Journal of African History,* XXIII, 1982, pp.415–6.

8. Hromnik, 'Goa and Mozambique', p.18.

9. Ibid.

10. Ibid.

11. Hromnik, *Indo-Africa,* p.81.

12. Ibid.

13. João de Barros, *Da Asia,* Lisbon, 1778–88, I, x, 3.

14. 'Albuquerque to king, Goa, 25 Oct 1514', in António da Silva Rego, et al., *Documentos sobre os Portugueses em Moçmbique e na Africa Central, 1497–1840,* Lisbon, 1962–89, 9 vols to date, III, 559–61 [hereafter DM].

15. Account of Almeida's voyage, DM, I, 533.

16. G.S.P. Freeman-Grenville, *The East African Coast: Select Documents from the first to the earlier nineteenth century,* London, 1962, p.75.

17. E.A. Alpers, 'Gujarat and the Trade of East Africa, *c.* 1500–1800', *International Journal of African Historical Studies,* IX, 1976, p.39. His estimate is based on Moreland's work from many years ago: we could do with a better attempt after all this time.

18. Tomé Pires, *The Suma Oriental of Tomé Pires,* ed. A. Cortesão, London, 1944, 2 vols, I, 42.

19. See, for example, Freeman-Grenville, *East African Coast,* pp.201–4; Bashir Ahmed Datoo, *Port Development in East Africa,* Nairobi, 1975, p.45; Neville Chittick, 'Indian Relations with East Africa before the arrival of the Portuguese', *Journal of the Royal Asiatic Society,* 1980, especially p.125.

20. Stanislaus I. Gorerazvo Mudenge, 'Afro-Indian Relations before 1900: a

Southeast African perspective', in Shanti Sadiq Ali and R.R. Ramchandani, eds *India and the Western Indian Ocean States,* New Delhi, 1981, pp.39–40.

21. James S. Kirkman, 'The Coast of Kenya as a Factor in the Trade and Culture of the Indian Ocean', in *Sociétés e compagnies de Commerce en Orient et dans l'Océan Indien,* ed. M. Mollat, Paris, 1970, *passim;* al-Biruni, *Alberuni's India,* ed. and trans. Edward Sachau, reprint, Delhi, 1964, II, 104; Gabriel Ferrand, ed. and trans., *Relations de voyages et textes géographiques Arabes, Persans et Turks relatifs a l'extréme-orient du VIIIe au XVIIIe siècles,* Paris, 1913, 2 vols, I, 173; Richard Wilding, *The Shorefolk: Aspects of the Early Development of Swahili Communities,* Fort Jesus Occasional Papers no. 2, mimeo, 1987, p.81.

22. A. Rita-Ferreira, *Fixação portuguesa e historia pre-colonial de Moçambique,* Lisbon, Instituto de investigação cientifica tropical, 1982, p.50.

23. Interview with Richard Wilding, Mombasa, 4 November 1991.

24. Interview with George Abungu, Mombasa, 4 November 1991; Wilding, *Shorefolk,* p.81; see also James de Vere Allen, *Swahili Origins: Swahili Culture and the Shungwaya Phenomenon,* ed. John Middleton, London, 1993, p.69 for a claim of very minor Indian influence.

25. M.C. Horton and T.R. Blurton, ' "Indian" Metal work in East Africa: the bronze lion statuette from Shanga', *Antiquity,* LXII, 1988, pp.21–2.

26. Wilding interview 4 Novmber 1991; Wilding, *Shorefolk,* p.81.

27. M.N. Pearson, 'Indian Seafarers in the Sixteenth Century', in *Coastal Western India: Studies from the Portuguese Records,* New Delhi, 1981, pp.116–47.

28. Many of these early Portuguese accounts are available in translation, especially in DM, and in G.M. Theal, *Records of South-Eastern Africa,* London, 1898–1903, 9 vols.

29. S.A.I. Tirmizi, *Indian Sources for African History,* vol. I, Delhi, 1988, p.17; for a good general overview see Wilding, *Shorefolk,* pp.81–9.

30. Account of da Gama's voyage in DM, I, 19.

31. Duarte Barbosa, *Livro,* London, 1918–21, 2 vols, I, 6–8.

32. Barbosa, *Livro,* I, 31.

33. Vasco da Gama, *A Journal of the First Voyage of Vasco da Gama,* London, 1898, pp.36, 39; Fernão Lopes de Castanheda, *História do descobrimento e conquista da India pelos Portugueses,* 3rd. ed., Coímbra, 1924–33, 9 vols, I, 9. For Calicut see M.N. Pearson, 'The Search for the Similar: Early Contacts between Portuguese and Indians,' in Jens Christian V. Johansen, Erling Ladewig Petersen and Henrik Stevnsborg, eds, *Clashes of Cultures: Essays in Honour of Niels Steensgaard,* Odense University Press, 1992, pp.144–59.

34. Castanheda, II, 6; account of Almeida's voyage in DM, I, 531–5; account of Almeida's voyage in Eric Axelson, *South East Africa, 1488–1530,* London, 1940, pp.235–6.

35. Barbosa, I, 21–2; Castanheda, I, x.

36. Da Gama, *Voyage,* pp.44–5; the same story in Luis de Albuquerque, *Crónica do descobrimento e conquista da India pelos Portugueses,* Coimbra, 1974, p.8.

37. Fr Sebastian Gonçalves, *Primeira Parte da Historia dos Religiosas da Companhia de Jesus,* ed. José Wicki, Coimbra, 1957–62, 3 vols, I, 83.

38. Barros, I, iv, 6.

39. Castanheda, I, 10, 12.

40. King of Portugal to king of Castile, Italian copy, printed in Rome 23 October 1505, DM, I, 47.

41. W.B. Greenlee, *The Voyage of Pedro Alvares Cabral to Brazil and India,* London, 1938, p.65.

42. James B. McKenna, *A Spaniard in the Portuguese Indies: The Narrative of Martín Fernández de Figueroa,* Cambridge, MA, 1967, p.73.

43. Register, Melinde, 20 March 1510, DM, II, 423.

44. Freeman-Grenville, *East African Coast,* pp.161–2.

45. See for example G.V. Scammell, 'Indigenous Assistance in the Establishment of Portuguese Power in the Indian Ocean', in John Correia-Afonso, ed., *Indo-Portuguese History: Sources and Problems,* Delhi, 1981, pp.163–73; G.V. Scammell, 'The Pillars of Empire: Indigenous Assistance and the Survival of the "Estado da India" *c.* 1600–1700', *Modern Asian Studies,* XXII, July 1988, pp.473–90; M.N. Pearson, 'Banyas and Brahmins: Their Role in the Portuguese Indian Economy', *Coastal Western India,* pp.93–115.

46. João dos Santos, *Ethiopia Oriental,* Lisbon, 1891, 2 vols, I, i, cap 2.

47. António da Silva, SJ, *Mentalidade missiológica dos Jesuítas em Moçambique antes de 1759,* Lisbon, 1967, 2 vols, I, 115; note that 'mestiço' refers to people of European and Indian blood, while an African and European mixture produced a mulatto.

48. Santos, I, iii, cap.4.

49. N. Buckeridge, *Journal and Letter Book of Nicholas Buckeridge, 1651–1654,* ed. J.R. Jenson, Minneapolis, 1973, pp.21. 65.

50. J.F. Mbwiliza, *A History of Commodity Production in Makuani, 1600–1900: Mercantalist Accumulation to Imperialist Domination,* Dar es Salaam, 1991, p.20.

51. Luis Frois, SJ, letter of 15 December 1561, Goa, DM, VIII, 41.

52. B. Leite, p.165; also Gonçalves, II, 400.

53. Monclaro's account of the Barreto expedition, DM, VIII, 399; also in *Documenta Indica,* VIII, 723; see also E.A. Axelson ed., 'Viagem que fez o Padre Antonio Gomes...ao Imperio de Manomotapa...', *Studia,* III, 1959, pp.155–242.

54. Alcantara Guerreiro, 'Inquerito em Mocambique no anno de 1573', *Studia,* 6, 1960, p.14.

55. Santos, I, ii, cap. 8.

56. Report on silver mines of Rios de Cuama by Fr Francisco de Avellar, 1617, in *Memoria dos documentos acerca dos Direitos de Portugal aos territórios de Machona e Nyassa,* Lisbon, 1890, p.95.

57. Axelson, 'Viagen...Gomes', pp.181, 220.

58. António Bocarro, 'Livro das plantas das fortalezas da India', *Arquivo Português Oriental,* ed. A.B. de Bragança Pereira, Bastorá, Goa, 1937–40, IV, 2, 1, pp.20–30.

59. Shanti Sadiq Ali, 'India and Mozambique: Past and Present', in *Purabhilekh–Puratatva,* VI, 1, 1988, p.12.

60. Eric Axelson, *Portuguese in Southeast Africa, 1600–1700,* Johannesburg, 1960, p.137. Newitt accepts this claim: M.D.D. Newitt, *A History of Mozambique,* London, 1994, p.182.

61. M.D.D. Newitt, *Portugal in Africa: the last hundred years,* London, 1981, p.10; M.D.D. Newitt, 'East Africa and the Indian Ocean Trade: 1500–1800', in Ashin Das Gupta and M.N. Pearson, eds, *India and the Indian Ocean, 1500–1800,* Calcutta, 1987, pp.213–4.

62. Oliveira Boleo, 'O "Regimento para o novo comercio de Mocambique" de 1673', *Studia,* III, 1959, pp.107–8.

63. King to viceroy, 20 March 1690, in P.S.S. Pissurlencar, ed., *Assentos do Conselho do Estado,* Bastorá, 1953–7, 5 vols, IV, 441--2.

64. Fr. António da Conceição, 'Tratado dos Rio de Cuama, 1696', *O Chronista de Tissuary,* II, 1867, pp.64–5, 68; for a brief mention of the situation in 1693 see Maria Manuela Sobral Blanco, 'O Estado Português da India: da rendição de Ormuz à perda de Cochim, (1622–1663),' University of Lisbon, Ph.D. dissertation, 1992, 3 vols, II, 762–9, an account by 'Pe Frey Phelipe de Assumpção por andar nas ditas terras quatorze annos.'

65. Prince to governors of India, 27 March 1679, in *Assentos,* IV, 569–70.

66. Viceroy to king, 24 January 1683, in *Assentos,* IV, 570.

67. S.S. Ali, 'India and Mozambique', p.11.

68. Conceição, 'Tratado', pp.86–7.

69. King to viceroy, 28 February 1698, in *Memoria dos documentos,* p.129.

70. See M.D.D. Newitt, *Portuguese Settlement on the Zambezi: Exploration, Land Tenure and Colonial Rule in Eastern Africa,* Harlow, 1973; Allen Isaacman, *Mozambique: the Africanization of a European Institution,* Madison, 1972; S.I.G. Mudenge, 'The Goans in the Zambezi Valley before 1900: an Outline', *Purabhilekh–Puratatva,* II, 2, 1984, pp.1–7.

71. See especially the various works of Malyn Newitt cited above, and A. Rita-Ferreira, 'Moçambique e os naturais da India Portuguesa', in Luis de Albuquerque and I. Guerreiro, eds, *II Seminário internacional de história Indo-Portuguesa,* Lisbon, 1985.

72. 'Livros das Monções', Historical Archives of Goa, vol.87, ff.96–, and published in *Arquivo Português Oriental,* ed. A.B. de Bragança Pereira, Bastorá, Goa, 1937–40, IV, 2, 2, pp.88–9.

73. Henrik Ellert, *Rivers of Gold,* Gweru, 1993, p.167; Rita–Ferreira, 'Moçambique e os naturais', *passim;* Isaacman, *Mozambique,* e.g. pp.59, 76, 84.

74. S.S. Ali, 'India and Mozambique', p.12.

75. Most notably in Ashin Das Gupta, *Indian Merchants and the Decline of Surat, c. 1700–1750,* Wiesbaden, 1979; also in my *Merchants and Rulers in Gujarat,* Berkely, 1976, and *Coastal Western India,* citied above.

76. 'Cartas e Ordens', Historical Archives of Goa, III, f.73.

77. Viceroy to king, 3 October 1671, in 'Livros das Monções,' Historical Archives of Goa, vol. 36, f.258.

78. Freeman-Grenville, *The East African Coast,* pp.161–2.

79. Petition from B.S. Correa, rendeiro of Goa alfandega, December 1639, in 'Livros das Fianças', Historical Archives of Goa, II, ff.143–4; Ibid., f.174, petition of July 1640; other evidence of this trade in Buckeridge, *Journal,* 57, 65. For an enthusiastic account of bania trade generally in East Africa see Alpers, 'Gujarat and the Trade of East Africa', *passim.*

80. For documentation see J.H. da Cunha Rivara, 'A India no governo do Vice-Rei Conde de Villa Verde, 1693–1698', *O Chronista de Tissuary,* II–III, 1867–8; Newitt, *History of Mozambique,* pp.318–23; and especially Frederico Dias Antunes, 'A crise no Estado da India no Final do Século XVII e a Criação das Companhias de Comércio das Indias Orientais e dos Baneanes de Diu', in *Portuguese India and its Northern Province, Proceedings of the 7th International Seminar on Indo-Portuguese History,* in *Mare Liberum,* no. 9, Lisbon, July 1995, pp.19–29.

81. Manuel Lobato, 'Relações comerciais entre a India e a costa Africana nos séculos XVI and XVII: o papel do Guzerate no Comércio de Moçambique', in *Portuguese India and its Northern Province, Proceedings of the 7th International Seminar on Indo-Portuguese History,* in *Mare Liberum,* no. 9, Lisbon, July 1995, p.157.

82. A. Rita–Ferreira, 'História Pré-Colonial do Sul de Moçambique: Tentativa de Síntese', *Studia,* no.41–2, 1979, pp.137–64, and no. 43–4, 1980, 283–324; no.41–2, p.156.

83. History Department, Universidade Eduardo Mondlane, *História de Moçambique, vol. I, Primeiras sociedades sendantarias e impacto dos mercadores (200/300–1886),* Maputo, 1988, 2nd ed., pp.89–93.

84. Mbwiliza, p.28.

85. Letter from capitão-mor dos Baneanes, Narsy Ranuhor, to governor and captain-general, Moçambique, *Documentário Trimestral,* no. 72, p.115; no. 75, n.d. but presumably eighteenth century, p.172.

86. See Rita-Ferreira 'Naturais', *passim;* History Department, pp.89–93; Martin Hall, *The Changing Past: Farmers, Kings and Traders in Southern Africa,* Cape Town, 1987, p.124.

87. Mbwiliza, pp.13–14.

88. Mbwiliza, p.64.

89. History Department, pp.89–93; Mbwiliza, p.28.

90. King to viceroy, 12 March 1746 and 13 December 1746, in J.H. da Cunha Rivara, ed., *Archivo Português Oriental,* Nova Goa, 1857–77, 9 vols, IV, 467–9.

91. See Gervase Clarence-Smith, *The Third Portuguese Empire,* Manchester, 1985, ch. 2; and Alpers, 'Gujarat and the Trade of East Africa'.

11

Edmund Burke and India: the Vicissitudes of a Reputation

P.J. MARSHALL

In his *Autobiography of an Unknown Indian,* Nirad C. Chaudhuri wrote of Edmund Burke:

> Towards Burke we felt nothing but whole-hearted reverence. We had heard that not only had he supported the American colonists but that he had impeached Warren Hastings for his oppression of the Indian people. The two bulky grey-blue volumes of his impeachment speeches in the cupboard were to our eyes the impressively concrete evidence of his championship of the downtrodden.[1]

In 1992 Dr Sara Suleri included two chapters on Burke in her *The Rhetoric of English India*. Underlying what Burke said or wrote about India, she sees 'a desire to conserve the imperial project'. More specifically, she argues that Burke provided 'imperial England with an idiom in which to articulate its emergent suspicion that the health of the colonizing project was dependent on a recognition of the potentially crippling structure of imperial culpability'.[2] Her essays are the most sophisticated, so far, of a number of studies which place Burke's writings firmly in the category of 'colonial discourse'.[3]

The shift from the approach to Burke of the young Nirad Chaudhuri to that of contemporary analyists of colonial discourse marks a great change in the study of India's colonial past. For Chaudhuri and for generations of British and Indian people going back to the late nineteenth century and on to 1947 and even beyond, to debate the history of India in the 18th century was to argue about issues which were still alive under continuing British rule or in its immediate aftermath. Was Britain using or had it used its power over India to India's detriment? Those who believed this to be the case, shared Chaudhuri's enthusiasm for Burke and saw him as the champion of the downtrodden. For liberal-minded British people as well as for many Indians, Burke's speeches were evidence of a conscience within the British empire and of aspirations for a different kind of colonial rule. Surendranath Banerjee put Burke first in a very strong field. Addressing 'a body of young men', he told them: 'You must live in a high and bold atmosphere fragrant with the breath of the gods, Burke, Mazzini, Jesus Christ, Buddha, Chaitanya, Ram Mohun Roy, Keshub Chunder Sen, must be your constant companions.'[4] Those who took Hastings's side in retrospect and saw him as wronged by Burke, envisaged colonial rule as essentially benevolent. Curzon was of course in no doubt about Burke's wrongheadedness. He was one of 'the three most powerful intellects in the sphere of British politics that have ever devoted themselves to the study of Indian problems' (Macaulay and Bright were the other two), but all three had been 'so wrong in their verdicts'.[5] The 18th century past was recognized to be so politically charged that John Morley, as Secretary of State for India, was advised in 1907 that Macaulay's essays on Clive and Hastings should be deleted 'from the text books commended to the ingenuous youth of India'.[6] For both sides the debate was about how Britain had used its political and economic power over India.

For those concerned with colonial discourse, especially since the publication in 1978 of Edward Said's *Orientalism,* the issues look rather different. The misuse of political and economic power is generally assumed without further question and instead attention is rivetted on the abuse of intellectual or cultural power, that is of the power to represent. In the simplest formulations, it is argued that colonial rule rested as much on the appropriation of knowledge as on the application of coercive force. To depict non-Europeans at all was to exercise power over them. Supposedly objective knowledge was assumed to be the prerogative of Europeans who represented the peoples subjected to them in terms that emphasized western superiority and eastern inferiority. This knowledge both legitimized colonial rule for those who ruled and helped to induce the ruled to acquiesce in their subordination to those wiser than themselves. For commentators, such as Sara Suleri, who have modified Said's first formulations, the colonial relationship was more complex than one simply involving the exercise of intellectual power over one side by the other. Colonizer and colonized shared a common predicament and deeply influenced one another. Dr Suleri's interpretation of Burke is a sensitive and sympathetic one, but he is still assessed for his contribution to colonial discourse about India. Burke offers a rich field for the analysis of representations. No European intellectual in the later eighteenth century, a period which Said sees as crucial in laying the foundations for what he called 'modern Orientalism',[7] engaged in depicting a non-European people on a comparable scale to Burke's involvement with India. He said things about Indians in hundreds of parliamentary speeches. He offered his readers elaborate assessments of India in some of the major speeches which were subsequently published, such as the speech on Fox's India Bill, or on the Nabob of Arcot's debts, the four-day opening of the impeachment of Hastings before the Lords and the nine-day closing speech. The corpus of Burke's published writings and recorded speech on India is a vast one dwarfing the rest of his output.

For 40 years I have worked on this great mass of material, first in a thesis on the impeachment of Warren Hastings,[8] then in editing the majority of the letters that referred to Indian matters in ten volumes of the new edition of Burke's correspondence published between 1957 and 1970 under the general editorship of a great American scholar, Thomas Copeland,[9] finally in producing what are at present two and will be three 'very bulky' blue volumes of the new Oxford University Press edition of the *Writings and Speeches of Edmund Burke.*[10] In theory, these last will replace Nirad Chaudhuri's two grey-blue volumes, although their prohibitive cost as well as a radically changed intellectual climate make it scarcely conceivable that they will be found in many Bengali families' cupboards.

As a young historian my concern was to establish the record of Burke's involvement with India rather than to analyse how he envisaged it. Starting work in the late 1950s, a very unideological period in British historical writing, and believing that colonial issues were now closed, I felt no obligation to take sides in my thesis with either Burke or Hastings. I wrote that since 1947 'the incentive to pass judgement on British India by acquitting or condemning Hastings is obviously much reduced, and the historian can concentrate on explanations rather than verdicts'. I pointed out the underlying similarities in the views of Burke and Hastings and argued that 'Detachment...makes it possible to do justice to the intentions of both Burke and Hastings and to appreciate the suffering inflicted by the impeachment on both of them.'[11] I have adhered to this approach over a very long period. In the most recent volume of Burke's Indian *Writings and Speeches,* which appeared in 1991, I still declined to judge between him and Hastings, opining that 'the old certainties about the duties of those who ruled empires' had evaporated long ago and that clear grounds for judgement had disappeared with them.[12]

Few were inclined to take issue with my approach which might be regarded as either commendably even-handed or as insipid and cowardly, according to taste. The old issues were still live ones in the 1950s, at least for Dr N.K. Sinha who then dominated the study of the eighteenth century in Bengal. He was keen, for instance, to demonstrate that Nandakumar had been judicially murdered.[13] But he treated me gently. Younger historians in India in the 1960s were extremely hostile to anything that seemed like an apologia for imperialism, but they gave little, if any, attention to Burke or Hastings. They were above all interested in economic history. My only critic in recent years has been Dr Conor Cruise O'Brien, who is robustly partisan about Burke, seeing him as the enemy of oppression in Ireland, America and India. Oppression, in Dr O'Brien's view, flourished under Hastings. In a courteous way, O'Brien chides me for being too gentle with oppression. Burke, in his view, exposed it and was instrumental in bringing it to an end. 'The people of India by the end of life were uncontestably better off by reason of his exertions on their behalf.'[14]

II

Few wish to engage in such controversies now. In as far as interest is currently being expressed in Burke and India it is in what Burke wrote about India rather than in whether he was 'right' about Hastings or was able to influence British rule for 'the better'. He is seen as contributing to the emergence in the second half of the eighteenth century 'of the discourse of colonialism. Or rather, discourses', since this was a period in which 'a network of intersecting and contending discourses about India' came into existence.[15]

In general terms, such a mode of analysis is obviously valid. Everyting that Burke wrote or said about India assumes the existence of British power over parts of India. He saw these provinces as part of what he recognized, with more clarity of definition than many of his contemporaries, to be a unitary British empire. He never advocated that empire in India should be relinquished. What are held to be the major premises of colonial discourse are also evident in his depiction of India. Indians cannot represent themselves; they must be represented. Burke's representation shows Indians to be different from Europeans. For him there is an Asia or an 'east', and Indians are part of that. Yet within these very loose terms of reference, Burke adopts positions that are highly idiosyncratic. His view of what constituted empire and his manner of representing Indians are very much his own.

Burke's active political career began when he entered Parliament in 1765, the year when the East India Company acquired the *diwani* of Bengal. Although there is clear evidence that Burke took an informed interest in Indian affairs from the outset, he was not drawn into close involvement with how the Company governed its new provinces for another ten years. During that period, Burke generally supported the East India Company as the appropriate body to exercise authority in India. He was sceptical about the motives that lay behind attempts to regulate the Company through state intervention or to prosecute its servants for misdeeds. Those who had 'so widely extended our empire and commerce', he said in 1772, should be cherished and fostered.[16] He defended Robert Clive when he was under attack.

Within a few years, Burke's opinions began to change. Through personal connections, he was drawn into the tangled affairs of the Company in southeast India. He quickly came to believe that British intervention was disrupting the political systems that had for centuries assured the prosperity of those who lived on the coastal plain of the Carnatic. His sympathies were especially engaged with the Maratha principality of Tanjore. By 1780 he was also investigating what was being done by the Company in Bengal. He again became convinced that British rule was profoundly disruptive and that disruption, and with it poverty, was spreading with British influence up the Ganges valley to engulf Benares and Awadh. Hastings as the Company's Governor-General must be called to account, while the Company itself was clearly unfit to administer an empire since it could not control its servants. The reform programme embodied in Fox's India Bills was defeated in 1783 and Burke formally spent the rest of his political career in opposition. From the opposition benches he continued to press the case against Hastings, persuading the House to bring him to impeachment in 1787. The trial lasted from 1788 until Hastings's acquittal in 1795, two years before Burke's death.

Thus, although Burke was directly responsible for an act of Parliament of 1781 dealing with the administration of justice in Bengal and was the principal draftsman of Fox's India Bills, which would have radically altered the structure of British rule in India, most of his Indian career was devoted to the unsuccessful pursuit of a single individual. After flaying the Pitt ministry in his speech on the Nabob of Arcot's debts in 1785, he had little to say in criticism of the way Britain was governing India. Later he was to claim some merit for this,[17] and was to refer approvingly to 'the beneficent government of Lord Cornwallis' in Bengal.[18]

Since Burke concentratd on a retrospective attack on an individual out of office, while apparently acquiescing in what was recognizably evolving into the Raj of nineteenth century, those who see him in the last resort as a defender of British colonialism in India clearly have a case. By making Hastings a 'repositary of ill doing', it has been argued, Burke could 'simultaneously protect the colonial project from being indicted for the larger ill of which Hastings was simply a herald'.[19] 'Hastings is made responsible for all the iniquities of colonialism in the hope that the larger project will be purged by his prosecution'.[20]

While Burke certainly had a colonial project, his speeches and writings show that it bore little relation to what the East India Company or any other British regime had ever done or was ever likely to do in India. For tactical reasons he may have acquiesced in the order being created by Henry Dundas and Lord Cornwallis, but his project was entirely different from theirs. It was inspired not by the quest for national power and wealth but by the obligation to fulfil the dictates of divine providence and to enhance the honour and reputation of Britain in the eyes of the world.

However gross the iniquities of the East India Company or its servants, Burke was convinced that the new Indian provinces must remain within the British empire. Britain could not relinquish what he now saw as an obligation imposed on it by God's providence. He regarded British ignorance about India as among many 'circumstances [which] are not, I confess very favourable to the idea of our attempting to govern India at all. But there we are; there we are placed by the Sovereign Disposer: and we must do the best we can in our situation. The situation of man is the preceptor of his duty.'[21] He did not consider that the murkiness of the origins of Britain's conquest of Bengal, be it by 'fraud or force or whether by a mixture of both', undermined its providential nature. Conquest was 'a more immediate designation of the hand of God'.[22] In 1791 he asked the House of Lords whether their judgement on Hastings would 'vindicate the dispensation of Providence that has committed so great an Empire to so remote a country'.[23]

Conquest had made the British rulers of Indian provinces and conferred on them obligations that they could in no way evade. Rule was not a simple exercise of power based on the will of the conqueror or his sense of his own advantage. 'The conqueror only succeeds to all the painful duties and subordination to the power of God which belonged to the Sovereign that held the country before'.[24] The new ruler, like his predecessor, was bound by God's law, the 'great, immutable, pre-existent law, prior to all our devices, and prior to all our contrivances, paramount to our very being itself, by which we are knit and connected in the eternal frame of the universe, out of which we cannot stir.'[25] The first precept of that great law was that the ruler must, above everything else, pursue the welfare of the ruled. 'The moment a sovereign removes the Idea of security and protection from his subjects...He is no longer sovereign; they are no longer subjects.'[26] 'All political power which is set over men...and for so much, a derogation from the natural equality of mankind at large, ought to be some way or other exercised ultimately for their benefit.'[27]

Burke believed that the British could best discharge their duty to the well-being of the ruled by limiting their intervention to the minimum. They must 'leave the Country on the foundations on which it stood, and if any change was made, it should be to fix property, to quiet litigation'.[28] Indian authority must be kept intact at every possible level. If the Mughal empire could not be restored, the British must preserve the rulers of the successor states which had come to power, together with the structures of local authority as he understood them. Burke saw no function for British Collectors, Magistrates or Judges. The questions to be asked of a British Governor of Bengal were: 'First, whether he has made the ancient Mahomedan families as easy as he could; secondly, whether he has made the Hindoo inhabitants, the zemindars and their tenants, as secure in their property and as easy in their tenure as he could'.[29]

The role of the British government was quite simply to protect. They must maintain an army to protect their provinces from invaders, but the greatest danger to the welfare of those provinces was from the British themselves. One of the most pressing tasks in the new government of India was to devise a system to control abuses by the British servants of the Company. Burke became convinced that attempts to do this by restoring the authority of the Directors of the Company over their servants, by creating a royal court in Calcutta or by prosecutions in the British courts had all failed. He did not believe that the creation of a new department of state in Britain to supervise the Company, such as Pitt's Board of Control, would work either. Only Parliament could effectively supervise Indian government by calling to account miscreants. Had Fox's India Bills become law, the Company would have been replaced by a parliamentary commission whose function was 'to regulate the administration of India upon the principles of a Court of Judicature'.[30] When the Bills were defeated, Burke considered that there was no alternative left but to resort to the process of parliamentary justice, trial by impeachment. Through it the British Parliament could redress the grievances of India.

The inspiration for this vision of an empire of protection enforced by Parliament seems clearly to lie in Cicero, whose example, above all in his prosecution of Verres, Burke frequently invoked. In *De Officiis*

Cicero wrote that 'as long as the empire of the Roman people was maintained through acts of kind service and not through injustice,...the senate was a haven and refuge for kings, for peoples, and for nations; moreover our magistrates and generals yearned to acquire the greatest praise from one thing alone, the fair and faithful defence of our provinces and our allies. In this way we could more truly have been titled a protectorate than an empire of the world.'[31]

Like Cicero, Burke believed that the empire must be conducted not only in accordance with the will of God but also to win the good opinion of men. For Britain to 'increase its commerce without increasing its honour and reputation' he described as 'a bad bargain for the Country'.[32] He told the Lords that 'the credit and honour of the British nation' was at stake in the Hastings trial. He frequently spoke of other European nations watching and judging Britain by its record in India. 'Situated as this Kingdom is—an object, thank God, of envy to the rest of the world for its greatness and its power—its conduct, in that very elevated situation to which it has arisen will undoubtedly be scrutinized'.[33] Britain's rule over India should have 'done honour to Europe, to our Cause, to our religion, done honour to all the circumstances of which we boast'.[34] This had not been the case, but he at least 'had laboured, though in vain, to rescue from ignominy and abhorrence the British name'.[35]

While the British must seek the good of their subjects above all things, in a properly conducted imperial relationship they could also legitimately derive material rewards for themselves. He believed that under an undisturbed Indian government, the Company's provinces would prosper, as they had done in the past. The British could then draw off a revenue 'ample enough beyond all the most extravagant expectations'.[36] British officials serving in India could expect 'moderate, safe, and proper emoluments' from the revenue.[37] It was possible for servants of the Company to come home 'Rich and innocent'.[38] Any revenue extracted by the British must, however, be the last claim on Indian resources. Of the Carnatic, he wrote that 'In order that the people, after a long period of vexation and plunder, may be in a condition to maintain government, government must begin by maintaining them.'[39] He denounced as 'the most flagitious rapacity' the level of taxation in Bengal, where 'Whatever taxes we paid, it seemed to be the system of our Indian Governors to impose the double of that burden on their subjects'.[40]

Britain could also expect to benefit commercially from its connection with India. Classical antiquity may have inspired Burke with a belief that empire should be built on principles of honour, but he was very much a man of his time in his conviction that trade between equals could only be mutually beneficial to both sides. He tried to demonstrate this in the Ninth Report of the Select Committee of 1783. Up to 1765, trade between Britain and India had indeed been of benefit to both. The Company had exported silver which had 'encouraged Industry, and promoted Cultivation to a high Degree' in India. In return for its silver, the Company had obtained commodities 'essential for animating all other Branches of Trade and for compleating the Commercial Circle...The English Company flourished under this Exportation for a very long Series of Years. The Nation was considerably benefited both in Trade and in Revenue.'[41] This happy situation came to an end in 1765 when the Company ceased to export silver and began to pay for its Indian cargoes out of the revenue of Bengal, while using its new political power to regulate the prices it paid for its exports. The result was not only that Bengal was impoverished but that the Company's trade was debased. The moral was that 'All Attempts...which tend to the Distress of India, must, and in a very short Time will, make themselves felt, even by those in whose Favour such Attempts have been made.'[42] If the Company put its trade back on 'a Bottom truly Commercial', based on *'the Principles of Profit and Loss',* it could legitimately expect to make a profit from that trade.[43] But 'The Prosperity of the Natives must be previously secured, before any Profit from them whatsoever is attemtped.'[44]

Given Burke's views on what British empire in India ought to be, why he made the punishment of Hastings an objective above all others becomes more explicable. Sara Suleri is only the most recent of innumerable commentators on Burke who see an obvious disproportion in his sense of outrage about what had happened in India and his insistence on pinning the blame on Hastings. To impute so much criminality to one man seems to be too much. The system that Hastings was required to operate must bear a major part of the guilt. Surely Burke recognized that. Dr Suleri argues that he did indeed know 'the colonial story too well' and recognised, at least subconsciously, that even he himself was caught up with Hastings in a 'shared intimacy of guilt' arising from the irredeemably contaminated nature of colonial rule in India.[45] Yet for Burke empire in India was by no means an inevitably corrupt colonialism. It was not merely the domination of one people over another for their own advantage. It was the performance by Britain of a providential obligation. Rulers who obeyed God's law and protected their subjects could expect to share the benefits of empire with them. Human misdeeds had, however, vitiated a relationship that was part of God's order. Misconduct by rulers in India was particularly heinous. A society whose institutions were, in Burke's view, fully sufficient to ensure its prosperity was peculiarly vulnerable to the tyranny of those in authority. The main task of British government was thus to protect Indians from such tyranny. When the Governor General himself proved to be a rapacious tyrant, punishment must be exemplary. For Burke it was not necessarily disproportionate to attribute all the misfortunes of India to the one man who, Burke insisted, had perverted the whole system of British government in India.

For recent commentators, the ferocity of Burke's indictment of Hastings indicated his anxiety about the effects on Britain of empire in India. For Burke, however, a properly conducted empire was a source of national virtue not of corruption. His anxiety therefore was about the consequences that would follow from abuses of imperial power that went uncorrected, rather than about the power itself. At the starkest, those who broke God's law would be punished by God in this world, let alone the next. 'A cry for vengeance had gone forth and reached his ears, who never could be inattentive to the distresses of his creature; and we could expect as little mercy from him as we had shewn to them'. The loss of the American colonies was a portent. 'As we had regarded the suffering and grievances of the Indians without mercy, our punishment would come without mitigation'.[46]

The dangers that could arise from an extensive empire of conquest were a very ancient commonplace of European political thought. An overgrown empire would let loose a flood of wealth that would corrupt the virtue of the citizens of the mother country. Its liberties were in danger from proconsuls in the outlying provinces who would use the mercenary armies under their command to overthrow a properly constituted authority at home. This was the history of imperial Rome. Of all species of empire, empire in Asia was held to be by far the most dangerous. Those who ruled in Asia would be corrupted by eastern luxury and oriental despotism and would transfer their corruption to Europe.

Burke accepted some if not all of this conventional wisdom. His stress was not on the inevitability of corruption through imperial expansion, but on the consequences of wrongdoing by individuals. This was his interpretation of the Roman example. 'The downfall of the greatest empire this world ever saw, had been, on all hands agreed upon to have originated in the mal-administration of its provinces. Rome never felt within herself the seeds of decline, till corruption from foreign misconduct impaired her vitals.'[47] He elaborated these dangers in his impeachment speeches. The threat came from men who had enriched themselves illegally and had adopted despotic doctrines. He hit on the figure of £40 million as the amount of money which he supposed British people had brought with them from India.[48] This wealth, he believed, had created an 'Indian influence' which now 'extended from the Needles off the Isle of Wight to John of Grott's house' in the far north of Scotland.[49] This hugely powerful interest was poised to take power, beginning with the House of Commons. 'We dread the operation of money. Do we not know that there are many men who wait, and who indeed hardly wait, the event of this prosecution to let loose all the corrupt wealth of India, acquired by the oppression of that country, for the corruption of all the liberties of this, and to fill the parliament with men who are now the object of its indignation?'[50] Men from India who gained positions of power in Britain would use that power in the despotic manner in which they had governed the Company's provinces. 'What may be our future moral and political condition when the persons who come from that school of pride, insolence, corruption and tyranny, are more intimately mixed up with us of purer morals...Every man in Great Britain will be contaminated and must be corrupted, if you let loose among us whole legions of men, generation after generation, tainted with these abominable vices, and avowing these detestable principles.'[51] Men who exercised arbitrary power in India were likely to be rebels in Britain, that is, presumably, Jacobins. A tyrant and a rebel were, in his view, two faces of the same thing. Both 'arise from a contempt of public order, and of the laws and institutions which curb mankind. They arise from a harsh, cruel and ferocious disposition, impatient of the rules of law, order, and morality.'[52]

Burke's anxiety about the effect on Britain of misrule in India has been interpreted as evidence that he saw India by its very nature as a threat to Britain. A sense 'of [the] unstoppable, pernicious, influence of the East', has been attributed to him. The British 'Self' would be transformed by empire into the Indian 'Other'.[53] One much quoted passage does indeed seem to support such an interpretation. If they connived in the acquisition of money by fraud and extortion in India, Burke said, 'the people of England' would cease to be 'an open-hearted, candid, liberal, plain, sincere people'. They would instead become 'a nation of concealers, a nation of dissemblers, a nation of liars, a nation of forgers;...in one word,...a people of *banyans*'.[54] Burke did indeed regard 'banyans', the business agents of British officials and merchants in Bengal, as wholly depraved. 'They know all the lurking holes, all the winding resources of the unfortunate, and they hunt out distress and misery, even to its last retreats.'[55] They were 'persons in the form and shape of men, but with all the character and disposition of beasts of prey'.[56] In other respects, however, it was not India that corrupted the British in India and through them the British at home; it was particular British people who corrupted India and would, unless they were curbed, corrupt Britain. Banyans apart, Burke did not argue that Indians were inherently corrupt. He went to great pains to demonstrate that Indian governments were in no sense despotic; they were governments according to law. Concepts of oriental despotism were the notions of ignorant travel writers and other superficial authors, which had been deliberately exploited by wicked men like Hastings for their own purposes. In short, Burke was deeply apprehensive about the effects on Britain of an ill-regulated imperial relationship, but he still maintained his vision of an innocent and indeed a mutually beneficial connection.

III

Assumptions about the nature of Indian society were crucial to Burke's view of what Britain's role in India ought to be. He did his best to ensure that his contemporaries would share his vision of India and accept the conclusions he drew from it.

Burke believed that there were special reasons why it was his duty to 'represent' Indians to British audiences and a British readership, not merely by describing them, but by literally representing their interests in Parliament. For him the British Parliament was an imperial Parliament in which the concerns of the people of the empire were in contemporary parlance 'virtually', if not actually, represented. Indians must be represented by others because, Burke believed, there was a 'confederacy' whose 'crooked policy', was 'to keep the poor natives wholly out of sight. We might hear enough about what great and illustrious exploits were daily performing on that conspicuous theatre by Britons: But...we were never to hear of any native's being an actor! '[57] 'Natives' could not speak for themselves in Britain and so he must defeat the conspiracy and speak for them.

Burke believed that Indians could not appear to plead their own cause, not because he deemed them incapable of such a thing, but for a precise reason. Hindus were prohibited from crossing the sea.

'Every head of a Great Empire has been known to throng with people from the Subject provinces who have come from curiosity, pleasure, complaint, solicitation of an interest, or for some common purpose. You would imagine that possessing a Country in India containing twenty four millions of People, that our streets would have been blackened by Indian faces'.[58] But it was not so. He himself had never 'seen the face of an Indian in this country', except for a Maratha envoy, whom he had induced to give evidence to a committee of the House of Commons.[59]

Burke's depictions of India embodied received opinion, often of great antiquity, which stressed differences between Asia and Europe. As was commonplace, he considered that Hindu civilization was unlike any other. Hindus had 'manners, religion, customs and usages, appropriate to themselves and in no ways resembling those of the rest of mankind.'[60] Burke also shared the conventional belief that Hindu civilization was fossilized antiquity, totally impervious to change. For Muslims too, he accepted some, but by no means all, the contemporary European stereotypes of what were thought to be the distinguishing features of Islamic regimes. He described the spread of Islam through 'enthusiasm' and 'despotism' as an 'era of great misfortune' to India and 'the world in general'.[61]

Yet the suggestion that Burke sought to 'Orientalize' India by rendering it 'radically "different" ' in the manner of the Arabian Nights or similar versions of the exotic seems to be misleading.[62] In general, Burke felt that his duty in representing a people who could not represent themselves was to stress similarity rather than difference. India must be 'approximated to our understandings, and if possible to our feelings; in order to awaken something of sympathy for the unfortunate natives'.[63] Those prosecuting Hastings, he said, had nothing to do with 'the fabulous regions of Indian mythology'. They wanted to 'vindicate the rights and privileges of the people of India. We wish to reinstate them in your sympathy. We wish you to respect a people as respectable as yourselves; a people who know as well as you what is rank, what is law, what is property;—a people who know how to feel disgrace, who know what equity, what reason, what proportion in punishments, what security of property is, just as well as any of your lordships.'[64]

Burke's strategy for trying to ensure that Indians should be 'approximated to our understandings' was to describe, to analyse, to use statistics, and to make comparisons with what would be familiar to his audiences. For instance, the Carnatic was depicted in concrete detail. The size of its cattle was evidence that it is 'not by the bounty of nature a fertile soil'. To demonstrate its dependence on irrigation Burke produced a map, from which he showed that in the district around Madras alone, there were 'up to eleven hundred' reservoirs, 'from the extent of two or three acres to five miles in circuit'.[65] The best known of his comparisons that related India to Europe was that with the political state of Germany in the Speech on Fox's India Bill. 'The Nabob of Oude might stand for the King of Prussia; the Nabob of Arcot I would compare as superior in territory and equal in revenue, to the Elector of Saxony.'[66] In analysing British society, Burke used the concept of 'interests', as in 'a great official, a great professional, a great military and naval interest'.[67] He described Bengal society in exactly the same way. Muslims constituted 'the official interest, the judicial interest, the court interest, and the military interest'. Hindus were 'the greatest part both of the landed and monied interest in that country'.[68] The burdens which the Company placed on the population of Bengal could best be appreciated by comparing their tax levels with those in England: Bengal's population were much poorer than England's but they paid a land tax and a salt tax double those in England.[69]

It has been suggested that Burke had a 'subterranean understanding' that his attempt to reduce India to mundane details and comparisons served only to 'dissolve rather than to consolidate the image of India' that he wished to convey, and that he felt he had no alternative but to invoke a 'sublime' that eluded such attempts.[70] Be that as it may, he persisted in his self–appointed task of explanation right through to the last of his impeachment speeches.

Those who choose the course of trying to explain another society in terms of measurement and comparison with Europe, rather than invoking the alien and exotic, inevitably face the accusation that in the process they reduce that society to an inferior model of Europe. Such accusations have been made against Burke. He is said to present Indians as 'pathetic, muted victims who must be championed and given a voice by the prosecution' of Hastings.[71] Much analysis of colonial discourse focusses on the way in which Asian societies were feminized in European representations of them, that is on their metaphorical depiction as female victims of aggression to be protected by their more virile western conquerors. Not only did Burke describe male Hindus as 'approaching almost to the feminine' in their manners,[72] but some of the most highly-charged passages in his later speeches dwelt on the suffering of Indian women.

In seeing Indians as people particularly vulnerable to oppressions, Burke had clearly absorbed much from travel accounts which were inevitably based almost entirely on the areas where Europeans had commercial contact, that is on Bengal, the Coromandel Coast and Gujarat. There, it seemed to Europeans, people who were industrious, technologically adept and commercially sophisticated were wholly unmartial and quite incapable of defending themselves. They had fallen victim to successive conquerors of whom the British were the most recent. Like many of his contemporaries, Burke was strongly impressed by recent developments in the military power of Europe and the capacity of what he called an army 'disciplined in the European manner'.[73] He believed that all Asians were now at the mercy of such power. Yet he also recognized military capacity in some Indian people. The Marathas, 'an injured, betrayed, and insulted people', had forced the surrender of a British army.[74] Most formidable of all was Haidar Ali of Mysore, whom he called an intended victim 'not of the passive kind'. 'He resolved in the gloomy recesses of a mind capacious of such things to leave the whole Carnatic an everlasting monument of vengeance' and unleashed 'a whirlwind of cavalry' that penned the British into the settlement of Madras.[75]

If Burke thought that most Indians were militarily vulnerable and needed British protection, he most emphatically did not believe that they were politically incapable and therefore in need of direct British rule. 'I am unable to regard the acquisition of Territory to the Company as matter of Merit', he wrote in 1781, 'until I find in some one instance, the condition of the Inhabitants has been improved by the revolution'.[76] By contrast, the examples of Tanjore, Benares or the Bengal *zamindaris* all convinced him that 'wherever the Hindoo Religion has been established, that Country has been flourishing'.[77] He believed that Hinduism instilled in rulers 'the ambition of an insatiable benevolence...to perpetuate themselves through generations, the guardians, the protectors, the nourishers of mankind'.[78] They promoted public works, above all the great irrigation projects on which agriculture depended, but also maintained 'inns and hospitals, where the traveller and the poor were relieved'.[79] The Hindu magistrate had a duty to protect property and was 'bound to govern by law'.[80] Under benevolent rulers, the natural industry and frugality of the Hindu artisan and cultivator produced an abundant prosperity.

Burke was less well disposed to Islamic government. He thought that the Muslim community in Bengal 'like Mahomedan settlers in many other countries' had 'fallen into decay'.[81] Rulers like Shuja-ud-daula of Awadh or Muhamad Ali of Arcot had intrigued with the British to extend their territory and their acquisitions, such as the lands of the Rohillas or Tanjore, had been despoiled. But Burke went to very great lengths to argue that Islamic government was not inherently despotic. Long sections of his opening and closing speeches in the impeachment were devoted to that point.[82] He called 'the Mahomedan law...a system of the wisest, the most learned, and most enlightened jurisprudence that perhaps ever existed in the world.'[83] He eventually came to regard even Shuja-ud-daula as a 'powerful, magnificent, and illustrious prince', who had 'long governed a happy and contented people' and was 'a wise and beneficent governor'.[84]

Burke even endowed Indian women, for whose sufferings he so often tried to arouse the chivalry of his male audiences, with political capacity. On the one hand, he described Indian women as, like women in general, forming 'the better and more virtuous part of mankind', but 'at the same time the least protected from the outrages to which this sensibility exposes them';[85] on the other, he argued that some Muslim ladies of rank were 'possessed of large Revenues, exercising high judicial authority and exercising the first authority in the Country'.[86]

Burke's India had recognizably the same contours as the European societies he tried to depict—France, Ireland and Britain itself. In the conventional terms of enlightenment social science, he saw India, like them, as a 'commercial' society that had passed through the earlier stages of human development. It was a society based on a hierarchy of rank and inequality of property, inequality being vindicated by the immense contribution made by the privileged to the common welfare. It was sanctified by religious establishments, Hindus enjoying 'That form of Religious Institution connected with Government and Policy that makes a people happy and a Government flourishing'.[87]

Although India was recognizably a commercial society, it had lost the capacity for continuing development that marked European commercial societies. Hindus had 'all the reverence for antiquity and...all the affection to their own institutions that other people have to novelty and change'.[88] Modern Islamic societies had atrophied. Neither could now stand up to the 'improved state of Europe, with the improved state of arts and the improved state of laws, and (which is much more material) the improved state of military discipline'.[89]

The consequence had been the ascendancy of 'a Nation the most enlightened of the enlightened part of Europe'.[90] Great benefits should have followed for India. The opposite had been the case. Rulers and aristocracies had been overthrown and 'men of great place, men of great rank, men of hereditary authority, cannot fall without a horrible crash upon all about them. Such towers cannot tumble without ruining their dependent cottages.'[91] There was mass impoverishment of the population as a whole. Even the land itself was degraded. In many vivid passages Burke contrasted the arcadian beauties of the smiling landscape of pre-British India with the howling wilderness that had ensued. The very 'physical works of God were desolated and destroyed by this man'.[92]

IV

It is not surprising that nationalist-minded Indian people in the later 19th century, such as Surendranath Banerjee or Dadabhai Naoraji, should have venerated Burke and used him as a stick with which to beat the imperial regime. Nor is it surprising that Indian opinion in the mid-20th century should have largely ignored Burke. They had long since ceased to have any expectations from a benevolent colonial presence and Burke's apparently conservative social principles seemed to offer nothing relevant to their struggle to generate economic growth and relieve poverty.

Those interested in Burke can only be grateful that the analysists of colonial discourse have rediscovered him at the end of the 20th century. They bring illumination through their sensitivity to language and literary strategies. Once their work has moved beyond the rigidities of 'self' and 'other', they have much to offer. Even so, Burke's 'colonial project' is one that eludes many of their formulations. Whatever else he may have been doing, he was not seeking to protect the emergent Raj with its mixture of good intentions and shabby compromises over revenue extraction, wars and the manipulation of Indian states. Nor does he seem to have been consumed with 'colonial anxiety'. His project was a glowing vision of peoples united through God's providence in a bond of protection and mutual benefit.

NOTES

1. Nirod C. Chaudhuri, *Autobiography of an Unknown Indian* (Delhi 1997 reprint), p.102.

2. Sara Suleri, *The Rhetoric of English India* (Chicago, 1992), pp.26, 28.

3. See also, David Musselwhite, 'The Trial of Warren Hastings', *Literature, Politics and Theory. Papers from the Essex Conference 1976–84,* Francis Barker et al., eds (London, 1986), pp.77–103; Kate Teltscher, *India Inscribed: European and British Writing on India 1600–1800* (Delhi, 1995), chap. 5.

4. *A Nation in Making* (London, 1925), p.141.

5. *Lord Curzon in India. Being a Selection of his Speeches as Viceroy and Governor-General of India 1898–1905,* Thomas Raleigh, ed. (London, 1906), p.55.

6. John Morley, *Recollections,* 2 vols (London, 1917), II. 240.

7. Said, *Orientalism,* p.122.

8. Published as a book under that title (Oxford, 1964).

9. *The Correspondence of Edmund Burke* (Cambridge and Chicago).

10. Vol. V, *India: Madras and Bengal 1774–1785* (Cambridge, 1981); vol. VI, *India: The Launching of the Hastings Impeachment 1786–1788* (Cambridge, 1991).

11. *Impeachment of Warren Hastings,* p.xiv.

12. Burke, *Writings and Speeches,* VI. 16–17.

13. 'The Trial o Maharaja Nandakumar', *Bengal Past and Present,* LXXVIII (1959).

14. *The Great Melody: A Thematic Biography of Edmund Burke* (London, 1992), p.583.

15. Teltscher, *India Inscribed,* p.2.

16. *The Writings and Speeches of Edmund Burke,* ed., Paul Langford, vol. II, *Party, Parliament and the American Crisis 1766–1774* (Oxfora, 1981), p.374.

17. *Correspondence,* VIII. 428.

18. *The Works of the Right Honourable Edmund Burke* (Bohn's British Classics), 8 vols (London, 1854–89), VIII. 101.

19. Suleri, *Rhetoric,* p.57.

20. Teltscher, *India Inscribed,* pp.166–7. See also Thomas R. Metcalf, *Ideologies of the Raj* (Cambridge, 1994), pp.19–20.

21. *Writings and Speeches,* V. 404.

22. Ibid., VI. 351.

23. British Library, Add MS, 24234, f.359.

24. *Writings and Speeches,* VI. 351.

25. Ibid., VI. 350.

26. Ibid., VI. 470.

27. Ibid., V. 385.

28. Ibid., VI. 35.

29. *Works,* VIII. 308.

30. *Writings and Speeches,* V. 444.

31. *De Officiis,* II, 26–7, translated as *Cicero on Duties,* by M.T. Griffin and E.M. Atkins (Cambridge, 1991), p.72.

32. *Writings and Speeches,* VI. 282.

33. Ibid., VI. 271, 277.

34. Ibid., VI. 315.

35. Ibid., V. 476.

36. Ibid., VI. 35.

37. *Works,* VIII. 308.

38. *Correspondence,* V. 257.

39. *Writings and Speeches,* V. 521.

40. Ibid., V. 467.
41. Ibid., V. 222–3.
42. Ibid., V. 258.
43. Ibid., V. 241.
44. Ibid., V. 221.
45. Suleri, *Rhetoric,* pp.46–7.
46. *Writings and Speeches,* V. 468.
47. Ibid., VI. 63.
48. Ibid., VI., 277; *Works,* VII. 458–9.
49. Speech, 14 February 1791, *Parliamentary History of England,* XXVIII. col. 1433.
50. *Works,* VII. 449.
51. Ibid., VII. 487.
52. Ibid., VIII. 58.
53. Teltscher, *India Inscribed,* p.169.
54. *Works,* VII. 449 'A twisting, shuffling prevaricating equivocating Nation —a Nation of Banians' (MS draft, Fitzwilliam MSS, Northamptonshire Record Office, A. XXX. 4).
55. *Writings and Speeches,* VI. 293.
56. *Works,* VIII. 416.
57. *Writings and Speeches,* VI. 460–1.
58. 21 May 1789, British Library, Add MS 24230, f.200.
59. *Writings and Speeches,* VI. 106.
60. Ibid., VI. 301.
61. Ibid., VI. 307.
62. Musselwhite, 'The Trial of Hastings', *Literature, Politics and Theory,* p.98.
63. *Writings and Speeches,* V. 390.
64. *Works,* VII. 502–3.
65. *Writings and Speeches,* V. 521–2.
66. Ibid., V. 390.
67. Ibid., II. 310.
68. *Works,* VIII, 307.
69. *Writings and Speeches,* V. 467.
70. Suleri, *Rhetoric,* pp.28–30.
71. Teltscher, *India Inscribed,* p.9.
72. *Writings and Speeches,* VI. 302.
73. Ibid., VIII. 308.
74. Ibid., V. 396.
75. Ibid., V. 518–9.
76. *Correspondence,* IV. 346.
77. *Writings and Speeches,* VI. 305.
78. Ibid., V. 522.
79. Ibid., V. 423.
80. *Works,* VII. 492.
81. *Works,* VIII, 306.

82. *Writings and Speeches,* VI. 353–65; *Works,* VII. 495–501.
83. Ibid., VIII. 4–5.
84. Ibid., VIII. 110.
85. Ibid., VIII. 274.
86. *Speeches and Writings,* VI. 478.
87. Ibid., VI. 305.
88. Ibid.
89. Ibid., VI. 283.
90. Ibid., VI. 315.
91. *Works,* VIII. 59.
92. Ibid., VIII. 306.

Bibliography of the Works of Ashin Das Gupta: A Note

This bibliography brings together Ashin Das Gupta's significant writings as a professional historian and as a contemporary commentator on his own society and polity in both English and Bengali. Most of his professional writing is in English while most of his social writing is in Bengali. When writing in Bengali, he wrote mostly for the Bengali literary magazine *Desh,* encouraged to do so, most graciously, by Sagarmoy Ghosh, its veteran editor. However, some of his serious historical writing in Bengali was written for the journal *Oitihasik,* steered single-handedly by Arun Kumar Das Gupta, who had dedicated himself to the task of publishing serious history writing in Bengali. I wish to acknowledge my debt to both these editors for bringing this inspiration and pleasure to my husband's work. Although a lover of Bengali literature himself, and in life as good a Bengali as any other, by habit and training he wrote in English till the early 1980s. At that juncture, and throughout the 80s and the 90s, he wrote many pieces in Bengali. Notable among them were his essays on Mahatma Gandhi, on religion and politics. At that time, in addition, he took on the task of editing a series called *Itihas Granthomala,* on the initiative of Ananda Publishers, Calcutta, to establish a clientele for serious history writing in Bengali. To this day he continues to take an active interest in advancing this series with the cooperation of authors invited to write for the series. The first book for the *Itihas Granthomala* was published in 1991, and four more titles have come out since then. Despite his illness of recent years, he spends much of his time energetically continuing his scholarly work and he enjoys writing or dictating his writing in Bengali, more than doing the same in English. An interesting fallout has been that his scholarly writings on the Indian merchant and the Indian Ocean have become more accessible to the interested general reader and brought down some barriers.

The bibliography below is a compilation of his publications under books, historical writings in English and Bengali, articles of general interest in both the languages, and book reviews. I have debated much as to whether I should include the book reviews. I came round to the view that those of the reviews that are important for future research in Indian maritime history deserve to be included. It is my hope that this short note introducing Ashin Das Gupta's work will reflect on his diversity as a scholar and a writer.

I wish to thank Amit Bandopadhyay for his invaluable assistance in compiling this bibliography. Amit has been a student of the Presidency College History (Honours) class of 1970, and we are fortunate to have him as a diligent research assistant over the last five years. Saktidas Ray, chief librarian of the Ananda Bazar group of publications, helped with his characteristic kindness in the compilation once I informed him about it. Finally, I wish to convey my gratitude to the joint editors of this volume of essays, Lakshmi Subrahmaniam and Rudrangshu Mukherjee. Both Rudrangshu and Lakshmi have certainly been among my husband's best students and they have themselves kept alive that bond in their hearts. It is by no means easy for Rudrangshu to take time off from his editorial work for *The Telegraph* to do anything else. Yet he did take this on for his teacher. In all of these endeavours we have turned often to our friend Peter Marshall and have received his help bountifully. I take this as my opportunity, also our son Amil's, to thank each one of them gratefully and also those who may remain unnamed but are no less remembered.

Calcutta, 18 April, 1997 Uma Das Gupta

Books in English:

1. *Merchants of Maritime India 1500–1800,* Variorum, U.K., Collected Study Series, 1994.

2. Edited with M.N. Pearson, *India and the Indian Ocean 1500–1800,* Oxford University Press, Delhi, 1987.

3. *Indian Merchants and the Decline of Surat c. 1700–1750,* Reprint with a new Preface, Manohar, New Delhi, 1994. The original edition was published in 1979, as a monograph of the Sudasien-Institut, Universitat Heidelberg: Weisbaden, Franz Steiner Verlag, 1979.

4. *Malabar in Asian Trade 1740–1800,* Cambridge University Press, Cambridge South Asian Studies, 1967.

Books in Bengali:

1. *Bishay Sadhinata o Anyanyo Bishay,* Ananda Publishers Limited, Calcutta, 1992.

2. *Itihas o Sahitya,* Ananda Publishers Limited, Calcutta, 1989.

Historical Essays in English:

'S. Arasaratnam and the Bay of Bengal: A note', *The Calcutta Historical Journal,* 17, 2, July–December 1995.

'Moreland hypothesis', *Mariners, Merchants and Oceans: Studies in Maritime History,* ed. K.S. Mathew, Manohar, New Delhi, 1995.

'Europeans in India before the empire', Professor Anil Chandra Bandopadhyay Memorial Lecture, 1992, Department of History, Jadavpur University, Calcutta, 1993.

'The maritime city', *Ports and their Hinterlands (1700–1950),* ed. Indu Banga, Manohar, New Delhi, 1992.*

'The broker at Mughal Surat, *c.* 1740', *The Asian Seas 1500–1800: Local Societies, European Expansion and the Portuguese, Revista de Cultura,* 13–14, Macau, 1991.*

'The changing face of the Indian maritime merchant', *Emporia, Commodities and Entrepreneurs in Asian Maritime Trade c. 1400–1750,* ed. R. Ptak and D. Rothermund, Weisbaden, Franz Steiner Verlag, 1991.*

'Pieter Phoonsen of Surat, *c.* 1730–1740', *Modern Asian Studies,* 22, Cambridge University Press, 1988.

'A note on the shipowning merchants of Surat, *c* 1700', *Marchands et hommes d'affaires asiatiques dans l'Ocean Indien et la Mer de Chine, 13–20 siecles:* ed. D. Lombard and Jean Aubin: Paris, *Editions de l'EHESS,* 1987.

'Indian merchants and the wesern Indian Ocean: the early 17th century', *Modern Asian Studies,* 19, Cambridge University Press, 1985.*

'Indian merchants in the age of partnership, 1500–1800', *Business Communities of India,* ed. D. Tripathi, Manohar, New Delhi, 1984.*

'Indian merchants and trade in the Indian Ocean, *c.* 1500–1700', *The Cambridge Economic History of India,* vol. 1: *c.* 1200–*c.* 1750, ed. T. Raychaudhuri and I. Habib, Cambridge University Press, 1982.*

'Some problems of reconstructing the history of India's west coast from European Sources', *Indo-Portuguese History,* ed. J. Correia-Afonso, Oxford University Press, India, 1981.*

'Gujarati merchants and the Red Sea trade 1700–1725', The Age of Partnership: *The Europeans in Asia before Dominion,* ed. B.B. Kling and M.N. Pearson, University of Hawaii Press, 1979.*

'On Narendra Krishna Sinha, the historian', *Bengal Past and Present,* 95, Calcutta, 1976.

'The maritime merchant of medieval India, *c.* 1500–1800', *Proceedings of the Indian History Congress, Presidential address to the medieval section, 35th session, Jadavpur University, Calcutta,* University of Delhi, 1974.*

'Trade and Politics in 18th century India', *Islam and the Trade of Asia,* ed. D.S. Richards, Oxford, Bruno Cassirer and University of Pennsylvania Press, 1970.*

'The merchants of Surat, *c.* 1700–50', *Elites in South Asia,* ed. E. Leach and S.N. Mukherjee, Cambridge University Press, 1970.*

'The crisis at Surat, 1730–32', *Bengal Past and Present,* 86, Calcutta, 1967.*

'The making of Travancore', *Bengal Past and Present,* 80, Calcutta, 1961.

'Malabar in 1740', *Bengal Past and Present,* 80, Calcutta, 1960.*

'A note on out-station factories (Bombay)', *Bengal Past and Present,* 76, Calcutta, 1957.

'Madras Commercial Records', *Bengal Past and Present,* 75, Calcutta, 1956.

'Studies in the Madras Records', *Bengal Past and Present,* 75, Calcutta, 1956.

* reprinted in *Merchants of Maritime in India 1500–1800* as cited under 'Books in English' of this bibliography.

Historical essays in Bengali:

'Arab Sagor, 1500–1800': Adhyapak Susobhan Chandra Sarkar smarak baktrita, 1996, Paschim Banga Itihas Sangsad, Calcutta, 1996.

'Somudra banik-er samriddhi', *Nandan,* November, 1996.

'Jarusalem-er swapno', *Nandan,* Puja sankhya, 1995.

'Bangoposagor': Indrani Ray memorial lecture, Pratikshan, Calcutta, 1989.

'Bharat Sagare jugasandhi', *Desh,* Calcutta, 27 July 1996.

'Bharat Sagare somudrobonik', *Desh,* Calcutta, 9 May 1995.

'Pyrenees-er rakhal', *Oitihasik,* 3, (2), April–June 1981.

'Montaillou': Pyrenees-er gram, *Oitihasik,* 2, (3–4), July–October 1980.

'Bonik o sainik', *Oitihasik,* Collected Essays, April 1976.

Articles of general interest in Bengali:

'Samprodayer daye', *Jignasa,* Calcutta, 14, (3), Kartik–Poush, 1400 B.S.

'Upohas', *Desh,* Calcutta, 25 September 1993.

'Ambedkar-er baktyobyo', *Desh,* Calcutta, 31 July 1993.

'Bapu', *Desh,* Calcutta, 30 January 1993.

'Prothom Gandhi', *Desh,* Calcutta, 3 October 1992.

'Robi Thakur-er dal', *Desh,* Calcutta, 25 August 1990.

'Sohishnutar itihsa', *Desh,* Calcutta, 20 January 1990.

'Akrur Datt-r poribar', *Desh,* Calcutta, Binodan sankhya, 1989.

'Maulana Azad-er baktabyo', *Desh,* Calcutta, 25 March 1989.

'Pharashi biplaber shotru', *Desh,* Calcutta, 15 July 1989.

'Jawaharlal Nehru ebong Bharatbarsho', *Desh,* Calcutta, 12 November, 1988.

'Bankim Chandra Chattopadhyay o Nibaran Chakrabarty', *Desh,* Calcutta, Sahitya sankhya, 1988.

'Monia', *Desh,* Calcutta, 7 February 1987.

'Ekti sonar pathor bati', *Desh,* Calcutta, 4 October 1986.

'Jaro Bhorot-er horin: Gandhi ebong Congress', *Desh,* Calcutta, Congress sankhya, 1985.

'Abu Sayeed Ayyub o Bharatbarsher itihas', *Desh,* Calcutta, 5 February 1983.

'Jukti bhito manush', *Samatat,* Calcutta, July–September, 1977.

'Buno Ramnath prasange', *Ananda Bazar Patrika,* Calcutta, Puja sankhya, 1976.

'Hindu dharmo o rajniti', *Kolkata,* August, 1969.

Articles of general interest in English:

'Historians and the problem of objectivity', *The Visva-Bharati Quarterly,* 35 (3–4), November 1979.

'Red herrings in the Indian Ocean', *Quest,* April–June, 1965.

'The historian in India', *Quest,* January–March, 1962.

Selected Book Reviews:

Sanjay Subrahmanyam, *The Career and legend of Vasco da Gama,* in *The Statesman,* 9 May 1997.

Anne Bulley, *Free Mariner: John Adolphus Pope in the East Indies 1786–1821,* in the *Journal of Imperial and Commonwealth History,* 21, 1993.

Sanjay Subrahmanyam, *Improvising empire: Portuguese trade and settlement in the Bay of Bengal 1500–1700,* in *The Telegraph,* 3 January 1992.

Antony Disney, *Twilight of the Pepper Empire,* in *The Journal of Asian Studies,* 39 (4), August 1980.

Sushil Chaudhuri, *Trade and commercial organization in Bengal, 1650–1720,* in *The Indian Historical Review,* 4 (2), January 1978.

M.N. Pearson, *Merchants and rulers in Gujarat: The response to the Portuguese in the sixteenth century,* in *The Journal of Asian Studies,* 36 (1), 1976.

Surendra Gopal, *Commerce and crafts in Gujarat, 16th and 17th centuries: A study on the impact of European expansion on precapitalist economy,* in *The Indian Historical Review,* 1976.

C.R. Boxer, *Mary and mysogyny, women in Iberian expansion overseas, 1415–1815, facts, fancies and personalities* in *The Indian Economic and Social History Review,* 13 (2), April–June 1976.

C.R. Boxer, *The Portuguese seaborne empire 1415–1825,* in *The indian Economic and Social History Review,* 9 (2), June 1972.

N.K. Sinha, *The economic history of Bengal 1793–1848,* Volume III, in *Bengal Past and Present,* 89 (167), January–June, 1970.

N.K. Sinha, *The economic history of Bengal from Plassey to the Permanent Settlement,* Volume II, in *Bengal Past and Present,* 81 (152), July–December 1962.

19 July 1997 Uma Das Gupta

Index